Ford & Mercury
Mid-size Models
Automotive
Repair
Manual

by Chaun Muir and John H Haynes

Member of the Guild of Motoring Writers

Models covered:

Ford: Torino; Gran Torino; Elite; Ranchero; LTD II; Thunderbird (1975 thru 1982); LTD (1983 thru 1986)

Mercury: Montego; Comet; Cougar (1975 thru 1982); Marquis (1983 thru 1986)

Lincoln: Versailles (1977 thru 1980)

Engines covered: 140 (2.3); 200 (3.3); 232 (3.8); 225 (4.2); 302 (5.0); 351 (5.8); 400 (6.6); 460 (7.5)

(8V6 – 733)   AB

Haynes Publishing Group
Sparkford Nr Yeovil
Somerset BA22 7JJ England

Haynes North America, Inc
861 Lawrence Drive
Newbury Park
California 91320 USA

Acknowledgements

We are grateful for the help and cooperation of the Ford Motor Company for their assistance with technical information, certain illustrations and vehicle photos, and the Champion Spark Plug Company supplied the illustrations of various spark plug conditions.

A book in the **Haynes Automotive Repair Manual Series**

Printed in the U.S.A.

ISBN 1 85010 388 7

Library of Congress Catalog Card Number 85-80232

Contents

1976 Ford Gran Torino

About this manual

Its purpose

The purpose of this manual is to help you get the best value from your vehicle. It can do so in several ways. It can help you decide what work must be done, even if you choose to have it done by a dealer service department or a repair shop; it provides information and procedures for routine maintenance and servicing; and it offers diagnostic and repair procedures to follow when trouble occurs.

It is hoped that you will use the manual to tackle the work yourself. For many simpler jobs, doing it yourself may be quicker than arranging an appointment to get the vehicle into a shop and making the trips to leave it and pick it up. More importantly, a lot of money can be saved by avoiding the expense the shop must pass on to you to cover its labor and overhead costs. An added benefit is the sense of satisfaction and accomplishment that you feel after having done the job yourself.

Using the manual

The manual is divided into Chapters. Each Chapter is divided into numbered Sections, which are headed in bold type between horizontal lines. Each Section consists of consecutively numbered paragraphs.

The two types of illustrations used (figures and photographs), are referenced by a number preceding their caption. Figure reference numbers denote Chapter and numerical sequence within the Chapter; (i.e. Fig. 3.4 means Chapter 3, figure number 4). Figure captions are followed by a Section number which ties the figure to a specific portion of the text. All photographs apply to the Chapter in which they appear and the reference number pinpoints the pertinent Section and paragraph; i.e., 3.2 means Section 3, paragraph 2.

Procedures, once described in the text, are not normally repeated. When it is necessary to refer to another Chapter, the reference will be given as Chapter and Section number i.e. Chapter 1/16). Cross references given without use of the word 'Chapter' apply to Sections and/or paragraphs in the same Chapter. For example, 'see Section 8' means in the same Chapter.

Reference to the left or right side of the vehicle is based on the assumption that one is sitting in the driver's seat, facing forward.

Even though extreme care has been taken during the preparation of this manual, neither the publisher nor the author can accept responsibility for any errors in, or omissions from, the information given.

Introduction to the Ford Mid-size passenger cars

This manual covers maintenance and repair operations for 1975 through 1986 Ford Mid-size passenger cars, with the exception of the Cougar and the Thunderbird, which are covered here only through 1982 due to major design changes in 1983.

Other models included in this manual are the Torino and Gran Torino, the Elite, Ranchero and XR-7, the Cougar Villager Wagon, the Versailles, the Marquis (1983 through 1986), the LTD (1983 through 1986) and the LTD II.

Over the years covered in this manual, Ford has utilized eight different engines, from the 2.3 liter four-cylinder to the 7.5 liter V-8. Your vehicle may have a fuel injection system or one of seven different carburetors. There are nine separate emissions control systems, two manual and six automatic transmissions, three types of differentials, manual steering, integral and non-integral power steering, three types of front suspension, two types of rear suspension and either disc or drum brakes.

1977 Ford Ranchero

1979 Ford Thunderbird

1979 Ford LTD II

1984 Ford LTD

1984 Mercury Grand Marquis

1FABP43F9DB100001

VEHICLE IDENTIFICATION NUMBER

MFD. BY FORD MOTOR CO. IN U.S.A.

DATE: 09-82

GVWR: 5347 LB — 2425 KG

FRONT GAWR: 2714 LB
1231 KG

REAR GAWR: 2683 LB
1216 KG

THIS VEHICLE CONFORMS TO ALL APPLICABLE FEDERAL MOTOR VEHICLE SAFETY AND BUMPER STANDARDS IN EFFECT ON THE DATE OF MANUFACTURE SHOWN ABOVE.

VEH. IDENT. NO. 1FABP43F9DB100001

TYPE PASSENGER

3H

EXTERIOR PAINT COLORS

F0276
R0141
482450
DSO

BODY	VR	MLDG.	INT. TRIM	A/C	R	S	AX	TR
54K	YB	84A	GB	A	2	B	8	XBBBB

(UNITED STATES)

Typical vehicle identification number label — 1973
shown, other years similar

- ① — WORLD MANUFACTURER IDENTIFIER (1, F, A)
- ⑧ — RESTRAINT SYSTEM TYPE (B)
- ⑫ — CONSTANT "P" (P)
- — LINE, SERIES, BODY TYPE (4, 3)
- — ENGINE TYPE (F)
- — CHECK DIGIT (9)
- — MODEL YEAR (D)
- — ASSEMBLY PLANT (B)
- ① — PRODUCTION SEQUENCE NUMBER (1, 0, 0, 0, 0, 1)

- ② — VEHICLE TYPE
- ③ — PAINT
- ④ — BODY TYPE CODE
- ⑤ — VINYL ROOF
- ⑥ — BODY SIDE MOULDING
- ⑦ — TRIM CODE — (FIRST CODE LETTER = FABRIC AND SEAT TYPE, SECOND CODE = COLOR)
- ⑧ — AIR CONDITIONING
- ⑨ — RADIO
- ⑩ — SUN/MOON ROOF
- ⑪ — AXLE RATIO
- ⑫ — TRANSMISSION
- ⑬ — SPRINGS — FRONT L. AND R., REAR L. AND R. (4 CODES)
- ⑭ — DISTRICT SALES OFFICE
- ⑮ — PTO/SPL ORDER NUMBER
- ⑯ — ACCESSORY RESERVE LOAD

FORD MOTOR COMPANY
VEHICLE EMISSION CONTROL INFORMATION

SET PARKING BRAKE AND BLOCK WHEELS. DISCONNECT AUTOMATIC PARKING BRAKE RELEASE (IF SO EQUIPPED). MAKE ALL ADJUSTMENTS WITH ENGINE AT NORMAL OPERATING TEMPERATURE, ACCESSORIES AND HEADLIGHTS OFF. PUT AIR CLEANER IN POSITION WHEN CHECKING ALL ENGINE SPEEDS.

MAKE ALL ADJUSTMENTS WITH TRANSMISSION IN NEUTRAL.

IGNITION TIMING-DISCONNECT AND PLUG DISTRIBUTOR VACUUM HOSE. ADJUST TIMING TO 10° BTDC, 800 RPM MAX. RECONNECT HOSE.

FAST IDLE-DISCONNECT AND PLUG EGR VALVE VACUUM HOSE. PUT FAST IDLE SCREW ON KICKDOWN STEP OF FAST IDLE CAM. RUN ENGINE UNTIL RADIATOR COOLING FAN COMES ON. ADJUST TO 2400 RPM (2200 RPM FOR VEHICLE WITH LESS THAN 100 MILES). RECONNECT EGR VACUUM HOSE.

CURB IDLE-
1. VACUUM OPERATED THROTTLE MODULATOR (VOTM) OFF— PUT FAST IDLE SCREW ON SECOND STEP OF FAST IDLE CAM AND RUN ENGINE UNTIL RADIATOR COOLING FAN COMES ON. ACCELERATE ENGINE MOMENTARILY. DISCONNECT AND PLUG VOTM VACUUM HOSE. ADJUST TO 800 RPM BY TURNING THROTTLE STOP ADJUSTING SCREW (700 RPM FOR VEHICLE WITH LESS THAN 100 MILES). ADJUST DASHPOT CLEARANCE TO
2. VOTM ON- PLACE HEATER SELECTOR ON HEAT, TEMPERATURE ON COOL AND BLOWER ON HIGH. CONNECT A VACUUM HOSE FROM MANIFOLD VACUUM TO THE VOTM. WITH RADIATOR COOLING FAN RUNNING, ADJUST TO 1200 RPM BY TURNING SCREW ON TOP OF VOTM (1100 RPM FOR VEHICLE WITH LESS THAN 100 MILES). RESTORE VOTM VACUUM CONNECTIONS.

SEE SHOP MANUAL FOR CHOKE AND IDLE MIXTURE ADJUSTMENT INFORMATION.

THIS VEHICLE CONFORMS TO U.S.E.P.A. REGULATIONS APPLICABLE TO 1983 MODEL YEAR NEW MOTOR VEHICLES. COMPLIANCE DEMONSTRATED AND DESIGNED FOR PRINCIPAL USE BELOW 4000 FEET. FOR NEW VEHICLE COMPLIANCE ABOVE 4000 FEET, SEE SERVICE PUBLICATIONS.

E3AE-9C485-DFS

CATALYST

SPARK PLUG :AWSF-32   GAP- .042-.046
1.6 LITER /3CM
DFM 1.6 V2GDK6   EGR/AIP/TWC

VACUUM HOSE ROUTING
—•— A/C ONLY
—•— NON A/C ONLY

FRONT OF VEHICLE

Typical vehicle emissions control label

Vehicle identification numbers

Modifications are a continuing and unpublicized process in vehicle manufacturing. Since spare parts manuals and lists are compiled on a numerical basis, the individual vehicle numbers are essential to correctly identify the component required.

The Vehicle Identification Number (VIN) is located on the driver's side of the dashboard where it meets the windshield and sometimes on the right fender panel in the engine compartment. A data plate including the date of production can be found on the latch post of the driver's door. An emissions hose routing diagram and tune-up information can be found on the underside of the hood on some models and on the engine valve cover on other models. In this book, this label will be referred to as the Emission Control Information Label.

General dimensions

Overall length	173 in
Overall width	66 in
Overall height	53 in
Wheelbase	101.2 in

Buying parts

Replacement parts are available from many sources, which generally fall into one of two categories – authorized dealer parts departments and independent retail auto parts stores. Our advice concerning these parts is as follows:

Retail auto parts stores: Good auto parts stores will stock frequently needed components which wear out relatively fast, such as clutch components, exhaust systems, brake parts, tune-up parts, etc. These stores often supply new or reconditioned parts on an exchange basis, which can save a considerable amount of money. Discount auto parts stores are often very good places to buy materials and parts needed for general vehicle maintenance such as oil, grease, filters, spark plugs, belts, touch-up paint, bulbs, etc. They also usually sell tools and general accessories, have convenient hours, charge lower prices and can often be found not far from home.

Authorized dealer parts department: This is the best source for parts which are unique to the vehicle and not generally available elsewhere (such as major engine parts, transmission parts, trim pieces, etc.).

Warranty information: If the vehicle is still covered under warranty, be sure that any replacement parts purchased – regardless of the source – do not invalidate the warranty!

To be sure of obtaining the correct parts, have engine and chassis numbers available and, if possible, take the old parts along for positive identification.

Maintenance techniques, tools and working facilities

Maintenance techniques

There are a number of techniques involved in maintenance and repair that will be referred to throughout this manual. Application of these techniques will enable the home mechanic to be more efficient, better organized and capable of performing the various tasks properly, which will ensure that the repair job is thorough and complete.

Fasteners

Fasteners are nuts, bolts, studs and screws used to hold two or more parts together. There are a few things to keep in mind when working with fasteners. Almost all of them use a locking device of some type, either a lock washer, locknut, locking tab or thread adhesive. All threaded fasteners should be clean and straight, with undamaged

Bolt strength markings (top — standard/SAE/USS; bottom — metric)

Grade	Identification
Hex Nut Grade 5	3 Dots
Hex Nut Grade 8	6 Dots

Standard hex nut strength markings

Class	Identification
Hex Nut Property Class 9	Arabic 9
Hex Nut Property Class 10	Arabic 10

Metric hex nut strength markings

CLASS 10.9   CLASS 9.8   CLASS 8.8

Metric stud strength markings

threads and undamaged corners on the hex head where the wrench fits. Develop the habit of replacing all damaged nuts and bolts with new ones. Special locknuts with nylon or fiber inserts can only be used once. If they are removed, they lose their locking ability and must be replaced with new ones.

Rusted nuts and bolts should be treated with a penetrating fluid to ease removal and prevent breakage. Some mechanics use turpentine in a spout-type oil can, which works quite well. After applying the rust penetrant, let it ''work'' for a few minutes before trying to loosen the nut or bolt. Badly rusted fasteners may have to be chiseled or sawed off or removed with a special nut breaker, available at tool stores.

If a bolt or stud breaks off in an assembly, it can be drilled and removed with a special tool commonly available for this purpose. Most automotive machine shops can perform this task, as well as other repair procedures (such as repair of threaded holes that have been stripped out).

Flat washers and lock washers, when removed from an assembly, should always be replaced exactly as removed. Replace any damaged washers with new ones. Always use a flat washer between a lock washer and any soft metal surface (such as aluminum), thin sheet metal or plastic.

Fastener sizes

For a number of reasons, automobile manufacturers are making wider and wider use of metric fasteners. Therefore, it is important to be able to tell the difference between standard (sometimes called U.S., English or SAE) and metric hardware, since they cannot be interchanged.

All bolts, whether standard or metric, are sized according to diameter, thread pitch and length. For example, a standard 1/2 — 13 x 1 bolt is 1/2 inch in diameter, has 13 threads per inch and is 1 inch long. An M12 — 1.75 x 25 metric bolt is 12 mm in diameter, has a thread pitch of 1.75 mm (the distance between threads) and is 25 mm long. The two bolts are nearly identical, and easily confused, but they are not interchangeable.

In addition to the differences in diameter, thread pitch and length, metric and standard bolts can also be distinguished by examining the bolt heads. To begin with, the distance across the flats on a standard bolt head is measured in inches, while the same dimension on a metric bolt is measured in millimeters (the same is true for nuts). As a result, a standard wrench should not be used on a metric bolt and a metric wrench should not be used on a standard bolt. Also, most standard bolts have slashes radiating out from the center of the head to denote the grade or strength of the bolt (which is an indication of the amount

of torque that can be applied to it). The greater the number of slashes, the greater the strength of the bolt (grades 0 through 5 are commonly used on automobiles). Metric bolts have a property class (grade) number, rather than a slash, molded into their heads to indicate bolt strength. In this case, the higher the number, the stronger the bolt (property class numbers 8.8, 9.8 and 10.9 are commonly used on automobiles).

Strength markings can also be used to distinguish standard hex nuts from metric hex nuts. Many standard nuts have dots stamped into one side, while metric nuts are marked with a number. The greater the number of dots, or the higher the number, the greater the strength of the nut.

Metric studs are also marked on their ends according to property class (grade). Larger studs are numbered (the same as metric bolts), while smaller studs carry a geometric code to denote grade.

It should be noted that many fasteners, especially Grades 0 through 2, have no distinguishing marks on them. When such is the case, the only way to determine whether it is standard or metric is to measure the thread pitch or compare it to a known fastener of the same size.

Standard fasteners are often referred to as SAE, as opposed to metric. However, it should be noted that SAE technically refers to a non-metric *fine thread* fastener only. Coarse thread non-metric fasteners are referred to as USS sizes.

Since fasteners of the same size (both standard and metric) may have different strength ratings, be sure to reinstall any bolts, studs or nuts removed from your vehicle in their original locations. Also, when replacing a fastener with a new one, make sure that the new one has a strength rating equal to or greater than the original.

Tightening sequences and procedures

Most threaded fasteners should be tightened to a specific torque value (torque is a twisting force). Over-tightening the fastener can weaken it and cause it to break, while under-tightening can cause it to eventually come loose. Bolts, screws and studs, depending on the material they are made of and their thread diameters, have specific torque values (many of which are noted in the Specifications at the beginning of each Chapter). Be sure to follow the torque recommendations closely. For fasteners not assigned a specific torque, a general torque value chart is presented here as a guide. As was previously mentioned, the size and grade of a fastener determine the amount of torque that can safely be applied to it. The figures listed on the next page are approximate for Grade 2 and Grade 3 fasteners (higher grades can tolerate higher torque values).

Standard (SAE and USS) bolt dimensions/grade marks

G Grade marks (bolt strength)
L Length (in inches)
T Thread pitch (number of threads per inch)
D Nominal diameter (in inches)

Metric bolt dimensions/grade marks

P Property class (bolt strength)
L Length (in millimeters)
T Thread pitch (distance between threads in millimeters)
D Diameter

Metric thread sizes	Ft-lb	Nm
M-6	6 to 9	9 to 12
M-8	14 to 21	19 to 28
M-10	28 to 40	38 to 54
M-12	50 to 71	68 to 96
M-14	80 to 140	109 to 154

Pipe thread sizes		
1/8	5 to 8	7 to 10
1/4	12 to 18	17 to 24
3/8	22 to 33	30 to 44
1/2	25 to 35	34 to 47

U.S. thread sizes		
1/4 — 20	6 to 9	9 to 12
5/16 — 18	12 to 18	17 to 24
5/16 — 24	14 to 20	19 to 27
3/8 — 16	22 to 32	30 to 43
3/8 — 24	27 to 38	37 to 51
7/16 — 14	40 to 55	55 to 74
7/16 — 20	40 to 60	55 to 81
1/2 — 13	55 to 80	75 to 108

Torque limits

Fasteners laid out in a pattern (i.e. cylinder head bolts, oil pan bolts, differential cover bolts, etc.) must be loosened or tightened in a sequence to avoid warping the component. This sequence will normally be shown in the appropriate Chapter. If a specific pattern is not given, the following procedures can be used to prevent warping. Initially, the bolts or nuts should be assembled finger-tight only. Next, they should be tightened one full turn each, in a crisscross or diagonal pattern. After each one has been tightened one full turn, return to the first one and tighten them all one-half turn, following the same pattern. Finally, tighten each of them one-quarter turn at a time until each fastener has been tightened to the proper torque. To loosen and remove the fasteners, the procedure would be reversed.

Component disassembly

Component disassembly should be done with care and purpose to help ensure that the parts go back together properly. Always keep track of the sequence in which parts are removed. Make note of special characteristics or marks on parts that can be installed more than one way (such as a grooved thrust washer on a shaft). It is a good idea to lay the disassembled parts out on a clean surface in the order that they were removed. It may also be helpful to make sketches or take instant photos of components before removal.

When removing fasteners from a component, keep track of their locations. Sometimes threading a bolt back in a part, or putting the washers and nut back on a stud, can prevent mix-ups later. If nuts and bolts cannot be returned to their original locations, they should be kept in a compartmented box or a series of small boxes. A cupcake or muffin tin is ideal for this purpose, since each cavity can hold the bolts and nuts from a particular area (i.e. oil pan bolts, valve cover bolts, engine mount bolts, etc.). A pan of this type is especially helpful when working on assemblies with very small parts, such as the carburetor, alternator, valve train or interior dash and trim pieces. The cavities can be marked with paint or tape to identify the contents.

Whenever wiring looms, harnesses or connectors are separated, it's a good idea to identify the two halves with numbered pieces of masking tape so they can be easily reconnected.

Gasket sealing surfaces

Throughout any vehicle, gaskets are used to seal the mating surfaces between two parts and keep lubricants, fluids, vacuum or pressure contained in an assembly.

Many times these gaskets are coated with a liquid or paste-type gasket sealing compound before assembly. Age, heat and pressure can sometimes cause the two parts to stick together so tightly that they are very difficult to separate. Often, the assembly can be loosened by striking it with a soft-faced hammer near the mating surfaces. A regular hammer can be used if a block of wood is placed between the hammer and the part. Do not hammer on cast parts or parts that could be easily damaged. With any particularly stubborn part, always recheck to make

sure that every fastener has been removed.

Avoid using a screwdriver or bar to pry apart an assembly, as they can easily mar the gasket sealing surfaces of the parts (which must remain smooth). If prying is absolutely necessary, use an old broom handle, but keep in mind that extra clean-up will be necessary if the wood splinters.

After the parts are separated, the old gasket must be carefully scraped off and the gasket surfaces cleaned. Stubborn gasket material can be soaked with rust penetrant or treated with a special chemical to soften it so it can be easily scraped off. A scraper can be fashioned from a piece of copper tubing by flattening and sharpening one end. Copper is recommended because it is usually softer than the surfaces to be scraped, which reduces the chance of gouging the part. Some gaskets can be removed with a wire brush, but regardless of the method used, the mating surfaces must be left clean and smooth. If for some reason the gasket surface is gouged, then a gasket sealer thick enough to fill scratches will have to be used during reassembly of the components. For most applications, a non-drying (or semi-drying) gasket sealer should be used.

Hose removal tips

Caution: *If the vehicle is equipped with air conditioning, do not disconnect any of the A/C hoses without first having the system depressurized by a dealer service department or an air conditioning specialist.*

Hose removal precautions closely parallel gasket removal precautions. Avoid scratching or gouging the surface that the hose mates against or the connection may leak. This is especially true for radiator hoses. Because of various chemical reactions, the rubber in hoses can bond itself to the metal spigot that the hose fits over. To remove a hose, first loosen the hose clamps that secure it to the spigot. Then, with slip-joint pliers, grab the hose at the clamp and rotate it around the spigot. Work it back and forth until it is completely free, then pull it off. Silicone or other lubricants will ease removal if they can be applied between the hose and the outside of the spigot. Apply the same lubricant to the inside of the hose and the outside of the spigot to simplify installation.

As a last resort (and if the hose is to be replaced with a new one anyway), the rubber can be slit with a knife and the hose peeled from the spigot. If this must be done, be careful that the metal connection is not damaged.

If a hose clamp is broken or damaged, do not reuse it. Wire-type clamps usually weaken with age, so it is a good idea to replace them with screw-type clamps whenever a hose is removed.

Tools

A selection of good tools is a basic requirement for anyone who plans to maintain and repair his or her own vehicle. For the owner who has few tools, if any, the initial investment might seem high, but when compared to the spiraling costs of professional auto maintenance and repair, it is a wise one.

To help the owner decide which tools are needed to perform the tasks detailed in this manual, the following tool lists are offered: *Maintenance and minor repair, Repair and overhaul* and *Special.* The newcomer to practical mechanics should start off with the *Maintenance and minor repair tool kit,* which is adequate for the simpler jobs performed on a vehicle. Then, as confidence and experience grow, the owner can tackle more difficult tasks, buying additional tools as they are needed. Eventually the basic kit will be expanded into the *Repair and overhaul tool set.* Over a period of time, the experienced do-it-yourselfer will assemble a tool set complete enough for most repair and overhaul procedures and will add tools from the *Special* category when it is felt that the expense is justified by the frequency of use.

Maintenance and minor repair tool kit

The tools in this list should be considered the minimum required for performance of routine maintenance, servicing and minor repair work. We recommend the purchase of combination wrenches (box-end and open-end combined in one wrench); while more expensive than open-ended ones, they offer the advantages of both types of wrench.

> *Combination wrench set (1/4 in to 1 in or 6 mm to 19 mm)*
> *Adjustable wrench — 8 in*
> *Spark plug wrench (with rubber insert)*
> *Spark plug gap adjusting tool*
> *Feeler gauge set*
> *Brake bleeder wrench*
> *Standard screwdriver (5/16 in x 6 in)*
> *Phillips screwdriver (No. 2 x 6 in)*
> *Combination pliers — 6 in*
> *Hacksaw and assortment of blades*
> *Tire pressure gauge*
> *Grease gun*
> *Oil can*
> *Fine emery cloth*
> *Wire brush*
> *Battery post and cable cleaning tool*
> *Oil filter wrench*
> *Funnel (medium size)*
> *Safety goggles*
> *Jackstands (2)*
> *Drain pan*

Note: *If basic tune-ups are going to be part of routine maintenance, it will be necessary to purchase a good quality stroboscopic timing light and combination tachometer/dwell meter. Although they are included in the list of Special tools, it is mentioned here because they are absolutely necessary for tuning most vehicles properly.*

Repair and overhaul tool set

These tools are essential for anyone who plans to perform major repairs and are in addition to those in the *Maintenance and minor repair tool kit.* Included is a comprehensive set of sockets which, though expensive, are invaluable because of their versatility (especially when various extensions and drives are available). We recommend the 1/2-inch drive over the 3/8-inch drive. Although the larger drive is bulky and more expensive, it has the capacity of accepting a very wide range of large sockets (ideally, the mechanic would have a 3/8-inch drive set and a 1/2-inch drive set).

> *Socket set(s)*
> *Reversible ratchet*
> *Extension — 10 in*
> *Universal joint*
> *Torque wrench (same size drive as sockets)*
> *Ball peen hammer — 8 oz*
> *Soft-faced hammer (plastic/rubber)*
> *Standard screwdriver (1/4 in x 6 in)*
> *Standard screwdriver (stubby — 5/16 in)*
> *Phillips screwdriver (No. 3 x 8 in)*
> *Phillips screwdriver (stubby — No. 2)*
> *Pliers — vise grip*
> *Pliers — lineman's*
> *Pliers — needle nose*
> *Pliers — snap-ring (internal and external)*
> *Cold chisel — 1/2 in*
> *Scriber*
> *Scraper (made from flattened copper tubing)*
> *Center punch*
> *Pin punches (1/16, 1/8, 3/16 in)*
> *Steel rule/straightedge — 12 in*
> *Allen wrench set (1/8 to 3/8 in or 4 mm to 10 mm)*
> *A selection of files*
> *Wire brush (large)*
> *Jackstands (second set)*
> *Jack (scissor or hydraulic type)*

Note: *Another tool which is often useful is an electric drill motor (with a chuck capacity of 3/8-inch) and a set of good-quality drill bits.*

Special tools

The tools in this list include those which are not used regularly, are expensive to buy, or which need to be used in accordance with their manufacturer's instructions. Unless these tools will be used frequently, it is not very economical to purchase many of them. A consideration would be to split the cost and use between yourself and a friend or friends. In addition, most of these tools can be obtained from a tool rental shop on a temporary basis.

This list contains only those tools and instruments widely available

Micrometer set

Dial indicator set

Dial caliper

Hand-operated vacuum pump

Timing light

Compression gauge with spark plug
hole adapter

Damper/steering wheel puller

General purpose puller

Hydraulic lifter removal tool

Valve spring compressor

Valve spring compressor

Ridge reamer

Piston ring groove cleaning tool

Ring removal/installation tool

Ring compressor

Cylinder hone

Brake hold-down spring tool

Brake cylinder hone

Clutch plate alignment tool

Tap and die set

to the public, and not those special tools produced by the vehicle manufacturer for distribution to dealer service departments. Occasionally, references to the manufacturer's special tools are included in the text of this manual. Generally, an alternative method of doing the job without the special tool is offered. However, sometimes there is no alternative to their use. Where this is the case, and the tool cannot be purchased or borrowed, the work should be turned over to the dealer service department or an automotive repair shop.

Valve spring compressor
Piston ring groove cleaning tool
Piston ring compressor
Piston ring installation tool
Cylinder compression gauge
Cylinder ridge reamer
Cylinder surfacing hone
Cylinder bore gauge
Micrometer(s) and/or dial calipers
Hydraulic lifter removal tool
Balljoint separator
Universal-type puller
Impact screwdriver
Dial indicator set
Stroboscopic timing light (inductive pick-up)
Hand-operated vacuum/pressure pump
Tachometer/dwell meter
Universal electrical multimeter
Cable hoist
Brake spring removal and installation tools
Floor jack

Buying tools

For the do-it-yourselfer who is just starting to get involved in vehicle maintenance and repair, there are a number of options available when purchasing tools. If maintenance and minor repair is the extent of the work to be done, the purchase of individual tools is satisfactory. If, on the other hand, extensive work is planned, it would be a good idea to purchase a modest tool set from one of the large retail chain stores. A set can usually be bought at a substantial savings over the individual tool prices (and they often come with a tool box). As additional tools are needed, add-on sets, individual tools and a larger tool box can be purchased to expand the tool selection. Building a tool set gradually allows the cost of the tools to be spread over a longer period of time and gives the mechanic the freedom to choose only those tools that will actually be used.

Tool stores will often be the only source of some of the special tools that are needed, but regardless of where tools are bought, try to avoid cheap ones (especially when buying screwdrivers and sockets) because they won't last very long. The expense involved in replacing cheap tools will eventually be greater than the initial cost of quality tools.

Care and maintenance of tools

Good tools are expensive, so it makes sense to treat them with respect. Keep them clean and in usable condition and store them properly when not in use. Always wipe off any dirt, grease or metal chips before putting them away. Never leave tools lying around in the work area. Upon completion of a job, always check closely under the hood for tools that may have been left there (so they don't get lost during a test drive).

Some tools, such as screwdrivers, pliers, wrenches and sockets, can be hung on a panel mounted on the garage or workshop wall, while others should be kept in a tool box or tray. Measuring instruments, gauges, meters, etc. must be carefully stored where they cannot be damaged by weather or impact from other tools.

When tools are used with care and stored properly, they will last a very long time. Even with the best of care, tools will wear out if used frequently. When a tool is damaged or worn out, replace it; subsequent jobs will be safer and more enjoyable if you do.

Working facilities

Not to be overlooked when discussing tools is the workshop. If anything more than routine maintenance is to be carried out, some sort of suitable work area is essential.

It is understood, and appreciated, that many home mechanics do not have a good workshop or garage available and end up removing an engine or doing major repairs outside. It is recommended, however, that the overhaul or repair be completed under the cover of a roof.

A clean, flat workbench or table of comfortable working height is an absolute necessity. The workbench should be equipped with a vise that has a jaw opening of at least four inches.

As mentioned previously, some clean, dry storage space is also required for tools, as well as the lubricants, fluids, cleaning solvents, etc. which soon become necessary.

Sometimes waste oil and fluids, drained from the engine or cooling system during normal maintenance or repairs, present a disposal problem. To avoid pouring them on the ground or into a sewage system, simply pour the used fluids into large containers, seal them with caps and take them to an authorized disposal site or recycling center. Plastic jugs (such as old antifreeze containers) are ideal for this purpose.

Always keep a supply of old newspapers and clean rags available. Old towels are excellent for mopping up spills. Many mechanics use rolls of paper towels for most work because they are readily available and disposable. To help keep the area under the vehicle clean, a large cardboard box can be cut open and flattened to protect the garage or shop floor.

Whenever working over a painted surface (such as when leaning over a fender to service something under the hood), always cover it with an old blanket or bedspread to protect the finish. Vinyl covered pads, made especially for this purpose, are available at auto parts stores.

Booster battery (jump) starting

Certain precautions must be observed when using a booster battery to 'jump start' a vehicle.

a) Before connecting the booster battery, make sure that the ignition switch is in the Off position.
b) Turn off the lights, heater and other electrical loads.
c) The eyes should be shielded; safety goggles are a good idea.
d) Make sure the booster battery is the same voltage as the dead one in the vehicle.
e) The two vehicles must not touch each other.
f) Make sure the transmission is in Neutral (manual transmission) or Park (automatic transmission).

Connect the red jumper cable to the *positive* (+) terminals of each battery.

Connect one end of the black jumper cable to the *negative* (−) terminal of the booster battery. The other end of this cable should be connected to a good ground on the vehicle to be started, such as a bolt or bracket on the engine block. Use caution to ensure that the cables will not come into contact with the fan, drivebelts or other moving parts of the engine.

Start the engine using the booster battery, then, with the engine running at idle speed, disconnect the jumper cables in the reverse order of connection.

Booster battery cable connections (note that the negative cable is *not* attached to the negative terminal of the dead battery)

Jacking and towing

Jacking

The jack supplied with the vehicle should only be used for raising the vehicle when changing a tire or placing jackstands under the frame. **Caution:** *Never work under the vehicle or start the engine while this jack is being used as the only means of support.*

The vehicle should be on level ground with the wheels blocked and the transmission in Park (automatic) or Reverse (manual). Pry off the hub cap (if equipped) using the tapered end of the lug wrench. Loosen the wheel nuts one-half turn and leave them in place until the wheel is raised off the ground.

Place the jack under the side of the vehicle in the indicated position and place the jack lever in the 'up' position. Raise the jack until the jack head groove fits into the rocker flange notch. Operate the jack with a slow, smooth motion, using your hand or foot to pump the handle until the wheel is raised off the ground. Remove the wheel nuts, pull off the wheel and replace it with the spare. (If you have a stowaway spare, refer to the instructions accompanying the supplied inflator.)

With the beveled side in, replace the wheel nuts and tighten them until snug. Place the jack lever in the 'down' position and lower the vehicle. Remove the jack and tighten the nuts in a crisscross sequence by turning the wrench clockwise. Replace the hub cap (if equipped) by placing it into position and using the heel of your hand or a rubber mallet to seat it.

Towing

The vehicle can be towed with all four wheels on the ground, provided that speeds do not exceed 35 mph and the distance is not over 50 miles, otherwise transmission damage can result.

Towing equipment specifically designed for this purpose should be used and should be attached to the main structural members of the vehicle and not the bumper or brackets.

Safety is a major consideration when towing and all applicable state and local laws must be obeyed. A safety chain system must be used for all towing.

While towing, the parking brake should be released and the transmission should be in Neutral. The steering must be unlocked (ignition switch in the Off position). Remember that power steering and power brakes will not work with the engine off.

CAR SHOULD BE TAKEN TO AVOID CONTACT WITH REAR STABILIZER BAR IF THE VEHICLE IS SO EQUIPPED.

RIGHT

WRONG

DO NOT ALLOW THE HOIST TO TOUCH THE CASTING

WHEN RAISING A VEHICLE ON A TWIN POST HOIST, CARE SHOULD BE TAKEN TO POSITION THE VEHICLE SO THAT THE HOISTING FORKS DO NOT DAMAGE THE AXLE CARRIER CASTING AND/OR REAR COVER.

Rear axle hoisting points

FRONT

Front suspension lift points for balljoint unloading. Note location of coil spring in different illustrations and match to spring location in your car

Typical frame contact lift points

Automotive chemicals and lubricants

A number of automotive chemicals and lubricants are available for use during vehicle maintenance and repair. They include a wide variety of products ranging from cleaning solvents and degreasers to lubricants and protective sprays for rubber, plastic and vinyl.

Cleaners

Carburetor and choke cleaner is a strong solvent for gum, varnish and carbon. Most carburetor cleaners leave a dry-type lubricant film which will not harden or gum up. Because of this film it is not recommended for use on electrical components.

Brake system cleaner is used to remove grease and brake fluid from the brake system where clean surfaces are absolutely necessary. It leaves no residue and often eliminates brake squeal caused by contaminants.

Electrical cleaner removes oxidation, corrosion and carbon deposits from electrical contacts, restoring full current flow. It can also be used to clean spark plugs, carburetor jets, voltage regulators any other parts where an oil-free surface is required.

Demoisturants remove water and moisture from electrical components such as alternators, voltage regulators, electrical connectors and fuse blocks. It is non-conductive, non-corrosive and non-flammable.

Degreasers are heavy-duty solvents used to remove grease from the outside of the engine and from chassis components. They can be sprayed or brushed on, and, depending on the type, are rinsed off either with water or solvent.

Lubricants

Motor oil is the lubricant specially formulated for use in engines. It normally contains a wide variety of additives to prevent corrosion and reduce foaming and wear. Motor oil comes in various weights (viscosity ratings) from 5 to 80. The recommended weight of the oil depends on the seasonal temperature and the demands on the engine. Light oil is used in cold climates and under light load conditions. Heavy oil is used in hot climates and where high loads are encountered. Multi-viscosity oils are designed to have characteristics of both light and heavy oils and are available in a number of weights from 5W-20 to 20W-50.

Gear oil is a specially designed oil used in differentials, manual transmissions and transfer cases, as well as other areas where high-friction, high-temperature lubrication is required.

Chassis and wheel bearing grease is a heavy grease used where increased loads and friction are encountered, such as for wheel bearings, balljoints, tie-rod ends and universal joints.

High temperature wheel bearing grease is designed to withstand the extreme temperatures encountered by wheel bearings in disc-brake equipped vehicles. It usually contains molybdenum disulfide (moly), which is a dry-type lubricant.

White grease is a heavy grease for metal-to-metal applications where water is a problem. White grease stays soft under both low and high temperatures (usually from −100 °F to + 190 °F, and will not wash off or dilute in the presence of water.

Silicone lubricants are used to protect rubber, plastic, vinyl and nylon parts.

Graphite lubricants are used where oils cannot be used due to contamination problems, such as in locks. The dry graphite will lubricate metal parts while remaining uncontaminated by dirt, water, oil or acids. It is electrically conductive and will not foul electrical contacts in locks such as the ignition switch.

Moly-penetrants loosen and lubricate frozen, rusted and corroded fasteners and prevent future rusting or freezing.

Heat-sink grease is a special electrically non-conductive grease that is used for mounting HEI ignition modules where it is essential that heat be transferred away from the module.

Sealants

RTV sealant is one of the most widely used gasket compounds. Made from silicone, RTV is air curing, it seals, bonds, waterproofs, fills surface irregularities, remains flexible, doesn't shrink, is relatively easy to remove, and is used as a supplementary sealer with almost all low and medium temperature gaskets.

Anaerobic sealant is much like RTV in that it can be used either to seal gaskets or to form gaskets by itself. It remains flexible, is solvent resistant and fills surface imperfections. The difference between an anaerobic sealant and an RTV-type sealant is in the curing. RTV cures when exposed to air, while an anaerobic sealant cures only in the absence of air. This means that an anaerobic sealant cures only after the assembly of parts, sealing them together.

Thread and pipe sealant is used for sealing hydraulic and pneumatic fittings and vacuum lines. It usually is made from a teflon compound, and comes in a spray, a paint-on liquid, and as a wrap-around tape.

Chemicals

Anti-seize compound prevents seizing, galling, cold welding, rust and corrosion in fasteners. High-temperature anti-seize, usually made with copper and graphite lubricants, is usually used for exhaust system and manifold bolts.

Anaerobic locking compounds are used to keep fasteners from vibrating or working loose, and cure only after installation, in the absence of air. Medium strength locking compound is used for small nuts, bolts and screws that you expect to be removing later. High strength locking compound is for large nuts, bolts and studs which you don't intend to be removing on a regular basis.

Oil additives range from viscosity index improvers to chemical treatments that claim to reduce internal engine friction. It should be noted that most oil manufacturers caution against using additives with their oils.

Gas additives perform several functions, depending on their chemical makeup. They usually contain solvents that help dissolve gum and varnish that build up on carburetor and intake parts. They also serve to break down carbon deposits that form on the inside surfaces of the combustion chambers. Some additives contain upper cylinder lubricants for valves and piston rings, and others chemicals to remove condensation from the gas tank.

Other

Brake fluid is a specially formulated hydraulic fluid that can withstand the heat and pressure encountered in brake systems. Care must be taken that this fluid does not come in contact with painted surfaces or plastics. An opened container should always be resealed to prevent contamination by water or dirt.

Weatherstrip adhesive is used to bond weatherstripping around doors, windows and trunk lids. It is sometimes used to attach trim pieces.

Undercoating is a petroleum-based tar-like substance that is designed to protect metal surfaces on the underside of the vehicle from corrosion. It also acts as a sound-deadening agent by insulating the bottom of the vehicle.

Waxes and polishes are used to help protect painted and plated surfaces from the weather. Different types of paint may require the use of different types of wax and polish. Some polishes utilize a chemical or abrasive cleaner to help remove the top layer of oxidized (dull) paint on older vehicles. In recent years many non-wax polishes that contain a wide variety of chemicals such as polymers and silicones have been introduced. These non-wax polishes are usually easier to apply and last longer than conventional waxes and polishes.

Safety first!

Regardless of how enthusiastic you may be about getting on with the job at hand, take the time to ensure that your safety is not jeopardized. A moment's lack of attention can result in an accident, as can failure to observe certain simple safety precautions. The possibility of an accident will always exist, and the following points should not be considered a comprehensive list of all dangers. Rather, they are intended to make you aware of the risks and to encourage a safety conscious approach to all work you carry out on your vehicle.

Essential DOs and DON'Ts

DON'T rely on a jack when working under the vehicle. Always use approved jackstands to support the weight of the vehicle and place them under the recommended lift or support points.

DON'T attempt to loosen extremely tight fasteners (i.e. wheel lug nuts) while the vehicle is on a jack — it may fall.

DON'T start the engine without first making sure that the transmission is in Neutral (or Park where applicable) and the parking brake is set.

DON'T remove the radiator cap from a hot cooling system — let it cool or cover it with a cloth and release the pressure gradually.

DON'T attempt to drain the engine oil until you are sure it has cooled to the point that it will not burn you.

DON'T touch any part of the engine or exhaust system until it has cooled sufficiently to avoid burns.

DON'T siphon toxic liquids such as gasoline, antifreeze and brake fluid by mouth, or allow them to remain on your skin.

DON'T inhale brake lining dust — it is potentially hazardous (see *Asbestos* below)

DON'T allow spilled oil or grease to remain on the floor — wipe it up before someone slips on it.

DON'T use loose fitting wrenches or other tools which may slip and cause injury.

DON'T push on wrenches when loosening or tightening nuts or bolts. Always try to pull the wrench toward you. If the situation calls for pushing the wrench away, push with an open hand to avoid scraped knuckles if the wrench should slip.

DON'T attempt to lift a heavy component alone — get someone to help you.

DON'T rush or take unsafe shortcuts to finish a job.

DON'T allow children or animals in or around the vehicle while you are working on it.

DO wear eye protection when using power tools such as a drill, sander, bench grinder, etc. and when working under a vehicle.

DO keep loose clothing and long hair well out of the way of moving parts.

DO make sure that any hoist used has a safe working load rating adequate for the job.

DO get someone to check on you periodically when working alone on a vehicle.

DO carry out work in a logical sequence and make sure that everything is correctly assembled and tightened.

DO keep chemicals and fluids tightly capped and out of the reach of children and pets.

DO remember that your vehicle's safety affects that of yourself and others. If in doubt on any point, get professional advice.

Asbestos

Certain friction, insulating, sealing, and other products — such as brake linings, brake bands, clutch linings, torque converters, gaskets, etc. — contain asbestos. *Extreme care must be taken to avoid inhalation of dust from such products since it is hazardous to health*. If in doubt, assume that they *do* contain asbestos.

Fire

Remember at all times that gasoline is highly flammable. Never smoke or have any kind of open flame around when working on a vehicle. But the risk does not end there. A spark caused by an electrical short circuit, by two metal surfaces contacting each other, or even by static electricity built up in your body under certain conditions, can ignite gasoline vapors, which in a confined space are highly explosive. Do not, under any circumstances, use gasoline for cleaning parts. Use an approved safety solvent.

Always disconnect the battery ground (–) cable *at the battery* before working on any part of the fuel system or electrical system. Never risk spilling fuel on a hot engine or exhaust component.

It is strongly recommended that a fire extinguisher suitable for use on fuel and electrical fires be kept handy in the garage or workshop at all times. Never try to extinguish a fuel or electrical fire with water.

Fumes

Certain fumes are highly toxic and can quickly cause unconsciousness and even death if inhaled to any extent. Gasoline vapor falls into this category, as do the vapors from some cleaning solvents. Any draining or pouring of such volatile fluids should be done in a well ventilated area.

When using cleaning fluids and solvents, read the instructions on the container carefully. Never use materials from unmarked containers.

Never run the engine in an enclosed space, such as a garage. Exhaust fumes contain carbon monoxide, which is extremely poisonous. If you need to run the engine, always do so in the open air, or at least have the rear of the vehicle outside the work area.

If you are fortunate enough to have the use of an inspection pit, never drain or pour gasoline and never run the engine while the vehicle is over the pit. The fumes, being heavier than air, will concentrate in the pit with possibly lethal results.

The battery

Never create a spark or allow a bare light bulb near a battery. They normally give off a certain amount of hydrogen gas, which is highly explosive.

Always disconnect the battery ground (–) cable *at the battery* before working on the fuel or electrical systems.

If possible, loosen the filler caps or cover when charging the battery from an external source (this does not apply to sealed or maintenance-free batteries). Do not charge at an excessive rate or the battery may burst.

Take care when adding water to a non maintenance-free battery and when carrying a battery. The electrolyte, even when diluted, is very corrosive and should not be allowed to contact clothing or skin.

Always wear eye protection when cleaning the battery to prevent the caustic deposits from entering your eyes.

Household current

When using an electric power tool, inspection light, etc., which operates on household current, always make sure that the tool is correctly connected to its plug and that, where necessary, it is properly grounded. Do not use such items in damp conditions and, again, do not create a spark or apply excessive heat in the vicinity of fuel or fuel vapor.

Secondary ignition system voltage

A severe electric shock can result from touching certain parts of the ignition system (such as the spark plug wires) when the engine is running or being cranked, particularly if components are damp or the insulation is defective. In the case of an electronic ignition system, the secondary system voltage is much higher and could prove fatal.

Conversion factors

Length (distance)

Inches (in)	X	25.4	= Millimetres (mm)	X 0.0394	= Inches (in)
Feet (ft)	X	0.305	= Metres (m)	X 3.281	= Feet (ft)
Miles	X	1.609	= Kilometres (km)	X 0.621	= Miles

Volume (capacity)

Cubic inches (cu in; in³)	X	16.387	= Cubic centimetres (cc; cm³)	X 0.061	= Cubic inches (cu in; in³)
Imperial pints (Imp pt)	X	0.568	= Litres (l)	X 1.76	= Imperial pints (Imp pt)
Imperial quarts (Imp qt)	X	1.137	= Litres (l)	X 0.88	= Imperial quarts (Imp qt)
Imperial quarts (Imp qt)	X	1.201	= US quarts (US qt)	X 0.833	= Imperial quarts (Imp qt)
US quarts (US qt)	X	0.946	= Litres (l)	X 1.057	= US quarts (US qt)
Imperial gallons (Imp gal)	X	4.546	= Litres (l)	X 0.22	= Imperial gallons (Imp gal)
Imperial gallons (Imp gal)	X	1.201	= US gallons (US gal)	X 0.833	= Imperial gallons (Imp gal)
US gallons (US gal)	X	3.785	= Litres (l)	X 0.264	= US gallons (US gal)

Mass (weight)

Ounces (oz)	X	28.35	= Grams (g)	X 0.035	= Ounces (oz)
Pounds (lb)	X	0.454	= Kilograms (kg)	X 2.205	= Pounds (lb)

Force

Ounces-force (ozf; oz)	X	0.278	= Newtons (N)	X 3.6	= Ounces-force (ozf; oz)
Pounds-force (lbf; lb)	X	4.448	= Newtons (N)	X 0.225	= Pounds-force (lbf; lb)
Newtons (N)	X	0.1	= Kilograms-force (kgf; kg)	X 9.81	= Newtons (N)

Pressure

Pounds-force per square inch (psi; lbf/in²; lb/in²)	X	0.070	= Kilograms-force per square centimetre (kgf/cm²; kg/cm²)	X 14.223	= Pounds-force per square inch (psi; lbf/in²; lb/in²)
Pounds-force per square inch (psi; lbf/in²; lb/in²)	X	0.068	= Atmospheres (atm)	X 14.696	= Pounds-force per square inch (psi; lbf/in²; lb/in²)
Pounds-force per square inch (psi; lbf/in²; lb/in²)	X	0.069	= Bars	X 14.5	= Pounds-force per square inch (psi; lbf/in²; lb/in²)
Pounds-force per square inch (psi; lbf/in²; lb/in²)	X	6.895	= Kilopascals (kPa)	X 0.145	= Pounds-force per square inch (psi; lbf/in²; lb/in²)
Kilopascals (kPa)	X	0.01	= Kilograms-force per square centimetre (kgf/cm²; kg/cm²)	X 98.1	= Kilopascals (kPa)
Millibar (mbar)	X	100	= Pascals (Pa)	X 0.01	= Millibar (mbar)
Millibar (mbar)	X	0.0145	= Pounds-force per square inch (psi; lbf/in²; lb/in²)	X 68.947	= Millibar (mbar)
Millibar (mbar)	X	0.75	= Millimetres of mercury (mmHg)	X 1.333	= Millibar (mbar)
Millibar (mbar)	X	0.401	= Inches of water (inH₂O)	X 2.491	= Millibar (mbar)
Millimetres of mercury (mmHg)	X	0.535	= Inches of water (inH₂O)	X 1.868	= Millimetres of mercury (mmHg)
Inches of water (inH₂O)	X	0.036	= Pounds-force per square inch (psi; lbf/in²; lb/in²)	X 27.68	= Inches of water (inH₂O)

Torque (moment of force)

Pounds-force inches (lbf in; lb in)	X	1.152	= Kilograms-force centimetre (kgf cm; kg cm)	X 0.868	= Pounds-force inches (lbf in; lb in)
Pounds-force inches (lbf in; lb in)	X	0.113	= Newton metres (Nm)	X 8.85	= Pounds-force inches (lbf in; lb in)
Pounds-force inches (lbf in; lb in)	X	0.083	= Pounds-force feet (lbf ft; lb ft)	X 12	= Pounds-force inches (lbf in; lb in)
Pounds-force feet (lbf ft; lb ft)	X	0.138	= Kilograms-force metres (kgf m; kg m)	X 7.233	= Pounds-force feet (lbf ft; lb ft)
Pounds-force feet (lbf ft; lb ft)	X	1.356	= Newton metres (Nm)	X 0.738	= Pounds-force feet (lbf ft; lb ft)
Newton metres (Nm)	X	0.102	= Kilograms-force metres (kgf m; kg m)	X 9.804	= Newton metres (Nm)

Power

Horsepower (hp)	X	745.7	= Watts (W)	X 0.0013	= Horsepower (hp)

Velocity (speed)

Miles per hour (miles/hr; mph)	X	1.609	= Kilometres per hour (km/hr; kph)	X 0.621	= Miles per hour (miles/hr; mph)

Fuel consumption*

Miles per gallon, Imperial (mpg)	X	0.354	= Kilometres per litre (km/l)	X 2.825	= Miles per gallon, Imperial (mpg)
Miles per gallon, US (mpg)	X	0.425	= Kilometres per litre (km/l)	X 2.352	= Miles per gallon, US (mpg)

Temperature

Degrees Fahrenheit = (°C x 1.8) + 32   Degrees Celsius (Degrees Centigrade; °C) = (°F - 32) x 0.56

*It is common practice to convert from miles per gallon (mpg) to litres/100 kilometres (l/100km),
where mpg (Imperial) x l/100 km = 282 and mpg (US) x l/100 km = 235

Troubleshooting

Contents

This section provides an easy-reference guide to the more common problems which may occur during the operation of your vehicle. These problems and possible causes are grouped under various components or systems i.e. Engine, Cooling system, etc., and also refer to the Chapter and/or Section which deals with the problem.

Remember that successful troubleshooting is not a mysterious 'black art' practiced only by professional mechanics; it's simply the result of a bit of knowledge combined with an intelligent, systematic approach to the problem. Always work by a process of elimination, starting with the simplest solution and working through to the most complex — and never overlook the obvious. Anyone can forget to fill the gas tank or leave the lights on overnight, so don't assume that you are above such oversights.

Finally, always get clear in your mind why a problem has occurred and take steps to ensure that it doesn't happen again. If the electrical system fails because of a poor connection, check all other connections in the system to make sure that they don't fail as well; if a particular fuse continues to blow, find out why — don't just go on replacing fuses. Remember, failure of a small component can often be indicative of potential failure or incorrect functioning of a more important component or system.

Engine

1   Engine will not rotate when attempting to start

1   Battery terminal connections loose or corroded. Check the cable terminals at the battery; tighten the cable or remove corrosion as necessary.
2   Battery discharged or faulty. If the cable connections are clean and tight on the battery posts, turn the key to the On position and switch on the headlights and/or windshield wipers. If they fail to function, the battery is discharged.
3   Automatic transmission not completely engaged in Park or clutch not completely depressed.
4   Broken, loose or disconnected wiring in the starting circuit. Inspect all wiring and connectors at the battery, starter solenoid and ignition switch.
5   Starter motor pinion jammed in flywheel ring gear. If manual transmission, place transmission in gear and rock the vehicle to manually turn the engine. Remove starter and inspect pinion and flywheel at earliest convenience.
6   Starter solenoid faulty (Chapter 5).
7   Starter motor faulty (Chapter 5).
8   Ignition switch faulty (Chapter 12).

2   Engine rotates but will not start

1   Fuel tank empty.
2   Battery discharged (engine rotates slowly). Check the operation of electrical components as described in previous Section.
3   Battery terminal connections loose or corroded. See previous Section.
4   Carburetor flooded and/or fuel level in carburetor incorrect. This will usually be accompanied by a strong fuel odor from under the hood. Wait a few minutes, depress the accelerator pedal all the way to the floor and attempt to start the engine.
5   Choke control inoperative (Chapter 4).
6   Fuel not reaching carburetor. With ignition switch in Off position, open hood, remove the top plate of air cleaner assembly and observe the top of the carburetor (manually move choke plate back if necessary). Have an assistant depress accelerator pedal and check that fuel spurts into carburetor. If not, check fuel filter (Chapter 1), fuel lines and fuel pump (Chapter 4).
7   Excessive moisture on, or damage to, ignition components (Chapter 5).
8   Worn, faulty or incorrectly gapped spark plugs (Chapter 5).
9   Broken, loose or disconnected wiring in the starting circuit (see previous Section).
10   Distributor loose, causing ignition timing to change. Turn the distributor as necessary to start the engine, then set ignition timing as soon as possible (Chapter 5).
11   Broken, loose or disconnected wires at the ignition coil or faulty coil (Chapter 5).

3   Starter motor operates without rotating engine

1   Starter pinion sticking. Remove the starter (Chapter 5) and inspect.
2   Starter pinion or flywheel teeth worn or broken. Remove the cover at the rear of the engine and inspect.

4   Engine hard to start when cold

1   Battery discharged or low. Check as described in Section 1.
2   Choke control inoperative or out of adjustment (Chapter 4).
3   Carburetor flooded (see Section 2).
4   Fuel supply not reaching the carburetor (see Section 4).
5   Carburetor/fuel injection system in need of overhaul (Chapter 4).
6   Fuel not reaching injector system. Check filter screens, lines and fuel pump.

5   Engine hard to start when hot

1   Choke sticking in the closed position (Chapter 4).
2   Carburetor flooded (see Section 2).
3   Air filter clogged (Chapter 4).
4   Fuel not reaching the carburetor (see Section 2).

6   Starter motor noisy or excessively rough in engagement

1   Pinion or flywheel gear teeth worn or broken. Remove the cover at the rear of the engine (if so equipped) and inspect.
2   Starter motor mounting bolts loose or missing.

7   Engine starts but stops immediately

1   Loose or faulty electrical connections at distributor, coil or alternator.
2   Insufficient fuel reaching the carburetor/fuel injector(s). Disconnect the fuel line at the carburetor/fuel injector(s) and remove the filter (Chapter 4). Place a container under the disconnected fuel line. Observe the flow of fuel from the line. If little or none at all, check for blockage in the lines and/or replace the fuel pump (Chapter 4).
3   Vacuum leak at the gasket surfaces of the intake manifold and/or carburetor/fuel injector unit(s). Make sure that all mounting bolts (nuts) are tightened securely and that all vacuum hoses connected to the carburetor/fuel injection unit(s) and manifold are positioned properly and in good condition.

8   Oil puddle under engine

1   Oil pan gasket and/or oil plug seal leaking. Check and replace if necessary.
2   Oil pressure sending unit leaking. Replace unit or seal threads with teflon tape (Chapter 5)
3   Valve cover gaskets leaking at front or rear of engine.
4   Engine oil seals leaking at front or rear of engine.

9   Engine lopes while idling or idles erratically

1   Vacuum leakage. Check mounting bolts (nuts) at the carburetor/fuel injection unit and intake manifold for tightness. Make sure that all vacuum hoses are connected and in good condition. Use a stethoscope or a length of fuel hose held against your ear to listen for vacuum leaks while the engine is running. A hissing sound will be heard. A soapy water solution will also detect leaks. Check the carburetor/fuel injection unit and intake manifold gasket surfaces.
2   Leaking EGR valve or plugged PCV valve (see Chapter 6).
3   Air filter clogged (Chapter 1).
4   Fuel pump not delivering sufficient fuel to the carburetor/fuel injector (see Chapter 4).
5   Carburetor out of adjustment (Chapter 4).
6   Leaking head gasket. If this is suspected, take the vehicle to a repair shop or dealer where the engine can be pressure checked.
7   Timing chain and/or gears worn (Chapter 2).
8   Camshaft lobes worn (Chapter 2).

10   Engine misses at idle speed

1   Spark plugs worn or not gapped properly (Chapter 5).
2   Faulty spark plug wires (Chapter 4).
3   Choke not operating properly (Chapter 4).

11   Engine misses throughout driving speed range

1   Fuel filter clogged and/or impurities in the fuel system (Chapter 4). Also check fuel output at the carburetor/fuel injector (see Section 7).

2 Faulty or incorrectly gapped spark plugs (Chapter 5).
3 Incorrect ignition timing (Chapter 5).
4 Check for cracked distributor cap, disconnected distributor wires and damaged distributor components (Chapter 5).
5 Leaking spark plug wires (Chapter 5).
6 Faulty emissions system components (Chapter 6).
7 Low or uneven cylinder compression pressures. Remove spark plugs and test compression with gauge (Chapter 1).
8 Weak or faulty ignition system (Chapter 5).
9 Vacuum leaks at carburetor/fuel injection unit, intake manifold or vacuum hoses (see Section 8).
10 Loose injector harness.

12 Engine stumbles on acceleration

1 Spark plugs fouled (Chapter 1). Clean and/or replace.
2 Carburetor needs adjustment or repair (Chapter 4).
3 Fuel filter clogged. Replace filter.
4 Incorrect ignition timing (Chapter 1).
5 Intake manifold air leak (Chapters 4 and 6).

13 Engine surges while holding accelerator steady (fuel-injected models only)

1 Intake air leak (Chapter 4)
2 Fuel pump faulty (Chapter 4).
3 Loose fuel injector harness connections.
4 Defective control unit.

14 Engine stalls

1 Idle speed incorrect (Chapter 4).
2 Fuel filter clogged and/or water and impurities in the fuel system (Chapter 4).
3 Choke improperly adjusted or sticking (Chapter 4).
4 Distributor components damp or damaged (Chapter 5).
5 Faulty emissions system components (Chapter 6).
6 Faulty or incorrectly gapped spark plugs (Chapter 5). Also check spark plug wires (Chapter 5).
7 Vacuum leak at the carburetor/fuel injection unit, intake manifold or vacuum hoses. Check as described in Section 8.
8 Valve clearances incorrectly set (Chapter 2).

15 Engine lacks power

1 Incorrect ignition timing (Chapter 5).
2 Excessive play in distributor shaft. At the same time, check for worn rotor, faulty distributor cap, wires, etc. (Chapter 5).
3 Faulty or incorrectly gapped spark plugs (Chapter 5).
4 Carburetor/fuel injection unit not adjusted properly or excessively worn (Chapter 4).
5 Faulty coil (Chapter 5).
6 Brakes binding (Chapter 9).
7 Automatic transmission fluid level incorrect (Chapter 7).
8 Clutch slipping (Chapter 7).
9 Fuel filter clogged and/or impurities in the fuel system (Chapter 4).
10 Emissions control system not functioning properly (Chapter 6).
11 Use of sub-standard fuel. Fill tank with proper octane fuel.
12 Low or uneven cylinder compression pressures. Test with compression tester, which will detect leaking valves and/or blown head gasket (Chapter 1).

16 Engine backfires

1 Emissions system not functioning properly (Chapter 6).
2 Ignition timing incorrect (Chapter 3).

3 Faulty secondary ignition system (cracked spark plug insulator, faulty plug wires, distributor cap and/or rotor) (Chapters 1 and 5).
4 Carburetor/fuel injection in need of adjustment or worn excessively (Chapter 4).
5 Vacuum leak at carburetor/fuel injection unit, intake manifold or vacuum hoses. Check as described in Section 8.
6 Valve clearances incorrectly set, and/or valves sticking (Chapter 2).

17 Pinging or knocking engine sounds during acceleration or uphill

1 Incorrect grade of fuel. Fill tank with fuel of the proper octane rating.
2 Ignition timing incorrect (Chapter 5).
3 Carburetor/fuel injection unit in need of adjustment (Chapter 4).
4 Improper spark plugs. Check plug type against Emissions Control Information label located in engine compartment. Also check plugs and wires for damage (Chapter 5).
5 Worn or damaged distributor components (Chapter 5).
6 Faulty emissions system (Chapter 6).
7 Vacuum leak. Check as described in Section 9.

18 Engine running with oil pressure light on

1 Low oil pressure. Check oil level and add oil if necessary (Chapter 1)
2 Idle rpm below specification (Chapter 1).
3 Short in wiring circuit. Repair or replace damaged wire.

19 Engine 'diesels' (continues to run) after switching off

1 Idle speed too high (Chapter 5).
2 Electrical solenoid at side of carburetor not functioning properly (not all models, see Chapter 4).
3 Ignition timing incorrectly adjusted (Chapter 5).
4 Air cleaner heat valve not operating properly (Chapter 4).
5 Excessive engine operating temperature. Probable causes of this are malfunctioning thermostat, clogged radiator, faulty water pump (Chapter 3).
6 EGR system malfunction (Chapter 6).

Engine electrical system

20 Battery will not hold a charge

1 Alternator drivebelt defective or not adjusted properly (Chapter 5).
2 Electrolyte level low or battery discharged (Chapter 12).
3 Battery terminals loose or corroded (Chapter 12).
4 Alternator not charging properly (Chapter 12).
5 Loose, broken or faulty wiring in the charging circuit (Chapter 12).
6 Short in vehicle wiring causing a continual drain on battery.
7 Battery defective internally.

21 Alternator light fails to go out

1 Fault in alternator or charging circuit (Chapter 5).
2 Alternator drivebelt defective or not properly adjusted (Chapter 5).
3 Alternator voltage regulator inoperative (Chapter 5).

22 Ignition light fails to come on when key is turned on

1 Warning light bulb defective (Chapter 12).
2 Alternator faulty (Chapter 5).
3 Fault in the printed circuit, dash wiring or bulb holder (Chapter 12).

Fuel system

23 Excessive fuel consumption

1 Dirty or clogged air filter element (Chapter 4).
2 Incorrectly set ignition timing (Chapter 5).
3 Choke sticking or improperly adjusted (Chapter 4).
4 Emissions system not functioning properly (not all vehicles, see Chapter 6).
5 Carburetor idle speed and/or mixture not adjusted properly (Chapter 4).
6 Fuel injection internal parts excessively worn or damaged (Chapter 4).
7 Low tire pressure or incorrect tire size (Chapter 10).

24 Fuel leakage and/or fuel odor

1 Leak in a fuel feed or vent line (Chapter 4).
2 Tank overfilled. Fill only to automatic shut-off.
3 Emissions system filter clogged (Chapter 6).
4 Vapor leaks from system lines (Chapter 4).
5 Carburetor/fuel injection internal parts excessively worn or out of adjustment (Chapter 4).

Engine cooling system

25 Overheating

1 Insufficient coolant in system (Chapter 3).
2 Water pump drivebelt defective or not adjusted properly (Chapter 2).
3 Radiator core blocked or radiator grille dirty and restricted (Chapter 3).
4 Thermostat faulty (Chapter 3).
5 Fan blades broken or cracked (Chapter 3).
6 Radiator cap not maintaining proper pressure. Have cap pressure tested by gas station or repair shop.
7 Ignition timing incorrect (Chapter 5).
8 Defective water pump (Chapter 3).

26 Overcooling

1 Thermostat faulty (Chapter 3).
2 Inaccurate temperature gauge (Chapter 12)

27 External coolant leakage

1 Deteriorated or damaged hoses. Loose clamps at hose connections (Chapter 3).
2 Water pump seals defective. If this is the case, water will drip from the 'weep' hole in the water pump body (Chapter 3).
3 Leakage from radiator core or header tank. This will require the radiator to be professionally repaired (see Chapter 3 for removal procedures).
4 Engine drain plugs or water jacket core plugs leaking (see Chapters 2 and 3).

28 Internal coolant leakage

Note: *Internal coolant leaks can usually be detected by examining the oil. Check the dipstick and inside of the rocker arm cover(s) for water deposits and an oil consistency like that of a milkshake.*

1 Leaking cylinder head gasket. Have the cooling system pressure-tested.
2 Cracked cylinder bore or cylinder head. Dismantle engine and inspect (Chapter 2).
3 Loose cylinder head bolts (Chapter 2).

29 Coolant loss

1 Too much coolant in system (Chapter 3).
2 Coolant boiling away due to overheating (see Section 25).
3 Internal or external leakage (see Sections 27 and 28).
4 Faulty radiator cap. Have the cap pressure-tested.

30 Poor coolant circulation

1 Inoperative water pump. A quick test is to pinch the top radiator hose closed with your hand while the engine is idling, then let it loose. You should feel the surge of coolant if the pump is working properly (Chapter 3).
2 Restriction in cooling system. Drain, flush and refill the system (Chapter 3). If necessary, remove the radiator (Chapter 3) and have it reverse-flushed.
3 Water pump drivebelt defective or not adjusted properly (Chapter 3).
4 Thermostat sticking (Chapter 3).

Clutch

31 Fails to release (pedal pressed to the floor — shift lever does not move freely in and out of Reverse)

1 Improper linkage free play adjustment (Chapter 8).
2 Clutch fork off ball stud. Look under the vehicle, on the left side of transmission.
3 Clutch plate warped or damaged (Chapter 8).

32 Clutch slips (engine speed increases with no increase in vehicle speed)

1 Linkage out of adjustment (Chapter 8).
2 Clutch plate oil soaked or lining worn. Remove clutch (Chapter 8) and inspect.
3 Clutch plate not seated. It may take 30 or 40 normal starts for a new one to seat.
4 Warped flywheel (Chapter 2)

33 Grabbing (chattering) as clutch is engaged

1 Oil on clutch plate lining. Remove (Chapter 8) and inspect. Correct any leakage source.
2 Worn or loose engine or transmission mounts. These units move slightly when clutch is released. Inspect mounts and bolts.
3 Worn splines on clutch plate hub. Remove clutch components (Chapter 8) and inspect.
4 Warped pressure plate or flywheel. Remove clutch components and inspect.
5 Hardened or warped clutch disc facing.

34 Squeal or rumble with clutch fully engaged (pedal released)

1 Improper adjustment; no free play (Chapter 8).
2 Release bearing binding on transmission bearing retainer. Remove clutch components (Chapter 8) and check bearing. Remove any burrs or nicks, clean and relubricate before reinstallation.
3 Weak linkage return spring. Replace the spring.
4 Cracked clutch disc.

35 Squeal or rumble with clutch fully disengaged (pedal depressed)

1 Worn, defective or broken release bearing (Chapter 8).
2 Worn or broken pressure plate springs (or diaphragm fingers) (Chapter 8).

36 Clutch pedal stays on floor when disengaged

1   Bind in linkage or release bearing. Inspect linkage or remove clutch components as necessary.
2   Linkage springs being over-extended. Adjust linkage for proper free play. Make sure proper pedal stop (bumper) is installed.

Manual transmission

37 Noisy in Neutral with engine running

1   Input shaft bearing worn.
2   Damaged main drive gear bearing.
3   Worn countershaft bearings.
4   Transmission oil deteriorated.

38 Noisy in all gears

1   Any of the above causes, and/or:
2   Insufficient lubricant (see checking procedures in Chapter 7A).
3   Worn or damaged output shaft or bearings.

39 Noisy in one particular gear

1   Worn, damaged or chipped gear teeth for that particular gear.
2   Worn or damaged synchronizer for that particular gear.

40 Slips out of gear

1   Transmission loose on clutch housing.
2   Shift rods interfering with engine mounts or clutch lever.
3   Shift rods not working freely.
4   Damaged mainshaft pilot bearing.
5   Dirt between transmission case and engine or misalignment of transmission (Chapter 8).
6   Worn or improperly adjusted linkage (Chapter 8).
7   Worn synchro units.

41 Difficulty in engaging gears

1   Clutch not releasing completely.
2   Loose, damaged or out-of-adjustment shift linkage. Make a thorough inspection, replacing parts as necessary (Chapter 8).

42 Oil leakage

1   Excessive amount of lubricant in transmission (see Chapter 1 for correct checking procedures). Drain lubricant as required.
2   Side cover loose or gasket damaged.
3   Rear oil seal or speedometer oil seal in need of replacement.

Automatic transmission

Note: *Due to the complexity of the automatic transmission, it is difficult for the home mechanic to properly diagnose and service this component. For problems other than the following, the vehicle should be taken to a dealer or reputable mechanic.*

43 Fluid leakage

1   Automatic transmission fluid is a deep red color. Fluid leaks should not be confused with engine oil, which can easily be blown by air flow to the transmission.
2   To pinpoint a leak, first remove all built-up dirt and grime from around the transmission. Degreasing agents and/or steam cleaning will achieve this. With the underside clean, drive the vehicle at low speeds so air flow will not blow the leak far from its source. Raise the vehicle and determine where the leak is coming from. Common areas of leakage are:

   a) Pan: Tighten mounting bolts and/or replace pan gasket as necessary (see Chapter 7B).
   b) Filler pipe: Replace the rubber seal where pipe enters transmission case.
   c) Transmission oil lines: Tighten connectors where lines enter transmission case and/or replace lines.

44 Transmission fluid brown or has burned smell

1   Transmission low on fluid. Replace fluid. Do not overfill.

45 General shift mechanism problems

1   Chapter 7B deals with checking and adjusting the shift linkage on automatic transmissions. Common problems which may be attributed to poorly adjusted linkage are:

   Engine starting in gears other than Park or Neutral.
   Indicator on shifter pointing to a gear other than the one actually being used.
   Vehicle moves when in Park.

2   Refer to Chapter 7B to adjust the linkage.

46 transmission will not downshift with accelerator pedal pressed to the floor

1   Chapter 7B deals with adjusting the automatic transmission kickdown.

47 Engine will start in gears other than 'P' (Park) or 'N' (Neutral)

1   Chapter 7B deals with adjusting the neutral start switches used with automatic transmissions.

48 Transmission slips, shifts rough, is noisy or has no drive in forward or reverse gears

1   There are many probable causes for the above problems, but the home mechanic should be concerned with only one possibility — fluid level.
2   Before taking the vehicle to a repair shop, check the level and condition of the fluid as described in Chapter 7B. Correct fluid level as necessary or change the fluid and filter if needed. If the problem persists, have a professional diagnose the probable cause.

Driveshaft

49 Leakage of fluid at front of driveshaft

1   Defective transmission rear oil seal. See Chapter 7B for replacement procedures. While this is done, check the splined yoke for burrs or a rough condition which may be damaging the seal. If found, these can be removed with emery cloth or a fine abrasive stone.

50 Knock or clunk when transmission is under initial load (just after transmission is put into gear)

1   Loose or disconnected rear suspension components. Check all mounting bolts and bushings (Chaptaer 11).
2   Loose driveshaft bolts. Inspect all bolts and nuts and tighten

to torque specifications (Chapter 8).
3   Worn or damaged universal joint bearings. Test for wear (Chapter 8).
4   Worn mainshaft splines.

51   Metallic grating sound consistent with road speed

1   Pronounced wear in the universal joint bearings. Test for wear (Chapter 8).

52   Vibration

Note: *Before it can be assumed that the driveshaft is at fault, make sure the tires are perfectly balanced and perform the following test.*

1   Install a tachometer inside the car to monitor engine speed as the car is driven. Drive the car and note the engine speed at which the vibration (roughness) is most pronounced. Now shift the transmission to a different gear and bring the engine speed to the same point.
2   If the vibration occurs at the same engine speed (rpm) regardless of which gear the transmission is in, the driveshaft is NOT at fault since the driveshaft speed varies.
3   If the vibration decreases or is eliminated when the transmission is in a different gear at the same engine speed, refer to the following probable causes.
4   Bent or dented driveshaft. Inspect and replace as necessary (Chapter 8).
5   Undercoating or built-up dirt, etc., on the driveshaft. Clean the shaft thoroughly and test.
6   Worn universal joint bearings. Remove and inspect (Chapter 8).
7   Driveshaft and/or companion flange out of balance. Check for missing weights on the shaft. Remove driveshaft (Chapter 8) and reinstall 180° from original position. Retest. Have driveshaft professionally balanced if problem persists (Chapter 8).
8   Driveshaft improperly installed (Chapter 8).
9   Worn transmission rear bushing (Chapter 7).

Rear axle

53   Noise — same when in drive as when vehicle is coasting

1   Road noise. No corrective procedures available.
2   Tire noise. Inspect tires and tire pressures (Chapter 10).
3   Front wheel bearings loose, worn or damaged (Chapter 10).
4   Insufficient differential oil. (Whining noise consistent with vehicle speed changes.)

54   Vibration

1   See probable causes under 'Driveshaft'. Proceed under the guidelines listed for the driveshaft. If the problem persists, check the rear wheel bearings by raising the rear of the car and spinning the wheels by hand. Listen for evidence of rough (noisy) bearings. Remove and inspect. (Chapter 8).

55   Oil leakage

1   Pinion oil seal damaged (Chapter 8).
2   Axle shaft oil seals damaged (Chapter 8).
3   Differential inspection cover leaking. Tighten mounting bolts or replace the gasket as required (Chapter 8).

Brakes

Note: *Before assuming that a brake problem exists, make sure that the tires are in good condition and inflated properly (see Chapter 10), that the front end alignment is correct and that the vehicle is not loaded with weight in an unequal manner.*

56   Vehicle pulls to one side during braking

1   Defective, damaged or oil contaminated disc brake pads on one side. Inspect as described in Chapter 1.
2   Excessive wear of brake pad material or disc on one side. Inspect and correct as necessary.
3   Loose or disconnected front suspension components. Inspect and tighten all bolts to the specified torque (Chapter 10).
4   Defective caliper assembly. Remove caliper and inspect for stuck piston or other damage (Chapter 9).

57   Noise (high-pitched squeal without the brakes applied)

1   Disc brake pads worn out. The noise comes from the wear sensor rubbing against the disc (does not apply to all vehicles). Replace pads with new ones immediately (Chapter 9).

58   Excessive brake pedal travel

1   Partial brake system failure. Inspect entire system (Chapter 9) and correct as required.
2   Insufficient fluid in master cylinder. Check (Chapter 1), add fluid and bleed system if necessary (Chapter 9).
3   Rear brakes not adjusting properly. Make a series of starts and stops while the vehicle is in Reverse. If this does not correct the situation, remove drums and inspect self-adjusters (Chapter 9).

59   Brake pedal feels spongy when depressed

1   Air in hydraulic lines. Bleed the brake system (Chapter 9).
2   Faulty flexible hoses. Inspect all system hoses and lines. Replace parts as necessary.
3   Master cylinder mounting bolts/nuts loose.
4   Master cylinder defective (Chapter 9).

60   Excessive effort required to stop vehicle

1   Power brake booster not operating properly (Chapter 9).
2   Excessively worn linings or pads. Inspect and replace if necessary (Chapter 9).
3   One or more caliper pistons or wheel cylinders seized or sticking. Inspect and rebuild as required (Chapter 9).
4   Brake linings or pads contaminated with oil or grease. Inspect and replace as required (Chapter 9).
5   New pads or shoes installed and not yet seated. It will take a while for the new material to seat against the drum (or rotor).

61   Pedal travels to the floor with little resistance

1   Little or no fluid in the master cylinder reservoir caused by leaking wheel cylinder(s), leaking caliper piston(s), loose, damaged or disconnected brake lines. Inspect entire system and correct as necessary.

62   Brake pedal pulsates during brake application

1   Wheel bearings not adjusted properly or in need of replacement (Chapter 10).
2   Caliper not sliding properly due to improper installation or obstructions. Remove and inspect (Chapter 9).
3   Rotor defective. Remove the rotor (Chapter 9) and check for excessive lateral runout and parallelism. Have the rotor resurfaced or replace it with a new one.

63 Parking brake does not hold

1 Mechanical parking brake linkage improperly adjusted. Adjust according to procedure in Chapter 9.

Suspension and steering systems

64 Vehicle pulls to one side

1 Tire pressures uneven (Chapter 10).
2 Defective tire (Chapter 10).
3 Excessive wear in suspension or steering components (Chapter 10).
4 Front end in need of alignment.
5 Front brakes dragging. Inspect brakes as described in Chapter 9.
6 Wheel bearings improperly adjusted.

65 Shimmy, shake or vibration

1 Tire or wheel out-of-balance or out-of-round. Have professionally balanced.
2 Loose, worn or out-of-adjustment wheel bearings (Chapter 10)
3 Shock absorbers and/or suspension components worn or damaged (Chapter 10).

66 Excessive pitching and/or rolling around corners or during braking

1 Defective shock absorbers. Replace as a set (Chapter 10).
2 Broken or weak springs and/or suspension components. Inspect as described in Chapter 10.

67 Excessively stiff steering

1 Lack of fluid in power steering fluid reservoir (Chapter 10).
2 Incorrect tire pressures (Chapter 10).
3 Lack of lubrication at steering joints (Chapter 10).
4 Front end out of alignment.
5 Air in power steering system.
6 Low tire pressure.

68 Excessive play in steering

1 Loose front wheel bearings (Chapter 10).
2 Excessive wear in suspension or steering components (Chapter 10).
3 Steering gearbox out of adjustment (Chapter 10).

69 Lack of power assistance

1 Steering pump drivebelt faulty or not adjusted properly (Chapter 10).
2 Fluid level low (Chapter 10).
3 Hoses or lines restricted. Inspect and replace parts as necessary.
4 Air in power steering system. Bleed system (Chapter 10).

70 Excessive tire wear (not specific to one area)

1 Incorrect tire pressures (Chapter 10).
2 Tires out of balance. Have professionally balanced.
3 Wheels damaged. Inspect and replace as necessary.
4 Suspension or steering components excessively worn (Chapter 11).

71 Excessive tire wear on outside edge

1 Inflation pressures incorrect (Chapter 10).
2 Excessive speed in turns.
3 Front end alignment incorrect (excessive toe-in). Have professionally aligned.
4 Suspension arm bent or twisted (Chapter 10).

72 Excessive tire wear on inside edge

1 Inflation pressures incorrect (Chapter 10).
2 Front end alignment incorrect (toe-out). Have professionally aligned.
3 Loose or damaged steering components (Chapter 10).

73 Tire tread worn in one place

1 Tires out of balance.
2 Damaged or buckled wheel. Inspect and replace if necessary.
3 Defective tire.

Chapter 1   Tune-up and routine maintenance

Refer to Chapter 13 for information related to 1985 and later models

Contents

Specifications

Recommended lubricants, fluids and capacities

Engine oil type	SAE grade SE or better
Engine oil viscosity	
40° to 100° F (4° to 38° C)	SAE 40W, 10W-30, 10W-40, 10W-50, 20W-40
20° to 100° F (–7° to 38° C)	SAE 20W-40, 20W-50, 10W-40, 10W-50
10° to 100° F (–14° to 38° C)	SAE 20W-30, 20W-40, 20W-50, 10W-40, 10W-50
0° to 100° F (–18° to 38° C)	SAE 10W-30, 10W-40, 10W-50
0° to 60° F (-18° to 17° C)	SAE 10W, 5W-30
Below –20° to 60° F (below –30° to 17° C)	SAE 5W-30, 5W-20, 10W-20, 10W-30, 10W
Below –20° to 20° F (below –30° to –7° C)	SAE 10 W, 5W-30, 5W-20
Engine oil capacity (with filter)	5.0 qts (4.7 liters)
Coolant type	50/50 mixture of ethylene glycol-based antifreeze and water
Brake fluid type	DOT 3
Manual transmission/rear axle oil type	SAE 80W-90 GL-5 gear oil
Automatic transmission	
Fluid type*	
Automatic overdrive (all)	Dexron II or Ford CJ
C3 (81 on)	
C4 (80 on)	
C6 (77 on)	
C5 (all)	Type H
All others	Type F
*The fluid type should be stamped on the transmission dipstick	
Fluid capacity	
AOD	12.3 qts (11.7 liters)
FMX	11 qts (10.4 liters)
C3	8 qts (7.6 liters)
C4	10.0 qts (9.46 liters)
C5	11.0 qts (10.4 liters)
C6	11.8 quts (11.2 liters)
Power steering fluid type	ATF type F
Front wheel bearing lubricant	EP lithium-base grease
Steering, shift and clutch linkage lubricant	EP lithium-base grease
Suspension balljoint lubricant	EP lithium-base grease
Radiator cap opening pressure	16 psi
Engine idle speed	See Emission Control Information label

Ignition system

Direction of distributor rotation

    V6 and V8 engines . . . . Counterclockwise

    Inline engines . . . . Clockwise

Firing order

    4.2, 5.0 and 7.5 liter V8 1-5-4-2-6-3-7-8

    5.8 and 6.6 liter V8 1-3-7-2-6-5-4-8

    V6 1-4-2-5-3-6

    Inline six-cylinder 1-5-3-6-2-4

    Four-cylinder 1-3-4-2

Spark plug type and gap . . . . See Emission Control Information label

Ignition timing . . . . See Emission Control Information label

Torque specifications   Ft-lbs (except where noted)

Oil pan drain plug . . . . 15 to 25

Spark plugs

    3.3L . . . . 17 to 22

    2.3L — 7.5L . . . . 5 to 10

    All others . . . . 10 to 15

Fuel charger to intake manifold (CFI) . . . . 120 in-lb.

Intake manifold-to-cylinder head bolts (V8 only)

    4.2, 5.0 and 5.8L . . . . 21 to 27

    6.6 and 7.5L . . . . 25 to 30

Distributor hold-down bolt 20

Manual transmission fill plug . . . . 15 to 30

Automatic transmission pan bolts . . . . 12 to 20

Rear axle filler/inspection plug . . . . 17 to 25

Wheel lug nuts . . . . 80 to 105

1

1 Introduction and routine maintenance

    This Chapter was designed to help the home mechanic maintain his (or her) vehicle for peak performance, economy, safety and long life.

    On the following pages you will find a maintenance schedule, along with sections which deal specifically with each item on the schedule. Included are visual checks, adjustments and item replacements.

    Servicing your vehicle, using the time/mileage maintenance schedule and the sequenced Sections, will give you a planned program of maintenance. Keep in mind that it is a full plan, and maintaining only a few items at the specified intervals will not give you the same results.

    You will find as you service your vehicle that many of the procedures can, and should, be grouped together, due to the nature of the job at hand. Examples of this are as follows:

    If the vehicle is fully raised for a chassis lubrication, for example, this is the ideal time for the following checks: exhaust system, suspension, steering and fuel system.

    If the tires and wheels are removed, as during a routine tire rotation, go ahead and check the brakes and wheel bearings at the same time.

    If you must borrow or rent a torque wrench, it is a good idea to service the spark plugs and check the carburetor or TBI mounting torque all in the same day to save time and money.

    The first step of this, or any, maintenance plan is to prepare yourself before the actual work begins. Read through the appropriate Sections for all work that is to be performed before you begin. Gather together all the necessary parts and tools. If it appears that you could have a problem during a particular job, don't hesitate to seek advice from your local parts man or dealer service department.

Routine maintenance intervals

    The following recommendations are given with the assumption that the vehicle owner will be doing the maintenance or service work (as opposed to having a dealer service department do the work). The following are factory maintenance recommendations. However, subject to the preference of the individual owner, interested in keeping his or her vehicle in peak condition at all times and with the vehicle's ultimate resale in mind, many of these operations may be performed more often. We encourage such owner initiative.

    When the vehicle is new it should be serviced initially by a factory authorized dealer service department to protect the factory warranty. In many cases the initial maintenance check is done at no cost to the owner.

Every 250 miles (400 km), weekly and before long trips

Check tire pressures (cold)

Check steering for smooth and accurate operation

Inspect tires for wear and damage

Check power steering reservoir fluid level

Check the brake fluid reservoir level. If the amount of fluid has dropped noticeably since the last check inspect all brake lines and hoses for leakage and condition

Check for satisfactory brake operation

Check the operation of the windshield wiper and washers

Check the windshield wiper condition

Check the operation of the horn

Check the operation of all instruments

Check the radiator coolant level and add coolant as needed

Check the battery electrolyte level and add distilled water as needed

Check the engine oil level and add oil as needed

Every 3000 miles (500 km) or 3 months, whichever comes first

Change the engine oil and filter

Check and replace if necessary the air cleaner filter element

Check the idle speed

Check engine drivebelt condition and tension

Check the exhaust heat control valve operation

Every 6000 miles (10000 km) or 6 months, whichever comes first

Check cooling system clamps and hoses

Check the exhaust system for loose or damaged components

Check the power steering fluid level and add fluid as necessary

Lubricate the steering linkage

Lubricate the clutch linkage (if so equipped)

Check the brake linings and pads

Check the differential oil level and add oil as necessary

Check the manual transmission oil level and add oil as necessary

Check the automatic transmission bands and adjust if necessary

Replace the fuel filter

A Inline four-cylinder

B Inline six-cylinder

C V6

D V8

Fig. 1.1 Typical engine compartment service points

1 Brake master cylinder	*7 Coolant reservoir*	*12 Power steering reservoir dipstick*
2 Engine oil filler cap	*8 Windshield washer reservoir*	* and filler tube*
3 Engine oil filter	*9 Air cleaner assembly*	*13 PCV valve and grommet*
4 Fuel filter	*10 Battery*	*14 Radiator cap*
5 Engine oil dipstick	*11 Automatic transmission dipstick*	*15 PCV filter*
6 Distributor	* and filler tube*	*16 Radiator cap (2.3L non-A/C)*

Check the operation of the temperature-controlled air cleaner

**Every 12000 miles (20000 km) or 12 months,
whichever comes first**

    Lubricate parking brake linkages, pivots and clevices
    Check the spark plug wires
    Check the operation of the EGR system and delay valve (if so
equipped)
    Check and clean the crankcase breather cap
    Inspect the brake lines and hoses
    Check the PCV valve
    Check the condition of the engine coolant

**Every 18000 miles (30000 km) or 18 months,
whichever comes first**

    Check and adjust the ignition timing
    Check the distributor cap and rotor
    Tighten the intake manifold nuts and bolts to the specified torque
    Replace the crankcase ventilation filter
    Replace the automatic transmission fluid
    Replace the spark plugs

Every 24000 miles (40000 km) or 24 months, whichever comes first

Drain and refill the cooling system with the specified coolant
Drain and refill the manual transmission with the specified lubricant
Drain and refill the differential
Check the evaporative system hoses, vapor lines and fuel filler cap
Check the engine compression

Severe operating conditions

Severe operating conditions are defined as follows:
Extended periods of idling or low speed operation
Towing trailers up to 1000 lbs (450 kg) for long distances
Operating when the outside temperatures remain below 10° F (−12° C) for 60 days or more
When most trips you make are less than ten miles (16 km) in duration
Operation in severe dust conditions
If your vehicle falls into the severe operation conditions category the maintenance schedule must be amended as follows:
a) Change the engine oil and filter every 2 months or 2000 miles (3200 km)
b) Check, clean and regap the spark plugs every 4000 miles (6400 km)
c) Service the automatic transmission bands every 5000 miles (8000 km) and drain and refill the transmission with fresh fluid every 2000 miles (32000 km)
d) If the vehicle is operated in severe dust conditions, check the paper-type air cleaner element every 1000 miles
f) Check and replace the cartridge-type fuel filter frequently when operating in dusty conditions

2 Tune-up sequence

The term *tune-up* is loosely used for any general operation that puts the engine back in its proper running condition. A tune-up is not a specific operation, but rather a combination of individual operations, such as replacing the spark plugs, adjusting the idle speed, setting the ignition timing, etc.

If, from the time the vehicle is new, the routine maintenance schedule (Section 1) is followed closely and frequent checks are made of fluid levels and high wear items, as suggested throughout this manual, the engine will be kept in relatively good running condition and the need for additional tune-ups will be minimized.

More likely than not, however, there will be times when the engine is running poorly due to lack of regular maintenance. This is even more likely if a used vehicle (which has not received regular and frequent maintenance checks) is purchased. In such cases an engine tune-up will be needed outside of the regular routine maintenance intervals.

The following operations are those most often needed to bring a generally poor running engine back into a proper state of tune.

Minor tune-up

Clean, inspect and test battery (Sec 5)
Check all engine-related fluids (Sec 4)
Check engine compression (Sec 31)
Check and adjust drivebelts (Sec 6)
Replace spark plugs (Sec 29)
Inspect distributor cap and rotor (Sec 30)
Inspect spark plug and coil wires (Sec 30)
Check and adjust idle speed (Sec 14)
Check and adjust timing (Sec 28)
Check and adjust fuel/air mixture (see underhood VECI label)
Replace fuel filter (Sec 17)
Check PCV valve (Chapter 6)
Check cooling system (Sec 7)

Major tune-up

The above operations plus those listed below)
Check EGR system (Chapter 6)

Check ignition system (Chapter 5)
Check charging system (Chapter 5)
Check fuel system (Sec 16)

3 Tire and tire pressure checks

1   Periodically inspecting the tires may not only prevent you from being stranded with a flat tire, but can also give you clues as to possible problems with the steering and suspension systems before major damage occurs.
2   Proper tire inflation adds miles to the lifespan of the tires, allows the vehicle to achieve maximum miles per gallon figures and contributes to the overall quality of the ride.
3   When inspecting the tires, first check the tread wear. Irregularities in the tread pattern (cupping, flat spots, more wear on one side than the other) are indications of front end alignment and/or balance problems. If any of these conditions are noted, take the vehicle to a reputable repair shop to correct the problem.
4   Check the tread area for cuts and punctures. Many times a nail or tack will embed itself into the tire tread and yet the tire will hold its air pressure for a short time. In most cases a repair shop or gas station can repair the punctured tire.
5   It is also important to check the sidewalls of the tires, both inside and outside. Check for deteriorated rubber, cuts and punctures. Also inspect the inboard side of the tire for signs of brake fluid leakage, indicating that a thorough brake inspection is needed immediately.
6   Incorrect tire pressure cannot be determined merely by looking at the tire. This is especially true for radial tires. A tire pressure gauge must be used. If you do not already have a reliable gauge it is a good idea to purchase one and keep it in the glovebox. Built-in pressure gauges at gas stations are often unreliable.
7   Always check tire inflation when the tires are cold. Cold, in this case, means the vehicle has not been driven more than one mile after sitting for three hours or more. It is normal for the pressure to increase four to eight pounds or more when the tires are hot.
8   Unscrew the valve cap protruding from the wheel or hubcap and press the gauge firmly onto the valve stem. Observe the reading on the gauge and compare the figure to the recommended tire pressure listed on the tire placard. The tire placard is usually attached to the driver's door or glove compartment door.
9   Check all tires and add air as necessary to bring them up to the recommended pressure levels. Do not forget the spare tire. Be sure to reinstall the valve caps (which will keep dirt and moisture out of the valve stem mechanism).

TIRE TREAD

TIRE WEAR INDICATOR

Fig. 1.2 Tread wear indicator at the replacement stage (Sec 3)

4 Fluid level checks

1   There are a number of components on a vehicle which rely on the use of fluids to perform their job. During normal operation of the vehicle these fluids are used up and must be replenished before damage occurs. See *Recommended lubricants and fluids* at the front of this Chapter for specific fluids to be used when addition is required. When checking fluid levels it is important to have the vehicle on a level surface.

ADD → SAFE ├── SPECIFICATION

NOTE: LUBRICANT LEVEL SHOULD ALWAYS BE
WITHIN THE SAFE RANGE.

Fig. 1.3 Typical engine oil dipstick marks (Sec 4)

Engine oil

2   The engine oil level is checked with a dipstick, which is located at the side of the engine block. The dipstick travels through a tube and into the oil pan to the bottom of the engine.

3   The oil level should be checked preferably before the vehicle has been driven, or about 15 minutes after the engine has been shut off. If the oil is checked immediately after driving the vehicle, some of the oil will remain in the upper engine components, producing an inaccurate reading on the dipstick.

4   Pull the dipstick from the tube and wipe all the oil from the end with a clean rag. Insert the clean dipstick all the way back into the oil pan and pull it out again. Observe the oil at the end of the dipstick. At its highest point, the level should be between the Add and Full marks.

5   It takes approximately one quart of oil to raise the level from the Add mark to the Full mark on the dipstick. Do not allow the level to drop below the Add mark as engine damage due to oil starvation may occur. On the other hand, do not overfill the engine by adding oil above the Full mark, since it may result in oil-fouled spark plugs, oil leaks or oil seal failures.

6   Oil is added to the engine after removing a twist-off cap located on the rocker arm cover. The cap is marked *Engine oil* or *Oil*. An oil can spout or funnel will reduce spills as the oil is poured in.

7   Checking the oil level can also be an important preventative maintenance step. If you find the oil level dropping abnormally it is an indication of oil leakage or internal engine wear which should be corrected. If there are water droplets in the oil, or if it is milky looking, component failure is indicated and the engine should be checked immediately. The condition of the oil can also be checked along with the level. With the dipstick removed from the engine, take your thumb and index finger and wipe the oil up the dipstick, looking for small dirt or metal particles which will cling to the dipstick. This is an indication that the oil should be drained and fresh oil added (Section 15).

Engine coolant

8   All vehicles covered by this manual are equipped with a pressurized coolant recovery system, which makes coolant level checks very easy (photo). A clear or translucent coolant reservoir, attached to the inner fender panel, is connected by a hose to the radiator cap. As the engine heats up during operation coolant is forced from the radiator, through the connecting tube, and into the reservoir. As the engine cools the coolant is automatically drawn back into the radiator to keep the level correct.

9   The coolant level should be checked when the engine is hot. Merely observe the level of fluid in the reservoir, which should be at or near the Full mark on the side of the reservoir. If the system is completely cool, also check the level in the radiator by removing the cap.

10   **Caution:** *Under no circumstances should the radiator cap or the coolant recovery reservoir cap be removed when the system is hot. Escaping steam and scalding liquid can cause serious personal injury.* In the case of the radiator cap, wait until the system has cooled completely, then wrap a thick cloth around the cap and turn it to the first stop. If any steam escapes, wait until the system has cooled further, then remove the cap. The coolant recovery cap may be removed carefully after it is apparent that no further 'boiling' is occurring in the recovery tank.

11   If only a small amount of coolant is required to bring the system up to the proper level, regular water can be used. However, to maintain the proper antifreeze/water mixture in the system, both should be mixed together to replenish a low level. **Note:** *High-quality antifreeze offering protection to −20°F should be mixed with water in the proportion specified on the container. Do not allow antifreeze to come in contact with your skin or painted surfaces of the vehicle. Flush contacted areas immediately with plenty of water.*

12   Coolant should be added to the reservoir until it reaches the Full Cold mark.

13   As the coolant level is checked, note the condition of the coolant. It should be relatively clear. If it is brown or a rust color, the system should be drained, flushed and refilled.

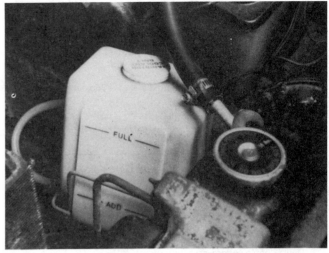

4.8   The coolant level should be near the Full mark on the reservoir

4.17   Remove the cell caps to check the battery electrolyte level

14   If the cooling system requires repeated additions to maintain the proper level, have the radiator cap checked for proper sealing ability. Also check for leaks in the system (cracked hoses, loose hose connections, leaking gaskets, etc.).

Windshield washer fluid

15   Fluid for the windshield washer system is located in a plastic reservoir. The level in the reservoir should be maintained at the Full mark, except during periods when freezing temperatures are expected, at which times the fluid level should be maintained no higher than 3/4 full to allow for expansion should the fluid freeze. The use of an additive will help lower the freezing point of the fluid and will result in better cleaning of the windshield surface. Do not use antifreeze because it will cause damage to the vehicle's paint.

16   To help prevent icing in cold weather, warm the windshield with the defroster before using the washer.

Battery electrolyte

17   To check the electrolyte level in the battery (non-maintenance-free batteries only), remove all the vent caps (photo). If the battery level is low, add distilled water until the level is above the cell plates. There is an indicator in each cell to help you judge when enough water has been added. Do not overfill.

Brake fluid

18   The master cylinder is mounted on the left side of the engine compartment firewall and has a cover which must be removed to check the fluid level (photo).

4.18   Checking the brake master cylinder fluid level

19   Before removing the cover use a rag to clean all dirt, grease, etc. from around the area. If foreign matter enters the master cylinder when the cover is removed blockage of the brake system lines can occur. Also, make sure all painted surfaces around the master cylinder are covered, as brake fluid will ruin paint.

20   Release the clip securing the cover to the top of the master cylinder. A screwdriver can be used to pry the wire clip free. Carefully lift the cover off the master cylinder and note the fluid level. It should be approximately 1/4-inch below the top edge of each reservoir. If a low level is found, fluid must be added.

21   When adding fluid, pour it carefully into the reservoir, taking care not to spill any onto surrounding painted surfaces. Be sure the specified fluid is used, since mixing different types of brake fluid can cause damage to the system. See *Recommended Lubricants and Fluids* or your owner's manual.

22   At this time the fluid and master cylinder can be inspected for contamination. Normally, the brake system will not need periodic draining and refilling, but if rust deposits, dirt particles or water droplets are seen in the fluid, the system should be dismantled, drained and refilled with fresh fluid.

23   After filling the reservoir to the proper level, make sure the lid is properly seated to prevent fluid leakage and/or system pressure loss.

24   The brake fluid in the master cylinder will drop slightly as the brake shoes or pads at each wheel wear down during normal operation. If the master cylinder requires repeated replenishing to keep it at the proper level, this is an indication of leakage in the brake system, which should be corrected immediately. Check all brake lines and connections, along with the wheel cylinders and booster.

25   If, upon checking the master cylinder fluid level, you discover one or both reservoirs empty or nearly empty, the brake system should be bled (Chapter 9).

Manual transmission oil

26   Manual shift transmissions do not have a dipstick. The fluid level is checked with the engine cold by removing a plug from the side of the transmission. Locate the plug and use a rag to clean the plug and the area around it, then remove the plug with a wrench.

27   If oil immediately starts leaking out, thread the plug back into the transmission because the oil level is correct. If there is no leakage, completely remove the plug and place your little finger inside the hole. The oil level should be just at the bottom of the plug hole.

28   If the transmission needs more oil use a syringe or squeeze bottle to add the appropriate lubricant until the level is correct.

29   Thread the plug back into the transmission and tighten it securely.

30   Drive the vehicle a short distance, then check to make sure the plug is not leaking.

Automatic transmission fluid

31   The level of the automatic transmission fluid should be carefully maintained. Low fluid level can lead to slipping or loss of drive, while

Fig. 1.4   **Releasing the retainer on the brake master cylinder cover (Sec 4)**

Fig. 1.5   **Effect of temperature on transmission fluid level (Sec 4)**

overfilling can cause foaming and loss of fluid.

32   With the parking brake set, start the engine, then move the shift lever through all the gear ranges, ending in Park. The fluid level must be checked with the vehicle level and the engine running at idle. **Note:** *Incorrect fluid level readings will result if the vehicle has just been driven at high speeds for an extended period, in hot weather in city traffic, or if it's been pulling a trailer. If any of these conditions apply, wait until the fluid has cooled (about 30 minutes).*

33   Locate the dipstick at the rear of the engine compartment on the passenger's side and pull it out of the filler tube.

34   Carefully touch the end of the dipstick to determine if the fluid is cool (about room temperature), warm, or hot (uncomfortable to the touch).

35   Wipe the fluid from the dipstick with a clean rag and push it back into the filler tube until the cap seats.

36   Pull the dipstick out again and note the fluid level.

37   If the fluid felt cool the level should be 1/8 to 3/8-inch below the Add mark. The two dimples below the Add mark indicate this range. Refer to the accompanying illustration showing the effect of temperature on the fluid level.

38   If the fluid felt warm, the level should be close to the Add mark (just above or below it).

39   If the fluid felt hot, the level should be near the Full mark.

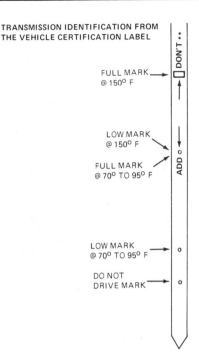

Fig. 1.6 Typical transmission fluid dipstick marks
(C6 transmission shown) (Sec 4)

4.43   Rear axle oil filler plug (arrow) (check the lubricant level with a bent wire gauge)

4.52   Power steering pump fluid level dipstick

Fig. 1.7 Typical power steering pump and dipstick marks
(Sec 4)

40 Add just enough of the recommended fluid to fill the transmission to the proper level. It takes about one pint to raise the level from the Add mark to the Full mark with a hot transmission, so add the fluid a little at a time and keep checking the level until it is correct.

41 The condition of the fluid should also be checked along with the level. If the fluid at the end of the dipstick is a dark reddish-brown color, or if the fluid has a burnt smell, the transmission fluid should be changed. If you are in doubt about the condition of the fluid, purchase some new fluid and compare the two for color and smell.

Rear axle oil

42 Like the manual transmission, the rear axle has an inspection and fill plug which must be removed to check the oil level.

43 Remove the plug, which is located either in the removable cover plate or on the side of the differential carrier (photo). Use your little finger to reach inside the axle housing to feel the oil level. It should be near the bottom of the plug hole.

44 If this is not the case, add the proper lubricant to the rear axle through the plug hole.

45 Make certain the correct lubricant is used, as regular and Traction-Lok rear axles require different lubricants. Refer to Chapter 8 to determine which type of rear axle you have.

46 Tighten the plug securely and check for leaks after the first few miles of driving.

Power steering fluid

47 Unlike manual steering, the power steering system relies on fluid which may, over a period of time, require replenishing.

48 The reservoir for the power steering pump is located on the front of the engine.

49 For the check the front wheels should be pointed straight ahead and the engine should be off.

50 Use a clean rag to wipe off the reservoir cap and the area around the cap. This will help prevent any foreign matter from entering the reservoir during the check.

51 Make sure the engine is at normal operating temperature.

52 Remove the dipstick (photo), wipe it off with a clean rag, reinsert it, then withdraw it and read the fluid level. The level should be between the Add and Full Hot marks.

53 If additional fluid is required, pour the specified type directly into the reservoir, using a funnel to prevent spills.

54 If the reservoir requires frequent fluid additions, all power steering hoses, hose connections, the power steering pump and the steering box should be carefully checked for leaks.

5.1 Eye and hand protection, baking soda, petroleum jelly and tools required for battery maintenance

5.5A Battery terminal corrosion usually appears as a white, fluffy powder

5.5B Removing a cable from the battery terminal post (always remove the ground cable first and hook it up last)

5.5C Cleaning a battery terminal post with the cleaning tool

5 Battery check and maintenance

Caution: *Certain precautions must be followed when checking or servicing the battery. Hydrogen gas, which is highly flammable, is always present in the battery cells so keep lighted tobacco and any other open flames or sparks away from the battery. The electrolyte inside the battery is actually dilute sulfuric acid, which can be hazardous to your skin and cause injury if splashed in the eyes. It will also ruin clothes and painted surfaces.*

1 Tools and materials required for battery maintenance include eye and hand protection, baking soda, petroleum jelly, a battery cable puller, cable/terminal post cleaning tools and a hydrometer (photo).

Checking
2 Check the battery for cracks and evidence of leakage.
3 To check the electrolyte level in the battery, remove all vent caps. If the battery level is low, add distilled water until the level is above the cell plates. There is an indicator in each cell to help you judge when enough water has been added. Do not overfill. **Note:** *Some models may be equipped with maintenance-free batteries which have no provision (or need) for adding water. Also, some models may be equipped with translucent batteries so the electrolyte level can be observed without removing any vent caps. On these batteries, the level should be between the upper and lower lines.*
4 Periodically check the specific gravity of the electrolyte with a hydrometer. This is especially important during cold weather. If the reading is below the specified range, the battery should be recharged.

5.5D Cleaning a battery cable clamp

Maintenance-free batteries have a built-in hydrometer which indicates the battery state-of-charge.
5 Check the tightness of the battery cable clamps to ensure good electrical connections. If corrosion is evident, remove the cables from the battery terminals (a puller may be required), clean them with a battery terminal brush, then reinstall them (photos). Corrosion can be kept to a minimum by applying a layer of petroleum jelly or grease to the terminal and cable clamps after they are assembled.

6   Inspect the entire length of each battery cable for corrosion, cracks and frayed conductors. Replace the cables with new ones if they are damaged (Chapter 5).
7   Make sure that the rubber protector over the positive terminal is not torn or missing. It should completely cover the terminal.
8   Make sure that the battery is securely mounted, but do not over-tighten the clamp bolts.
9   The battery case and caps should be kept clean and dry. If corrosion is evident, clean the battery as explained in Step 12.
10   If the vehicle is not being used for an extended period, disconnect the battery cables and have the battery charged approximately every six weeks.

Cleaning

11   Corrosion on the battery hold-down components and inner fender panels can be removed by washing with a solution of water and baking soda. Once the area has been thoroughly cleaned, rinse it with clean water.
12   Corrosion on the battery case and terminals can also be removed with a solution of water and baking soda and a stiff brush. Be careful that none of the solution is splashed into your eyes or onto your skin (wear protective gloves). Do not allow any of the baking soda and water solution to get into the battery cells. Rinse the battery thoroughly once it is clean.
13   Metal parts of the vehicle which have been damaged by spilled battery acid should be painted with a zinc-based primer and paint. Do this only after the area has been thoroughly cleaned and dried.

Charging

14   As mentioned before, if the battery's specific gravity is below the specified amount, the battery must be recharged.
15   If the battery is to remain in the vehicle during charging, disconnect the cables from the battery to prevent damage to the electrical system.
16   When batteries are being charged, hydrogen gas (which is very explosive and flammable) is produced. Do not smoke or allow an open flame near a charging or a recently charged battery. Also, do not plug in the battery charger until the connections have been made at the battery posts.
17   The average time necessary to charge a battery at the normal rate is from 12 to 16 hours (sometimes longer). Always charge the battery slowly. A quick charge or boost charge is hard on a battery and will shorten its life. Use a battery charger that is rated at no more than 1/10 the amp/hour rating of the battery.
18   Remove all of the vent caps and cover the holes with a clean cloth to prevent the spattering of electrolyte. Hook the battery charger leads to the battery posts (positive to positive, negative to negative), then plug in the charger. Make sure it is set at 12 volts if it has a selector switch.
19   Watch the battery closely during charging to make sure that it does not overheat.
20   The battery can be considered fully charged when it is gassing freely and there is no increase in specific gravity during three successive readings taken at hourly intervals. Overheating of the battery during charging at normal charging rates, excessive gassing and continual low specific gravity readings are an indication that the battery should be replaced with a new one.

6   Drivebelt check and adjustment

1   The drivebelts, or V-belts as they are sometimes called, are located at the front of the engine and play an important role in the overall operation of the vehicle and its components. Due to their function and material make-up, the belts are prone to failure after a period of time and should be inspected and adjusted periodically to prevent major engine damage.
2   The number of belts used on a particular vehicle depends on the accessories installed. Drivebelts are used to turn the generator/alternator, power steering pump, water pump and air-conditioning compressor. Depending on the pulley arrangement, a single belt may be used to drive more than one of these components.
3   With the engine off, open the hood and locate the various belts at the front of the engine. Using your fingers (and a flashlight, if necessary), move along the belts checking for cracks and separation of the belt plies. Also check for fraying and glazing, which gives the

Fig. 1.8   Engine drivebelt defects (Sec 6)

Fig. 1.9   Engine drivebelt tension check (Sec 6)

belt a shiny appearance. Both sides of the belt should be inspected, which means you will have to twist the belt to check the underside.
4   **Note:** *Steps 4 through 9 pertain to all engines except the 232 cu in V6. If your vehicle is equipped with a V6 refer to Steps 10 through 12.*
5   The tension of each belt is checked by pushing on the belt at a distance halfway between the pulleys. Push firmly with your thumb and see how much the belt moves down (deflects). A rule of thumb is that if the distance from pulley center-to-pulley center is between 7 and 11 inches, the belt should deflect 1/4-inch. If the belt is longer and travels between pulleys spaced 12 to 16 inches apart, the belt should deflect 1/2-inch.
6   If it is necessary to adjust the belt tension, either to make the belt tighter or looser, it is done by moving the belt-driven accessory on the bracket.
7   For each component there will be an adjustment or strap bolt and a pivot bolt. Both bolts must be loosened slightly to enable you to move the component.
8   After the two bolts have been loosened, move the component away from the engine (to tighten the belt) or toward the engine (to loosen the belt). Hold the accessory in position and check the belt tension. If it is correct, tighten the two bolts until just snug, then recheck the tension. If it is correct, tighten the bolts.
9   It will often be necessary to use some sort of pry bar to move the accessory while the belt is adjusted. If this must be done to gain the proper leverage, be very careful not to damage the component being moved or the part being pried against.
10   On V6 engines loosen the two idler bracket bolts (refer to the accompanying illustration) and turn the adjusting bolt until the belt is adjusted properly. Turning the wrench to the right tightens the belt and turning the wrench to the left loosens the belt.
11   Tighten the two idler pulley bolts and recheck the belt tension.
12   Replacement procedures for drivebelts are basically the same as the adjustment procedures. When installing new belts make sure they are properly seated in their pulley grooves. On V6 engines make sure that all V grooves make proper contact with the pulleys (refer to the accompanying illustration).

Fig. 1.10 Drivebelts and adjustment hardware on the inline six-cylinder engine (Sec 6)

Fig. 1.11 Drivebelts and adjustment locations on the 7.5L (460ci) V8 engine (Sec 6)

Fig. 1.12 Typical drivebelt and adjustment locations on all V8 engines except the 7.5L engine (Sec 6)

Fig. 1.13 Drivebelt and adjustment hardware locations on the V6 engine (Sec 6)

Fig. 1.14 The V6 drivebelt must fully engage the pulley (left) to prevent slippage and excessive wear (Sec 6)

Fig. 1.15 Radiator cap and filler neck inspection points
(Sec 7)

7 Cooling system check

1   Many major engine failures can be attributed to a faulty cooling system. If the vehicle is equipped with an automatic transmission, the cooling system also plays an important role in prolonging transmission life.

2   The cooling system should be checked with the engine cold. Do this before the vehicle is driven for the day or after it has been shut off for at least three hours.

3   Remove the radiator cap and thoroughly clean the cap (inside and out) with clean water. Also clean the filler neck on the radiator. All traces of corrosion should be removed.

4   Carefully check the upper and lower radiator hoses along with the smaller diameter heater hoses. Inspect each hose along its entire length, replacing any hose which is cracked, swollen or shows signs of deterioration. Cracks may become more apparent if the hose is squeezed.

5   Make sure that all hose connections are tight. A leak in the cooling system will usually show up as white or rust colored deposits on the areas adjoining the leak.

6   Use compressed air or a soft brush to remove bugs, leaves, etc. from the front of the radiator or air-conditioning condenser. Be careful not to damage the delicate cooling fins or cut yourself on them.

7   Finally, have the cap and system pressure tested. If you do not have a pressure tester, most gas stations and repair shops will do this for a minimal change.

8 Underhood hose check and replacement

Caution: *Replacement of air-conditioner hoses must be left to a dealer or air-conditioning specialist who can depressurize the system and perform the work safely.*

1   The high temperatures present under the hood can cause deterioration of the numerous rubber and plastic hoses.

2   Periodic inspection should be made for cracks, loose clamps and leaks because some of the hoses are part of the emissions control systems and can affect the engine's performance.

3   Remove the air cleaner, if necessary, and trace the entire length of each hose. Squeeze each hose to check for cracks and look for swelling, discoloration or leaks.

4   If the vehicle has considerable mileage or if one or more of the hoses is suspect, it is a good idea to replace all of the hoses at one time.

5   Measure the length and inside diameter of each hose and obtain and cut the replacement to size. Since original equipment hose clamps are often good for only one or two uses, it is a good idea to replace them with screw-type clamps.

6   Replace each hose one at a time to eliminate the possibility of confusion. Hoses attached to the heater and radiator contain coolant, so newspapers or rags should be kept handy to catch the spills when they are disconnected.

7   After installation, run the engine until it reaches operating temperature, shut it off and check for leaks. After the engine has cooled, retighten all of the screw-type clamps.

ALWAYS CHECK hose for chafed or burned areas that may cause an untimely and costly failure.

SOFT hose indicates inside deterioration. This deterioration can contaminate the cooling system and cause particles to clog the radiator.

HARDENED hose can fail at any time. Tightening hose clamps will not seal the connection or stop leaks.

SWOLLEN hose or oil soaked ends indicate danger and possible failure from oil or grease contamination. Squeeze the hose to locate cracks and breaks that cause leaks.

Fig. 1.16 Check all coolant hoses periodically as shown
(Sec 7)

9 Chassis lubrication

1   A grease gun and a cartridge filled with the proper grease (see *Recommended Lubricants and Fluids*) are usually the only equipment necessary to lubricate the chassis components. In some chassis locations, plugs may be installed rather than grease fittings, in which case grease fittings will have to be purchased and installed.

2   Refer to the accompanying illustration, which shows where the various grease fittings are located. Look under the vehicle to find these components and determine if grease fittings or solid plugs are installed. If there are plugs, remove them with a wrench and buy grease fittings, which will thread into the component. A Ford dealer or auto parts store will be able to supply replacement fittings. Straight, as well as angled, fittings are available.

3   For easier access under the vehicle, raise it with a jack and place jackstands under the frame. Make sure the vehicle is securely supported by the stands.

4   Before proceeding, force a little of the grease out of the nozzle to remove any dirt from the end of the gun. Wipe the nozzle clean with a rag.

5   With the grease gun, plenty of clean rags and the diagram, crawl under the vehicle and begin lubricating the components.

1

STEERING LINKAGE
REMOVE PLUGS TO LUBRICATE

BALL JOINTS
REMOVE PLUGS
TO LUBRICATE

FRONT WHEEL BEARINGS
INSPECT

STEERING STOP PADS
LUBRICATE SURFACES

AXLE

PARKING BRAKE LINKAGE (DRUM REAR BRAKES)
LUBRICATE CABLE GUIDES, LEVERS AND LINKAGE AS REQUIRED

▲ LUBRICATION POINT

Fig. 1.17 Typical chassis lubrication points (Sec 9)

9.6   Clean the grease fitting before attaching to the pump nozzle to keep dirt from being forced into the assembly

6   Wipe the grease fitting nipple clean and push the nozzle firmly over the fitting nipple. Squeeze the trigger on the grease gun to force grease into the component (photo). **Note:** *The control arm balljoints should be lubricated until the rubber reservoir is firm to the touch. Do not pump too much grease into these fittings as it could rupture the reservoir. For all other suspension and steering fittings, continue pumping grease into the nipple until grease seeps out of the joint between the two components. If the grease seeps out around the grease gun nozzle, the nipple is clogged or the nozzle is not seated on the fitting nipple. Resecure the gun nozzle to the fitting and try again. If necessary, replace the fitting.*
7   Wipe the excess grease from the components and the grease fitting. Follow the procedures for the remaining fittings.
8   While you are under the vehicle, clean and lubricate the parking brake cable, along with the cable guides and levers. This can be done by smearing some of the chassis grease onto the cable and its related parts with your fingers. Place a few drops of light engine oil on the transmission shift linkage rods and swivels.
9   Lower the vehicle to the ground for the remaining body lubrication process.
10   Open the hood and smear a little chassis grease on the hood latch mechanism. If the hood has an inside release, have an assistant pull the release knob from inside the vehicle as you lubricate the cable at the latch.
11   Lubricate all the hinges (door, hood, etc.) with a few drops of light engine oil to keep them in proper working order.
12   Finally, the key lock cylinders can be lubricated with spray-on graphite, which is available at auto parts stores.

10   Exhaust system check

1   With the engine cold (at least three hours after the vehicle has been driven), check the complete exhaust system from its starting point at the engine to the end of the tailpipe. This should be done on a hoist where unrestricted access is available.
2   Check the pipes and connections for signs of leakage and/or corrosion, indicating a potential failure. Make sure that all brackets and hangers are in good condition and tight.
3   At the same time, inspect the underside of the body for holes, corrosion, open seams, etc. which may allow exhaust gases to enter the passenger compartment. Seal all body openings with silicone or body putty.
4   Rattles and other noises can often be traced to the exhaust system, especially the mounts and hangers. Try to move the pipes, muffler and catalytic converter (if so equipped). If the components can come in contact with the body or suspension parts, secure the exhaust system with new mounts.
5   This is also an ideal time to check the running condition of the engine by inspecting inside the very end of the tailpipe. The exhaust

Fig. 1.18 Measuring balljoint radial play (Sec 11)

deposits here are an indication of engine state-of-tune. If the pipe is black and sooty or coated with white deposits, the engine is in need of a tune-up (including a thorough carburetor inspection and adjustment).

11   Suspension and steering check

1   Whenever the front of the vehicle is raised for service it is a good idea to visually check the suspension and steering components for wear.
2   Indications of a fault in these systems are excessive play in the steering wheel before the front wheels react, excessive sway around corners, body movement over rough roads or binding at some point as the steering wheel is turned.
3   Before the vehicle is raised for inspection, test the shock absorbers by pushing down to rock the vehicle at each corner. If you push down and the vehicle does not come back to a level position within one or two bounces, the shocks/struts are worn and must be replaced. As this is done, check for squeaks and strange noises coming from the suspension components. Information on suspension components can be found in Chapter 10.
4   Raise the front end of the vehicle and support it firmly on jackstands placed under the frame rails. Because of the work to be done, make sure the vehicle cannot fall from the stands.
5   Grab the top and bottom of the front tire with your hands and rock the tire/wheel on the spindle. If there is movement of more than 0.005 inch, the wheel bearings should be serviced.
6   Crawl under the vehicle and check for loose bolts, broken or disconnected parts and deteriorated rubber bushings on all suspension and steering components. Look for grease or fluid leaking from around the steering box. Check the power steering hoses and connections for leaks. Check the balljoints for wear.
7   Have an assistant turn the steering wheel from side-to-side and check the steering components for free movement, chafing and binding. If the steering does not react with the movement of the steering wheel, try to determine where the slack is located.

12   Brake check

Note: *For detailed illustrations of the brake system refer to Chapter 9.*
1   The brakes should be inspected every time the wheels are removed or whenever a defect is suspected. Indications of a potential brake system defect are: the vehicle pulls to one side when the brake pedal is depressed; noises coming from the brakes when they are applied; excessive brake pedal travel; pulsating pedal; and leakage of fluid, usually seen on the inside of the tire or wheel.

12.13 When checking the brake shoe lining thickness, note the amount remaining above the rivet heads (arrows)

12.6 The disc brake pad lining thickness can be checked by looking through the inspection hole in the caliper (arrow)

Disc brakes

2   Disc brakes can be visually checked without removing any parts except the wheels.

3   Raise the vehicle and place it securely on jackstands. Remove the wheels (see *Jacking and Towing* at the front of the manual, if necessary).

4   The disc brake calipers, which contain the pads, are now visible. There is an outer pad and an inner pad in each caliper. All pads should be inspected.

5   The inner pads on the front wheels are equipped with a wear sensor. This is a small, bent piece of metal which is visible from the in-board side of the brake caliper. When the pads wear to the danger limit, the metal sensor rubs against the rotor and makes a screeching sound.

6   Check the pad thickness by looking at each end of the caliper and through the inspection hole in the caliper body (photo). If the wear sensor clip is very close to the rotor, or if the lining material is 1/16-inch or less in thickness, the pads should be replaced. Keep in mind that the lining material is riveted or bonded to a metal backing shoe, and the metal portion is not included in this measurement.

7   Since it will be difficult, if not impossible, to measure the exact thickness of the remaining lining material, remove the pads for further inspection or replacement if you are in doubt as to the quality of the pad.

8   Before installing the wheels check for leakage around the brake hose connections leading to the caliper and damage (cracking, splitting, etc.) to the brake hose. Replace the hose or fittings as necessary, referring to Chapter 9.

9   Check the condition of the rotor. Look for scoring, gouging and burnt spots. If these conditions exist, the hub/rotor assembly should be removed for servicing (Chapter 9).

Drum brakes

10   Using a scribe or chalk, mark the drum and hub so they can be reinstalled in the same relationship to each other.

11   Pull the brake drum off the axle and brake assembly. If this proves difficult, make sure the parking brake is released, then squirt some penetrating oil around the hub area. Allow the oil to soak in and try to pull the drum off again. If the drum cannot be pulled off, the brake shoes will have to be retracted. This is done by first removing the rubber or metal plug in the backing plate. With the plug removed, pull the lever off the adjuster and use a small screwdriver to turn the adjuster wheel, which will move the shoes away from the drum.

12   With the drum removed, carefully brush away any accumulations of dirt and dust. **Warning:** *Do not blow the dust out with compressed air. Make an effort not to inhale the dust because it contains asbestos and is harmful to your health.*

12.14 Make sure the springs are connected and in good condition (arrows)

13   Note the thickness of the lining material on both the front and rear brake shoes (photo). If the material has worn to within 1/16-inch of the recessed rivets or metal backing, the shoes should be replaced. If the linings look worn, but you are unable to determine their exact thickness, compare them with a new set at an auto parts store. The shoes should also be replaced if they are cracked, glazed (shiny surface) or contaminated with brake fluid.

14   Check to see that all the brake assembly springs are connected and in good condition (photo).

15   Check the brake components for signs of fluid leakage. With your finger, carefully pry back the rubber cups on the wheel cylinder located at the top of the brake shoes. Any leakage is an indication that the wheel cylinders should be overhauled immediately (Chapter 9). Also check the hoses and connections for signs of leakage.

16   Wipe the inside of the drum with a clean rag and denatured alcohol. Again, be careful not to breathe the dangerous asbestos dust.

17   Check the inside of the drum for cracks, scores, deep scratches and hard spots, which will appear as small discolored areas. If imperfections cannot be removed with fine emery cloth, the drum must be taken to a machine shop for resurfacing.

18   After the inspection process, if all parts are found to be in good condition, reinstall the brake drum (remember to replace the rubber plug in the backing plate). Install the wheel and lower the vehicle to the ground.

Parking brake

19   The easiest way to check the operation of the parking brake is to park the vehicle on a steep hill with the parking brake set and the transmission in Neutral. If the parking brake cannot prevent the vehicle from rolling, it is in need of adjustment (see Chapter 9).

13.3 Choke plate location (arrow) (if the choke is working properly, the plate will be closed when the engine is cold and completely open when the engine reaches normal operating temperature)

14.4 Typical idle speed adjustment screw (4350-4V carburetor shown — see Chapter 4 for detailed drawings of other carburetors)

13   Carburetor choke check

1   The choke only operates when the engine is cold, so this check should be performed before the engine has been started for the day.
2   Open the hood and remove the top plate of the air cleaner assembly. It is held in place by nuts or a wing nut. If any vacuum hoses must be disconnected, make sure you tag them to ensure reinstallation in their original positions. Place the top plate and nuts aside, out of the way of moving engine components.
3   Look at the top of the carburetor at the center of the air cleaner housing. You will notice a flat plate at the carburetor opening (photo).
4   Have an assistant press the accelerator pedal to the floor. The plate should close completely. Start the engine while you observe the plate at the carburetor. **Caution:** *Do not position your face directly over the carburetor, because the engine could backfire and cause serious burns.* When the engine starts, the choke plate should open slightly.
5   Allow the engine to continue running at idle speed. As the engine warms up to operating temperature the plate should slowly open, allowing more air to enter through the top of the carburetor.
6   After a few minutes, the choke plate should be all the way open to the vertical position.
7   You will notice that engine speed corresponds with the plate opening. With the plate completely closed the engine should run at a fast idle. As the plate opens, the engine speed will decrease.
8   If a malfunction is detected during the above checks, refer to Chapter 4 for specific information related to adjusting and servicing choke components.

14   Engine idle speed check and adjustment

1   Engine idle speed is the speed at which the engine operates when no accelerator pedal pressure is applied. This speed is critical to the performance of the engine itself, as well as many engine sub-systems.
2   A hand-held tachometer must be used when adjusting the idle speed to get an accurate reading. The exact hook-up for these meters varies with the manufacturer, so follow the directions included with your unit.
3   Since these models were equipped with many different carburetors in the time period covered by this manual, and each has its own peculiarities when setting idle speed, it would be impractical to cover all types in this Section. Chapter 4 contains information on each individual carburetor used. However, all vehicles covered in this manual should have a tune-up decal or Emission Control Information label in

the engine compartment, usually placed near the top of the radiator. The printed instructions for setting idle speed can be found on this decal or label, and should be followed since they are for your particular engine.
4   For most applications the idle speed is set by turning an adjustment screw located at the side of the carburetor (photo). Turning the screw changes the position of the throttle valve in the carburetor. This screw may be on the linkage itself or may be part of the idle stop solenoid. Refer to the tune-up decal or Chapter 4.
5   Once you have located the idle speed screw, experiment with different length screwdrivers until the adjustments can easily be made without coming into contact with hot or moving engine components.
6   Follow the instructions on the tune-up decal or Emission Control Information label, which may include disconnecting certain vacuum or electrical connections. To plug a vacuum hose after disconnecting it, insert a bolt or golf tee into the opening or cover the open end with tape to prevent any vacuum loss through the hose.
7   If the air cleaner is removed, the vacuum hose to the snorkel should be plugged.
8   Make sure the parking brake is firmly set and the wheels blocked to prevent the vehicle from rolling. This is especially true if the transmission is to be in Drive. An assistant inside the vehicle holding the brake pedal down is the safest method.
9   For all applications, the engine must be completely warmed-up to operating temperature, which will automatically render the choke fast idle inoperative.
10   Turn the idle speed screw in or out, as required, until the idle speed listed on the Emission Control Information label is attained.

15   Engine oil and filter change

1   Frequent oil changes may be the best form of preventative maintenance available to the home mechanic. When engine oil ages, it becomes diluted and contaminated, leading to premature engine wear.
2   Although some sources recommend oil filter changes every other oil change, we feel that the minimal cost of an oil filter and the relative ease with which it is installed dictate that a new filter be used whenever the oil is changed.
3   The tools necessary for a normal oil and filter change are a wrench to fit the drain plug at the bottom of the oil pan, an oil filter wrench to remove the old filter, a container with at least a six-quart capacity to drain the old oil into and a funnel or oil can spout to help pour fresh oil into the engine (photo).
4   In addition, you should have plenty of clean rags and newspapers handy to mop up any spills. Access to the underside of the vehicle

15.3   Typical example of tools required to perform the engine oil and filter change

15.9   Engine oil drain plug (arrow) (V8 engine shown)

1

is greatly improved if the vehicle can be lifted on a hoist, driven onto ramps or supported by jackstands. **Warning:** *Do not work under a vehicle which is supported only a bumper, hydraulic or scissors-type jack.*

5   If this is your first oil change on the vehicle, it is recommended that you crawl underneath and familiarize yourself with the locations of the oil drain plug and the oil filter. The engine and exhaust components will be warm during the actual work, so it is a good idea to figure out any potential problems before the engine and accessories are hot.

6   Allow the engine to warm up to normal operating temperature. If the new oil or any tools are needed, use this warm-up time to gather everything necessary for the job. The correct type of oil to buy for your application can be found in *Recommended Lubricants and Fluids* near the front of this manual.

7   With the engine oil warm (warm engine oil will drain better and more built-up sludge will be removed with the oil), raise and support the vehicle on jackstands.

8   Move all necessary tools, rags and newspapers under the vehicle. Position the drain pan under the drain plug. Keep in mind that the oil will initially flow from the pan with some force, so place the pan accordingly.

9   Being careful not to touch any of the hot exhaust components, use the wrench to remove the drain plug near the bottom of the oil pan (photo). Depending on how hot the oil has become, you may want to wear gloves while unscrewing the plug the final few turns.

10   Allow the old oil to drain into the pan. It may be necessary to move the pan farther under the engine as the oil flow slows to a trickle.

11   After all the oil has drained, wipe off the drain plug with a clean rag. Small metal particles may cling to the plug and would immediately contaminate the new oil.

12   Clean the area around the drain plug opening and reinstall the plug. Tighten the plug securely with the wrench. If a torque wrench is available, use it to tighten the plug.

13   Move the drain pan into position under the oil filter.

14   Use the filter wrench to loosen the oil filter (photo). Chain or metal band-type filter wrenches may distort the filter canister, but this is of no concern as the filter will be discarded.

15   Sometimes the oil filter is on so tight it cannot be loosened, or it is positioned in an area which is inaccessible with a filter wrench. As a last resort, you can punch a metal bar or long screwdriver directly through the side of the canister and use it as a T-bar to turn the filter. If you do so, be prepared for oil to spurt out of the canister as it is punctured.

16   Completely unscrew the old filter. Be careful, it is full of oil. Empty the oil inside the filter into the drain pan.

17   Compare the old filter with the new one to make sure they are the same type.

18   Use a clean rag to remove all oil, dirt and sludge from the area where the oil filter mounts to the engine. Check the old filter to make sure the rubber gasket is not stuck to the engine mounting surface. If the

15.14   Removing the oil filter (use strips of sandpaper or cloth tape between the filter and the wrench band if you can't get a good grip on the filter)

gasket is stuck to the engine (use a flashlight if necessary), remove it.

19   Open one of the cans of new oil and apply a light coat of oil to the rubber gasket of the filter.

20   Attach the filter to the engine, following the tightening directions printed on the filter canister or packing box. Most filter manufacturers recommend against using a filter wrench due to the possibility of over-tightening and damage to the seal.

21   Remove all tools, rags, etc. from under the vehicle, being careful not to spill the oil in the drain pan, then lower the vehicle.

22   Move to the engine compartment and locate the oil filler cap on the engine. In most cases there will be a screw-off cap on the rocker arm cover. The cap will most likely be labeled *Engine Oil* or *Oil.*

23   If an oil can spout is used, push the spout into the top of the oil can and pour the fresh oil through the filler opening. A funnel may also be used.

24   Pour three quarts of fresh oil into the engine. Wait a few minutes to allow the oil to drain into the pan, then check the level on the oil dipstick (see Section 4 if necessary). If the oil level is at or near the lower Add mark, start the engine and allow the new oil to circulate.

25   Run the engine for only about a minute and then shut it off. Immediately look under the vehicle and check for leaks at the oil pan drain plug and around the oil filter. If either is leaking, tighten with a bit more force.

26   With the new oil circulated and the filter now completely full, recheck the level on the dipstick and add enough oil to bring the level to the Full mark on the dipstick.

27 During the first few trips after an oil change, make it a point to check frequently for leaks and proper oil level.

28 The old oil drained from the engine cannot be reused in its present state and should be disposed of. Oil reclamation centers, auto repair shops and gas stations will normally accept the oil, which can be refined and used again. After the oil has cooled it can be drained into a suitable container (capped plastic jugs, topped bottles, milk cartons, etc.) for transport to one of these disposal sites.

16 Fuel system check

Warning: *There are certain precautions to take when inspecting or servicing the fuel system components. Work in a well-ventilated area and do not allow open flames (cigarettes, appliance pilot lights, etc.) to get near the work area. Mop up spills immediately and do not store fuel-soaked rags where they could ignite.*

1 If your vehicle is equipped with fuel injection, refer to the fuel injection pressure relief procedure (Chapter 4) before servicing any component of the fuel system.

2 The fuel system is under a small amount of pressure, so if any fuel lines are disconnected for servicing, be prepared to catch the fuel as it spurts out. Plug all disconnected fuel lines immediately after disconnection to prevent the tank from emptying.

3 The fuel system is most easily checked with the vehicle raised on a hoist so the components underneath the vehicle are readily visible and accessible.

4 If the smell of gasoline is noticed while driving or after the vehicle has been in the sun, the system should be thoroughly inspected immediately.

5 Remove the gas filler cap and check for damage, corrosion or a broken sealing imprint on the gasket. Replace the cap with a new one, if necessary.

6 With the vehicle raised, inspect the gas tank and filler neck for punctures, cracks or other damage. The connection between the filler neck and the tank is especially critical. Sometimes a rubber filler neck will leak due to loose clamps or deteriorated rubber, problems a home mechanic can usually rectify. **Warning:** *Do not, under any circumstances, try to repair a fuel tank yourself (except rubber components) unless you have had considerable experience. A welding torch or any open flame can easily cause the fuel vapors to explode if the proper precautions are not taken.*

7 Carefully check all rubber hoses and metal lines leading away from the fuel tank. Check for loose connections, deteriorated hoses, crimped lines or other damage. Follow the lines up to the front of the vehicle, carefully inspecting them all the way. Repair or replace damaged sections as necessary.

8 If a fuel odor is still evident after the inspection check the Evaporative Control System (ECS). If the fuel odor persists, the carburetor or fuel injection system should be serviced (Chapter 4).

17 Fuel filter replacement

1 On these models, the fuel filter is located close to the fuel inlet at the carburetor. It is usually made of pleated paper and cannot be cleaned or reused.

2 The job should be done with the engine cold (after sitting at least three hours). The necessary tools include open-end wrenches to fit the fuel line nuts. Flare nut wrenches (which wrap around the nut) should be used if available. In addition, you will have to obtain the replacement filter (make sure it is for your specific vehicle and engine) and some clean rags.

3 Remove the air cleaner assembly. If vacuum hoses must be disconnected, be sure to note their positions and/or tag them to ensure that they are reinstalled correctly.

4 Follow the fuel line to the point where it enters the carburetor. In most cases the fuel line will be metal all the way from the fuel pump to the carburetor.

Carburetor-mounted type

5 Place some rags under the fuel inlet fittings to catch spilled fuel as the fittings are disconnected.

6 With the proper size wrench, hold the fitting immediately next to the carburetor and loosen the fitting at the end of the fuel line. A flare

Fig. 1.19 Vehicles with carburetor types 2700VV and 7200VV have filters which must be disassembled for filter replacement

17.6 Typical carburetor-mounted fuel filter (arrow)

nut wrench on this fitting will help prevent slipping and possible damage. However, an open-end wrench should do the job. Make sure the fitting next to the carburetor is held securely while the fuel line is disconnected. Some models may have a screw-in type filter and a rubber hose instead of a metal line (photo). The hose is attached to the filter inlet with a spring clamp. This clamp can be removed with pliers. Be sure to check rubber fuel hoses for cracks or deterioration.

7 After the fuel line is disconnected, move it aside for better access to the inlet fitting. Do not crimp the fuel line.

8 Unscrew the fuel inlet fitting, which was previously held steady. As this fitting is drawn away from the carburetor body, be careful not to lose the thin washer-type gasket on the nut or the spring, located behind the fuel filter. Also, pay close attention to how the filter is installed.

9 Compare the old filter with the new one to make sure they are the same length and design.

10 Reinstall the spring in the carburetor body.

11 Place the new filter in position behind the spring. It will have a rubber gasket and check valve at one end, which should point away from the carburetor.

12 Install a new washer-type gasket on the fuel fitting (a gasket is usually supplied with the new filter) and tighten the fitting. Make sure it is not cross-threaded. Tighten it securely. If a torque wrench is available, tighten the fitting to 7-10 ft-lbs (10-14 Nm). Do not overtighten it, as the hole can strip easily, causing fuel leaks.

13 Hold the fuel inlet fitting securely with a wrench while the fuel line is connected. Again, be careful not to cross-thread the connector. Tighten the fitting securely.

14 Plug the vacuum hose which leads to the air cleaner snorkel motor so the engine can be run.

15 Start the engine and check carefully for leaks. If the fuel line connector leaks, disconnect it, using the above procedures, and check for stripped or damaged threads. If the fuel line connector has stripped threads, remove the entire line and have a repair shop install a new

Fig. 1.20 Inline fuel filter installation (Sec 17)

Fig. 1.21 Inline fuel filter installation (fuel-injected models only) (Sec 17)

fitting. If the threads look all right, purchase some thread sealing tape and wrap the connector threads with it. Now reinstall and tighten it securely. Inlet repair kits are available at most auto parts stores to overcome leaking at the fuel inlet filter nut.

16 Reinstall the air cleaner assembly, connecting the hoses in their original positions.

Inline type

17 To install an inline-type fuel filter, remove the spring clamps and rubber hoses and discard them.

18 Cut new hoses to the proper length, install the clamps and push one end of the hose onto the filter inlet and the other onto the outlet. Push the inlet side of the hose onto the metal line from the fuel pump, and the other onto the carburetor inlet fitting.

19 Position the spring-type clamps with pliers.

20 Run the engine, check for leaks and reinstall the air cleaner assembly, connecting all hoses to their original fittings.

Fuel-injected models

21 Fuel is filtered at three different points on fuel-injected models. All filters used are of one-piece construction and cannot be cleaned. Replace the filter if it becomes clogged. Fuel is first filtered inside the tank at the fuel pump inlet. Servicing of this filter requires removal of the fuel pump, the procedure for which can be found in Chapter 4.

22 Fuel is again filtered at an inline-type filter found downstream of the fuel tank. This filter is attached to the underbody just forward of the right wheel well. Before removing this filter depressurize the fuel line by disconnecting it at the engine. Use plenty of rags to soak up the fuel which will squirt out. Be careful not to damage the nylon fuel line or the plastic connectors during this operation, as they will have to be replaced.

23 Remove the quick-connect fittings at both ends of the filter.

Fig. 1.22 Thermo-controlled air cleaner assembly (Sec 18)

18.7 Checking the thermo-controlled air cleaner vacuum motor (the valve should remain closed with the vacuum fitting plugged)

24 Remove the filter and retainer from the metal bracket. Remove the rubber insulator ring from the filter, then remove the filter from the retainer. Note the arrow on the side of the filter which indicates the direction of fuel flow and should point towards the open end of the retainer. Discard the filter.

25 When installing the new filter replace the rubber insulator rings if the filter moves freely after installation of the retainer. Replace the retainer on the bracket and tighten the retaining bolts to between 51 and 60 in-lb (5.8 to 6.8 Nm). Push the quick connect fittings onto the filter ends and reconnect the fuel line at the engine.

26 Start the engine and check for leaks.

---

18 Thermo-controlled air cleaner check

---

1 The thermostatically controlled air cleaner draws air to the carburetor from different locations, depending upon engine temperature.

2 This is a simple visual check. If access is limited, a small mirror may have to be used.

3 Open the hood and locate the butterfly valve inside the air cleaner assembly. It will be located inside the long snorkel of the metal air cleaner housing.

4 If there is a flexible air duct attached to the end of the snorkel, leading to an area behind the grille, disconnect it at the snorkel. This will enable you to look through the end of the snorkel and see the damper.

5 The check should be done when the engine and outside air are cold. Start the engine and look through the snorkel at the valve, which should move to a closed position. With the valve closed, air cannot enter through the end of the snorkel, but instead enters the air cleaner through the flexible duct attached to the exhaust manifold (photo).

6 As the engine warms up to operating temperature, the valve should open to allow air through the snorkel end. Depending upon ambient temperature, this may take 10 to 15 minutes. To speed up the check you can reconnect the snorkel air duct, drive the vehicle and then check to see if the damper is completely open.

7 If the thermo-controlled air cleaner is not operating properly see Chapter 6 for more information.

BIAS and BIAS-BELTED TIRES   RADIAL PLY TIRES

**Fig. 1.23 Proper tire rotation for radial and bias-belted tires
(Sec 19)**

19   Tire rotation

1   The tires should be rotated at the specified intervals and whenever uneven wear is noticed. Since the vehicle will be raised and the tires removed anyway, this is a good time to check the brakes and wheel bearings.
2   Refer to the accompanying illustrations of tire rotation patterns.
3   Refer to the information in *Jacking and Towing* at the front of this manual for the proper procedures to follow when raising the vehicle and changing a tire. However, if the brakes are to be checked, do not apply the parking brake as stated. Make sure the tires are blocked to prevent the vehicle from rolling.
4   Preferably, the entire vehicle should be raised at the same time. This can be done on a hoist or by jacking up each corner and then lowering the vehicle onto jackstands placed under the frame rails. Always use four jackstands and make sure the vehicle is firmly supported.
5   After rotation, check and adjust the the tire pressures as necessary and be sure to check the lug nut tightness.

20   Clutch pedal free play check and adjustment

All manual-transmission-equipped vehicles come with a self-adjusting clutch mechanism which requires only periodic lubrication.

21   Rear axle oil change

1   To change the oil in the rear axle it is necessary to remove the cover plate on the differential housing. Because of this, purchase a new gasket at the same time the gear lubricant is bought.
2   Move a drain pan, rags, newspapers and wrenches under the rear of the vehicle. With the drain pan under the differential cover, loosen each of the inspection plate bolts.
3   Remove the bolts on the lower half of the plate, but use the upper bolts to keep the cover loosely attached to the differential. Allow the oil to drain into the pan, then completely remove the cover.
4   Using a lint-free rag, clean the inside of the cover and the accessible areas of the differential housing. As this is done, check for chipped gears and metal particles in the oil, indicating that the differential should be thoroughly inspected and repaired (see Chapter 8 for more information).
5   Thoroughly clean the gasket mating surface on the cover and the differential housing. Use a gasket scraper or putty knife to remove all traces of the old gasket.
6   Apply a thin film of RTV-type gasket sealant to the cover flange and then press a new gasket into position on the cover. Make sure the bolt holes align properly.
7   Place the cover on the differential housing and install the bolts. Tighten the bolts a little at a time, working across the cover in a diagonal fashion until all bolts are tight. If a torque wrench is available, tighten

the bolts to the specified torque.
8   Remove the inspection plug on the side of the differential housing (or inspection cover) and fill the housing with the proper lubricant until the level is 1/2-inch below the bottom of the plug hole.
9   Securely install the plug.

22   Cooling system servicing

1   Periodically the cooling system should be drained, flushed and re-filled to replenish the antifreeze mixture and prevent formation of rust and corrosion, which can impair the performance of the cooling system and ultimately cause engine damage.
2   At the same time the cooling system is serviced, all hoses and the radiator cap should be inspected and replaced if defective (see Section 8).
3   Since antifreeze is a corrosive and poisonous solution, be careful not to spill any of the coolant mixture on the paint or your skin. If this happens, rinse immediately with plenty of clean water. Also, consult your local authorities about the dumping of antifreeze before draining the cooling system. In many areas reclamation centers have been set up to collect automobile oil and drained antifreeze/water mixtures, rather than allowing them to be added to the sewage system.
4   With the engine cold, remove the radiator cap.
5   Move a large container under the radiator to catch the coolant as it is drained.
6   Drain the radiator. Most models are equipped with a drain plug at the bottom. If this drain has excessive corrosion and cannot be turned easily, or if the radiator is not equipped with a drain, disconnect the lower radiator hose to allow the coolant to drain. Be careful that none of the solution is splashed on your skin or into your eyes.
7   If accessible, remove the engine coolant drain plugs.
8   Disconnect the hose from the coolant reservoir and remove the reservoir. Flush it out with clean water.
9   Place a garden hose in the radiator filler neck and flush the system until the water runs clear at all drain points.
10   In severe cases of contamination or clogging of the radiator, remove it (see Chapter 3) and reverse flush it. This involves simply inserting the hose in the bottom radiator outlet to allow the clear water to run against the normal flow, draining through the top. A radiator repair shop should be consulted if further cleaning or repair is necessary.
11   When the coolant is regularly drained and the system refilled with the correct antifreeze/water mixture, there should be no need to use chemical cleaners or descalers.
12   To refill the system, reconnect the radiator hoses and install the drain plugs securely in the engine. Special thread-sealing tape (available at auto parts stores) should be used on the drain plugs. Install the reservoir and the overflow hose, where applicable.
13   Fill the radiator to the base of the filler neck and then add more coolant to the reservoir until it reaches the mark.
14   Run the engine until normal operating temperature is reached and, with the engine idling, add coolant up to the Full level. Install the radiator cap so that the arrows are in alignment with the overflow hose. Install the reservoir cap.
15   Always refill the system with a mixture of high quality antifreeze and water in the proportion called for on the antifreeze container or in your owner's manual. Chapter 3 also contains information on antifreeze mixtures.
16   Keep a close watch on the coolant level and the various cooling system hoses during the first few miles of driving. Tighten the hose clamps and/or add more coolant as necessary.

23   Automatic transmission fluid change

1   At the specified intervals the transmission fluid should be changed and the filter replaced. Since there is no drain plug, the transmission oil pan must be removed from the bottom of the transmission to drain the fluid. On some models of the C4 transmission, the fluid is drained by disconnecting the filler tube from the transmission pan. Check to see if your model has this connection. We recommend, however, that the pan be removed anyway to make a thorough cleaning possible.
2   Before beginning work, purchase the specified transmission fluid (see *Recommended Fluids* at the front of this Chapter) and a new filter. The necessary gaskets should be included with the filter. If not, pur-

chase an oil pan gasket and a strainer-to-valve body gasket.

3   Other tools necessary for this job include jackstands to support the vehicle in a raised position, a wrench to remove the oil pan bolts, a standard screwdriver, a drain pan capable of holding at least 8 pints, newspapers and clean rags.

4   The fluid should be drained immediately after the vehicle has been driven. This will remove any built-up sediment better than if the fluid were cold. Because of this, it may be wise to wear protective gloves (fluid temperature can exceed 350° in a hot transmission).

5   After the vehicle has been driven to warm up the fluid, raise it and place it on the jackstands for access underneath.

6   Move the necessary equipment under the vehicle, being careful not to touch any of the hot exhaust components.

7   Place the drain pan under the transmission oil pan and loosen, but do not remove, the bolts at one end of the pan.

8   Moving around the pan, loosen all the bolts a little at a time. Be sure the drain pan is in position, as fluid will begin dripping out. Continue in this manner until all of the bolts are removed, except for one at each of the corners.

9   Remove the two bolts at the back of the pan and allow the pan to sag downwards, spilling fluid into the drain pan. If the pan has not broken loose, use a screwdriver to carefully separate the pan from the transmission body. Be careful not to scratch the gasket mating surface. While supporting the pan, remove the remaining bolts and lower the pan. Drain the remaining fluid into the drain pan. As this is done, check the fluid for metal particles, which may be an indication of internal failure.

10 Now visible on the bottom of the transmission is the filter/strainer.

11 Remove the filter and gasket.

12 Thoroughly clean the transmission oil pan with solvent. Check for metal filings or foreign material. Dry with compressed air if available. It is important that all remaining gasket material be removed from the oil pan mounting flange. Use a gasket scraper or putty knife for this.

13 Clean the filter mounting surface on the valve body. Again, this surface should be smooth and free of any leftover gasket material.

14 Clean the screen assembly with solvent, then dry it thoroughly (use compressed air if available). Paper or felt type filters should be replaced with new ones.

15 Place the new or cleaned filter in position, with a new gasket between it and the transmission valve body. Install the mounting screws and tighten them securely.

16 Apply a light bead of gasket sealant around the pan mounting surface, with the sealant to the inside of the bolt holes. Press the new gasket into place on the pan, making sure all the holes line up with the holes in the pan.

17 Lift the pan up to the bottom of the transmission and install the mounting bolts. Tighten the bolts in a diagonal fashion, working around the pan. Using a torque wrench, tighten the bolts to the specified torque.

18 Lower the vehicle.

19 Open the hood and remove the transmission fluid dipstick.

20 It is best to add a little fluid at a time, continually checking the level with the dipstick. Allow the fluid time to drain into the pan. Add fluid until the level just registers on the end of the dipstick. In most cases, a good starting point will be four to five pints added to the transmission through the filler tube.

21 With the selector lever in Park, apply the parking brake and start the engine without depressing the accelerator pedal (if possible). Do not race the engine at high speed; run at slow idle only.

22 Depress the brake pedal and shift the transmission through each gear. Place the selector back in Park and check the level on the dipstick with the engine still idling. Look under the vehicle for leaks around the transmission oil pan.

23 Push the dipstick firmly back into its tube and drive the vehicle to reach normal operating temperature. Park the vehicle on a level surface and check the fluid level on the dipstick with the engine idling and the transmission in Park. The level should now be at the Full Hot mark on the dipstick. If not, add more fluid to bring the level up to this point. Do not overfill.

---

24   Air filter and PCV filter replacement

Air filter

1   At the specified intervals the air filter and PCV filter should be

24.2   The air filter (A) and the crankcase ventilation filter (B) can be changed after removing the air cleaner top plate

replaced with new ones. A thorough program of preventative maintenance would call for the two filters to be inspected between changes.

2   The air filter is located inside the air cleaner housing on the top of the engine. The filter is generally replaced by removing the wing nut at the top of the air cleaner assembly and lifting off the top plate (photo).

3   While the top plate is off, be careful not to drop anything down into the carburetor.

4   Lift the air filter element out of the housing.

5   To check the filter, hold it up to strong sunlight or place a flashlight or droplight on the inside of the filter. If you can see light coming through the paper element, the filter is all right. Check all the way around the filter.

6   Wipe out the inside of the air cleaner housing with a clean rag.

7   Place the old filter (if in good condition) or the new filter (if the specified interval has elapsed) into the air cleaner housing. Make sure it seats properly in the bottom of the housing.

8   Connect any disconnected vacuum hoses to the top plate and reinstall the plate.

PCV filter

9   The PCV filter is also located inside the air cleaner housing. Remove the top plate and air filter as described previously, then locate the PCV filter on the side of the housing.

10 Remove the retaining clip from outside the housing, then remove the PCV filter.

11 Install a new PCV filter, then reinstall the retaining clip, air filter, top plate and any hoses which were disconnected.

---

25   Positive Crankcase Ventilation (PCV) valve check

1   The PCV valve is located in the rocker arm cover (photo). A hose connected to the valve runs to either the carburetor or intake manifold.

2   When purchasing a replacement PCV valve make sure it is for your particular vehicle, model year and engine size.

3   Pull the valve (with hose attached) from the rocker arm cover.

4   Loosen the retaining clamp and pull the PCV valve from the end of the hose, noting its installed position and direction.

5   Compare the old valve with the new one to make sure they are the same.

6   Push the valve into the end of the hose until it is seated and reinstall the clamp.

25.1   On most engines, the PCV valve (arrow) is located in the rocker arm cover

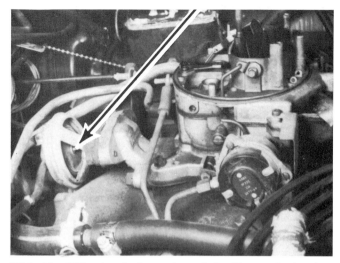

26.1   The EGR valve diaphragm (arrow) should move freely when pressure is applied and return to its original position when pressure is released

7   Inspect the rubber grommet for damage and replace it with a new one if faulty.

8   Push the PCV valve and hose securely into position.

9   More information on the PCV system can be found in Chapter 6.

26   Exhaust Gas Recirculation (EGR) valve check

1   The EGR valve is located on the intake manifold, adjacent to the carburetor (photo) or fuel injection unit. Most of the time, when a problem develops in this emissions system, it is due to a stuck or corroded EGR valve.

2   With the engine cold to prevent burns, reach under the EGR valve and manually push on the diaphragm. Using moderate pressure, you should be able to move the diaphragm within the housing.

3   If the diaphragm does not move or moves only with much effort, replace the EGR valve with a new one. If in doubt about the quality of the valve, compare the free movement of your EGR valve with a new valve.

4   Refer to Chapter 6 for more information on the EGR system.

27   Evaporative control system (ECS) check

1   The function of the ECS emissions system is to draw fuel vapors from the fuel tank and carburetor, store them in the charcoal canister (photo), and then burn them during normal engine operation.

2   If a strong fuel odor is detected, the canister, purge control valve and system hoses should be inspected for deterioration.

3   The purge control valve controls the flow of fuel vapors into and out of the charcoal canister. If the control valve malfunctions or becomes clogged, the vapors will back up in the canister.

4   The purge control valve is difficult to test without special equipment, so if a fault is suspected replace the valve with a new one.

5   For further information on this system, see Chapter 6.

28   Ignition timing check and adjustment

Note: *Ignition timing on Duraspark III ignition systems is controlled by an Electronic Engine Control (EEC) and is not adjustable. The information which follows is applicable only to vehicles equipped with the Duraspark or Duraspark II ignition system. The process for checking and adjusting ignition timing requires the use of a stroboscopic-type timing light. These are available at auto parts stores and rental yards. Timing an engine 'by ear' and static timing procedures are not acceptable with today's tight emissions controls and should only be used to initially start and run an engine after it has been disassembled or the distributor has been removed.*

Fig. 1.24 EGR valve and carburetor spacer plate locations (Sec 26)

27.1   Typical ECS canister location

CARBON DEPOSITS

Symptoms: Dry sooty deposits indicate a rich mixture or weak ignition. Causes misfiring, hard starting and hesitation.

Recommendation: Check for a clogged air cleaner, high float level, sticky choke and worn ignition points. Use a spark plug with a longer core nose for greater anti-fouling protection.

OIL DEPOSITS

Symptoms: Oily coating caused by poor oil control. Oil is leaking past worn valve guides or piston rings into the combustion chamber. Causes hard starting, misfiring and hesition.

Recommendation: Correct the mechanical condition with necessary repairs and install new plugs.

TOO HOT

Symptoms: Blistered, white insulator, eroded electrode and absence of deposits. Results in shortened plug life.

Recommendation: Check for the correct plug heat range, over-advanced ignition timing, lean fuel mixture, intake manifold vacuum leaks and sticking valves. Check the coolant level and make sure the radiator is not clogged.

PREIGNITION

Symptoms: Melted electrodes. Insulators are white, but may be dirty due to misfiring or flying debris in the combustion chamber. Can lead to engine damage.

Recommendation: Check for the correct plug heat range, over-advanced ignition timing, lean fuel mixture, clogged cooling system and lack of lubrication.

HIGH SPEED GLAZING

Symptoms: Insulator has yellowish, glazed appearance. Indicates that combustion chamber temperatures have risen suddenly during hard acceleration. Normal deposits melt to form a conductive coating. Causes misfiring at high speeds.

Recommendation: Install new plugs. Consider using a colder plug if driving habits warrant.

GAP BRIDGING

Symptoms: Combustion deposits lodge between the electrodes. Heavy deposits accumulate and bridge the electrode gap. The plug ceases to fire, resulting in a dead cylinder.

Recommendation: Locate the faulty plug and remove the deposits from between the electrodes.

NORMAL

Symptoms: Brown to grayish-tan color and slight electrode wear. Correct heat range for engine and operating conditions.

Recommendation: When new spark plugs are installed, replace with plugs of the same heat range.

ASH DEPOSITS

Symptoms: Light brown deposits encrusted on the side or center electrodes or both. Derived from oil and/or fuel additives. Excessive amounts may mask the spark, causing misfiring and hesitation during acceleration.

Recommendation: If excessive deposits accumulate over a short time or low mileage, install new valve guide seals to prevent seepage of oil into the combustion chambers. Also try changing gasoline brands.

WORN

Symptoms: Rounded electrodes with a small amount of deposits on the firing end. Normal color. Causes hard starting in damp or cold weather and poor fuel economy.

Recommendation: Replace with new plugs of the same heat range.

DETONATION

Symptoms: Insulators may be cracked or chipped. Improper gap setting techniques can also result in a fractured insulator tip. Can lead to piston damage.

Recommendation: Make sure the fuel anti-knock values meet engine requirements. Use care when setting the gaps on new plugs. Avoid lugging the engine.

SPLASHED DEPOSITS

Symptoms: After long periods of misfiring, deposits can loosen when normal combustion temperature is restored by an overdue tune-up. At high speeds, deposits flake off the piston and are thrown against the hot insulator, causing misfiring.

Recommendation: Replace the plugs with new ones or clean and reinstall the originals.

MECHANICAL DAMAGE

Symptoms: May be caused by a foreign object in the combustion chamber or the piston striking an incorrect reach (too long) plug. Causes a dead cylinder and could result in piston damage.

Recommendation: Remove the foreign object from the engine and/or install the correct reach plug.

1

Fig. 1.25 Engine timing marks and cylinder firing order (Sec 28)

Fig. 1.26 Typical inductive pick-up timing light hook-up (Sec 28)

29.2 Typical example of tools required to change the spark plugs

1   Start the engine and bring it to normal operating temperature.
2   Shut the engine off and connect the timing light according to the manufacturer's instructions. At the same time, refer to the Emissions Control Information label (located inside the engine compartment) for the proper engine timing specifications. Make sure the wiring leads for the timing light are not contacting the exhaust manifolds and that they are routed away from any moving parts such as the cooling fan.
3   Remove and block any vacuum hoses leading to the distributor if this is dictated by the instructions on the Emissions Control Information label. Use a golf tee, pencil or bolt to block any disconnected vacuum lines. **Caution:** *Make sure that you have no dangling articles of clothing such as ties or jewelry which can be caught in the moving components of the engine.*
4   Start the engine and make sure that it is idling at the proper speed, according to the Emissions Control Information label. If not, see Section 14.
5   Aim the timing light at the timing marks. If the timing marks do not show up clearly, it may be necessary to stop the engine and clean the timing pointer and crankshaft pulley with a rag.
6   Compare the position of the timing marks with the timing specifications for your vehicle. If the marks line up, the ignition timing is correct and no adjustment is necessary. If the timing is incorrect, turn off the engine.
7   Loosen the distributor holddown bolt with a wrench or special distributor bolt tool.
8   Restart the engine and rotate the distributor very slowly in either direction while pointing the timing light at the timing marks.
9   Be sure that the timing marks are aligned correctly and turn off the engine.
10 Tighten the distributor holddown bolt.
11 Restart the engine and check the timing to make sure it has not changed while tightening down the distributor bolt.
12 Recheck the idle speed to make sure it has not changed significantly. If the idle speed has changed, reset the idle speed and recheck the timing, as timing will vary with engine rpm.
13 Reconnect all vacuum hoses.

29 Spark plug replacement

1   The spark plugs are located on both sides of V6 and V8 engines and on one side of inline engines. They may or may not be easily accessible for removal. If the vehicle is equipped with air conditioning or power steering, some of the plugs may be tricky to remove. Special extension or swivel tools may be necessary. Make a survey under the hood to determine if special tools will be needed.
2   In most cases, tools necessary for a spark plug replacement include a plug wrench or spark plug socket, which fits onto a ratchet

wrench (this special socket will be insulated inside to protect the plug) and a wire-type feeler gauge to check and adjust the spark plug gap (photo). Also, a special spark plug wire removal tool is available for separating the wires from the spark plugs . To simplify installation, obtain a piece of 3/16-inch inside diameter rubber hose, 8 to 12 inches in length, to use in starting the plugs into the head.
3   The best procedure to follow when replacing the spark plugs is to purchase the new spark plugs beforehand, adjust them to the proper gap, and then replace each plug one at a time. When buying the new spark plugs, it is important to obtain the correct plugs for your specific engine. This information can be found on the Emissions Control Information label located under the hood or in the owner's manual. If differences exist between these sources, purchase the spark plug type specified on the Emissions Control label because the information was printed for your specific engine.
4   With the new spark plugs at hand, allow the engine to cool completely before attempting plug removal. During this time, each of the new spark plugs can be inspected for defects and the gaps can be checked.
5   The gap is checked by inserting the proper thickness gauge between the electrodes at the tip of the plug. The gap between the electrodes should be the same as that given on the Emissions Control label. The wire should just touch each of the electrodes. If the gap is incorrect, use the notched adjuster on the feeler gauge body to bend the curved side electrode slightly until the proper gap is achieved. If the side electrode is not exactly over the center electrode, use the notched adjuster to align the two.
6   Cover the fenders of the vehicle to prevent damage to the paint.
7   With the engine cool, remove the spark plug wire from one spark plug. Do this by grabbing the boot at the end of the wire, not the wire itself. Sometimes it is necessary to use a twisting motion while the boot and plug wire are pulled free. Using a plug wire removal tool is the easiest and safest method.
8   If compressed air is available, use it to blow any dirt or foreign material away from the spark plug area. A common bicycle pump will also work. The idea here is to eliminate the possibility of material falling into the cylinder as the spark plug is removed.
9   Place the spark plug wrench or socket over the plug and remove it from the engine by turning in a counterclockwise direction.
10 Compare the spark plug with those shown in the accompanying color photos to get an indication of the overall running condition of the engine.
11 Due to the angle at which the spark plugs must be installed on most engines, installation will be simplified by inserting the plug wire terminal of the new spark plug into the 3/16-inch rubber hose, mentioned previously, before it is installed in the cylinder head. This procedure serves two purposes: the rubber hose gives you flexibility for establishing the proper angle of plug insertion in the head and, should the threads be improperly lined up, the rubber hose will merely slip on the spark plug terminal when it meets resistance, preventing damage to the cylinder head threads.
12 After installing the plug to the limit of the hose grip, tighten it with the socket. It is a good idea to use a torque wrench for this to ensure that the plug is seated correctly. The correct torque figure is included in the Specifications.

30.4 Check the spark plug wire ends for corrosion and lubricate them with silicone grease before reinstalling them

13 Before pushing the spark plug wire onto the end of the plug, inspect it following the procedures outlined elsewhere in this Chapter.
14 Attach the plug wire to the new spark plug, again using a twisting motion on the boot until it is firmly seated on the spark plug. Make sure the wire is routed away from the exhaust manifold.
15 Follow the above procedure for the remaining spark plugs, replacing them one at a time to prevent mixing up the spark plug wires.

30 Spark plug wires, distributor cap and rotor check

1 The spark plug wires should be checked whenever new spark plugs are installed in the engine.
2 The wires should be inspected one at a time to prevent mixing up the order, which is essential for proper engine operation. Each original plug wire is numbered to help identify its location. If a number is illegible, a piece of tape can be marked with the correct number and wrapped around the plug wire.
3 Disconnect the plug wire from the spark plug. A removal tool can be used for this purpose or you can grab the rubber boot, twist slightly and pull the wire free. Do not pull on the wire itself, only on the rubber boot.
4 Check inside the boot for corrosion, which will look like a white crusty powder (photo). Some vehicles use a conductive white grease which should not be mistaken for corrosion. **Note:** *When any spark plug wire on an electronic ignition system is detached from a spark plug, distributor or coil terminal, silicone grease (Ford No. D7AZ-19A331-A or equivalent electronic application grease) should be applied to the interior surface of the boot before reattaching the wire to the component.*
5 Now push the wire and boot back onto the end of the spark plug. It should be a tight fit on the plug end. If not, remove the wire and use pliers to carefully crimp the metal connector inside the wire boot until the fit is snug.
6 Using a clean rag, wipe the entire length of the wire to remove built-up dirt and grease. Once the wire is clean, check for burns, cracks and other damage. Do not bend the wire, since the conductor might break.
7 Disconnect the wire from the distributor. Again, pull only on the rubber boot. Check for corrosion and a tight fit in the same manner as the spark plug end. Replace the wire in the distributor.
8 Check the remaining spark plug wires, making sure they are securely fastened at the distributor and spark plug when the check is complete.
9 If new spark plug wires are required, purchase a set for your specific engine model. Wire sets are available pre-cut, with the rubber boots already installed. Remove and replace the wires one at a time to avoid mix-ups in the firing order.
10 Check the distributor cap and rotor for wear. Look for cracks, carbon tracks and worn, burned or loose contacts. Replace the cap and rotor with new parts if defects are found. It is common practice to install a new cap and rotor whenever new spark plug wires are installed. When installing a new cap, remove the wires from the old cap one at

a time and attach them to the new cap in the exact same location — do not simultaneously remove all the wires from the old cap or firing order mix-ups may occur.

31 Compression check

1 A compression check will tell you what mechanical condition the upper portion (pistons, rings, valves, etc.) of your engine is in. Specifically, it can tell you if the compression is down due to leakage caused by worn piston rings, defective valves and seats or a blown head gasket.
2 Begin by cleaning the area around the spark plugs before you remove them. This will keep dirt from falling into the cylinders while you are performing the compression test.
3 Disconnect the ignition switch feed wire at the distributor. This is the pink wire coming from the ignition coil. Block the throttle and choke valves open.
4 With the compression gauge in the number one spark plug hole, crank the engine over at least four compression strokes and observe the gauge (the compression should build up quickly). Low compression on the first stroke, which does not build up during successive strokes, indicates leaking valves or a blown head gasket (a cracked head could also be the cause). Record the highest gauge reading obtained.
5 Repeat the procedure for the remaining cylinders and compare the results to the Specifications. Compression readings approximately 10% above or below the specified amount can be considered normal.
6 Pour a couple of teaspoons of engine oil (a squirt can works great for this) into each cylinder, through the spark plug hole, and repeat the test.
7 If the compression increases after after the oil is added, the piston rings are definitely worn. If the compression does not increase significantly, the leakage is occurring at the valves or head gasket. Leakage past the valves may be caused by burned valve seats or faces, warped, cracked or bent valves or incorrectly adjusted valves.
8 If two adjacent cylinders have equally low compression, there is a strong possibility that the head gasket between them is blown. The appearance of coolant in the combustion chambers or the crankcase would verify this condition.
9 If the compression unusually high, the combustion chambers are probably coated with carbon deposits. If that it the case, the cylinder head(s) should be removed and decarbonized.
10 If compression is way down or varies greatly between cylinders, it would be a good idea to have a leak-down test performed by a reputable automotive repair shop. This test will pinpoint exactly where the leakage is occurring and how severe it is.

32 Exhaust heat control valve check

Many earlier models are equipped with an exhaust heat control valve, which is located near the junction of the exhaust manifold and the exhaust pipe. When the engine is cold, this valve redirects hot exhaust gasses through a passage in the intake manifold to increase the vaporization of fuel.

To check the heat control valve, move it by hand and make sure it opens and closes freely. This is done by pressing gently on the actuator lever. If the valve action is not smooth, apply lithium grease to the actuator lever shaft and operate the lever manually several times to distribute the lubricant.

Fig. 1.27 Typical exhaust heat control valve (Sec 32)

Fig. 1.29 C4 transmission — adjusting the intermediate band (A) and the low reverse band (B) (Sec 34)

Fig. 1.28 Adjusting the front band on a C3 transmission (Sec 34)

1

Fig. 1.30 C5 transmission – adjusting the intermediate band (right) and the low reverse band (left) (Sec 34)

33 Intake manifold (V8) bolt torque check

1 The carburetor or fuel-injection throttle body, depending on which your vehicle has, is mounted on the top of the intake manifold. The intake manifold is attached to the head on inline engines, or to both heads on V-type engines. Many models also have an aluminum spacer plate at the top of the intake manifold to aid in heat transfer. Vacuum leaks can occur at the junction of any of these components, and usually are caused by loose nuts or bolts.

2 To tighten the mounting nuts or bolts, a torque wrench is necessary. If you don't own one, they can usually be rented on a daily basis.

3 Remove the air cleaner assembly, tagging all hoses and connections to simplify reassembly.

4 Locate the mounting nuts or bolts at the base of the carburetor or fuel injection throttle body and tighten them a little at a time and in a criss-cross pattern with the torque wrench. See the Chapter 4 Specifications for the torque values on your particular carburetor. Do the same with the fasteners at the base of the intake manifold.

5 If you still suspect a vacuum leak in this area, a simple stethoscope can be fashioned from a length of rubber hose. With the car running and one end of the hose held to your ear, probe the suspected area with the opposite end. You will hear a hissing sound if a leak exists.

6 If, after all the mounting nuts or bolts have been properly torqued, a leak still exists, the carburetor or fuel injection throttle body or the intake manifold must be removed and a new gasket installed.

7 Reinstall the air cleaner and hoses in their original positions.

34 Automatic transmission band adjustment

1 To determine which type of automatic transmission your vehicle has, check the identification codes on the vehicle identification label. General information on this label can be found in the front of this book.

2 Regardless of which transmission you have, it will be necessary to raise the vehicle. You will also need an accurate torque wrench, which can be rented if you don't own one.

C3 transmission — front band adjustment

3 Get under the vehicle and clean away any dirt or debris from the band adjustment screw area. The screw is located on the driver's side, just behind that big, bowl-shaped housing at the front of the transmission.

4 Remove and discard the adjustment screw locknut.

5 Install a new locknut on the adjusting screw and tighten the adjusting screw with a torque wrench to 10 ft-lbs. Back off the adjusting screw exactly 1-1/2 turns. Hold the screw and tighten the locknut.

C4 transmission — intermediate band adjustment

6 Clean the area around the adjusting screw. The screw is located on the driver's side of the transmission just above the midpoint of the pan.

7 Remove and discard the locknut. Install a new locknut and tighten the adjusting screw to 10 ft-lbs with the torque wrench. Back off the screw exactly 1-3/4 turns.

8 While holding the adjusting screw, tighten the locknut.

Fig. 1.31 FMX transmission — adjusting the front band (A) and the rear band (B) (Sec 34)

C4 transmission — low/reverse band adjustment

9   The adjusting screw is located near the left front corner of the pan. Follow the same procedure as for the intermediate band screw, but back off the adjusting screw three full turns before tightening the locknut.

C5 transmission — intermediate band adjustment

10   Clean all the dirt from the area around the adjusting screw. The screw is located on the driver's side of the transmission, just above the mid-point of the pan.
11   Remove the locknut and discard it. Install a new locknut, but do not tighten it yet.
12   Tighten the adjusting screw to 10 ft-lbs, then slowly back it off exactly 4-1/4 turns. Hold the adjusting screw and tighten to locknut.

C5 transmission — low/reverse band adjustment

13   The adjusting screw is located near the left front corner of the pan.
14   Follow the same procedure as for the intermediate band, but back off the adjusting screw three full turns before tightening the locknut.

C6 transmission — intermediate band adjustment

15   Follow the same procedure as described for the C4 transmission intermediate band, but back off the adjusting screw exactly 1-1/2 turns before tightening the locknut.

FMX transmission — front band adjustment

16   The transmission fluid must be drained before the front band adjust-ment can be made (Section 24). Use a clean drain pan and a 100-mesh screen if the fluid is to be reused.
17   You will also need to fabricate a spacer to substitute for a special tool Ford uses for this adjustment. The spacer should be made from 1/4-inch thick steel bar, approximately one inch wide by three inches long. The important thing is the 1/4-inch thickness.
18   Remove the pan and the fluid screen and clip from the transmission. Clean the screen and pan and remove all traces of gasket material from the face of the pan and the transmission case.
19   Loosen the locknut on the front servo adjusting screw. Pull back on the actuating rod and insert the 1/4 inch spacer between the adjusting screw and the stem of the servo piston.
20   Tighten the adjusting screw to 10 in-lbs and remove the spacer. Now tighten the screw an additional 3/4 turn and hold it in position as you tighten the locknut.
21   Install the transmission fluid screen and clip, then install the pan using a new gasket.
22   Refill the transmission with the specified fluid.

FMX transmission — rear band adjustment

23   Remove any built-up grease or dirt from around the adjustment screw threads. Lubricate the threads with light oil.
24   Loosen the reverse band adjusting screw locknut. Back off the adjusting screw, then retighten it to 10 ft-lbs.
25   Back off the adjusting screw exactly 1-1/2 turns. Hold the screw stationary as you tighten the locknut.

Chapter 2 Part A
2.3 liter four-cylinder engine

Contents

Specifications

Camshaft

Lobe lift	
Intake	0.2437 in
Exhaust	0.2437 in
Allowable lobe lift loss	0.005 in maximum
Theoretical valve lift @ zero lash	
Intake	0.3997 in
Exhaust	0.3997 in
Endplay	0.001 to 0.007 in
Service limit	0.009 in
Journal-to-bearing clearance	0.001 to 0.003 in
Service limit	0.006 in
Journal diameter	
No. 1	1.7713 to 1.7720 in
No. 2	1.7713 to 1.7720 in
No. 3	1.7713 to 1.7720 in
No. 4	1.7713 to 1.7720 in
Runout limit	0.005 in
Out-of-round limit	0.005 in
Front bearing location	0.000 to 0.010. Distance in inches that front bearing is installed below front face of bearing tower.

Torque specifications

	Ft-lbs
Oil pan bolts	8 to 10
Oil pan drain plug	15 to 25
Oil pump-to-block bolts	14 to 21
Oil pump cover bolts	6 to 8
Oil pump pickup tube-to-oil pump bolts	14 to 21
Rocker arm cover bolts	6 to 8
Outer timing cover bolts	6 to 9
Inner timing cover bolts	14 to 21
Crankshaft pulley hub bolt	100 to 120
Camshaft thrust plate-to-block bolts	6 to 9

Torque specifications (continued)

	Ft-lbs
Timing belt tensioner pivot bolt	28 to 40
Timing belt tensioner adjustment bolt	14 to 21
Auxiliary shaft sprocket bolt	28 to 40
Auxiliary shaft cover bolts	6 to 9
Intake manifold-to-cylinder head bolts	14 to 21
Exhaust manifold-to-cylinder head bolts	16 to 23
Cylinder head bolts	80 to 90
Spacer plate-to-manifold nuts/bolts	14 to 21
EGR valve-to-spacer plate bolts	14 to 21
Carburetor-to-spacer plate nuts	10 to14
Fuel pump-to-block bolts	14 to 21
Distributor holddown bolt	14 to 21
Distributor vacuum tube-to-manifold bolt	5 to 8
Water outlet housing bolts	14 to 21
Water pump-to-block bolts	14 to 21
Fan and pulley-to-water pump bolts	14 to 21
Water jacket drain plug	23 to 28
Temperature sending unit-to-block	8 to 18
Flywheel-to-crankshaft bolts	56 to 64
Front engine mounts-to-engine bolts	33 to 45
Front engine mount studs-to-crossmember nuts	50 to 65
Front engine damper-to-crossmember bolt	35 to 50
Rear mount-to-transmission bolt	50 to 70
Rear mount-to-crossmember nuts	25 to35
Rear crossmember-to-frame nuts/bolts	35 to 50

1   General Information

This Part of Chapter 2 is devoted to repair procedures for the 2.3 liter engine. The latter Sections in this Part of Chapter 2 involve the removal and installation procedures for the 2.3 liter engine. All information concerning engine block and cylinder head servicing can be found in Part E of this Chapter.

Many of the repair procedures included in this Part are based on the assumption that the engine is still installed in the vehicle. Therefore, if this information is being used during a complete engine overhaul, with the engine already out of the vehicle and on a stand, many of the steps included here will not apply.

The specifications included in this Part of Chapter 2 apply only to the engine and procedures found here. For specifications regarding other engines, see Part B, C or D, whichever applies. Part E of Chapter 2 contains the specifications necessary for engine block and cylinder head rebuilding procedures.

The 2.3 liter engine is an inline configuration and is constructed of cast iron. The crankshaft is supported on five main bearings and the camshaft by four bearings. All main bearings, connecting rod, camshaft and auxiliary shaft bearings are replaceable. The valves are actuated by a single overhead camshaft and hydraulic valve lash adjusters.

The camshaft in the 2.3 liter engine is driven from the crankshaft by a toothed belt, which also operates the auxiliary shaft. The auxiliary shaft drives the oil pump, distributor and fuel pump. Tension on the belt is maintained by a preloaded idler pulley, which runs on the outside of the belt.

The water pump and alternator are driven separately from the crankshaft by a conventional V-belt. V-belts are also used to provide power for the engine-driven accessories.

2   Rocker arm cover — removal and installation

1   Remove the air cleaner assembly, tagging each hose as it is disconnected with pieces of numbered tape to simplify reinstallation.
2   Remove the PCV valve from the rocker arm cover.
3   Remove the rocker arm cover bolts.
4   Remove the rocker arm cover as shown in the accompanying illustration. **Note:** *If the cover sticks to the cylinder head, use a block of wood and a hammer to dislodge it. If the cover still will not come loose, pry on it carefully, but do not distort the sealing flange surface.*
5   Prior to installation of the cover clean all dirt, oil and old gasket material from the sealing surfaces of the cover and cylinder head with a scraper and degreaser.
6   Apply a continuous 3/16-inch (5 mm) diameter bead of RTV-type

Fig. 2A.1   Rocker arm cover and gasket installation (Sec 2)

Fig. 2A.2 Rocker arm cover bolt tightening sequence (Sec 2)

Fig. 2A.3 Compressing the valve spring with a special Ford service tool. This tool is also used for valve lash adjustment as shown (Sec 3)

Fig. 2A.4 Valve train components — exploded view (earlier models do not incorporate the basket-shaped spring seat shown above) (Sec 3)

sealant to the sealing flange of the cover. Be sure to apply the sealant inboard of the bolt holes.

7   Place the rocker arm cover on the cylinder head while the sealant is still wet and install the mounting bolts. Tighten the bolts a little at a time to the specified torque in the sequence shown in the accompanying illustration.

8   Complete the installation by reversing the removal procedure.

3   Valve train components — replacement (cylinder head installed)

1   Remove the rocker arm cover as described in Section 2.

2   If the valve springs are to be removed, remove the spark plugs from the affected cylinders.

3   There are two methods which will allow the valve to remain in place while the valve spring is removed. If you have access to compressed air, install an air hose adapter in the spark plug hole. When air pressure is applied to the adapter (at least 100 psi) the valves will be held in place by the pressure. If the air pressure does not hold the valve in place, the valve is damaged or burned and the cylinder head must be removed and the valves serviced.

4   If you do not have access to compressed air, bring the piston of the affected cylinder to slightly before top dead center (TDC) on the compression stroke. Feed a long piece of 1/4-inch nylon cord in through the spark plug hole until it fills the combustion chamber. Be sure to leave the end of the cord hanging out of the spark plug hole so it can be removed easily.

5   Using tool T74P-6565-A or an equivalent tool, as shown in the accompanying illustration, collapse the lash adjuster and depress the valve spring. Slide the cam follower over the lash adjuster and out. Lift out the hydraulic lash adjuster. Compress the spring just enough to remove the spring keepers, spring retainer, valve spring and spring seat (if so equipped), as shown in the accompanying illustration. Remove the valve stem oil seal and discard it.

6   Inspection procedures for valve train train components are covered in Chapter 2, Part E.

7   Installation of the valve train components is the reverse of removal procedure. Always use new valve stem oil seals whenever the spring keepers have been disturbed. Place the hydraulic lash adjuster in position in its bore and, using the same compressing tool, collapse the lash adjuster to position the cam follower over the lash adjuster and the valve stem. It may also be necessary to compress the valve spring with the tool.

8   Install the rocker arm cover as outlined in Section 2 of this Chapter.

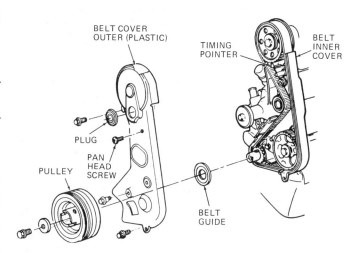

Fig. 2A.5 Timing belt outer cover, crankshaft belt guide and pulley installation (Sec 4)

4   Camshaft front cover and drivebelt — removal and installation

Removal

1   It is possible to remove the camshaft drivebelt with the engine in place, but experience shows that this type of belt is very reliable and unlikely to break or stretch. However, during major overhaul it is recommended that a new belt be installed.

2   Drain the cooling system, loosen the top hose clamps and remove the top coolant hose.

3   Loosen the alternator mounting bolts and push the alternator toward the engine. Remove the accessory drivebelts. **Note:** *Vehicles equipped with a Thermactor pump or an air-conditioning compressor will need to have the drivebelts for these accessories removed.*

4   Remove the bolts securing the camshaft drivebelt outer cover to the front of the engine and lift away the cover as shown in the accompanying illustration.

2A

Fig. 2A.6 Camshaft drivebelt, sprocket and tensioner installation (Sec 4)

Fig. 2A.8 Cylinder head bolt tightening sequence (which should also be used when loosening the bolts) (Sec 5)

Fig. 2A.7 When installing the drivebelt it is necessary that everything be aligned as shown (Sec 4)

5   Loosen the belt tensioner mounting plate securing bolt and release the tension on the belt.
6   Place the transmission in gear and apply the parking brake. Remove the bolt and plain washer which secures the crankshaft pulley to the nose of the crankshaft.
7   Using a puller carefully remove the pulley.
8   Remove the large diameter belt guide washer and pull the drivebelt away from the engine.
9   To replace the front oil seal it is not necessary to remove the front cover from the engine.
10   Remove the seal from the cover using the special seal-removing tool. When assembling the engine or reinstalling the front cover, install the cover on the engine without the seal then press the seal into place using the base of a large socket. This will avoid damage to the lip of the seal.
11   Before installing the front cover and tightening the bolts, be sure that the inside diameter of the seal is positioned evenly in relation to the crankshaft. Tighten the bolts to the specified torque. The positioning procedure will assure that the timing belt does not interfere with the front cover during engine operation.

Installation

12   Rotate the camshaft until the index mark on the sprocket is aligned with the timing pointer on the inner belt cover.
13   Rotate the crankshaft until the number one piston is at TDC.
14   Without disturbing the crankshaft and camshaft positions, install the belt tensioner but do not tighten the bolts.
15   Install the timing belt over the crankshaft sprocket, the auxiliary

shaft and camshaft sprockets, then behind the tensioner jockey wheel as shown in the accompanying illustration. If you experience difficulty, use a lever to pull the tensioner jockey wheel away from the belt.
16   Rotate the crankshaft two (2) full turns in a clockwise direction to remove all slack from the belt.
17   Check that the timing marks are correctly aligned as shown in the accompanying illustration, then tighten the adjuster and bolts to the specified torque.
18   Further reassembly is the reverse of disassembly.

5   Cylinder head — removal and installation

Note: *The procedure for camshaft removal and installation is in Section 6. Valve servicing instructions are found in Section 3.*

Removal — engine out of the vehicle
1   Remove the carburetor from the intake manifold.
2   Remove the carburetor base gasket, the EGR spacer and the second gasket.
3   Remove any emission control system hoses and fittings from the intake manifold, carefully noting their installed positions to simplify reassembly.
4   Loosen the intake manifold bolts 1/2-turn each, in the reverse order to that shown in Figure 2A.10 (Section 7). When they have all been loosened remove the bolts completely and lift away the manifold.
5   Remove the timing belt outer cover. Note the spacers used with two of the bolts adjacent to the auxiliary shaft sprocket.
6   If major engine disassembly is going to be carried out, remove the nut and washer retaining the crankshaft pulley.
7   Draw off the pulley with a puller and remove the belt guide.
8   Loosen the timing belt tensioner adjustment bolt to relieve the belt tension.
9   Remove the timing belt by drawing it off the sprockets.
10   Remove the timing belt tensioner.
11   Remove the single stud and washer from the upper mounting point of the inner timing belt cover.
12   Remove the rocker arm cover.
13   Loosen each cylinder head bolt slightly in the reverse order to that shown in the accompanying illustration. Then remove all the bolts with

the exception of 7 and 8, which should be unscrewed so that only about two threads are engaged.

14   Using the exhaust manifold for leverage, lift up to break the cylinder head gasket seal.

15   Loosen the exhaust manifold bolts in the reverse order to that shown in Figure 2A.11 (Section 8). Remove the bolts while supporting the manifold, then remove the manifold from the engine.

16   Remove the two remaining cylinder head bolts and lift off the head. Transfer it to a workbench for further disassembly. Remove the old gasket from the block.

17   Refer to Chapter 2E for further cylinder head disassembly and valve servicing procedures.

Removal — engine in the vehicle

18   Removal of the cylinder head with the engine in the vehicle is very similar to the procedure given above. However, the following points should be noted:

   a) First remove the hood for improved access.
   b) Disconnect the negative cable from the battery.
   c) Drain the engine coolant and remove the hoses connected to the cylinder head. Refer to Chapters 1 and 3, if necessary.
   d) Remove the air cleaner, carburetor and emission control system items attached to the carburetor and manifold. Refer to Chapter 4 if necessary. It is recommended that a sketch be made showing the various connections to avoid confusion.
   e) The camshaft drivebelt does not have to be completely removed unless it is to be replaced. This means that the crankshaft pulley and belt guide do not have to be removed.
   f) Remove the drivebelts from the engine accessories to permit the drivebelt outer cover to be removed.
   g) If air-conditioning refrigerant lines must be disconnected, it must be done by a qualified air-conditioning technician.
   h) Detach the spark plug leads and the oil pressure gauge wire.

Installation

19   If a new cylinder head is being installed, transfer all external parts.

20   If not already done, thoroughly clean the gasket surfaces on the cylinder head and the engine block. Do not gouge or otherwise damage the gasket surfaces.

21   To get the proper torque readings the threads of the head bolts must be clean. This also applies to the threaded holes in the engine block. Run a tap through the holes then blow them out with compressed air to ensure that they are clean.

22   Place the gasket in position over the engine block dowel pins.

23   Carefully lower the cylinder head onto the engine, over the dowel pins and the gasket.

24   Coat the threads of each cylinder head bolt and the point at which the head and the bolt meet with a sealing compound and install the bolts finger tight.

25   Tighten each of the bolts a little at a time in the sequence shown in the accompanying illustration. Continue tightening in this sequence until the proper torque reading is obtained. As a final check, work around the head in a front-to-rear sequence to make sure none of the bolts have been left out of the sequence.

26   The remaining installation steps are the reverse of removal.

---

6   Camshaft — removal and installation

Removal

1   Before the camshaft can be removed the cam followers must be removed.

2   Remove the rocker arm cover, the timing belt cover and the timing belt.

3   Remove the spring clip from the hydraulic valve lash adjuster end of the cam followers.

Fig. 2A.9 Components involved in camshaft installation (Sec 6)

4   Using special tool T74P-6565-A inserted beneath the camshaft, as shown in Fig. 2A.3 (Section 3), compress the lash adjuster of the first valve to be removed, ensuring that the cam lobe is facing away from the follower. This will permit the cam followers to be removed. Keep the cam followers in order so they can be reinstalled in their original positions. **Note:** *On some valves it may be necessary to compress the valve spring slightly to remove the cam follower.*
5   Lift out the hydraulic lash adjusters, keeping each one with its respective cam follower.
6   Using a metal bar, lock the camshaft drive sprocket. Remove the mounting bolt and washer.
7   Draw off the sprocket with a puller then remove the belt guide.
8   Remove the sprocket locating key from the end of the camshaft.
9   Remove the camshaft retaining plate from the rear bearing pedestal.
10   Using a hammer and a brass or aluminum drift, drive out the camshaft toward the front of the engine, taking the front seal with it. Be very careful not to damage the camshaft bearings and journals as it is pushed out.

Camshaft and bearings — inspection
11   After the camshaft has been removed from the engine, cleaned with solvent and dried, inspect the bearing journals for uneven wear, pitting or evidence of seizure. If the journals are damaged, the bearing inserts in the head are probably damaged as well. Both the camshaft and bearings will have to be replaced with new ones. Measure the inside diameter of each camshaft bearing and record the results (take two measurements, 90° apart, at each bearing).
12   Measure the bearing journals with a micrometer to determine if they are excessively worn or out-of-round. If they are more than 0.005-inch out-of-round, the camshaft should be replaced with a new one. Subtract the bearing journal diameters from the corresponding bearing inside diameter measurements to obtain the clearance. If it is excessive, new bearings must be installed. **Note:** *camshaft bearing replacement requires special tools and expertise that place it outside the scope of the do-it-yourselfer. Take the head to an automotive machine shop to ensure that the job is done correctly.*
13   Check the camshaft lobes for heat discoloration, score marks, chipped areas, pitting or uneven wear. If the lobes are in good condition the camshaft can be reused.
14   Make sure that the camshaft oilways are clear and clean.
15   To check the thrust plate for wear, install the camshaft in the cylinder head and position the thrust plate at the rear. Using a dial indicator, check the total end play by tapping the camshaft carefully back-and-forth. If the endplay is outside the specified limit, replace the thrust plate with a new one.

Cam followers — inspection
16   The faces of the cam followers which bear on the camshaft should show no signs of pitting, scoring or other forms of wear. They should not be a loose fit on the pivot bolt.
17   Inspect the face which bears on the valve stem. If it is pitted, the cam follower must be replaced with a new one.
18   If excessive cam follower wear is evident (and possibly excessive cam lobe wear), it may be due to a malfunction of the valve drive lubrication tube. If this has occurred, replace the tube and the cam follower. If more than one cam follower is excessively worn, replace the camshaft, all the cam followers and the lubrication tube. This also applies where excessive cam lobe wear is found.
19   During any operation which requires removal of the arm rocker cover, make sure that oil is being discharged from the lubrication tube nozzles by cranking the engine with the starter motor.

Installation
20   Liberally coat the camshaft journals and bearings with engine assembly lube, then carefully install the shaft in the cylinder head as shown in the accompanying illustration.
21   Install the retainer plate and bolts.
22   Lubricate a new camshaft seal with engine oil and carefully tap it into position at the front of the cylinder head.
23   Install the belt guide and pin at the front end of the camshaft, then carefully tap on the sprocket.
24   Install a new sprocket bolt.
25   Coat the hydraulic lash adjusters with engine assembly lube, then install each one into its respective position.
26   Coat the surface of the camshaft lobes and cam followers with engine assembly lube.

27   Using special tool T74P-6565-B to compress each lash adjuster, position each cam follower on its respective valve end and adjuster, ensuring that the camshaft is rotated as necessary. Install the retaining spring clips. **Note:** *On some valves it may be necessary to compress the valve spring slightly when fitting the cam follower.*

7   Intake manifold — removal and installation

1   Disconnect the battery cable from the negative terminal of the battery.
2   Drain the cooling system by following the procedure in Chapter 1.
3   Remove the air cleaner assembly, tagging each hose to be disconnected with a piece of numbered tape to simplify reinstallation.
4   Remove the PCV valve and hose.
5   Disconnect vacuum hoses as required.
6   Remove the oil dipstick and disconnect the heat tube at the EGR valve. The EGR valve is connected to a spacer plate between the carburetor and the intake manifold.
7   Label and disconnect the fuel line, vacuum lines and any electrical leads from the carburetor assembly. When disconnecting the fuel line be prepared to catch some fuel, then plug the fuel line with a golf tee or pencil.
8   Disconnect the throttle cable.
9   Remove the dipstick tube bolt from the intake manifold.
10   Disconnect the coil wire and remove the two distributor cap retaining screws.
11   Remove the intake manifold bolts and separate the manifold from the engine.
12   When separating the manifold from the cylinder head, do not pry between the manifold and the head as damage to the gasket sealing surfaces may result.
13   Remove the manifold gasket.
14   If the intake manifold is replaced with another one, transfer all accessories and components still attached to the old manifold to the new one.
15   Before installing the manifold, clean the cylinder head and manifold gasket surfaces.
16   Apply a thin bead of RTV-type sealant to the intake manifold and cylinder head mating surfaces. Make certain that the sealant will not spread into the air or coolant passages when the manifold is installed.
17   Place a new intake manifold gasket on the manifold, place the manifold in position against the cylinder head and install the mounting bolts finger tight.
18   Tighten the mounting bolts a little at a time in the sequence shown in the accompanying illustration until they are all at the specified torque.
19   Install the remaining components in the reverse order of removal.
20   Refill the engine and radiator with coolant. Start the engine and check for coolant and fuel leaks.
21   Adjust the ignition timing and idle speed as necessary (Chapter 1).

2A

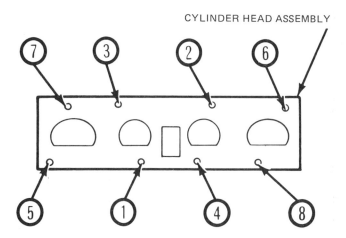

CYLINDER HEAD ASSEMBLY

Fig. 2A.10 Intake manifold bolt tightening sequence (Sec 7)

TIGHTEN THE MANIFOLD BOLTS TO SPECIFICATIONS IN
TWO PROGRESSIVE STEPS IN THE SEQUENCE SHOWN

**Fig. 2A.11 Exhaust manifold bolt tightening sequence
(Sec 8)**

Fig. 2A.12 Oil pan bolt tightening sequence (Sec 9)

---

8   Exhaust manifold — removal and installation

1   If the vehicle is equipped with air-conditioning, carefully examine the routing of the hoses and the mounting of the compressor. You may be able to remove the exhaust manifold without disconnecting the system. If you are in doubt, take the vehicle to a Ford dealer or automotive repair shop to have the system depressurized. **Caution:** *Do not disconnect any air-conditioning system lines while the system is under pressure.*
2   Disconnect the negative cable from the battery.
3   Remove the air cleaner assembly, tagging each hose to be disconnected with a piece of numbered tape to simplify reinstallation.
4   Remove the engine oil dipstick and dipstick tube.
5   Remove the hose from the Thermactor check valve.
6   Label the four spark plug wires then disconnect them and secure them to the side out of the way.
7   Disconnect the exhaust pipe from the exhaust manifold. You may have to apply penetrating oil to the fastener threads as they are usually corroded. The exhaust pipe can be hung from the frame with a piece of wire.
8   Remove the exhaust manifold end bolts first, then remove the center bolts and separate the exhaust manifold from the engine.
9   Remove the exhaust manifold gasket.
10   Before reinstalling the manifold, clean the gasket mating surfaces on the cylinder head and manifold. All old gasket material and carbon deposits must be removed.
11   Place a new exhaust manifold gasket in position on the cylinder head, then hold the manifold in place while installing the mounting bolts finger tight.
12   Tighten the mounting bolts a little at a time in the sequence shown in the accompanying illustration until all of the bolts are at the specified torque.
13   Install the remaining components in the reverse order of removal, using new gasket whenever one has been removed.
14   Start the engine and check for exhaust leaks between the manifold and cylinder head and between the manifold and exhaust pipe.

---

9   Oil pan — removal and installation

Note: *The oil pan is most easily removed if the engine is first removed from the vehicle.*
1   Disconnect the cable from the negative battery terminal.
2   Raise the vehicle on a hoist or place it securely on jackstands and drain the engine oil (refer to Chapter 1 if necessary).
3   Drain the cooling system (Chapter 1).
4   Remove the right and left engine support through-bolts.
5   Using a hoist or jack, raise the engine as far as it will go. Place

wood blocks between the mounts and the number two crossmember pedestal brackets. Remove the jack.
6   Remove the steering gear retaining nuts and bolts (see Chapter 10 for more information on the steering system).
7   Remove the bolt retaining the steering flex coupling to the steering gear. Position the steering gear forward and down.
8   Disconnect the starter cable and remove the starter (Chapter 5).
9   Remove the engine rear support-to-crossmember nuts.
10   Position a jack under the transmission and raise the transmission and engine assembly enough to remove the oil pan bolts.
11   Separate the oil pan from the block.
12   Clean the pan with solvent and remove old sealant and gasket material from the block and pan sealing surfaces.
13   Remove and clean the oil pick-up tube and screen assembly. After cleaning, reinstall them.
14   Apply sealant to the depressions where the end seals meet the block.
15   Position the oil pan gasket and end seals on the cylinder block, as shown in the accompanying illustration, using RTV sealant. Position the oil pan on the cylinder block and install the bolts.
16   Tighten the bolts to the specified torque, alternating between A and B in the directions shown in the accompanying illustration.
17   Lower the jack under the transmission and install the crossmember nuts. Remove the jack.
18   The remaining steps are the reverse of the removal procedure.
19   When the operation is complete, start the engine and check for oil and coolant leaks.

---

10   Engine mounts — replacement with engine in vehicle

Note: *Whenever self-locking bolts or nuts are removed, they must be replaced with new self-locking units. Prior to installing new self-locking bolts or nuts (which have factory-applied thread adhesive), hardened residual adhesive must be removed from the engine block bosses with an M10 x 1.5 bottoming tap.*
1   If the rubber mounts have become hardened, split or separated from the metal brackets, they must be replaced. This operation may be carried out with the engine/transmission still in the vehicle. See Section 9, *Oil pan — removal and installation,* for the recommended method of raising the engine while it is still in place.

Front mounts
2   To remove the engine mounts, remove the bolt that attaches the lower end of the engine damper to the number two crossmember bracket.
3   Remove the through-bolt nut and washer assemblies attaching both rubber mounts to the number two crossmember pedestal bracket. If the vehicle is equipped with a fuel pump shield, remove the attaching screw and the shield before removing the mounts.
4   Disconnect the shift linkage and raise the engine enough to disengage the mounting studs from the crossmember pedestal bracket.
5   Remove the bolts attaching the mount and bracket assembly to the engine. On the Thunderbird and Cougar models, loosen the addi-

DRAIN PLUG

FRONT SUMP OIL PAN

REAR SUMP OIL PAN

M6X 16.0 MM LONG SCREW
AND WASHER – 18 PLACES

OIL PAN

2A

M8X 20.0 MM LONG
SCREW AND WASHER
4 PLACES

PAN GASKET (R)

PAN GASKET (L)

SEAL
(REFER TO NOTE BELOW)

(SEE BONDING NOTE BELOW)

GUIDE PINS

SEAL

HOLE A

OIL-RESISTANT SEALER APPROX. 0.125" WIDE BEAD
TO JOINT OF BLOCK AND FRONT COVER

OIL PAN GASKET

BLOCK

FRONT

FRONT COVER
OR REAR CAP

SEAL TAB

1. APPLY GASKET ADHESIVE (ESE-M2G52-A OR B OR EQUIVALENT) EVENLY TO OIL
   PAN SIDE GASKETS. ALLOW ADHESIVE TO DRY PAST WET STAGE, THEN
   INSTALL GASKETS TO OIL PAN.

2. APPLY SEALER (ESE-M4G195-A OR EQUIVALENT) TO JOINT OF BLOCK AND
   FRONT COVER. INSTALL SEALS TO FRONT COVER AND REAR BEARING
   CAP AND PRESS SEAL TABS FIRMLY INTO BLOCK. BE SURE TO INSTALL THE
   REAR SEAL BEFORE THE REAR MAIN BEARING CAP SEALER HAS CURED.

3. POSITION 2 GUIDE PINS AND INSTALL THE OIL PAN. SECURE THE PAN WITH
   THE FOUR M8 BOLTS SHOWN ABOVE.

4. REMOVE THE GUIDE PINS AND INSTALL AND TORQUE THE EIGHTEEN M6
   BOLTS, BEGINNING AT HOLE A AND WORKING CLOCKWISE AROUND THE
   PAN.

Fig. 2A.13   Oil pan and gasket installation (Sec 9)

Fig. 2A.14 Engine supports on LTD and Marquis models (Sec 10)

Fig. 2A.15 Engine supports on all models other than LTD and Marquis (Sec 10)

tional upper damper bracket fasteners and remove the insulator and bracket assembly.
6   To install the mounts, position the mount and bracket assembly on the engine. Install the attaching bolts and tighten them to the specified torque.
7   Lower the engine into position, making sure that the mounts are seated flat on the number two crossmember and that the mounting studs are at the bottom of the slots.
8   Attach the mount to the number two crossmember mount studs. Tighten the flange nut to the specified torque.
9   Install the fuel pump shield to the left side engine support (if so equipped).
10 On LTD and Marquis models, attach the engine damper to the number two crossmember bracket attaching bolt. Tighten the bolt to the specified torque. On Thunderbird and Cougar models tighten the additional upper damper bracket fasteners.
11 Install the shift linkage.

Rear mounts

12 The rear support is located at the transmission extension housing. Replace any self-locking nuts and bolts you remove with new ones.
13 Support the transmission with a jack and wood blocks. Remove the two nuts attaching the rear rubber mount to the crossmember.
14 Remove the two bolts and nuts attaching the crossmember to the body brackets and remove the crossmember after raising the transmission slightly with the jack.
15 Remove the two bolts attaching the rear mount to the transmission and remove the mount and retainer.
16 To install the mount, position it and the retainer on the transmission. Install the two bolts and tighten them to the specified torque.
17 Attach the crossmember to the body brackets and tighten the nuts and bolts to the specified torque.
18 Lower the transmission and attach the insulator to the crossmember. Tighten the nuts to the specified torque.

11   Oil pump and strainer — removal and installation

1   Remove the oil pan (Section 9).
2   Remove the bolt securing the oil pump pick-up pipe support bracket to the block as shown in the accompanying illustration.
3   Using special tool 21-020, available at tool rental shops, remove the two bolts securing the oil pump to the block. These special bolts can not be removed with any replacement tool without damaging the bolt. The special tool is necessary for oil pump removal.
4   Lift away the oil pump and strainer assembly.

M8 X 25.0 LONG SCREW AND WASHER (14-21 LB-FT) 19.0-29 N·m 2 PLACES

OIL PUMP MUST BE FREE TO ROTATE AFTER INSTALLATION

OIL PUMP

32.0 mm (1.26")

M10 NUT (28-40 LB-FT) 38-54 N·m

ATTACH TO STUD ON NO. 4 MAIN BEARING CAP

SHAFT ASSEMBLY OIL PUMP INTERMEDIATE

Fig. 2A.16 Oil pump and strainer assembly (Sec 11)

5   Carefully detach the oil pump, making a special note of its position.
6   The oil pump should not be dismantled or repaired in any way. If there is any obvious damage, if the engine has high mileage, or in the case of major engine overhaul, a replacement pump should be installed.
7   Detach the oil intake pipe and screen and clean the parts thoroughly with solvent.
8   Reinstall the intake pipe and screen, using a new gasket.
9   Clean the mating faces of the oil pump and the block.
10 Insert the hexagonal driveshaft into the end of the oil pump.
11 Install the oil pump and the two bolts, using the special tool and a torque wrench to tighten the two bolts to the specified torque.
12 Reinstall the bolt that secures the oil pump pick-up pipe support bracket to the block.
13 Install the oil pan, fill the crankcase with oil (Chapter 1), check the operation of the oil pressure light and look for leaks.

12   Auxiliary shaft — removal, inspection and installation

2A

1   Remove the belt cover and the camshaft drivebelt according to the procedure outlined in Section 4.
2   Using a metal bar or a large screwdriver to lock the auxiliary shaft sprocket in place, remove the sprocket retaining bolt and washer.
3   Pull out the sprocket using a universal puller and remove the sprocket locking key from the shaft.
4   Remove the three screws from the auxiliary shaft cover and remove the cover.
5   Remove the shaft retaining plate screws and the retaining plate.
6   Withdraw the shaft. If it is tight, reinstall the bolt and washer. Use a pry bar and spacer block to pry out the shaft. Be extremely careful not to damage the bearings as you pull the shaft out of the block.
7   Examine the auxiliary shaft bearing for scoring and pitting. Replacement will have to be dealt with by a shop, for although it is easy to remove the old bearing, the correct installation of the new one requires special tools. See your local Ford dealer or machine shop for this work. The auxiliary shaft may show signs of wear on the bearing journal or the eccentric. Any signs of scoring or damage to the bearing journals cannot be removed by grinding. If in doubt, ask your service department to check the auxiliary shaft and give advice on replacement. Examine the gear teeth for wear and damage. If either is evident, a replacement shaft must be obtained.
8   Dip the auxiliary shaft completely in engine oil before installing it into the block. Tap it in gently with a soft-faced hammer to ensure that it is seated. Install the retaining plate and the auxiliary shaft cover as shown in the accompanying illustration.
9   The remainder of the procedure is the reverse of removal. Make sure that the auxiliary shaft key is in place before installing the sprocket. After the sprocket is installed, tighten the bolt to the specified torque.

13   Engine — removal

The engine may be lifted out either on its own or with the transmission. On models equipped with an automatic transmission, it is recommended that the engine be lifted out on its own because of the weight factor. If the engine and transmission are removed together they have to be lifted out at a very steep angle, so make sure that there is sufficient lifting height available.

Removal (without transmission)

Note: *If equipped with air-conditioning, have a refrigeration technician discharge the system.*
1   Raise the hood and disconnect the battery cables from the battery, starting with the negative cable.
2   Mark the position of the hood hinges with a pencil or scribe. Remove the retaining bolts and remove the hood.
3   Remove the air cleaner and exhaust manifold shroud.
4   If air-conditioning is involved, remove the compressor unit from the engine mounting bracket but do not disconnect the refrigerant hoses. Position the pump out of the way without straining the hoses.
5   Drain the oil from the oil pan.
6   Drain the coolant then remove the bottom radiator hose.
7   Remove the top hose and transmission oil cooler hoses (if equipped) from the radiator. Remove the mounting bolts and lift out the radiator.

GEAR AND FUEL PUMP
ECCENTRIC MUST NOT BE
ALLOWED TO TOUCH
BEARING SURFACES
DURING INSTALLATION

AUXILIARY SHAFT — 6K230

RETAINING PLATE-6A222

BEARING-6A753- 6B862

PIN

DIP SHAFT COMPLETELY IN ENGINE
OIL BEFORE INSTALLING

NOTE: CUT GASKET
FOR SEPARATE
REMOVAL OR
INSTALLATION OF
COVERS

AUXILIARY SHAFT
COVER — 6E007

VIEW A

GASKET-6020

COVER ALIGNMENT
PADS -3 PLACES

CYLINDER FRONT
COVER-6059

FRONT COVER
ALIGNMENT TOOL
(T74P-6019-B)

Fig. 2A.17 Auxiliary shaft and bearings and cylinder front cover assembly (note alignment of front cover during installation) (Sec 12)

8   Disconnect the power lead to the fan motor then remove the fan and shroud assembly.
9   Jack up the front of the vehicle and support it on jackstands.
10 Where applicable, remove the engine shield.
11 Remove the starter motor. Further details will be found in Chapter 5, if required.
12 On automatic transmission models, remove the torque converter bolt access plug.
13 Remove the converter housing cover and disconnect the converter from the flexplate.
14 On manual transmission models, remove the flywheel cover.
15 Detach the exhaust pipe from the exhaust manifold. Remove the packing washer.
16 Remove the nuts from the engine mounts, and remove the nuts and through-bolts retaining the rear engine support crossmember.
17 Detach the fuel lines from the fuel pump, plugging the lines to prevent fuel spillage.
18 Where applicable, remove the power steering pump drivebelt and draw off the pulley. Refer to Chapter 10 for further information on the pump.
19 Remove the lower bolt securing the power steering pump to the bracket.
20 Lower the vehicle to the ground.
21 Disconnect the heater and vacuum hoses from the engine. It is recommended that a sketch be made showing the various connections to avoid confusion during installation.
22 Disconnect the power brake hose.
23 Remove the oil pressure union from the connection on the left rear side of the cylinder head.
24 Detach the carburetor cable(s).
25 Disconnect the wire to the throttle solenoid and choke heater.
26 Detach the wire from the coolant temperature sender on the left rear side of the block.
27 Disconnect the lines from the vacuum amplifier.
28 Disconnect the coil wire and vacuum line from the distributor.
29 Pull off the multi-plug from the alternator, followed by the ground wire.
30 Remove the bolt from the alternator adjusting arm.
31 Remove the remaining power steering pump-to-bracket bolts, and remove the pump (if equipped).
32 Support the weight of the transmission on a jack, with a wood block between the jack and the transmission.
33 Attach the hoist hooks to the engine lifting brackets and lift the engine slightly.
34 Draw the engine forward to disengage the transmission; make sure that the transmission is still supported.
35 Lift the engine out, ensuring that no damage occurs to the hoses, etc., in the engine compartment or to the engine mounting equipment.

Removal (with transmission)

36 The procedure for removing the engine and transmission together is basically similar to that described above. However, the following differences should be noted:
    a) Disconnect the gearshift linkage from the transmission, referring to Chapter 7 if necessary.
    b) Detach the driveshaft following the procedure given in Chapter 8.
    c) Disconnect the clutch operating cable from the release arm.
    d) Do not remove the clutch housing bolts. These items are removed after the assembly has been removed from the vehicle. Further information on this will be found in Chapte 8.
    e) Remove the speedometer drive cable and the transmission electrical connections.
    f) Support the weight of the transmission with a jack and a block of wood while the rear mounting is being detached.
    g) It is a good idea to do the preliminary cleaning of the engine with the transmission still attached.

---

14 Flywheel and rear cover plate — removal and installation

1   Remove the engine from the vehicle without the transmission as described in Section 13.
2   Remove the pressure plate and the clutch disk from the rear of the flywheel as described in Chapter 8.
3   With the clutch removed, lock the flywheel using a large

screwdriver in mesh with the starter ring gear and remove the six bolts securing the flywheel to the crankshaft. The bolts should be removed a quarter turn at a time in a diagonal and progressive manner.
4   Mark the mating position of the flywheel and crankshaft flange and then remove the flywheel as shown in the accompanying illustration.
5   Remove the engine rear cover plate bolts and ease the rear cover plate over the two dowel pins. Remove the cover plate.
6   If the flywheel ring gear is badly worn or has teeth missing, it should be replaced by an automotive machine shop.
7   Installation of the flywheel and clutch is the reverse of the removal procedure. Be sure to tighten all bolts to the specified torque. For further information on clutch servicing, see Chapter 8.

APPLY FORD POLYETHYLENE GREASE DOAZ-19584-A OR EQUIVALENT TO CRANKSHAFT PILOT HOLE

AUTOMATIC TRANSMISSION

FLYWHEEL

REINFORCING PLATE

REAR COVER PLATE

Fig. 2A.18 Flywheel and rear cover plate — exploded view (Sec 14)

---

15 Engine — installation

Without transmission

1   Raise the engine on the hoist and position it over the engine compartment with the rear end sloping down.
2   Lower the engine until the exhaust manifold lines up approximately with the exhaust pipe.
3   Automatic transmission: Start the converter pilot into the crankshaft.
4   Manual transmission: Start the transmission input shaft into the clutch hub. If necessary, rotate the engine slightly to align the splines.
5   Make sure that the engine is settled on its mounts, then detach the hoist chain.
6   From beneath the vehicle, install the flywheel housing or converter upper attaching bolts.
7   Automatic transmission: Attach the converter to the flexplate. Refer to Chapter 7 for further information, if necessary. Install the converter bolt access plug.
8   Install the front engine mount nuts.
9   Connect the exhaust pipe to the manifold, using a new gasket (if applicable).
10 Reinstall the starter motor and wires.
11 Remove the plugs from the fuel lines and reconnect them to the fuel pump. If not already done, reconnect the fuel line to the carburetor.
1   Position the power steering pump on its brackets and install the upper bolts.
13 Install the engine shield.
14 From inside the engine compartment, install the power steering pump pulley.
15 Reconnect the engine ground lead.
16 Install the alternator adjusting arm bolt and the electrical connector(s).
17 Connect the wire to the electrically assisted choke.

18   Connect the coil wire and vacuum hose to the distributor.
19   Connect the vacuum amplifier.
20   Connect the wire to the coolant temperature sender in the block.
21   Connect the idle solenoid wires.
22   Position the throttle cable on the ball stud and install the ball stud on the clip. Snap the bracket clip into position on the bracket. Where applicable, install the kickdown cable.
23   Reinstall the line on the oil pressure sender.
24   Reinstall the brake vacuum unit hose.
25   Reconnect the engine heater and vacuum hoses.
26   Reinstall the drivebelts. Refer to Chapter 1 for the correct tension.
27   Reinstall the radiator. Refer to Chapter 3 if necessary.
28   Reinstall the oil cooler lines (where applicable).
29   Reinstall the radiator hoses.
30   Reinstall the fan shroud.
31   Refill the cooling system with the correct amount of colant. Refer to Chapter 1 if necessary.
32   Fill the crankcase with the specified amount and type of oil.

33   Reinstall the air cleaner and the vacuum hoses. Refer to Chapter 4 if necessary.
34   Connect the battery leads.
35   Have a last look around the engine compartment to make sure that no hoses or electrical connections have been left off.

With manual transmission

36   The procedure for reinstalling the engine and manual transmission is basically as described above. However, the following differences should be noted:

    a) Support the weight of the transmission with a hydraulic jack prior to reinstalling the rear mounts.

    b) Do not forget to reconnect the speedometer cable and transmission electrical connections. Refer to Chapter 7 for further information if necessary.

    c) When reconnecting the driveshaft, make sure that the index marks are correctly aligned. Refer to Chapter 8 for further information if necessary.

Chapter 2 Part B
3.3 liter inline six-cylinder engine

Contents

Specifications

Camshaft endplay	0.009 in max
Torque specifications	**Ft-lbs**
Camshaft sprocket-to-camshaft	35 to 45
Camshaft thrust plate-to-block	12 to 18
Cylinder front cover bolts	6 to 9
Cylinder head bolts	
Step 1	50 to 55
Step 2	60 to 65
Damper-to-crankshaft	85 to 100
Fuel pump-to-block or front cover	12 to 18
Flywheel-to-crankshaft	75 to 85
Exhaust manifold-to-cylinder head	18 to 24
Oil filter insert-to-block	10 to 15
Oil pan-to-block	7 to 9
Oil pump tube and screen-to-oil pump	10 to 15
Oil pump-to-block	10 to 15
Pulley-to-damper bolt	35 to 50
Rocker arm shaft-to-cylinder head	30 to 35
Rocker arm cover	3 to 5
Alternator bracket-to-block bolt	35 to 50
Alternator adjusting arm-to-block	15 to 20
Alternator adjusting arm-to-alternator	24 to 34
Thermactor pump bracket-to-block	12 to 18
Thermactor pump pivot bolt	22 to 32
Thermactor pump adjusting arm-to-pump	24 to 34
Thermactor pump adjusting arm-to-block	12 to 18
Thermactor pump pulley-to-pump hub	130 to 180 in-lbs
Fan-to-water pump hub bolt	12 to 18
Distributor clamp holddown bolt	17 to 25
Engine mounts	70 to 100
Engine damper mount (LTD and Marquis)	35 to 60
Transmission crossmember nuts	30 to 50
Transmission mount-to-transmission	50 to 70
Transmission mount-to-crossmember	25 to 35

Fig. 2B.1 3.3L inline six-cylinder engine — block and related parts (Sec 1)

1 General Information

This part of Chapter 2 is devoted to repair procedures for the inline six-cylinder engine. The latter Sections in this part of Chapter 2 involve the removal and installation procedures. All information concerning engine block and cylinder head servicing can be found in Part E of this Chapter.

Many repair procedures included in this part are based on the assumption that the engine is still installed in the vehicle. Therefore, if this information is being used during a complete engine overhaul, with the engine already out of the vehicle and on a stand, many of the steps included here will not apply.

The specifications included in this part of Chapter 2 apply only to the engine and procedures found here. For specifications regarding engines other than the inline six-cylinder, see Part A, C or D, whichever applies. Part E of Chapter 2 contains the specifications necessary for engine block and cylinder head rebuilding procedures.

The 3.3 liter six-cylinder engine is an inline design, with overhead valves operated by hydraulic lifters and pushrods.

The camshaft is located to the right of the crankshaft and is driven by the crankshaft via a multi-link timing chain. The camshaft rides on four replaceable bearings.

The crankshaft is held in place by seven main bearings. Each main bearing consists of two replaceable sections.

The engine is lubricated by a pressurized oiling system. Oil is held in the oil pan where it is splashed on lower engine surfaces, as well as being pumped to the top of the engine (to the valve train), then forced downward through the other components of the engine until it returns to the oil pan.

Because various components rub against one another, a certain amount of wear will take place. The rate of component wear depends on the cleanliness of the oil and filter and the replacement of all other filters at the specified intervals. Oversize components are available to prolong the operational life of the engine. They include oversize pistons, pushrods, valve guides and connecting rod and main bearings.

2 Rocker arm cover and rocker arms — removal and installation

Removal

1   Remove the air cleaner assembly and the crankcase ventilation system (Chapter 6).

Fig. 2B.2 When removing and installing the rocker arm shaft, loosen and tighten the bolts in the sequence shown (Sec 2)

2   Remove the accelerator cable bracket.

3   Remove the rocker arm cover bolts and separate the rocker arm cover from the engine. Discard the rocker arm cover gasket.

4   Remove the rocker arm shaft support bolts by loosening the bolts 1/2-turn at a time in the sequence shown in Fig. 2B.2.

5   Remove the rocker arm shaft assembly. Make sure the pushrods are identified before removal so they can be returned to the same location when they are installed.

6   Remove the pushrods.

Installation

7   Apply polyethylene grease or engine assembly lube to both ends of the pushrods and to the valve stem tips.

8   Install the pushrods and position the rocker arm shaft assembly on the cylinder head.

9   Install and tighten all the rocker arm support bolts 1/2-turn at a time in the sequence shown in Fig. 2B.2 until the supports contact the cylinder head.

10 Tighten the bolts to the specified torque in the sequence shown in the accompanying illustration.

11 If any part which could affect the valve clearance has been changed, check the valve clearance following the procedure in Chapter 2E.

12 Clean the rocker arm cover and cylinder head gasket surfaces.

13 Install a new gasket in the cover making sure all the gasket tangs are engaged in the notches provided in the cover.

14 Tighten the cover bolts in two steps. First tighten the bolts to five

2B

Fig. 2B.3 Rocker arm shaft components — exploded view (Sec 2)

ft-lbs, then retighten them to five ft-lbs again two minutes later.

15 Install the accelerator cable bracket.

16 Install the crankcase ventilation system and air cleaner assembly.

3   Valve spring, retainer and seal — replacement (on vehicle)

Note: *Broken valve springs and retainers or defective valve stem seals can be replaced without removing the cylinder head on engines that have no damage to the valves or valve seats. Two special tools and a compressed air source are required to perform this operation, so read through this Section carefully and rent or buy the tools before beginning this job.*

1   Remove the air cleaner.

2   Remove the accelerator cable return spring.

3   Remove the accelerator cable linkage at the carburetor.

4   Disconnect the choke cable at the carburetor.

5   Remove the PCV valve from the rocker arm cover and remove the rocker arm cover.

6   Remove the spark plug from the cylinder which has the bad component.

7   Crank the engine until the piston in the cylinder with the bad component is at top dead center on the compression stroke.

8   Install a special air line adapter, which will screw into the spark plug hole and connect to a compressed air source. Loosen the rocker arm shaft support bolts until valve spring tension is relieved. Remove both pushrods from the cylinder to be serviced.

9   Apply compressed air to the cylinder in question. Unless the valve or seat is damaged this will hold the valves closed. It is important that once the valve spring is removed the air pressure be maintained and the valve not be accidentally knocked off the seat until it can be secured. If air pressure drops or the valve is knocked off the seat before the valve stem is secured it could allow the valve to drop down into the engine.

10 Compress the valve spring with the special tool designed for this purpose.

11 Remove the keepers, spring retainer and valve spring, then remove the valve stem seal as shown in the accompanying illustration. **Note:** *If air pressure fails to hold the valve in the closed position during this operation, there is apparently damage to the seat or valve. If this condition exists, remove the cylinder head and have the valves serviced (see Chapter 2E).*

12 Wrap a rubber band, tape or string around the top of the valve stem so the valve can not fall into the combustion chamber. At this point the air pressure can be released.

13 Inspect the valve stem for damage. Rotate the valve in its guide and check the valve stem tip for eccentric movement (which would indicate a bent valve).

Fig. 2B.4 Removing a valve spring seal (Sec 3)

14 Move the valve up and down through its normal travel and make sure that the valve guide and stem do not bind. If the valve stem binds, either the valve is bent or the guide is damaged and the cylinder head will have to be removed for repair.

15 Reapply air pressure to the cylinder to retain the value in the closed position and remove the rubber band or tape.

16 Lubricate the valve stem with engine oil and install a new valve stem seal.

17 Install the spring in position over the valve. Make sure that the closed coil end of the spring is correctly positioned against the cylinder head.

18 Install the valve spring retainer. Compress the valve spring, using the valve spring compressor, and install the spring keepers. Remove the compressor tool and make sure that the keepers are installed correctly.

19 Apply engine oil or assembly lube to both ends of the pushrod.

20 Install the pushrod.

21 Apply engine oil or assembly lube to the tip of the valve stem.

22 Apply engine oil to the rocker arm support shaft.

23 Position the rocker arm over the pushrod and valve stem and tighten the support shaft bolts to the specified torque.

24 Remove the air source and the adapter from the spark plug hole.

25 Install the spark plug and connect the spark plug wire.

26 Insert a new rocker arm cover gasket into the cover and install the rocker arm cover on the head.

27 Connect the accelerator cable to the carburetor.

28 Install the accelerator cable return spring and connect the choke cable to the carburetor.

29 Install the PCV valve in the rocker arm cover and make sure that the line connected to the PCV valve is positioned correctly on both ends.

30 Install the air cleaner.

4   Cylinder head — removal and installation

Removal

Note: *If the engine has been removed from the vehicle you can skip Steps 1 through 14.*

1   Drain the cooling system (Chapter 2).

2   Remove the air cleaner and connections leading to the air cleaner.

3   Disconnect the PCV valve from the rocker arm cover and remove the valve.

4   Remove the vent hose from the intake manifold inlet tube.

5   Disconnect and remove the carburetor fuel inlet line leading from the fuel pump.

6   Remove all vacuum lines from the carburetor.

7   Disconnect the choke cable at the carburetor and position the choke cable and housing out of the way.

8   Disconnect the accelerator cable or accelerator linkage from the carburetor. Remove the accelerator return spring.

9   Disconnect the kickdown link at the carburetor.

10 Remove the upper radiator hose from the thermostat outlet.

11 Remove the heater hose at the coolant outlet elbow.

12 Remove the nuts securing the exhaust pipe to the exhaust manifold and support the pipe out of the way.

13 Mark the wires leading to the coil and disconnect them. Remove the coil bracket bolt and secure the coil and bracket out of the way.

14 Remove the rocker arm cover.

15 Remove the rocker arm shaft support bolts by loosening the bolts 1/2-turn at a time in sequence shown in Fig. 2B.2. Remove the rocker arm shaft assembly.

16 Remove the pushrods and label them so they can be installed in their original locations. A numbered box or rack will keep them properly organized.

17 Disconnect the spark plug wires at the spark plugs.

18 Remove the cylinder head bolts. If you have an engine hoist or similar device handy, attach eyelet bolts at the ends of the cylinder head in the holes provided and lift the cylinder head off of the engine block. If equipment of this nature is not available, use a helper and pry the cylinder head up off of the engine block. **Caution:** *Do not wedge any tools between the cylinder head and block gasket mating surfaces.*

19 Turn the cylinder head upside down and place it on a workbench or in a cylinder head holding device. **Note:** *New and rebuilt cylinder heads are commonly available for engines at dealerships and auto parts*

stores. Due to the fact that some specialized tools are necessary for the dismantling and inspection of the head, and replacement parts may not be readily available, it may be more practical and economical for the home mechanic to purchase a replacement head and install it.
20 Another alternative at this point is to take the cylinder head to a competent automotive machine shop or shop specializing in cylinder heads and exchange them or leave your head for the overhaul process.
21 If the complete engine is being overhauled this time, however, it may be wise to wait until the other components have been inspected.
22 If you are attempting to repair a part of the cylinder head assembly or if you are going to inspect the components yourself, refer to Chapter 2, Part E.

Installation

23 Make sure that the cylinder head and block mating surfaces are clean, flat and prepared for the new cylinder head gasket. Clean the exhaust manifold to exhaust pipe gasket surfaces.
24 Position the gasket over the dowel pins on the block, making sure that it is facing the right direction and that the correct surface is exposed. Gaskets are often marked *front* and *this side up* to aid the installer.
25 Using the previously installed lifting hooks (or two people), carefully lower the cylinder head into place on the block. Take care not to move the head sideways or to scrape it across the surface, as it can dislodge the gasket and/or damage the mating surfaces.
26 Coat the cylinder head retaining bolts with light engine oil and thread the bolts into the block. Tighten the bolts following the cylinder head bolt tightening sequence shown in the accompanying illustration. Work up to the final torque in two steps to avoid warping the head.
27 Apply a coat of engine oil to the rocker arm pivots and pushrod and valve ends.
28 Install the pushrods, the rocker arms, support shafts and the retaining bolts. Tighten them to the specified torque.
29 Install the rocker arm cover. The remaining steps are the reverse of the removal procedure.
30 Start the engine and allow it to reach operating temperature. Shut it off, allow it to cool down and retorque the head bolts.

Fig. 2B.5 Follow the above sequence when tightening or loosening the cylinder head bolts (Sec 4)

5   Exhaust manifold — removal and installation

Removal

1 Remove the air cleaner assembly and related parts.
2 Tag all electrical connections and vacuum lines to simplify reassembly. On later models a light-off catalyst is bolted directly to the outlet of the exhaust manifold. Four studs on the exhaust manifold flange are used to mount the light-off catalyst. Disconnect the light-off catalyst from the exhaust manifold.
3 Remove or disconnect the EGR tube and all other emission components which would interfere with the removal of the exhaust manifold.
4 Remove the exhaust manifold mounting bolts and nuts. It may be necessary to apply penetrating oil to the threads.
5 Remove the manifold.

Installation

6 Clean the mating surfaces of the exhaust manifold and cylinder head.
7 Position the exhaust manifold on the cylinder head and install the

bolts. Tighten the bolts and studs in the sequence shown to the specified torque.
8 Position the light-off catalyst unit on the manifold.
9 Install and tighten the mounting nuts.
10 Install or connect the emission component vacuum lines and electrical connectors previously disconnected.
11 Install the air cleaner assembly and related parts.
12 Start the engine and check for exhaust leaks.

Fig. 2B.6 Exhaust manifold bolt tightening sequence (follow the same sequence when loosening the bolts) (Sec 5)

6   Cylinder front cover and timing chain — removal and installation

Removal

1 Drain the cooling system and disconnect the hoses. Remove the cooling fan, drivebelts, and the crankshaft and water pump drive pulleys.
2 Remove the front cover by removing all bolts on the cover at the engine block and oil pan. Carefully pry the cover away from the engine block at the top. Be sure not to nick or gouge the mating surface of the engine block.
3 Scrape any gasket material left from the above procedure from the engine block.
4 Before removing the timing chain and sprockets the chain deflection must be checked. Turn the crankshaft in a counterclockwise direction and take up the slack on the left side of the chain. Establish a reference point to the left of the timing chain. Measure the distance from the reference point to the center of the left side of the chain. Turn the crankshaft in a clockwise direction and take up the slack on the right side of the timing chain. Press the slack chain on the *left side* toward the center with your thumb and measure the distance from your reference point to the center of the slack chain on the left side. Subtract the smaller figure from the larger and the difference will be the total deflection. If the deflection of the timing chain is greater than 1/4-inch the timing chain and sprockets must be replaced. Never replace just the chain or sprockets, replace them as a set.
5 Rotate the crankshaft until the two timing marks on the sprockets align. Remove the camshaft sprocket bolt and pull both sprockets evenly from the front of the engine.
6 Clean the chain and sprockets in solvent if you have decided to reuse them. Inspect the sprocket teeth for damage and wear and the chain for a distinctive wear pattern. If a wear pattern shows on the chain or the sprockets, we recommend that you replace the sprockets and chain with new parts.

Installation

7 Place the camshaft sprocket and the crankshaft sprocket in place and check to see that the timing marks on the sprockets are still aligned.
8 Remove the sprockets and place them inside the timing chain.
9 Slide the two sprockets, complete with the timing chain, onto the ends of the crankshaft and camshaft.
10 Install the camshaft sprocket bolt and tighten it to the specified torque.
11 Before installing the front cover, check the condition of the oil seal. If the seal is dried or has been leaking, it must be replaced (see Sec-

2B

Fig. 2B.7 Camshaft and related parts — exploded view (Sec 7)

tion 11).

12 Apply RTV-type sealant to the new front cover gasket and position the gasket on the cover. Coat all exposed portions of the gasket with sealant.

13 Install the cover. To prevent damage to the seal as it contacts the Woodruff key on the crankshaft, place a thin-walled socket over the crankshaft end. Make sure the outside diameter of the socket is less than the inside diameter of the seal.

14 Tighten all mounting bolts to the specified torque.

7   Camshaft and lifters — removal and installation

1 Remove the cylinder head.

2 Using a magnet, remove the lifters by inserting the magnet into the tops of the pushrod tubes and contacting the top of the lifter. Work from the front of the engine to the back and keep the lifters in the order of their removal. It is important to match the valve train components for proper engine life.

3 If the lifters are held in place by sludge or gum it will be necessary to remove them with pliers or a claw-type tool. Ford sells one such tool under part number T70L-6500-A. Tool shops and auto parts stores can supply reasonable alternatives.

4 Do not disassemble or mix-up the lifters.

5 Remove the front cover but not the timing chain.

6 Check camshaft endplay before removing the camshaft. Install a dial indicator on the front of the engine so the plunger of the indicator rests on the end of the camshaft. Push the camshaft as far to the rear of the engine block as it will go and zero the indicator. Push the camshaft to the front of the block as far as it will go and record the measurement indicated on the dial indicator. This is the endplay. If the endplay exceeds the service limit given in the specifications the thrust plate will have to be replaced.

7 Remove the timing chain and sprockets.

8 Remove the camshaft thrust plate.

9 Carefully pull the camshaft out of the block, being careful not to damage the camshaft lobes or the cam bearings.

10 Camshaft and lifter installation procedures are the reverse of those used for removal.

8   Oil pan and oil pump — removal and installation

Note: *This procedure is for removal and installation of the oil pan with the engine in the vehicle only. If the engine has been removed for an overhaul, use only Step 10 and Steps 14 through 26.*

Removal

1 Drain the engine oil and disconnect the negative cable at the battery. Remove the oil dipstick.

2 Drain the cooling system.

3 Remove the radiator as described in Chapter 3.

4 Raise the vehicle and support it securely on jackstands. Disconnect the starter cable at the starter.

5 Remove the starter from the bellhousing.

6 Remove the four nuts and bolts attaching the sway bar to the chassis and allow the sway bar to hang down.

7 Remove the engine front insulator to support bracket retaining nuts. Loosen the two rear engine support bolts and loosen the fan shroud to prevent fan blade damage.

8 Raise the front of the engine with a jack. Place a thick wooden block between the jack and the oil pan.

9 Place one inch wood blocks between the front support insulators and the supporting brackets.

10 Lower the engine onto the spacer blocks and remove the jack.

11 Remove the oil pan bolts.

12 Lower the pan to the crossmember.

13 Remove the two oil pump inlet tube to oil pump retaining bolts.

14 Remove the oil pump inlet assembly and allow it to rest in the oil pan.

15 Remove the oil pan from the vehicle. It may be necessary to rotate the crankshaft for the counterweights to clear the pan.

16 Clean all old gasket material from the mating surfaces of the block and the pan.

Installation

17 Remove the rear main bearing cap oil pan seal.

18 Remove the timing cover oil pan seal.

19 Clean all mating surfaces and seal grooves.

20 Install a new oil pan to front cover oil seal.

21 Install a new rear main bearing cap seal.

22 Install new oil pan side gaskets on the block as shown in the accompanying illustration. Apply a thin coat of RTV-type sealant to both sides of the gaskets.

23 Make sure the tabs of the front and rear seals fit properly into the mating slots on the oil pan side seals. A small amount of RTV-type sealant at each mating junction will help prevent leaks at these critical spots.

24 Clean the inlet tube and screen assembly and place it in the oil pan.

25 Position the oil pan underneath the engine.

26 Lift the inlet tube and screen assembly from the oil pan and secure it to the oil pump with a new gasket as shown in the accompanying illustration. Tighten the two retaining bolts to the specified torque.

27 Attach the oil pan to the engine block and install the bolts. Tighten the bolts to the specified torque, starting from the center and working out in each direction.

28 Raise the engine with a jack and a block of wood underneath the oil pan and remove the wood spacers previously installed under the support brackets.

29 Lower the engine to the correct installed position and install the nuts on the insulator studs. Reattach the sway bar to the chassis.

30 Install the starter and connect the starter cable.

31 Lower the vehicle.

32 Install the radiator according to the instructions in Chapter 3.

33 Fill the cooling system with coolant and check for leaks.

34 Fill the engine crankcase with oil and hook up the negative battery cable.

35 Start the engine and check carefully for leaks at the oil pan gasket sealing surfaces.

Fig. 2B.8 Oil pan gaskets and seals — note the location of the oil pump and strainer (Sec 8)

2B

Fig. 2B.9 Oil pump and inlet tube/strainer assembly (Sec 8)

Fig. 2B.10 Tightening sequence for flywheel bolts (use the same sequence when removing the flywheel) (Sec 9)

9   Flywheel — removal, inspection and installation

Note: *these instructions are valid only if the engine has been removed from the vehicle. If the engine is still in the vehicle, the transmission, the bellhousing and clutch assembly must be removed to expose the flywheel (refer to Chapter 7). Automatic transmission equipped vehicles are equipped with a flexplate rather than a flywheel. The flywheel or flexplate can be separated from the crankshaft by removing the mounting bolts. If the ring gear teeth are worn or damaged or if the flywheel or flexplate is damaged, replace it with a new one and tighten the mounting bolts to the specified torque.*

1   Mark the flywheel and the crankshaft end with a center punch to ensure installation in the same relative position.
2   To keep the crankshaft from turning, wedge a large screwdriver or pry bar between the ring gear teeth and the engine block (it must be positioned so that as the crankshaft moves, the tool bears against

the block). Make sure that the tool is not pushing against the oil pan. Another method of preventing crankshaft rotation involves holding the front pulley retaining bolt with a large wrench or socket and breaker bar. This method may require a helper. **Caution:** *Support the flywheel before performing the following step as it could fall off and be damaged or cause injury.*

3   Remove the flywheel retaining bolts from the crankshaft flange as shown in the accompanying illustration.
4   Remove the flywheel from the crankshaft by pulling straight back.
5   Inspect the flywheel clutch disc mating surface for scoring, heat marks, cracks or warpage. If any of these conditions exist, the flywheel should be taken to an automotive machine shop to be resurfaced (or replaced with a new one). If the flywheel is cracked it must be replaced with a new one.
6   Installation is the reverse of removal. The retaining bolts should be coated with a thread-locking compound and tightened in a crisscross pattern to the specified torque.

78

Fig. 2B.11 Engine mount assembly on vehicles with floor-mounted gearshift levers (Sec 10)

Fig. 2B.12 Engine mount assembly on vehicles with steering column-mounted gearshift levers (Sec 10)

10   Engine mounts — removal and installation

Front mounts

Removal

1   The engine front and rear supports and insulators can be replaced without removing the engine from the vehicle.
2   The engine front supports are located on each side of the cylinder block. Whenever self-locking mounting bolts and nuts are removed they must be replaced with new self-locking mounting bolts (with adhesive on the threads). The hardened residual bolt adhesive must be removed from the engine block bosses with an M10 by 1.5 bottoming tap.
3   Remove the fan shroud mounting screws.
4   Support the engine using a jack and wood block placed under the oil pan.
5   Remove the bolt that attaches the lower end of the engine damper to the number two crossmember bracket.
6   Remove both mounts from the number two crossmember.
7   Raise the engine with the jack just enough to disengage the mount studs from the crossmember.
8   Remove the mount to engine bracket nuts and remove the mount.

Installation

9   Install the mount assembly on the engine.
10   Tighten the nuts to the torque specified in the accompanying illustration.
11   Lower the engine into position, making sure that the mounts are seated flat on the number two crossmember and that the mount studs are at the bottom of the slots.
12   Install the mount nuts and tighten them to the specified torque.
13   Attach the engine damper to the number two crossmember bracket bolt (LTD and Marquis only). Tighten the bolt to the specified torque.
14   Install the fan shroud.

Rear mounts

Removal

15   The rear support is located on the transmission extension housing.
16   Support the transmission with a jack and wood block.
17   Remove the two nuts attaching the rear mount to the crossmember.
18   Remove the two bolts and nuts attaching the crossmember to the body brackets and remove the crossmember by raising the transmission slightly with the jack.
19   Remove the two bolts attaching the rear mount to the transmission.
20   Remove the mount and the retainer.

Installation

21   Position the rear mount and retainer on the transmission.
22   Install the two bolts and tighten to the specified torque.
23   Attach the crossmember to the body brackets and tighten the nuts to the specified torque.
24   Lower the transmission and install the mount to crossmember nuts.
25   Tighten the nuts to the specified torque.

11   Crankshaft oil seals — replacement

Front seal

Note: *The following operation requires a special tool for proper seal installation.*

1   Drain the cooling system and oil pan.
2   Remove the radiator.
3   Remove the crankshaft pulley and the timing cover (see Section 6).
4   Drive out the oil seal with a pin punch.
5   Clean out the recess in the cover.
6   Coat the outer edge of the new seal with grease and install it using the special tool designed for this operation as shown in the accompanying illustration. As an alternative, a large piece of pipe or a socket can be used to push the new seal in. However, use extreme caution as the seal can be damaged easily. Drive in the seal until it is completely seated in the recess. Make sure that the spring is properly positioned within the seal.
7   Installation is the reverse of the removal procedure.

Rear seal

Note: *If rear crankshaft oil seal replacement is the only operation being*

Fig. 2B.13 Replacing the crankshaft front oil seal (a large socket may be used in place of the Ford service tool) (Sec 11)

T80T-4000-W

TOOL— T60K-6700-A

OIL SEAL

performed, it can be accomplished with the engine in the vehicle. If, however, the oil seal is being replaced along with the rear main bearing, the engine must be removed.

8   Disconnect the negative battery cable from the battery, then remove the starter.
9   Remove the transmission (Chapter 7).
10   On manual transmission equipped vehicles, remove the pressure plate, disc and clutch assembly. On automatic transmission equipped vehicles, remove the flexplate.
11   Remove the flywheel mounting bolts and remove the flywheel and engine rear cover plate. **Note:** *Some models incorporate a two-piece split-lip seal which requires removal of the rear main bearing cap. If this is the case with your vehicle, turn to the procedure in Chapter 2E. One-piece seals can be serviced as follows:*
12   Use an awl to punch two holes in the seal. Punch the holes on opposite sides of the crankshaft, just above the bearing cap to engine block junction.
13   Thread a sheet metal screw into each punched hole.
14   Use two large screwdrivers or small pry bars to pry against both screws at the same time, removing the seal. A block or blocks of wood placed against the engine will provide additional leverage.
15   Be very careful when performing this operation that you do not damage the seal contact surfaces.
16   Clean the oil recess in the rear of the engine block and the main bearing cap surface of the crankshaft.
17   Inspect and clean the oil seal contact surfaces of the crankshaft.
18   Coat the new oil seal with engine oil.
19   Coat the crankshaft with engine oil.
20   Start the seal into the cavity in the back of the engine with the seal lip facing forward, using the special drive tool. Make sure that the tool stays in alignment with the crankshaft until the tool contacts the block. See Step 6 for seal installation alternatives.
21   Install the engine rear cover plate.
22   Attach the flywheel (or flexplate) to the crankshaft.
23   The remainder of the installation is the reverse of the removal procedure.

12   Engine — removal and installation

Removal without transmission

1   Raise the hood and disconnect the battery cables, negative cable first.

2B

2 Mark the position of the hood hinges with a pencil or scribe. Remove the retaining bolts and the hood.
3 Remove the air cleaner and exhaust manifold shroud.
4 If air-conditioning is installed, remove the compressor unit from the engine mounting bracket but do not disconnect the refrigerant hoses. Position the pump out of the way without straining the hoses. **Note:** *If it is necessary to remove the compressor from the vehicle, the hoses should be disconnected by an air conditioning technician.*
5 Remove the oil pan drain plug and drain the oil.
6 Remove the bottom radiator hose and drain the coolant.
7 Remove the top hose and transmission oil cooler hoses (if equipped) from the radiator. Remove the radiator.
8 Remove the fan.
9 Jack up the front of the vehicle and support it on jackstands.
10 Where applicable, remove the engine shield.
11 Remove the starter motor. Further details will be found in Chapter 5, if required.
12 On automatic transmission models, remove the torque converter bolt access plug. Remove the three flexplate to converter bolts.
13 Remove the converter housing cover and disconnect the converter from the flexplate.
14 On manual transmission models, remove the flywheel cover.
15 Remove the flywheel or converter housing cover, as applicable.
16 Detach the exhaust pipe from the exhaust manifold. Remove the packing washer.
17 Remove the nuts from the engine mounts.
18 Detach the fuel lines from the fuel pump, plugging the lines to prevent fuel spillage.
19 Where applicable, remove the power steering pump drivebelt and draw off the pulley.
20 Remove the lower bolt securing the power steering pump to the bracket.
21 Lower the vehicle to the ground.
22 Disconnect the heater and vacuum hoses from the engine. It is recommended that a sketch be made showing the various connections to avoid confusion during installation.
23 Disconnect the power brake hose.
24 Remove the oil pressure union from the connection on the left rear of the cylinder head.
25 Detach the carburetor cable(s).
26 Disconnect the wires to the throttle solenoid and choke heater.
27 Detach the wire from the water temperature sender on the left rear of the block.
28 Disconnect the lines from the vacuum amplifier.
29 Disconnect the coil wire and vacuum line from the distributor.
30 Pull the multi-plug from the alternator, followed by the ground wire.
31 Remove the bolt from the alternator adjusting arm.
32 Remove the remaining power steering pump bolts and remove the pump (if fitted).
33 Support the weight of the transmission on a suitable jack, with a wood block interposed between the jack head and the transmission.
34 Attach the hoist hooks to the engine lifting bracket and lift the engine a little.
35 Draw the engine forward to disengage the transmission, ensuring that the transmission is still satisfactorily supported.
36 Lift the engine out, being careful not to damage the hoses or other components in the engine compartment. Transfer the engine to a suitable work area and detach the accessories.
37 Clean the outside of the engine using a water soluble solvent. On the assumption that engine overhaul is to be carried out, remove the fuel pump, oil filter, spark plugs, distributor, fan, water pump, thermostat, oil pressure and water temperature senders, emission control units, etc. Refer to the appropriate Sections in this and other Chapters for further information.

Removal with manual transmission
38 The procedure for removing the engine and manual transmission together is basically similar to that described in the previous Section. However, the following differences should be noted:
 a) Disconnect the gearshift linkage from the transmission, referring to Chapter 7 as necessary.
 b) Detach the driveshaft following the procedure given in Chapter 8.
 c) Disconnect the clutch operating cable from the release arm.
 d) Do not remove the clutch housing bolts. These are removed after the assembly has been removed from the vehicle. Further

information on this will be found in Chapter 8.
 e) Remove the speedometer drive cable and the transmission electrical connections.
 f) Support the weight of the transmission in a similar manner to that described in the previous Section, paragraph 33, while the rear mount is being detached.
 g) It is a good idea to do the preliminary cleaning of the engine with the transmission still attached.

Installation without transmission
39 Raise the engine on the hoist and position it over the engine compartment so that the back of the engine is sloping downwards.
40 Lower the engine and guide it into the engine compartment until the exhaust manifold lines up with the exhaust pipe.
41 Automatic transmission: Start the converter pilot into the crankshaft.
42 Manual transmission: Start the transmission input shaft into the clutch hub. If necessary rotate the engine slightly to align the splines.
43 Make sure that the engine is settled on its mounts, then detach the hoist chains.
44 From beneath the vehicle install the flywheel housing or converter housing upper attaching bolts.
45 Automatic transmission: Attach the converter to the flexplate. Refer to Chapter 7 for further information, if necessary. Install the converter bolt access plug.
46 Install the front engine mount nuts.
47 Connect the exhaust pipe to the manifold, using a new gasket (if applicable).
48 Install the starter motor and wires.
49 Remove the plugs from the fuel lines and reconnect them to the fuel pump and carburetor.
50 Position the power steering pump on its brackets and install the upper bolts.
51 Install the engine shield.
52 From inside the engine compartment install the power steering pump pulley.
53 Reconnect the engine ground lead.
54 Install the alternator adjusting arm bolt and the electrical connectors.
55 Connect the wire to the electrically controlled choke.
56 Connect the coil wire and vacuum hose to the distributor.
57 Connect the vacuum amplifier.
58 Connect the wire to the coolant temperature sender in the block.
59 Connect the idle solenoid wires.
60 Position the accelerator cable on the ball stud and install the ball stud on the clip. Snap the bracket clip into position on the bracket. Where applicable, install the kickdown cable.
61 Attach the line to the oil pressure sender.
62 Install the brake vacuum unit hose.
63 Reconnect the engine heater and vacuum hoses.
64 Install the drivebelts on the accessories. Refer to Chapter 1 for the correct tension.
65 Install the radiator. Refer to Chapter 3 if necessary.
66 Install the oil cooler lines (where applicable).
67 Install the radiator hoses.
68 Where applicable, install the fan shroud.
69 Refill the cooling system with the correct amount of coolant mixture. Refer to Chapter 1 as necessary.
70 Fill the crankcase with the specified amount and type of oil.
71 Install the air cleaner and the vacuum hoses. Refer to Chapter 4 if necessary.
72 Connect the battery leads.

Installation with manual transmission
73 The procedure for installing the engine and manual transmission is basically as described in the previous Section. However, the following differences should be noted:
 a) Support the weight of the transmission with a hydraulic jack prior to installing the rear mounts.
 b) Do not forget to reconnect the speedometer cable and transmission electrical connections.
 c) Check the clutch adjustment after the cable has been reconnected. Refer to Chapter 8 for further information.
 d) When reconnecting the driveshaft, make sure that the index marks are correctly aligned. Refer to Chapter 8 for further information if necessary.

Chapter 2 Part C 3.8 liter V-6 engine

Refer to Chapter 13 for specifications related to 1985 and later models

Contents

Specifications

Torque specifications	Ft-lbs
Camshaft sprocket bolts	15 to 22
Front cover bolts	15 to 22
Oil inlet tube-to-main bearing cap nuts	30 to 40
Oil inlet tube-to-cylinder block bolts	15 to 22
Oil pan bolts	6 to 9
Oil pump cover bolts	18 to 22
Cylinder head bolts	
Step 1	47
Step 2	55
Step 3	63
Step 4	74
Step 5	Back off all bolts 2 turns
Step 6	Repeat Steps 1 through 4
Rocker arm fulcrum bolt	
Step 1	5 to 11
Step 2	18 to 26
Intake manifold bolts	
Step 1	5
Step 2	10
Step 3	18
Rocker arm cover bolts............................	3 to 5
Spark plugs	17 to 22
Flywheel bolts	54 to 64
Distributor holddown bolt	20 to 29
Crankshaft pulley bolts	20 to 28
Crankshaft damper bolt	93 to 121
Spark knock sensor-to-adapter	14 to 17
Spark knock sensor adapter-to-intake manifold	26 to 33
Vacuum fittings-to-intake manifold	26 to 33
Thermostat housing bolts	15 to 22
Heater tube-to-intake manifold stud bolt	15 to 22
Pressure plate bolts	15 to 19
Carburetor holddown stud	6
Carburetor holddown nuts	9 to 11

Torque specifications (continued)

EGR spacer-to-intake manifold bolts	6 to 9
EGR spacer stud	3 to 6
EGR adapter-to-EGR spacer nuts	15 to 22
EGR adapter stud	2 to 7
EGR valve-to-EGR adapter nuts	15 to 22
EGR tube end nuts	31 to 39
Thermactor check valve bolts	8 to 11
Vacuum tree-to-intake manifold	6 to 10
Clutch housing bolts	40 to 50
Alternator bracket bolts	30 to 40
Exhaust manifold bolts	15 to 22
Engine damper bracket-to-exhaust manifold nuts	15 to 22
Engine bracket brace-to-engine bracket nuts	60 to 80
Engine bracket brace-to-engine bracket bolts	35 to 50
Fan clutch assembly-to-water pump bolts	12 to 18
Flexplate-to-torque converter bolts	20 to 34
Transmission bolts	41 to 51
Engine mount insulator and bracket	33 to 45
Engine mounts-to-crossmember	70 to 100
Engine damper-to-crossmember (LTD and Marquis)	35 to 50
Rear mount to transmission	50 to 70
Transmission crossmember-to-body brackets	35 to 40
Transmission mount-to-crossmember	25 to 35

1 General Information

This part of Chapter 2 is devoted to repair procedures for the V6 engine. The latter Sections in this part of Chapter 2 involve the removal and installation procedures for the V6 engine. All information concerning engine block and cylinder head servicing can be found in Part E of this Chapter.

Many of the repair procedures included in this part are based on the assumption that the engine is still installed in the vehicle. Therefore, if this information is being used during a complete engine overhaul, with the engine already out of the vehicle and on a stand, many of the steps included here will not apply.

The specifications included in this part of Chapter 2 apply only to the engine and procedures found here. For specifications regarding engines other than the V6, see Part A, B or D, whichever applies. Part E of Chapter 2 contains the specifications necessary for engine block and cylinder head rebuilding procedures.

The 232 cubic inch V6 is similar to the V8s in construction and components used. However, important differences do exist. In the following paragraphs, similarities and differences between the V6 and V8 will be noted.

Fuel is delivered by a mechanical fuel pump mounted on the right side of the front (timing) cover assembly. The carburetor is mounted on an aluminum manifold which is bolted to aluminum cylinder heads. Service procedures related to these components remain similar to those for the V8.

The crankshaft is supported by four main bearings, with the number three bearing acting as thrust bearing.

The camshaft is supported by four bearings. Thrust loads and end-play are limited by a thrust button and spring installed in front of the camshaft. The spring-loaded button bears against the inside surface of the front cover, with lubrication supplied by oil splash from the timing chain. Immediately behind the thrust button bore are the distributor drive gear and the fuel pump eccentric.

The rotary gear type oil pump is located in the front cover assembly. The pump driven gear is rotated by the distributor shaft through an intermediate shaft.

Many of the component mating surfaces which are sealed with a gasket in V8 engines are sealed with RTV-type sealant in the V6. The surfaces sealed in this manner include the oil pan sides and front where they mate with the cylinder block and front cover; the thermostat housing to the intake manifold; the rocker arm covers to the cylinder head; both ends of the intake manifold to the cylinder block; along the rear main bearing cap and cylinder block parting line; and the thermactor air injection secondary cover to the intake manifold. When applying this sealant, always use the bead size specified and join the components within 15 minutes of application. After that time, the sealant begins to set-up and its sealing effectiveness may be reduced.

Because this engine is equipped with aluminum cylinder heads, a special corrosion inhibited coolant formulation is required to avoid radiator damage (see Chapter 3).

Accessories mounted on the front of the engine are driven by a single, serpentine drivebelt. The belt is routed over each accessory pulley and is driven by a pulley bolted to the crankshaft damper. It is held against the drive pulleys by a spring-loaded tensioner mounted on the upper right corner of the engine (see Chapter 1 for service procedures, including tensioning).

2 Rocker arm covers — removal and installation

1   Disconnect the spark plug wires.
2   Remove the spark plug wire routing clips from the rocker arm cover studs.
3   If the left rocker arm cover is being removed, remove the oil filter cap. If equipped with a speed control, reposition the air cleaner assembly and disconnect the servo chain at the carburetor. Remove the servo bracket bolts and nuts and position the servo and bracket aside.
4   If the right rocker arm cover is being removed, reposition the air cleaner assembly and heat tube, remove the PCV valve, then disconnect and remove the thermactor diverter valve and hose assembly at the bypass valve downstream air tube and the engine-mounted check valve.
5   Remove the rocker arm cover bolts.
6   Loosen the silicone rubber gasket material by inserting a putty knife under the cover flange. Work the cover loose and remove it. Note: *Pry carefully, as the plastic covers will break if excessive force is applied.*
7   Installation is the reverse of removal. Apply a 1/8 to 3/16-inch bead of RTV-type sealant to the rocker arm cover before placing it on the head. Make sure the sealer fills the channel in the cover flange and complete the installation within 15 minutes of sealer application.
8   Tighten the bolts in a crisscross pattern, a little at a time, until they are all at the specified torque.

3 Valve train components — replacement (cylinder head installed)

Note: *Broken valve springs, retainers or defective valve stem seals can be replaced without removing the cylinder head on engines that have no damage to the valves or valve seats. Two special tools are required for this operation, so read through the instructions carefully and rent or purchase the tools before starting work.*

1   Remove the air cleaner and related components.
2   Remove the accelerator cable return spring.

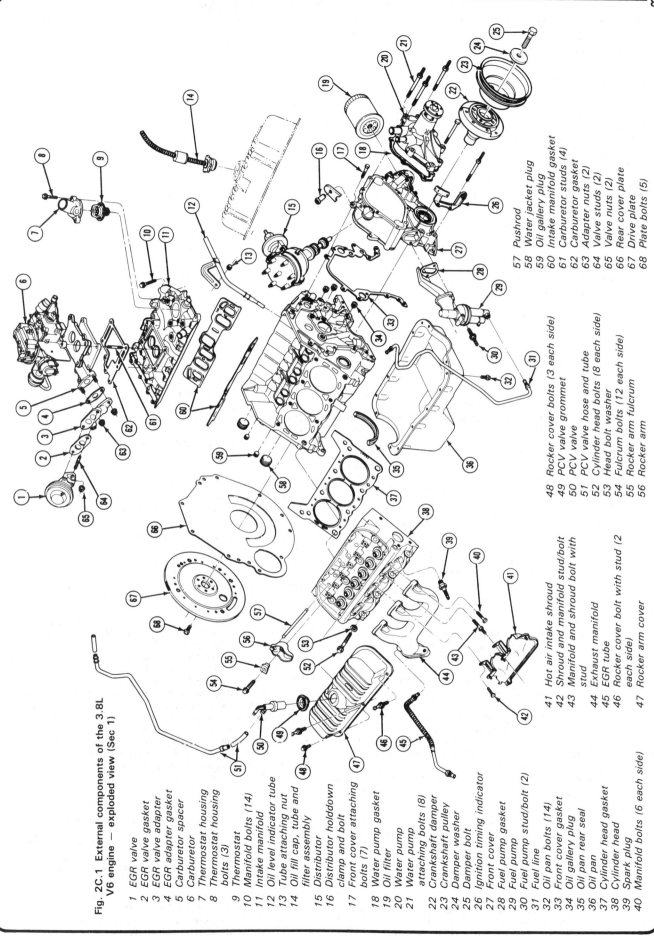

2C

Fig. 2C.1 External components of the 3.8L
V6 engine — exploded view (Sec 1)

1   EGR valve
2   EGR valve gasket
3   EGR valve adapter
4   EGR adapter gasket
5   Carburetor spacer
6   Carburetor
7   Thermostat housing
8   Thermostat housing
    bolts (3)
9   Thermostat
10 Manifold bolts (14)
11 Intake manifold
12 Oil level indicator tube
13 Tube attaching nut
14 Oil fill cap, tube and
    filter assembly
15 Distributor
16 Distributor holddown
    clamp and bolt
17 Front cover attaching
    bolts (7)
18 Water pump gasket
19 Oil filter
20 Water pump
21 Water pump
    attaching bolts (8)
22 Crankshaft damper
23 Crankshaft pulley
24 Damper washer
25 Damper bolt
26 Ignition timing indicator
27 Front cover
28 Fuel pump gasket
29 Fuel pump
30 Fuel pump stud/bolt (2)
31 Fuel line
32 Oil pan bolts (14)
33 Front cover gasket
34 Oil gallery plug
35 Oil pan rear seal
36 Oil pan
37 Cylinder head gasket
38 Cylinder head
39 Spark plug
40 Manifold bolts (6 each side)

41 Hot air intake shroud
42 Shroud and manifold stud/bolt
43 Manifold and shroud bolt with
    stud
44 Exhaust manifold
45 EGR tube
46 Rocker cover bolt with stud (2
    each side)
47 Rocker arm cover

48 Rocker cover bolts (3 each side)
49 PCV valve grommet
50 PCV valve
51 PCV valve hose and tube
52 Cylinder head bolts (8 each side)
53 Head bolt washer
54 Fulcrum bolts (12 each side)
55 Rocker arm fulcrum
56 Rocker arm

57 Pushrod
58 Water jacket plug
59 Oil gallery plug
60 Intake manifold gasket
61 Carburetor studs (4)
62 Carburetor gasket
63 Adapter nuts (2)
64 Valve studs (2)
65 Valve nuts (2)
66 Rear cover plate
67 Drive plate
68 Plate bolts (5)

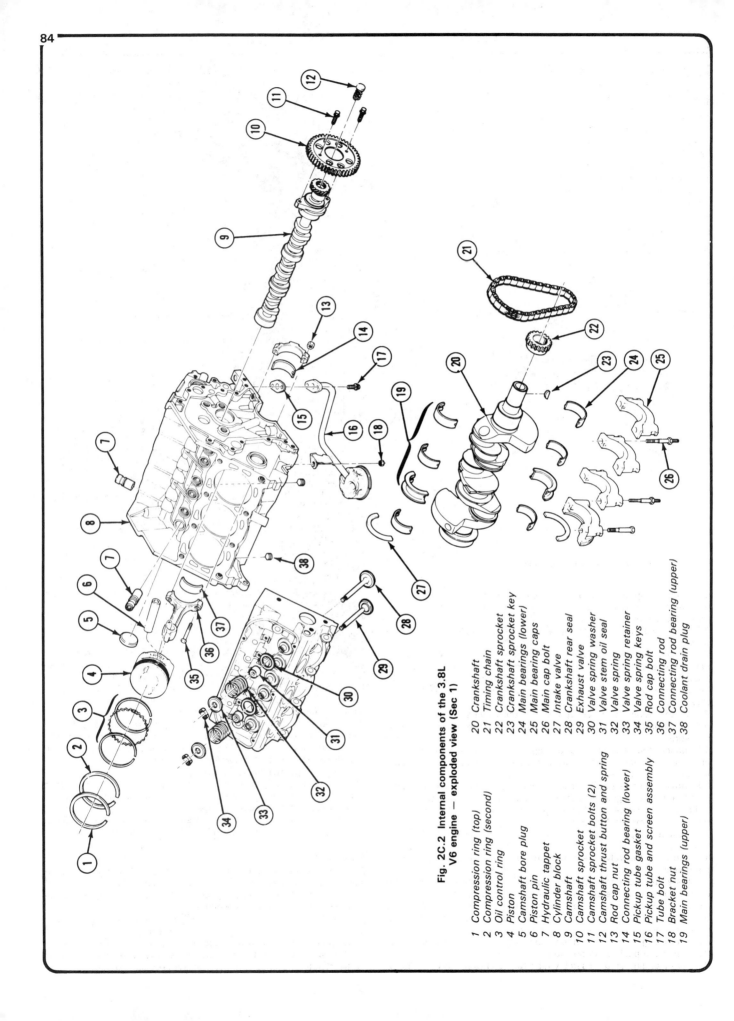

Fig. 2C.2 Internal components of the 3.8L V6 engine — exploded view (Sec 1)

1 Compression ring (top)
2 Compression ring (second)
3 Oil control ring
4 Piston
5 Camshaft bore plug
6 Piston pin
7 Hydraulic tappet
8 Cylinder block
9 Camshaft
10 Camshaft sprocket
11 Camshaft sprocket bolts (2)
12 Camshaft thrust button and spring
13 Rod cap nut
14 Connecting rod bearing (lower)
15 Pickup tube gasket
16 Pickup tube and screen assembly
17 Tube bolt
18 Bracket nut
19 Main bearings (upper)
20 Crankshaft
21 Timing chain
22 Crankshaft sprocket
23 Crankshaft sprocket key
24 Main bearings (lower)
25 Main bearing caps
26 Main cap bolt
27 Intake valve
28 Crankshaft rear seal
29 Exhaust valve
30 Valve spring washer
31 Valve stem oil seal
32 Valve spring
33 Valve spring retainer
34 Valve spring keys
35 Rod cap bolt
36 Connecting rod
37 Connecting rod bearing (upper)
38 Coolant drain plug

3 Remove the accelerator cable linkage at the carburetor.
4 Disconnect the choke cable at the carburetor.
5 Remove the rocker arm cover (see Section 2).
6 Remove the spark plug from the cylinder which has the bad component.
7 Crank the engine until the piston in the cylinder with the bad component is slightly before top dead center on the compression stroke (see Chapter 2B, Section 3).
8 Install the special air line adapter (which will screw into the spark plug hole and connect to a compressor). Remove the rocker arm stud bolt, fulcrum seat, rocker arm and pushrod as shown in the accompanying illustration.

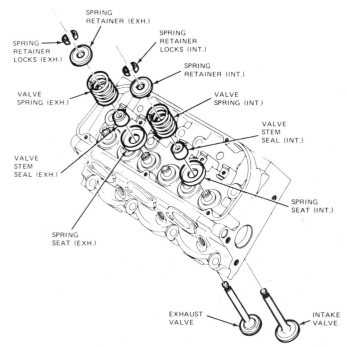

Fig. 2C.3 Valve train components (Sec 3)

9 Apply compressed air to the cylinder in question. This will, assuming that the valves and seats are in good condition, hold the valves against the seats.
10 Compress the valve spring with a head-installed valve spring compressor.
11 Remove the keepers, spring retainer and valve spring. Remove the valve stem seal. **Note:** *If air pressure fails to hold the valve in the closed position during this operation, there is apparently damage to the seat or the valve. If this condition exists, remove the cylinder head for further repair.*
12 Wrap a rubber band or tape around the valve stem so the valve will not drop through into the combustion chamber. Release the air pressure.
13 Inspect the valve stem for damage. Rotate the valve in its guide and check the valve stem tip for eccentric movement, which would indicate a bent valve.
14 Move the valve up and down through its normal travel and make sure that the valve guide and stem do not bind. If the valve stem binds, either the valve is bent and/or the guide is damaged and the head will have to be removed for repair.
15 Reapply air pressure to the cylinder to retain the valve. Remove the rubber band or tape holding the valve.
16 Lubricate the valve stem with engine oil and install a new valve stem seal.
17 Install the spring in position over the valve. Make sure that the closed coil end of the spring is against the cylinder head.
18 Install the valve spring retainer. Compress the valve spring using the valve spring compressor and install the keepers. Remove the compressor tool and make sure that the keepers are installed correctly.
19 Apply engine oil or assembly lube to both ends of the pushrod.
20 Install the pushrod in position.
21 Apply engine oil or assembly lube to the end of the valve stem.

22 Oil the fulcrum seats and socket. Install the rocker arm, fulcrum and bolt. Tighten the bolt to the specified torque.
23 Remove the air source and the adapter from the spark plug hole.
24 Install the spark plug and reconnect the spark plug wire.
25 Place a new rocker arm cover gasket in the cover and install the rocker arm cover.
26 Connect the accelerator cable to the carburetor.
27 Install the accelerator cable return spring. Connect the choke cable to the carburetor.
28 Install the air cleaner.
29 Start and run the engine. Make sure that there are no leaks and that there are no unusual sounds coming from the valve components.

4 Manifolds — removal and installation

Intake manifold

Removal
1 Drain the cooling system and disconnect the cable from the negative battery terminal.
2 Remove the air cleaner assembly including the air intake duct and heat tube.
3 Disconnect the accelerator cable at the carburetor.
4 If so equipped, disconnect the transmission linkage at the carburetor.
5 Remove the bolts from the accelerator cable mounting bracket and position the cable so it will not interfere with manifold removal.
6 If equipped with a speed control, disconnect the chain at the carburetor and remove the servo bracket assembly mounting nuts. Position the assembly so it will not interfere with manifold removal.
7 Disconnect the carburetor bowl vent hose at the carburetor.
8 Disconnect the thermactor air supply hose at the check valve located at the back of the intake manifold.
9 Disconnect the upper radiator hose at the thermostat housing.
10 Disconnect the fuel inlet line at the carburetor.
11 Disconnect the coolant bypass hose at the manifold.
12 Disconnect the heater tube at the intake manifold and remove the tube support bracket nut.
13 Label and disconnect the vacuum lines at the carburetor and intake manifold.
14 Disconnect all necessary electrical connectors.
15 If equipped with air conditioning, remove the compressor support bracket attached to the left front intake manifold bolt.
16 Remove the EGR tube.
17 Disconnect the PCV hose at the carburetor.
18 Unbolt and remove the carburetor.
19 Remove the three EGR spacer mounting screws from the manifold.
20 With the EGR adapter and valve attached, work the EGR spacer loose from the manifold and remove the spacer and gasket.
21. Remove the PCV hose.
22 Remove the intake manifold mounting bolts by reversing the order shown in the accompanying illustration.
23 Remove the intake manifold. **Note:** *The manifold is sealed at each end with RTV-type sealant. To break the seal it may be necessary to pry on the front of the manifold with a screwdriver. If so, use care to prevent damage to the machined surfaces.*
24 Remove the manifold side gaskets.
25 If the manifold is to be disassembled, remove the thermostat housing and thermostat, water temperature sending unit, thermactor check valve and all vacuum fittings.
26 The heater outlet and water bypass tubes are pressed in and are not serviceable. If they are damaged, replace the manifold with a new one.

Installation
27 If the intake manifold was disassembled, apply a coat of pipe sealant to the temperature sending unit, all vacuum fittings, the spark knock sensor/adapter (if so equipped) and the electric PVS (if so equipped) and install them in the manifold.
28 Install the thermostat in the manifold with the outlet side up.
29 Apply a 1/16-inch bead of RTV-type sealant to the thermostat housing and tighten it to the specified torque.
30 Position and install the thermactor check valve and a new gasket in the manifold. Tighten the bolts to the specified torque.

Fig. 2C.4 Intake manifold installation details (note the bolt
tightening sequence numbers) (Sec 4)

Fig. 2C.5 Left exhaust manifold installation details (earlier
models are not equipped with an EGO sensor) (Sec 4)

Fig. 2C.6 Exhaust manifold installation details (Sec 4)

31 Apply a bead of contact adhesive to each cylinder head mating
surface and press new intake manifold gaskets into place.
32 Apply a 1/8-inch bead of RTV-type sealant at each corner where
the cylinder head joins the cylinder block and a 1/4-inch bead at each
end of the block where the manifold seats against it.
33 Carefully lower the manifold into position on the block and cylinder
heads.
34 Apply a thin coat of pipe sealant to the manifold bolt threads and
to the underside of the bolt heads.
35 Install the 12 bolts and two stud bolts and tighten them in the
numerical sequence shown in the accompanying illustration.
36 Install the remaining components in the reverse order of removal.
37 Fill the cooling system with the specified coolant (see Chapter 1).
38 Start and run the engine and allow it to reach operating
temperature, checking carefully for leaks.
39 Shut the engine off and retighten the manifold bolts while the
engine is still warm.

Exhaust manifold — left side
40 Remove the oil level dipstick tube support bracket.
41 If equipped with a speed control, reposition the air cleaner assembly

APPLY SEALANT
TO THESE BOLTS

(TIGHTENING SEQUENCE)

BOLT WASHER

CYLINDER
HEAD

Fig. 2C.7 Cylinder head installation details (note the bolt tightening sequence numbers) (Sec 5)

GASKET

FRONT OF ENGINE

ALIGNMENT
DOWELS

and disconnect the servo chain at the carburetor.
42 Remove the servo bracket bolts and nuts and position the servo and bracket out of the way.
43 If so equipped, disconnect the EGO sensor at the wiring connector.
44 Disconnect the spark plug wires.
45 Raise the front of the vehicle and place it securely on jackstands.
46 Remove the manifold to exhaust pipe nuts.
47 Remove the jackstands and lower the vehicle.
48 Remove the exhaust manifold mounting bolts and the manifold.
49 Installation is the reverse of removal. **Note:** *When installing the bolts, install the pilot bolt (lower front bolt on no. 5 cylinder) first.*
50 A slight warpage in the exhaust manifold may cause a misalignment between the bolt holes in the head and manifold. If so, elongate the holes in the exhaust manifold as necessary to correct the misalignment, but do not elongate the pilot hole.

Exhaust manifold — right side
51 Remove the air cleaner assembly and heat tube.
52 Disconnect the thermactor hose from the downstream air tube check valve.
53 Remove the downstream air tube bracket bolt at the rear of the right cylinder head.
54 Disconnect the coil secondary wire from the coil and the wires from the spark plugs.
55 Remove the spark plugs and the outer heat shroud.
56 Raise the front of the vehicle and place it securely on jackstands.
57 Remove the transmission dipstick tube, if so equipped.
58 Remove the manifold to exhaust pipe nuts.
59 Remove the jackstands and lower the vehicle.
60 Remove the exhaust manifold mounting bolts, then remove the manifold, inner heat shroud and EGR tube as an assembly.
61 Installation is the reverse of removal. If bolt holes are misaligned, see Step 50, but do not elongate the pilot hole (lower rear bolt hole on no. 2 cylinder).

---

5   Cylinder heads — removal and installation

1   Drain the coolant into a clean container.
2   Disconnect the cable from the negative battery terminal.
3   Remove the air cleaner assembly, including the air intake duct and heat tube.
4   Loosen the accessory drivebelt idler, then remove the drivebelt (see Chapter 1 if necessary).
5   If the left cylinder head is being removed, refer to Steps 6 through 9 and Steps 17 through 30.
6   If equipped with power steering, remove the pump mounting bracket bolts.

7   Leaving the hoses connected, place the pump/bracket assembly aside, making sure that it is in a position to prevent the fluid from leaking out.
8   If equipped with air conditioning, remove the mounting bracket bolts.
9   Leaving the hoses connected, position the compressor aside. **Note:** *Under no circumstances should the air conditioning hoses be disconnected except by an authorized air conditioning service technician, as personal injury and equipment damage may result.*
10 If the right cylinder head is being removed, refer to Steps 11 through 30.
11 Disconnect the thermactor diverter valve and hose assembly at the bypass valve and downstream air tube, then remove the assembly.
12 Remove the accessory drive idler.
13 Remove the alternator.
14 Remove the thermactor pump pulley and pump.
15 Remove the alternator bracket.
16 Remove the PCV valve.
17 Remove the intake manifold (see Section 4).
18 Remove the rocker arm cover(s) (see Section 2).
19 Remove the exhaust manifold(s) (see Section 4).
20 Remove the pushrods and store them separately so that they can be reinstalled in their original positions.
21 Remove the cylinder head bolts, then remove the cylinder head(s).
22 Remove and discard the old cylinder head gasket(s) and discard the cylinder head bolts.
23 Refer to Chapter 2E for cylinder head disassembly and inspection procedures.
24 Position new head gasket(s) on the block using the dowels for alignment.
25 Position the head on the block.
26 Apply a thin coat of pipe sealant to the threads of the short cylinder head bolts (nearest to the exhaust manifold). Do not apply sealant to the long bolts.
27 Lightly oil the cylinder head bolt flat washers and install the flat washers and cylinder head bolts. **Note:** *Always use new cylinder head bolts.*
28 Tighten the bolts in the sequence shown in the accompanying illustration.

29 When the cylinder head bolts have been tightened to the specified torque in the steps indicated, it is not necessary to retighten the head bolts after engine operation. However, the bolts may be checked for tightness if desired.

30 The remaining installation steps are the reverse of those for removal. Be sure to use the proper coolant (see Chapter 1) when refilling the cooling system.

6   Timing chain — deflection check

1   Remove the right rocker arm cover (refer to Section 2).
2   Loosen the number three exhaust rocker arm and rotate it to one side. (The number three cylinder is the rear cylinder on the right side.)
3   Install a dial indicator on the end of the pushrod (see the accompanying illustration).
4   Turn the crankshaft clockwise until the number one piston is at TDC. The damper timing mark should point to TDC on the timing degree indicator as shown in the accompanying illustration. This will also take up the slack in the right side of the chain.
5   Zero the dial indicator.
6   Slowly turn the crankshaft counterclockwise until the slightest movement is seen on the dial indicator. Stop and note how far the timing mark has moved from TDC (refer to the accompanying illustration.
7   If the reading on the timing chain degree indicator exceeds 6°, replace the timing chain and sprockets (refer to Section 7).

7   Front cover and timing chain — removal and installation

Removal

1   Disconnect the cable from the negative battery terminal.
2   Drain the cooling system.
3   Remove the air cleaner assembly and air intake duct.
4   Remove the fan shroud mounting screws.
5   Remove the fan/clutch assembly mounting bolts.
6   Remove the fan/clutch assembly and shroud.
7   Loosen the accessory drivebelt idler (see Chapter 1 if necessary).
8   Remove the drivebelt.
9   Remove the water pump pulley.
10 If equipped with power steering, remove the pump mounting bracket bolts.
11 Leaving the hoses connected, place the pump bracket assembly aside, making sure that it is positioned to prevent fluid from leaking out.
12 If equipped with air conditioning, remove the compressor front support bracket, leaving the compressor in place. Do not attempt to disconnect the air conditioning hoses, as personal injury and/or equipment damage may result.
13 Disconnect the engine coolant bypass hose at the water pump.
14 Disconnect the heater hose at the water pump.
15 Disconnect the radiator upper hose at the thermostat housing.
16 Disconnect the coil wire from the distributor cap, then remove the cap with the spark plug wires attached.
17 Remove the distributor holddown clamp and lift the distributor out of the front cover.
18 Raise the vehicle and place it securely on jackstands.
19 Remove the crankshaft damper with a puller as shown in the accompanying illustration.
20 Remove the fuel pump shield, if so equipped.
21 Disconnect the fuel pump to carburetor fuel line at the fuel pump.
22 Remove the fuel pump mounting bolts, pull the pump out of the front cover and lay the pump aside with the flexible line attached.
23 Remove the oil filter.
24 Disconnect the lower radiator hose at the water pump.
25 Remove the oil pan (refer to Section 9). **Note:** *The front cover cannot be removed without lowering the oil pan.*
26 Remove the jackstands and lower the vehicle.
27 Remove the front cover bolts. It is not necessary to remove the water pump. **Note:** *Do not overlook the cover bolt located behind the oil filter adapter. The front cover will break if pried on before all bolts have been removed.*
28 Remove the ignition timing indicator from the front cover.
29 Remove the front cover and water pump as an assembly.
30 Remove the camshaft thrust button and spring from the end of

Fig. 2C.8 Installing a dial indicator on a pushrod to check timing chain deflection (Sec 6)

Fig. 2C.9 Checking timing chain deflection (note damper timing mark at TDC) (Sec 6)

Fig. 2C.10 Measuring the number of degrees (from TDC) of timing chain deflection (Sec 6)

the camshaft.
31 Remove the camshaft sprocket bolts.
32 Remove the camshaft sprocket, crankshaft sprocket and timing chain as shown in the accompanying illustration. If the crankshaft sprocket is difficult to remove, pry the sprocket off the shaft using two large screwdrivers positioned on each side of the sprocket.
33 The front cover contains the oil pump and oil pump intermediate shaft. If a new front cover is being installed, remove the water pump, oil pump, oil filter adapter and the oil pump intermediate shaft from the old cover. Refer to Section 10 for procedures involving the oil pump assembly. Refer to Chapter 3 for procedures involving the water pump.

Fig. 2C.11 Removal and installation of the crankshaft damper and pulley (Sec 7)

DAMPER

SEAL/DAMPER INSTALLER T82L-6316-A AND ADAPTER T70P-68070-A

PULLEY

CRANKSHAFT SPROCKET

TIMING CHAIN

Fig. 2C.12 Timing chain and sprockets — exploded view (note the position of the crankshaft sprocket key) (Sec 7)

CAMSHAFT SPROCKET

LUBRICATE WITH CLEAN ENGINE OIL BEFORE INSTALLATION

2C

CAMSHAFT SPROCKET TIMING MARK

CRANKSHAFT SPROCKET TIMING MARK

CRANKSHAFT KEYWAY

Installation

34   Lightly oil all bolt and stud threads before installation, except those requiring special sealant.

35   If reusing the front cover, replace the crankshaft front oil seal (refer to Section 11).

36   If a new front cover is being used, install the oil pump, oil filter adapter, oil pump intermediate shaft and water pump.

37   Rotate the crankshaft as necessary to position piston number one at TDC and the crankshaft keyway at the 12 o'clock position as shown in the accompanying illustration.

38   Lubricate the timing chain with clean engine oil.

39   Install the camshaft sprocket, crankshaft sprocket and timing chain, making sure the timing marks are aligned opposite each other.

40   Install the camshaft sprocket bolts and tighten them to the specified torque.

41   Lubricate the camshaft thrust button with polyethylene grease and install the thrust button and spring in the front of the camshaft. **Note:** *The thrust button and spring must be bottomed in the camshaft seat. Make sure that the thrust button and spring do not fall out during the installation of the front cover.*

Fig. 2C.13 Before removal or installation of the timing chain and sprockets the timing marks must be aligned as shown (Sec 7)

Fig. 2C.14 Front cover bolt tightening sequence (Sec 7)

42 Lubricate the crankshaft front oil seal with clean engine oil.
43 Position a new cover gasket on the block and install the front cover/water pump assembly, using the dowels for alignment. Adhesive may be used to hold the gasket in position while the front cover is installed.
44 Attach the ignition timing indicator to the front cover.
45 Coat the front cover bolts with pipe sealant and install the front cover, tightening the bolts in the order shown in the accompanying illustration to the specified torque.
46 Raise the vehicle and position it securely on jackstands.
47 Install the oil pan (refer to Section 9).
48 Connect the lower radiator hose and tighten the clamp securely.
49 Install the oil filter.
50 Turn the crankshaft 180° clockwise to position the fuel pump eccentric away from the fuel pump actuating arm. **Note:** *Failure to turn the crankshaft can result in the threads being stripped out of the front cover when the fuel pump attaching bolts are installed.*
51 Position a new gasket on the fuel pump and install the pump.
52 Connect the fuel line to the fuel pump.

53 Coat the crankshaft damper sealing surface with clean engine oil.
54 Position the crankshaft pulley key in the crankshaft keyway.
55 Using a special seal/damper tool (Ford tool T82L-6316-A or equivalent), install the crankshaft damper.
56 Install the damper washer and bolt and tighten both to the specified torque. **Note:** *This bolt may be used to push the damper onto the crankshaft if the proper installation tool is unavailable.*
57 Install the crankshaft pulley and tighten the bolts to the specified torque.
58 Turn the crankshaft 180° counterclockwise to bring piston number one back to TDC.
59 Remove the jackstands and lower the vehicle.
60 The remaining installation procedures are the reverse of removal. When installing the distributor, make sure the rotor is pointing at the number one distributor cap tower (refer to Chapter 5).
61 Start the engine and check for coolant, oil or fuel leaks.
62 Check the ignition timing and idle speed and adjust as required (refer to Chapters 1 and 4, respectively).

8 Camshaft and lifters — removal and installation

Removal

Note: *If the engine is in the vehicle and is equipped with air conditioning, the condenser must be removed. This requires discharging of the air conditioning system by an authorized air conditioning system technician. Under no circumstances should the home mechanic attempt to discharge the system or disconnect any of the air conditioning system lines while they are still pressurized, as this can cause serious personal*

Fig. 2C.15 Oil pan installation details (note the use of sealer on the gasket mating surfaces) (Sec 9)

injury as well as damage to the air conditioning system.
1 Disconnect the cable from the negative battery terminal.
2 Drain the coolant from the radiator.
3 Remove the radiator (refer to Chapter 3).
4 If equipped with air conditioning, see the note at the beginning of this Section.
5 Remove the grille (see Chapter 10).
6 Remove the intake manifold (refer to Section 4).
7 Remove the rocker arm covers (refer to Section 2).
8 Loosen the rocker arm nuts and rotate the rocker arms to the side.
9 Mark the pushrods if they are to be reused and remove them from the engine.
10 Remove the valve lifters from the engine using a special tool designed for this purpose. Sometimes they can be removed with a magnet if there is no varnish buildup or wear. If they are stuck in their bores you will have to obtain a special tool designed for grasping lifters internally and work them out.
11 Remove the timing cover, chain and gears (refer to Section 7).
12 Remove the oil pan (refer to Section 9).
13 Remove the camshaft from the front of the engine by slowly withdrawing it, being careful not to damage the bearings with the cam lobes. For inspection procedures, see Chapter 2E.

Fig. 2C.16 Oil pump components — exploded view (Sec 10)

Installation

14 Lubricate the cam lobes and bearing surfaces with engine assembly lube.

15 The remaining installation procedures are the reverse of those for removal.

---

9 Oil pan — removal and installation

---

1 Disconnect the cable from the negative battery terminal.

2 Remove the air cleaner assembly.

3 Remove the bolts attaching the fan shroud to the radiator and position the shroud over the fan.

4 Remove the engine oil dispstick.

5 Raise the vehicle and place it securely on jackstands.

6 Remove the oil filter.

7 Disconnect the exhaust pipes from the exhaust manifolds.

8 Remove the clamp attaching the inlet pipe to the converter pipe and remove the inlet pipe from the vehicle.

9 Disconnect the transmission shift linkage at the transmission (see Chapter 7, if necessary).

10 If so equipped, disconnect the transmission cooler lines at the radiator.

11 Remove the nuts attaching the engine supports to the chassis brackets.

12 Using a jack and a block of wood, lift the engine and place wood blocks between the engine supports and the chassis brackets, then remove the jack.

13 Remove the oil pan bolts and lower the oil pan. Unbolt the oil pickup and tube assembly and let them lay in the pan, then remove the pan from the vehicle. Remove the old gaskets and rear pan seal.

14 Clean the oil pan and engine block gasket sealing surfaces. Inspect the gasket sealing surfaces for damage and distortion due to over-tightening of the bolts. Repair and straighten the pan flanges as required.

15 Trial fit the pan to the cylinder block. Make sure enough clearance exists to allow the pan to be installed without the sealant scraping off when the pan is positioned for final installation.

16 Rest the oil pan on the frame crossmember.

17 Using a new gasket, install the oil pickup and tube assembly. Make sure that the support bracket engages the stud on the number two main bearing cap bolt.

18 Tighten the pickup and tube assembly nuts and bolts to the specified torque.

19 Install a new rear seal in the seal groove of the rear main cap, working it into place with a small screwdriver.

20 Apply a 1/8-inch bead of RTV-type sealant to the seam where the front cover and block join, to each end of the rear seal where the rear main cap and block join, and along the oil pan rails on the cylinder block as shown in the accompanying illustration. Where the bead crosses the front cover, increase the bead width to 1/4-inch.

21 Position the oil pan on the bottom of the engine and attach it with the bolts. Tighten the bolts to the specified torque.

22 Raise the engine and remove the wood blocks.

23 The remaining installation procedures are the reverse of those for removal.

---

10 Oil pump — removal, inspection and installation

---

1 Remove the front cover assembly (refer to Section 7).

2 Remove the oil pump cover bolts, then remove the cover.

3 Lift the pump gears out of the pocket in the cover.

4 If the engine has high mileage or is being rebuilt, replace the oil pump with a new one.

5 To assemble the oil pump, lightly pack the gear pocket with petroleum jelly or heavy oil. **Note:** *Do not use chassis lubricant.*

6 Install the gears in the cover pocket, making sure that the petroleum jelly fills all the voids between the gears and the pocket. **Note:** *Failure to properly coat the oil pump gears may result in failure of the pump to prime when the engine is started, leading to severe engine damage.*

7 Position the cover gasket and install the pump cover.

8 Tighten the pump cover bolts to the specified torque.

9 Using an electric drill, drill a small hole through the center of the relief valve plug.

10 Remove the plug with a sheet metal screw and slide hammer or by prying it out with an ice pick or similar tool.

11 Remove the spring and valve from the bore as shown in the accompanying illustration.

12 Thoroughly clean the valve bore and valve to remove any metal chips which may have entered the bore as a result of drilling the plug.

13 Lubricate the relief valve with engine oil and install it in the bore.

14 Position the spring in the bore.

15 Tap a new plug into the bore using a soft-faced hammer. Make

Fig. 2C.17 Oil pressure relief valve location (Sec 10)

Fig. 2C.18 Locaton of the oil pump drive intermediate shaft in the front cover (Sec 10)

Fig. 2C.19 Removing the damper from the front of the crankshaft (Sec 11)

sure the plug is flush with the machined surface.

16 Remove the clip from the intermediate shaft and slide the shaft out of the cover (refer to the accompaning illustration).

17 Before installing the shaft, measure and mark the shaft one inch from the end.

18 Position the shaft in the cover, making sure that it is seated in the oil pump drive gear.

19 Install the clip on the shaft so the top of the clip is just below the mark made in step 17. Use a screwdriver blade to snap the clip onto the shaft.

20 Install the front cover assembly (refer to Section 7).

---

11   Crankshaft oil seals — replacement

Front seal

1 Disconnect the cable from the negative battery terminal.

Fig. 2C.20 Installing the crankshaft front seal (Sec 11)

2 Remove the fan shroud screws.

3 Remove the fan/clutch assembly bolts.

4 Remove the fan/clutch assembly and shroud.

5 Loosen the accessory drivebelt idler.

6 Raise the vehicle and place it securely on jackstands.

7 Disengage the accessory drivebelt and remove the crankshaft pulley.

8 Using a puller, remove the crankshaft damper as shown in the accompanying illustration.

9 Remove the seal from the front cover using a large screwdriver or pry bar. Be careful not to damage the front cover or crankshaft.

10 Inspect the front cover and crankshaft damper for nicks, burrs and other roughness which may cause the seal to fail. If defects are found,

Fig. 2C.21 Typical engine mount assemblies (Sec 12)

replace the damaged components with new ones.

11 Lubricate the new seal lip with engine oil and install the seal with the special seal/damper installing tool available from Ford as shown in the accompanying illustration.

12 Lubricate the damper seal nose with engine oil and install the damper with the special tool.

13 Install the damper bolt and tighten it to the specified torque.

14 Position the crankshaft pulley and tighten the bolts to the specified torque.

15 Position the accessory drivebelt over the crankshaft pulley.

16 Remove the jackstands and lower the vehicle.

17 The remaining installation procedures are the reverse of those for removal.

18 Adjust the drivebelt tension (refer to Chapter 1).

19 Start the engine and check for oil leaks.

Rear seal – two-piece

20 The two-piece rear oil seal can be replaced with the engine in the vehicle. To gain access to the rear seal, remove the oil pan (refer to Section 9).

Note: *The oil pump does not have to be removed on this engine.*

21 *Refer to Chapter 2E to complete the procedure.*

Rear seal – one-piece

22 To replace the one-piece rear seal it is necessary to remove the transmission (see Chapter 7) and flywheel or flexplate.

23 Refer to Chapter 2E, Section 20, to complete the procedure.

---

12 Engine mounts – replacement with engine in vehicle

Front mounts

1 The engine front and rear supports and insulators can be replaced without removing the engine from the vehicle.

Fig. 2C.22 Typical rear engine mount (Sec 12)

2 The engine front supports are located on each side of the cylinder block. Whenever self-locking mounting bolts and nuts are removed they must be replaced with new self-locking bolts and nuts. Prior to installing the new self-locking mounting bolts (with adhesive on the threads) the hardened residual bolt adhesive must be removed from the engine block bosses with an M10 x 1.5 bottoming tap. Refer to the accompanying illustrations for removal of engine mount components.

3 Remove the fan shroud mounting screws to prevent damage to the fan when the engine is raised.

4 Support the engine with a jack and wood block placed under the oil pan.

5 Remove the nuts attaching the engine mounts to the number two crossmember.

6   On LTD and Marquis models only, remove the bolt that attaches the lower end of the engine damper to the number two crossmember bracket.

7   Raise the engine high enough to clear the engine mount studs from the crossmember.

8   Remove the fuel pump shield, if so equipped, from the right side of the engine.

9   Remove the starter ground cable and oil cooler line clips from the right engine support bracket.

10 Remove the bolts attaching the insulator and bracket assembly to the engine.

11 Remove the rubber insulator and bracket assembly.

12 To install a new insulator and bracket, position the insulator and bracket assembly on the engine. Install the bolts and tighten them to the specified torque.

13 Install the starter ground cable attaching a clip to the upper right front engine mount support bracket bolt.

14 Attach the fuel pump shield, if equipped, to the right side of the engine.

15 Lower the engine into position, making sure that the insulators are seated flat on the number two crossmember and that the insulator studs are at the bottom of the slots.

16 Attach the rubber insulators to the number two crossmember, being sure to use the washer and nut assemblies. Tighten the nuts to the specified torque.

17 On LTD and Marquis models only, install the bolt which attaches the engine damper to the number two crossmember bracket. Tighten the bolt to the specified torque.

18 Install the fan shroud mounting screws.

Rear mount

19 Support the transmission with a jack and wood block.

20 Remove the two rear nuts attaching the rear insulator to the crossmember.

21 Remove the two bolts and nuts attaching the crossmember to the body brackets.

22 Remove the crossmember by raising the transmission slightly with a jack.

23 Remove the two bolts attaching the rear insulator to the transmission.

24 Remove the insulator and the retainer.

25 To install a new rubber insulator and retainer, position the insulator and retainer assembly on the transmission.

26 Install the two bolts and tighten them to the specified torque.

27 Install the crossmember to body brackets.

28 Tighten the nuts to the specified torque.

29 Lower the transmission and install the insulator to crossmember nuts. Tighten the nuts to the specified torque.

---

13   Engine — removal and installation

Note: *The engine must be removed alone, with the transmission left in place in the vehicle. Also, due to the wide range of vehicle models covered by this manual, the following instructions are of general nature and may cover some steps not applicable to your vehicle.*

Removal

1   Remove the battery cables (negative first, then positive) from the battery.

2   Mark the position of the hood with a scribe or marking pen so it can be installed in the same position relative to the hinges and latch. Remove the hood. Cover the fenders for protection.

3   Remove the air cleaner along with the related emissions control and supply hoses from the carburetor. Cover the carburetor inlet with a clean cloth.

4   Remove all vacuum lines from the intake manifold area. Some of these lines will connect the automatic transmission modulator, speed control and emission control related systems. Clearly mark all lines to prevent confusion when the engine is reinstalled.

5   Remove the fuel feed hose from the fuel pump. Use caution when performing this step as gasoline is flammable and all precautions pertaining to flammable liquids should be observed. Plug the feed hose with a clamp and bolt if the fuel tank level is above the fuel feed line level.

6   **Note:** *Mark any electrical wires for proper installation before disconnecting them.* Disconnect the electrical connection(s) at the rear of the engine. In most cases, this will be a large multi-wire connector. However, some vehicles will be equipped with individual wires leading to components such as the engine operating sensors, ignition coil and emissions control related items such as the throttle positioner and choke heater. Remove the starter cable from the starter and position it out of the way. Remove the spark plug wires and the distributor cap as a unit.

7   Remove the speed control actuating cable from the carburetor linkage.

8   Remove the choke cable from the carburetor at its holddown clamp and the connecting linkage.

9   Disconnect the transmission kickdown cable from its connecting point at the carburetor linkage and at the transmission bellcrank connector.

10 Remove the throttle linkage from the carburetor connecting point and from the throttle pedal bellcrank (in some cases this is a cable system which will have a cable holddown clamp on the intake manifold and a connector at the carburetor linkage). Remove the throttle linkage return spring.

11 Drain the engine oil and remove the oil filter.

12 Drain the coolant from the engine and radiator drain plugs.

13 Remove the heater hoses from their connecting points at the water pump and intake manifold. Position the heater hoses out of the way.

14 Remove the radiator hoses from the engine. Remove the radiator hoses from the radiator if there is not enough clearance for the radiator to be removed with the hoses still in place.

15 Remove the fan shroud from the radiator and slide it back over the fan assembly.

16 Remove the transmission cooler lines from bottom of the radiator.

17 Loosen the alternator adjusting bolt and remove the drivebelt from the pulleys. Remove all drivebelts attached to the water pump/fan drive pulley.

18 Remove the bolts retaining the fan and spacer (or fan clutch drive assembly) to the water pump.

19 Remove the fan assembly and fan shroud by lifting them straight up and out of the engine compartment.

20 Remove the radiator to saddle retaining bolts.

21 Remove the radiator. Remove the alternator retaining bolt and position the alternator and wiring out of the way. It is important to secure the alternator in place to prevent damage to the wiring connector at the rear of the alternator. Never allow the alternator to hang from the wiring.

22 In some cases the air conditioning system will not need discharging, since the hoses leading to the compressor unit are long enough for it to be swung out of the way and secured to the fender well. Disconnect the air conditioning hoses only if the system has been discharged. Remember that the system can only be discharged by a qualified specialist.

23 Remove the air conditioning compressor from the mounting brackets and secure it out of the way.

24 Remove the power steering pump belt.

25 Remove the power steering pump from the mounting bracket, position it out of the way and secure it. **Note:** *The following steps will be performed with the vehicle raised. Make sure that it is supported securely on jackstands.*

26 Remove the starter (Chapter 5).

27 Remove the automatic transmission dipstick tube retaining bolt from the rear of the cylinder head or from the rear of the bellhousing retaining lug. Remove the automatic transmission dipstick and tube.

28 Remove the lower bellhousing retaining bolts.

29 Remove the engine mount to frame insulator retaining nuts.

30 Support the transmission assembly.

31 Remove the flywheel inspection cover.

32 Remove the torque converter drain plug cover.

33 Remove the torque converter to flexplate retaining nuts. The crankshaft will have to be rotated 90° to position each retaining nut for removal.

34 Remove the bolts retaining the exhaust pipes to the exhaust manifolds. Remove the exhaust pipes from the exhaust manifolds.

35 Remove the upper bellhousing to engine retaining bolts.

36 Lower the vehicle. Make sure the transmission is supported securely.

37 Install an engine lifting sling or chain. There are several methods which can be used to accomplish this. Metal eye hooks can be attached

with bolts positioned at diagonally opposite corners of the cylinder heads, but because the V6 heads are made of aluminum, special caution should be exercised. Make sure that the bolts attaching the eye hooks are threaded well into the heads, preventing thread damage when the engine is lifted. A sling can be fashioned from a short piece of chain connected to open-end hooks. A cable and bracket arrangement would also work well.

38 Raise the engine high enough for the engine mount studs to clear the frame bracket insulators.

39 Double check all attachment points to ensure that all of the retaining bolts holding the engine to the transmission have been removed.

40 Separate the engine from the bellhousing (or torque converter housing) making sure that the flywheel/clutch assembly (torque converter flexplate) pulls straight out of the housing without binding. You may need to adjust the engine height and angle for the two components to separate cleanly. A small wedge-type tool can be used between the housing and the engine block to separate them. However, if resistance if felt, check to make sure no retaining bolts are left in the engine. Do not force any parts during this removal procedure. If the engine is stuck to the transmission assembly, a fastener is probably holding them together.

41 Pull the engine straight forward and away from the transmission. Take care not to damage the transmission input shaft while performing this step.

42 When the transmission input shaft or torque converter has com-

pletely cleared the clutch assembly or flexplate, raise the engine and remove it from the engine compartment. There should be no connections between the engine and the vehicle.

43 Place the engine on an engine stand or other support for further disassembly.

Installation

44 Lift the engine off the engine stand with a hoist. The chains should be positioned as on removal, with the engine sitting level.

45 Lower the engine into place inside the engine compartment, closely watching clearances. On manual transmissions, carefully guide the engine onto the transmission input shaft. The two components should be at the same angle.

46 Install the engine mount through-bolts and the bellhousing bolts.

47 Install the remaining engine components in the reverse order of removal.

48 Fill the cooling system with the proper coolant and water mixture (Chapter 1).

49 Fill the engine with the correct grade of engine oil (Chapter 1).

50 Check the transmission fluid level, adding fluid as necessary.

51 Connect the positive battery cable, followed by the negative cable. If sparks or arcing occur as the negative cable is connected to the battery, check that all electrical accessories are turned off (check dome light first). If arcing still occurs, check that all electrical wiring is connected properly to the engine and transmission.

2C

Chapter 2 Part D
4.2, 5.0, 5.8, 6.6 and 7.5 liter V-8 engines
Refer to Chapter 13 for specifications related to 1985 and later models

Contents

Specifications

4.2L, 5.0L and 5.8LW engines

Torque specifications	Ft-lbs
Camshaft sprocket bolts	40 to 45
Camshaft thrust plate bolts	9 to 12
Timing cover bolts	12 to 18
Cylinder head bolts	
255 and 302	
1st step..........................	55 to 65
2nd step	65 to 72
351W	
1st step..........................	85
2nd step	95
3rd step	105 to 112
Crankshaft damper bolts...........................	70 to 90
EGR valve-to-carburetor spacer bolts	12 to 18
Fuel pump-to-block or timing cover	19 to 27
Flywheel bolts	75 to 85
Intake manifold bolts	23 to 25
Exhaust manifold bolts	18 to 24
Intake manifold vacuum fittings	
Aluminum	6 to 10
Cast iron	23 to 28
Intake manifold pipe fittings	
Aluminum	12 to 18
Cast iron	23 to 28
Oil inlet tube-to-main bearing cap bolts	22 to 32
Thermactor pump bracket bolts	30 to 45
Oil filter insert-to-cylinder block adapter	20 to 30
Oil filter	1/2 turn after oiled gasket contacts sealing surface
Oil pump inlet tube...............................	10 to 15
Oil pan drain plug................................	15 to 25
Oil pan bolts	9 to 11
Oil pump bolts	22 to 32
Crankshaft pulley bolts	35 to 50
Rocker arm stud/bolt-to-cylinder head	18 to 25
Rocker arm stud nut..............................	17 to 23
Spark plugs	10 to 15
Rocker arm cover bolts............................	3 to 5
Water outlet housing	9 to 12
Water pump-to-block/timing cover	12 to 18
Alternator bracket-to-block bolt	12 to 18
Alternator adjusting arm-to-alternator bolt	14 to 40
Thermactor pump pivot bolt	22 to 32
Thermactor pump adjusting arm-to-pump	22 to 32
Thermactor pump pulley-to-pump hub	12 to 18

5.8LM and 6.6L engines

Torque specifications	Ft-lbs
Camshaft sprocket	40 to 45
Camshaft thrust plate	9 to 12
Timing cover	12 to 18

Torque specifications (continued)

Cylinder head bolts	
1st step	75
2nd step	95 to 105
Crankshaft damper bolt	70 to 90
EGR valve-to-carburetor spacer	12 to 18
Fuel pump-to-block or timing cover	
Nut	14 to 20
Bolt	10 to 15
Flywheel bolts	75 to 85
Intake manifold bolts	
3/8 in	22 to 32
5/16 in	19 to 25
Exhaust manifold bolts	18 to 24
Oil filter insert-to-block/adapter	20 to 30
Oil filter-to-adapter or block	1/2 turn after oiled gasket contacts sealing surface
Oil inlet-to-main bearing	22 to 32
Thermactor pump bracket-to-cylinder block	30 to 45
Intake manifold vacuum fittings	6 to 10
Oil pan drain plug	15 to 25
Oil pump bolts	22 to 32
Oil pan bolts	7 to 9
Crankshaft pulley bolt	35 to 50
Rocker arm stud/bolt-to-cylinder head	18 to 25
Spark plugs	10 to 15
Rocker arm cover bolts	3 to 5
Water outlet housing	12 to 18
Water pump-to-block/timing cover	12 to 18
Alternator bracket-to-block bolt	15 to 20
Alternator adjusting arm-to-block bolt	15 to 20
Alternator adjusting arm-to-alternator bolt	24 to 40
Thermactor pump pivot bolt	35 to 45
Thermactor pump adjusting arm-to-pump	22 to 32
Thermactor pump pulley-to-pump hub	12 to 18

7.5L engine

Torque specifications	**Ft-lbs**
Camshaft sprocket	40 to 45
Camshaft thrust plate	9 to 12
Timing cover (5/16 in bolt)	15 to 21
Cylinder head bolts	
1st step	80
2nd step	110
3rd step	130 to 140
Crankshaft damper bolt	70 to 90
EGR valve-to-carburetor spacer	12 to 18
Fuel pump-to-block or timing cover	19 to 27
Flywheel bolts	75 to 85
Intake manifold bolts	22 to 32
Intake manifold vacuum fittings	6 to 10
Exhaust manifold bolts	28 to 33
Oil filter insert-to-block/adapter	45 to 55
Oil filter adapter-to-block	40 to 50
Oil filter-to-adapter or block	1/2 turn after oiled gasket contacts sealing surface
Oil inlet tube-to-pump	12 to 18
Oil inlet tube-to-main bearing cap	22 to 32
Oil pan drain plug	15 to 25
Oil pan bolts	
1/4 in bolts	7 to 9
5/16 in bolts	9 to 11
Oil pump-to-cylinder block	22 to 32
Pulley-to-damper bolt	35 to 50
Rocker arm stud/bolt-to-cylinder head	18 to 25
Spark plugs	5 to 10
Rocker arm cover bolts	5 to 6
Water outlet housing	12 to 18
Alternator bracket-to-block bolt	35 to 50
Alternator pivot bolt	45 to 57
Alternator adjusting arm-to-block bolt	35 to 50
Alternator adjusting arm-to-cylinder bolt	24 to 40
Thermactor pump bracket-to-cylinder block	35 to 50
Thermactor pump pivot bolt	35 to 50
Thermactor pump adjusting arm-to-pump	22 to 32
Engine mount to engine bolt	40 to 60
Engine mount insulator nuts	20 to 35

2D

RH REAR FOR 4.2L
22 (255CID), 5.8L (351 CID)
AND 5.0L (302 CID)

Fig. 2D.1 External components of the 255, 302 and 351W V8 engines — exploded view

1 Cylinder block
2 Front cover assembly
3 Front cover gasket
4 Timing pointer
5 Cylinder head
6 Cylinder head gasket
7 Cylinder head bolt
8 Camshaft rear bearing plug
9 Flywheel assembly
10 Flywheel housing

11 Rocker arm cover
12 Rocker arm cover gasket
13 PCV elbow and valve
    assembly
14 Oil pan
15 Front cover seal
16 Oil filter
17 Oil level dipstick
18 Oil level dipstick tube

19 Oil filler cap
20 PCV hose
21 Oil pan gasket set
22 Crankcase ventilation
    grommet
23 Rear engine plate
24 Water outlet connection
    gasket
25 Water pump

26 Water pump housing gasket
27 Water pump cover
28 Water pump cover gasket
29 Thermostat
30 Water outlet connection
31 Fuel pump
32 Fuel pump mounting gasket
33 Intake manifold
34 Intake manifold gasket

35 Exhaust manifold
36 Intake manifold gasket seals
37 Carburetor gasket
38 Carburetor mounting flange
39 Distributor cap
40 Distributor assembly
41 Spark plug wire set
42 Distributor holddown clamp
43 Spark plug
44 Hot water connector elbow

Fig. 2D.2 Internal components of the 255, 302 and 351W V8 engines — exploded view

1 Engine block
2 Front cover assembly
3 Cylinder head
4 Piston assembly
5 Piston pin
6 Piston ring set
7 Connecting rod assembly
8 Connecting rod bearing
9 Connecting rod nut
10 Connecting rod bolt
11 Camshaft
12 Camshaft bearing assembly
13 Camshaft sprocket
14 Camshaft front bearing
15 Camshaft center bearing
16 Camshaft rear bearing
17 Camshaft front intermediate bearing
18 Timing chain
19 Camshaft thrust plate
20 Camshaft rear intermediate bearing
21 Camshaft sprocket washer
22 Camshaft fuel pump eccentric
23 Crankshaft
24 Crankshaft sprocket
25 Crankshaft flywheel mounting flange
26 Crankshaft outer pulley
27 Crankshaft damper
28 Crankshaft main bearing
29 Crankshaft center main bearing
30 Crankshaft main bearing cap bolt
31 Main bearing cap
32 Flywheel
33 Crankshaft pulley washer
34 Flywheel bolt
35 Flywheel ring gear
36 Hydraulic lifter
37 Exhaust valve
38 Intake valve
39 Valve spring
40 Valve spring retainer
41 Valve spring retainer key
42 Rocker arm fulcrum
43 Valve stem seal
44 Oil deflector
45 Rocker arm attaching bolt
46 Rocker arm
47 Pushrod
48 Oil pump
49 Oil pump rotor and shaft assembly
50 Oil pump body plate
51 Oil pump relief valve plug
52 Oil pump intermediate shaft
53 Oil pump screen, tube and cover assembly
54 Oil pump inlet tube gasket
55 Oil pump intermediate shaft ring
56 Oil pump relief valve spring
57 Oil pump relief valve plunger
58 Front cover oil seal
59 Crankshaft rear seal
60 Engine rear plate
61 Bolt (5/8-18 x 2)
62 Bolt (3/8-16 x 1)
63 Bolt (3/8-16 x 1-1/2)
64 Bolt (1/4-20 x 5/8)
65 Dowel pin (5/16 x 1-3/8)
66 Woodruff key (1-3/4 x 3/16)
67 Bolt (5/16-18 x 5/8)

2D

Fig. 2D.3 External components of the 351M and 400 V8 engines — exploded view

1 Engine block
2 Front cover gasket
3 Timing pointer
4 Cylinder head
5 Cylinder head gaskets
6 Cylinder head bolt
7 Front cover plate
8 Camshaft rear bearing plug
9 Crankshaft pulley
10 Crankshaft damper
11 Flywheel
12 Flywheel housing
13 Left rocker cover assembly
13A Right rocker cover assembly
14 Rocker cover gasket
15 PCV assembly
16 Oil pan
17 Front cover oil seal
18 Oil pan drain plug
19 Oil filter
20 Drain plug gasket
21 Oil level dipstick
22 Dipstick tube
23 Oil filler cap
24 Crankcase ventilation hose
25 Oil pan gasket set
26 Oil filter mounting bolt insert
27 PCV grommet
28 Rear engine plate
29 Water outlet connection gasket
30 Water pump
31 Water pump housing gasket
32 Bolt (7/16-14 x 2-9/16)
33 Thermostat
34 Water outlet connection
35 Fuel pump
36 Fuel pump mounting gasket
37 Intake manifold
38 Intake manifold rear seal
39 Intake manifold front seal
40 Exhaust manifold
41 Intake manifold valley baffle
42 Carburetor mounting gasket
43 Distributor cap
44 Distributor
45 Spark plug wire set
46 Distributor holddown clamp
47 Spark plug
48 Screw and lockwasher (5/16-18 x 3/4)
49 Hex head bolt (5/16-18 x 2)
50 Washer head bolt (3/8-16 x 2)
51 Bolt (5/16-18 x 1-1/4)
52 Screw (5/16-18 x 1-1/4)
53 Screw (5/16-18 x 2-7/8)
54 Washer head bolt (5/16-18 x 1-7/8)
55 Washer head bolt (5/16-18 x 2-7/8)
56 Bolt (3/8-16 x 1)
57 Washer head bolt (1/4-20 x 5/8)
58 Bolt (5/16-18 x 3/4)
59 Lock washer (5/16 x 19/32 x 5/64)
60 Bolt (5/16-18 x 7/8)
61 Elbow (115° x 0.58 OD)
62 PCV system hose
63 Elbow grommet
64 PCV system tube

Fig. 2D.4 Internal componets of the 351M and 400 V8 engines — exploded view

1 Engine block
2 Cylinder head
3 Front engine plate
4 Piston assembly
5 Piston pin
6 Piston ring set
7 Connecting rod assembly
8 Connecting rod bearing
9 Connecting rod nut
10 Connecting rod bolt
11 Camshaft
12 Camshaft bearing assembly
13 Camshaft sprocket
14 Camshaft front bearing
15 Camshaft center bearing
16 Camshaft rear bearing
17 Camshaft front intermediate bearing
18 Timing chain
19 Camshaft thrust plate
20 Camshaft rear intermediate bearing
21 Camshaft sprocket washer
22 Camshaft fuel pump eccentric
23 Crankshaft
24 Crankshaft sprocket
25 Crankshaft oil slinger
26 Crankshaft damper
27 Crankshaft main bearing
28 Crankshaft center bearing
29 Crankshaft main bearing bolt
30 Main bearing cap
31 Flywheel
32 Crankshaft pulley retaining washer
33 Flywheel bolt
34 Flywheel ring gear
35 Hydraulic tappet
36 Exhaust valve
37 Intake valve
38 Valve spring
39 Valve spring retainer
40 Valve spring retainer key
41 Pushrod oil deflector baffle
42 Rocker arm support bolt
43 Rocker arm fulcrum seat
44 Rocker arm
45 Pushrod
46 Oil pump
47 Oil pump drive rotor and shaft assembly
48 Oil pump body plate
49 Oil pump intermediate shaft
50 Oil pump screen, tube and cover assembly
51 Oil pump mounting gasket
52 Oil pump relief valve plug
53 Oil pump relief valve spring
54 Oil pump relief valve plunger
55 Front engine seal
56 Crankshaft rear seal
57 Rear engine plate
58 Slotted head bolt (3/8-16 x 1-1/2)
59 Bolt (3/4-16 x 1-3/32)
60 Woodruff key (1-3/4 x 3/16)
61 Bolt (1/4-20 x 5/8)
62 Bolt (3/8-16 x 1-1/4)
63 Valve stem oil seal

Fig. 2D.5 External components of the 460 V8 engine — exploded view

1   Cylinder block
2   Front cover assembly
3   Front cover gasket
4   Timing pointer
5   Cylinder head
6   Cylinder head gasket
7   Cylinder head bolt
8   Camshaft rear bearing plug
9   Flywheel assembly
10 Flywheel housing
11 Rocker arm cover
12 Rocker arm cover gasket
13 Oil filler pipe hose
14 Oil pan
15 Front cover seal
16 Oil filter
17 Oil level dipstick
18 Oil level dipstick tube
19 Oil filler cap
20 Oil filler pipe hose
21 Oil pan gasket set
22 Oil filler adapter
23 Rear engine plate
24 Water outlet connection gasket
25 Water pump
26 Water pump housing gasket
27 Water pump cover
28 Water pump cover gasket
29 Thermostat
30 Water outlet connection
31 Fuel pump
32 Fuel pump mounting gasket
33 Intake manifold
34 Lockwasher (7/16)
35 Exhaust manifold
36 Intake manifold gasket seals
37 Carburetor gasket
38 Carburetor-to-intake manifold spacer
39 Distributor cap assembly
40 Distributor assembly
41 Spark plug wire set
42 Distributor holddown clamp
43 Spark plug
44 Hot water connection tube
45 Washer head bolt
46 Bolt (5/16-18 x 11/16)
47 Oil filter adapter assembly
48 Intake manifold valley gasket
49 Filler hose-to-carburetor hose

O-RING

2D

Fig. 2D.6 Internal components of the 460 V8 engines — exploded view

1 Engine block
2 Front cover assembly
3 Cylinder head
4 Piston assembly
5 Piston pin
6 Piston ring set
7 Connecting rod assembly
8 Connecting rod bearing
9 Connecting rod nut
10 Connecting rod bolt
11 Camshaft
12 Camshaft bearing assembly
13 Camshaft sprocket
14 Camshaft front bearing
15 Camshaft center bearing
16 Camshaft rear bearing
17 Camshaft front intermediate
   bearing
18 Timing chain
19 Camshaft thrust plate
20 Camshaft rear intermediate
   bearing
21 Camshaft sprocket washer
22 Camshaft fuel pump eccentric
23 Crankshaft
24 Crankshaft sprocket
25 Crankshaft-to-flywheel
   mounting flange
26 Crankshaft outer pulley
27 Crankshaft damper
28 Crankshaft main bearing
29 Crankshaft center main
   bearing
30 Crankshaft main bearing cap
   bolt
31 Main bearing cap
32 Flywheel
33 Crankshaft pulley retaining
   washer
34 Flywheel bolt
35 Flywheel ring gear
36 Hydraulic tappet
37 Exhaust valve
38 Intake valve
39 Valve spring
40 Valve spring retainer
41 Valve spring retainer key
42 Rocker arm fulcrum
43 Valve stem seal
44 Oil deflector
45 Rocker arm attaching bolt
46 Rocker arm
47 Pushrod
48 Oil pump

49 Oil pump rotor and shaft
   assembly
50 Oil pump body plate
51 Oil pump relief valve plug
52 Oil pump intermediate shaft
53 Oil pump screen, tube and
   cover assembly
54 Oil pump inlet tube gasket
55 Oil pump intermediate shaft
   ring
56 Oil pump relief valve spring
57 Oil pump relief valve plunger
58 Front cover oil seal
59 Crankshaft rear packing
60 Engine rear plate

61 Bolt (5/8-18 x 2)
62 Bolt (3/8-16 x 1)
63 Bolt (3/8-16 x 1-1/2)
64 Bolt (1/4-20 x 5/8)
65 Dowel pin (5/16 x 1-3/8)
66 Woodruff key (1-3/4 x 3/16)
67 Bolt (5/16-18 x 7/8)
68 Crankshaft pulley spacer

1   General information

This Part of Chapter 2 is devoted to repair procedures for V8 engines. The latter Sections in this part of Chapter 2 involve removal and installation procedures for V8 engines. All information concerning engine block and cylinder head servicing can be found in Part E of this Chapter.

Many of the repair procedures included in this part are based on the assumption that the engine is still installed in the vehicle. Therefore, if this information is being used during a complete engine overhaul, with the engine already out of the vehicle and on a stand, many of the steps included here will not apply.

The specifications included in this part of Chapter 2 apply only to the engines and procedures found here. For specifications regarding engines other than the V8, see Part A, B or C, whichever applies. Part E of Chapter 2 contains the specifications necessary for engine block and cylinder head rebuilding procedures.

Several V8s of various displacements are used in the model years covered by this manual. All are gasoline fueled with overhead valves actuated by hydraulic lifters and have five main bearing crankshafts.

Although all the V8s are of the same fundamental design, they are divided into the following three families. The 4.2L (255 ci), 5.0L (302 ci) and 5.8LW (351 ci) constitute one family. The 5.9LM (351 ci) and 6.6L (400 ci) belong to the second family, known for its high performance characteristics. The final family, known as the *Big-Block* group, contains the largest displacement engine available in Ford passenger cars, the 7.5L (460 ci) engine.

2   Rocker arm covers — removal and installation

1   Remove the air cleaner and intake duct assembly.
2   Remove the crankcase ventilation hoses and lines where applicable. Make sure that all lines and hoses have been removed from the rocker arm covers and position them out of the way.
3   Remove the PCV valve from the oil filler cap or rocker arm cover.
4   Remove the vacuum line and electric solenoid on 302 unleaded fuel engines.
5   Remove the vacuum solenoid mounted on the left rocker arm cover (if so equipped).
6   Disconnect the spark plug wires. Mark them so they can be installed in their original locations.
7   Remove the spark plug wires clipped to the rocker arm covers and position them out of the way.
8   Remove the clips retaining the wiring looms running along the left rocker arm cover.
9   Remove the rocker arm cover retaining bolts (photo).
10   Remove the rocker arm cover.
11   Remove all old gasket material and sealant from the rocker arm cover and cylinder head surfaces (photo).

12   Make sure the gasket surfaces of the rocker arm covers are flat and smooth, particularly around the bolt holes. Use a hammer and a block of wood to flatten them if they are deformed.
13   Attach a new rocker arm cover gasket to the cover. Notice that there are tabs provided in the cover to retain the gasket. It may be necessary to apply RTV-type gasket sealant to the corners of the cover to retain the gasket.
14   Install the rocker arm cover onto the cylinder head, making sure that the bolt holes are aligned correctly.
15   Install the rocker arm cover retaining bolts finger tight.
16   Working from the center of the rocker arm cover, tighten the retaining bolts to the correct torque. **Caution:** *Do not overtighten the bolts or the covers will warp and the gaskets will be pushed out of position, causing leaks.*
17   The remainder of the installation procedure is the reverse of removal.
18   Start the engine and run it until it reaches normal operating temperature, then make sure that there are no leaks.

3   Valve train components — replacement (cylinder head installed)

Note: *Broken valve springs and retainers or defective valve stem seals can be replaced without removing the cylinder head on engines that have no damage to the valves or valve seats. Two special tools and a compressed air source are required to perform this operation, so read through this Section carefully and rent or buy the tools before beginning this job.*

1   Remove the air cleaner.
2   Remove the accelerator cable return spring.
3   Remove the accelerator cable linkage at the carburetor.
4   Disconnect the choke cable at the carburetor.
5   Remove the PCV valve from the rocker arm cover and remove the rocker arm cover.
6   Remove the spark plug from the cylinder which has the bad component.
7   Turn the crankshaft until the piston in the cylinder with the bad component is almost at top dead center on the compression stroke.
8   Install an air line adapter which screws into the spark plug hole and connects to a compressed air source. Remove the rocker arm stud nut, fulcrum seat, rocker arm and pushrod (photo).
9   Apply compressed air to the cylinder.
10   Compress the valve spring with the valve spring tool.
11   Remove the keepers, spring retainer and valve spring, then remove the valve stem seal as shown in the accompanying illustration. **Note:** *If air pressure fails to hold the valve in the closed position during this operation there is probably damage to the seat or valve. If this condition exists, remove the cylinder head for further repair operations.*
12   Wrap a rubber band or tape around the top of the valve stem so

2.9   The rocker arm cover may be removed after first unscrewing the bolts around its perimeter

2.11   Being careful not to damage the mating surface of the cylinder head, carefully remove the rocker arm cover gasket with a gasket scraper or putty knife

that the valve will not fall through into the combustion chamber. Release the air pressure.

13   Inspect the valve stem for damage. Rotate the valve in its guide and check the valve stem tip for eccentric movement, which would indicate a bent valve.

14   Move the valve up and down through its normal travel and check that the valve guide and stem do not bind. If the valve stem binds, either the valve is bent or the guide is damaged and the head will have to be removed for repair.

15   Reapply air pressure to the cylinder to retain the valve in the closed position.

16   Lubricate the valve stem with engine oil and install a new valve stem seal.

17   Install the spring in position over the valve. Make sure that the closed coil end of the spring is correctly positioned against the cylinder head.

18   Install the valve spring retainer. Compress the valve spring and install the valve spring keepers. Remove the spring tool and make sure that the valve spring keepers are installed correctly.

19   Apply engine oil to both ends of the pushrod.

20   Install the pushrod.

21   Apply engine oil to the tip of the valve stem.

22   Apply engine oil to the fulcrum seat and socket.

23   Install the rocker arm, fulcrum seat and stud nut. Adjust the valve clearance following the procedure in Chapter 2E (no adjustment is necessary on 1979 models. Torque the valve fulcrum nut to the specified torque).

24   Remove the air source and the adapter from the spark plug hole.

25   Install the spark plug and connect the spark plug wire.

26   Install a new rocker arm cover gasket and attach the rocker arm cover to the engine.

27   Connect the accelerator cable to the carburetor.

28   Install the accelerator cable return spring. Connect the choke cable to the carburetor.

29   Install the PCV valve in the rocker arm cover and make sure that the line connected to the PCV valve is positioned correctly on both ends.

30   Install the air cleaner.

31   Start and run the engine, making sure that there are no oil leaks and that there are no unusual sounds coming from the valve assembly.

---

4   Manifolds — removal and installation

Intake manifold

Removal

Note: *Due to the weight and bulk of the large displacement engine intake manifolds, it is recommended that an engine hoist or puller device coupled with lifting hooks available from hardware stores be used to lift these manifolds from the engine. They can be removed by hand.*

Fig. 2D.7 Typical valve components used on Ford V8 engines (Sec 3)

However, the aid of a helper is suggested to avoid damaging engine components or causing personal injury.

1   Drain the cooling system.

2   Remove the air cleaner and intake duct assemblies.

3   Carefully mark and remove any emissions control connections at the air cleaner.

4   Disconnect the upper radiator hose from the thermostat housing and remove the thermostat housing.

5   Disconnect the heater hose and the water pump bypass hose at the intake manifold connections (photo).

6   Disconnect the spark plug wires at the spark plugs.

7   Unclip and remove the distributor cap together with the spark plug wires.

8   Disconnect the primary wiring leads to the coil and mark them so they can be reinstalled correctly.

3.8   Access to the pushrod and valve components can be gained by loosening the rocker arm bolt (arrow) and turning the rocker arm to the side

4.5   The heater hose (A) and water pump bypass hose (B) must be removed before removing the intake manifold

9   Remove the coil mounting bracket and mounting bolt (photo).
10 Remove the carburetor fuel inlet line from the carburetor and position it out of the way. It may be necessary to disconnect the line or loosen it at the fuel pump if the line is steel.
11 Disconnect the vacuum advance hose(s) from the distributor and mark them for proper installation.
12 Remove the distributor holddown bolt, then mark the position of the distributor and the rotor for correct installation (photo). Position the number one piston at top dead center when performing this operation (Section 9, Chapter 2E).
13 Remove the distributor from the engine, taking care that the distributor to oil pump driveshaft remains in the engine and connected to the oil pump. Plug the hole with a clean rag to prevent debris from entering the engine.
14 Remove the wire from the coolant temperature sender unit (photo).
15 Remove the wires from any sensors mounted in the intake manifold or the thermostat housing.
16 Remove the throttle cable or linkage connection at the carburetor (see Chapter 4).
17 Remove the kickdown cable at the carburetor if the vehicle is equipped with an automatic transmission.
18 Remove the pull cable and activating unit from the intake manifold if the vehicle is equipped with a cruise control unit.
19 Remove the vacuum hose leading to the power brake booster (photo). Secure this hose to the firewall, out of the way.
20 Remove the carburetor from the intake manifold if the carburetor is to be serviced separately.

21 Remove any wiring leading to components located on the intake manifold. Locate the wires where they won't be damaged.
22 Disconnect the crankcase vent hose leading from the manifold to the rocker arm cover.
23 Remove the bolts retaining the intake manifold to the cylinder heads.
24 Attach the lifting hooks at opposite corners and lift the intake manifold from the engine. It may be necessary to pry the manifold away from the cylinder heads. Use caution not to damage the mating surfaces.
25 Clean the mating surfaces of the intake manifold and cylinder heads. Take care not to allow any material to fall into the intake ports.
26 Remove the end gaskets from the top of the engine block.
27 Remove the oil gallery splash pan from the engine (if so equipped).

Disassembly and reassembly
255, 302, 351 and 400 cu in engines
28 If the manifold assembly is to be disassembled, identify all vacuum hoses before disconnecting them. Remove the coolant outlet housing gasket and the thermostat. Remove the ignition coil, temperature sending unit, carburetor (if not previously removed), spacer (on EEC engines remove the EGR cooler and related parts), gasket, vacuum fitting, accelerator return spring bracket and choke cable bracket.

460 cu in engine
29 If the manifold assembly is to be disassembled, identify all vacuum hoses before disconnecting them. Remove the coolant outlet housing, gasket and thermostat. Remove the automatic choke jet tubes, carbur-

4.9   The coil can be disconnected from the manifold by removing the bracket retaining bolt (arrow)

4.12   Mark the location of the distributor rotor before releasing the distributor holddown bolt (arrow) and removing the distributor

4.14   Coolant temperature sender electrical connector (7.5L engine shown)

4.19   The power brake booster vacuum hose connects to the intake manifold (arrow)

etor (if not previously removed), spacer and gaskets. Remove the thermostatic choke heater tube, the engine temperature sending unit and the EGR valve and gasket. Discard all gaskets.

Installation

30 If the manifold was disassembled, reassemble it by reversing the disassembly procedure. When installing the temperature sending unit, coat the threads with electrically conductive sealer and coat the thermostat gasket with water resistant sealer.

31 Apply RTV-type gasket sealant to the mating points at the junctions of the cylinder heads and engine block. **Note:** *Do not apply sealer to the waffle section of the end seals on 351W and 400 engines as the sealer will rupture the seals.*

32 Position new seals on the engine block and press the seal locating tabs into the holes in the mating surface as shown in the accompanying illustration. This is a very critical step as correct intake manifold sealing depends on the correct installation of these gaskets.

33 Apply RTV-type gasket sealant to the ends of the intake manifold seal as shown in the accompanying illustration. For 351W and 400 engines, see the note in Step 31.

34 Position the intake manifold gasket on the block and cylinder heads with the alignment notches fitting onto the dowels on the block (photo). Be sure that all of the holes in the gasket are aligned with the corresponding holes in the cylinder heads.

35 Lower the intake manifold into position using either a lift or two people, being careful not to disturb the gaskets. After the manifold is in place, run a finger around the seal area to make sure that the seals are in place. If the seals are not in place, remove the manifold and reposition the seals.

4.34   Align the new intake manifold gaskets by seating them over the dowel pins or studs in the cylinder head (arrows)

2D

Fig. 2D.8 Intake manifold gasket and seals (be sure the end seal locating tabs and pegs are completely seated before installing the manifold) (Sec 4)

Fig. 2D.9 RTV-type sealant must be applied to the locations shown before and after installing the intake manifold end seals (Sec 4)

36 Install the intake manifold retaining bolts finger tight. Tighten the intake manifold bolts in the sequence shown in the accompanying illustrations (note that different engines have different bolt tightening sequences). Work up to the final torque in three steps to avoid warping the manifold.
37 Install the remaining components in the reverse order of removal.
38 Start and run the engine and allow it to reach operating temperature. After it has reached operating temperature, check carefully for leaks.
39 Shut the engine off and retighten the manifolds while the engine is still warm.

Exhaust manifolds

Removal
40 If the right exhaust manifold is being removed, remove the air cleaner, intake duct and heat stove.
41 If the left exhaust manifold is being removed, remove the engine oil filter on 351M and 400 models. Remove the speed control bracket (if so equipped), and, on all engines except the 460, remove the oil dipstick and tube assembly.
42 On vehicles equipped with a column selector and automatic transmission, disconnect the cross lever shaft for the automatic transmission selector to provide the clearance necessary to remove the manifold.
43 Disconnect the retaining bolts holding the exhaust pipe to the exhaust manifolds.
44 Remove the spark plug heat shields if so equipped.

45 Remove the exhaust manifold retaining bolts.
46 Remove the exhaust manifold.
47 Clean the mating surfaces of the exhaust manifold and the cylinder head.
48 Clean the mounting flange of the exhaust manifold and the exhaust pipe.

Installation
49 Apply graphite grease to the mating surface of the exhaust manifold.
50 Position the exhaust manifold on the head and install the attaching bolts. Tighten the bolts to the specified torque in three steps, working from the center to the ends.
51 If so equipped, install the spark plug heat shields.
52 Install the gasket or spacer between the exhaust pipe and the exhaust manifold outlet.
53 Connect the exhaust pipe to the exhaust manifold using new retaining nuts.
54 Tighten the retaining nuts, making sure that the exhaust pipe is situated squarely in the exhaust manifold outlet.
55 Install the oil filter if the left exhaust manifold was removed (351M or 400 engine).
56 If removed, install the oil dipstick assembly.
57 Install the automatic transmission selector cross shaft at the chassis and the engine block if the vehicle is equipped with a column shifter.
58 If the right exhaust manifold was replaced, install the air cleaner heat stove, air cleaner and intake duct.
59 Start the engine and check for exhaust leaks.

Fig. 2D.10 Intake manifold tightening sequence — 4.2L, 5.0L and 5.8LW engines (Sec 4)

Fig. 2D.11 Intake manifold bolt tightening sequence — 5.8LM and 6.6L engines (Sec 4)

Fig. 2D.12 Intake manifold bolt tightening sequence — 7.5L engine (Sec 4)

Fig. 2D.13 Typical right exhaust manifold and heat shroud (Sec 4)

5   Rocker arms and pushrods — removal and installation

Removal

1   Remove the rocker arm covers as described in Section 2.
2   Remove the rocker arm fulcrum bolts.
3   Remove the oil deflectors (351M, 400 and 460 engines only), fulcrums, fulcrum guides (255, 302 and 351W engines only) and the rocker arms. If only the pushrods are being removed, loosen the fulcrum retaining bolts and rotate the rocker arms out of the way of the pushrods.

Installation

4   Apply engine oil or assembly lube to the top of the valve stem and the pushrod guide in the cylinder head.
5   Apply engine oil to the rocker arm fulcrum seat and the fulcrum seat socket in the rocker arm.
6   Install the pushrods.
7   Install the fulcrum guides (255, 302 and 351W engines only), rocker arms, fulcrums, oil deflector (351M and 400 engines only) and fulcrum bolts or nuts.
8   Tighten the fulcrum bolts or nuts to the specified torque.
9   Replace the rocker arm covers and gaskets as described in Section 2.
10   Start the engine and check for roughness and/or noise. Refer to Section 23 of Chapter 2E for any corrections that may have to be made for either a rough running or excessively noisy engine.

6   Cylinder heads — removal and installation

Removal

1   Remove the intake manifold and carburetor as an assembly as described previously.
2   Remove the rocker arm covers.
3   If the left cylinder head is being removed on a vehicle equipped with factory air conditioning, detach the compressor and support it securely to the side of the engine compartment. **Caution:** *Do not disconnect the air conditioning hoses, as serious injury or damage to the system will result.*
4   If the left cylinder head is being removed and the vehicle is equipped with power steering, remove the power steering bracket retaining bolt from the left cylinder head.
5   Position the power steering pump out of the way so it will not leak fluid.
6   If the right cylinder head is being removed, remove the alternator mounting bracket through-bolt.
7   Remove the air cleaner inlet tube (if so equipped) from the right cylinder head.

8   Remove the ground wire connected to the rear of the cylinder head.
9   Disconnect the exhaust manifold retaining bolts.
10   Remove the rocker arms or rocker arm assemblies as described previously. Remove the pushrods. Be sure to mark them, as they will need to be reinstalled in their original locations (photo).
11   Loosen the cylinder head retaining bolts by reversing the order shown in the tightening sequence diagram, then remove the bolts from the heads. Keep them in order so they can be installed in their original locations.
12   Using a hoist (or two people), carefully remove the cylinder head from the block, using care to avoid damaging the gasket mating surfaces (photo).
13   For cylinder head inspection procedures, see Chapter 2, Part E.

Installation

14   Make sure that the cylinder head and engine block mating surfaces are clean and flat.
15   Position a new head gasket over the dowel pins on the block. Make sure that the head gasket is facing the right direction and that the correct surface is exposed. Gaskets are sometimes marked *front* and *top*.
16   Using a hoist (or two people), carefully lower the cylinder head into place on the block. Take care not to move the head sideways or scrape it across the block as it can dislodge the gasket and/or damage the gasket surfaces.

6.10   A perforated cardboard box provides ideal pushrod storage

6.12   Recommended method of attaching the hoist to the cylinder head for removal

6.15   Be certain that the cylinder head gaskets are correctly positioned right side up (note the *Front* mark on the type used here)

2D

17 Coat the cylinder head retaining bolts with light engine oil and thread them into the block.
18 Tighten the bolts finger tight.
19 Tighten the bolts in the sequence shown in the accompanying illustration. Work up gradually in three steps to the final torque, going through the pattern completely on each step.
20 Apply engine oil to the rocker arm fulcrum seat and sockets or the rocker arm assemblies.
21 The remainder of the installation procedure is the reverse of removal.
22 Start and run the engine and check carefully for leaks and unusual noises.

7 Engine front cover and timing chain — removal and installation

Removal
1 Drain the cooling system.
2 Remove the screws attaching the radiator shroud to the radiator.
3 Remove the bolts attaching the fan to the water pump shaft.
4 Remove the fan and the radiator shroud.
5 Disconnect the upper radiator hose at the thermostat housing.
6 Disconnect the lower radiator hose at the water pump outlet.
7 Disconnect the transmission oil cooler lines at the radiator (if so equipped) (photo).

Fig. 2D.14 Cylinder head bolt tightening sequence — all models (Sec 6)

8 Loosen the alternator mounting and adjusting bolts to relieve the tension on the drivebelt. If the vehicle is equipped with air conditioning, loosen the air conditioning idler pulley.
9 Remove the air pump.
10 Remove the drivebelts and the water pump pulley.
11 Remove the bolt attaching the air conditioning compressor support, water pump and compressor. Remove the compressor support.
Caution: *Do not loosen or remove the air conditioning hoses, as serious personal injury or damage to the system could result.*

7.7 A flare-nut wrench is recommended for disconnecting the transmission oil cooler lines from the radiator

7.14 Remove the crankshaft damper with a puller as shown

7.20 Fuel pump location (7.5L shown)

7.21 When removing the engine front cover, remove only those bolts from the oil pan that attach directly to the cover

12 Remove the bolts and washers retaining the crankshaft pulley to the vibration damper. Remove the crankshaft pulley.

13 Remove the large bolt and washer retaining the damper to the crankshaft.

14 Remove the crankshaft damper with a puller (photo).

15 Remove the bypass hose from the top of the water pump.

16 Disconnect the heater return hose or tube at the water pump.

17 Remove and plug the fuel line at the fuel pump.

18 Disconnect the fuel line at the carburetor.

19 Remove the fuel feed line from the fuel pump.

20 Remove the fuel pump (photo).

21 Remove the retaining bolts holding the timing cover to the engine block and those holding the oil pan to the timing cover (photo).

22 Use a thin blade knife or similar tool to cut the oil pan seal flush with the engine block mating surface (photo).

23 Remove the timing cover and water pump as an assembly.

24 Remove the timing cover gasket and oil pan seal.

25 Remove the water pump from the timing cover if the cover is being replaced with a new one.

26 Check the timing chain deflection by rotating the crankshaft in a counterclockwise direction to take up the slack on the left side of the chain (photo).

27 Establish a reference point on the block and use a ruler to check the distance from the reference point to the left side of the chain.

28 Rotate the crankshaft in the opposite direction to take up the slack on the opposite (or right) side of the chain.

29 Force the left side of the chain out and measure the distance between the reference point and the chain. This will give you the deflection. If the deflection exceeds 1/2-inch, the timing chain and sprockets should be replaced with new parts.

30 If the timing chain and sprockets are being removed, turn the engine until the timing marks are aligned as shown in the accompanying illustration.

31 Remove the camshaft sprocket retaining bolt, washer, fuel pump eccentric (two-piece on 460 engines) and front oil slinger (if present) from the crankshaft.

32 Slide the timing chain and sprockets forward and off of the camshaft and crankshaft as an assembly (photo).

Installation

33 Assemble the timing chain and sprockets so the timing marks are in alignment.

34 Install the chain and sprockets onto the camshaft and crankshaft as an assembly. Make sure that the timing marks remain in proper alignment during the installation procedure.

35 Install the oil slinger (if so equipped) over the nose of the crankshaft.

36 Install the fuel pump eccentric, camshaft sprocket retaining bolt and washer. Tighten the retaining bolt to the proper torque. Lubricate the timing chain and gears with engine oil.

37 Clean the old gasket material from the gasket mating surface on the oil pan.

38 Coat the gasket surface of the oil pan with RTV-type gasket sealant.

2D

7.22 Be careful not to destroy the front cover to oil pan gasket during removal — it will be used to cut matching pieces from the new gasket

7.26 Checking the timing chain deflection (note that the timing chain here is extremely stretched and will be replaced with a new one)

Fig. 2D.15 Aligning timing gear marks before removing the timing chain assembly (Sec 7)

7.32 Remove both timing gears and the chain as a unit (be sure to align the timing gear marks first)

Cut and position the required sections of new front cover to oil pan seal on the oil pan.

39 Apply sealant at the corners of the mating surfaces (photo).

40 Coat the gasket surfaces of the cover with sealant and install a new gasket. Coat the mating surface on the block with sealant.

41 Position the timing cover on the block after installing a new front crankshaft seal.

42 Use care when installing the cover to avoid damaging the front crankshaft seal.

43 Install the cover alignment tool to position the cover properly. If no alignment tool is available you will have to use the crankshaft pulley to position the seal. It may be necessary to force the cover down slightly to compress the oil pan seal. This can be done by inserting a punch into the retaining bolt holes.

44 Coat the threads of the retaining bolts with RTV-type sealant and install them.

45 While holding the cover in alignment, tighten the oil pan to front cover retaining bolts.

46 Remove the alignment punch.

47 Tighten the retaining bolts holding the cover to the engine block.

48 Apply a thin coat of grease to the vibration damper seal contact surface.

49 Install the crankshaft spacer.

50 Install the Woodruff key in the crankshaft and slide the crankshaft damper into position.

51 Install the crankshaft damper retaining bolt and washer.

52 This bolt may be used to push the damper onto the crankshaft if the proper installation tool is not available.

53 Attach the crankshaft pulley to the damper and install the pulley retaining bolts.

54 Install the fuel pump with a new gasket.

55 Connect the fuel lines to the fuel pump.

56 The remainder of the installation procedure is the reverse of removal. Make sure that all bolts are tightened securely.

57 If any coolant entered the oil pan when separating the timing chain cover from the block, the crankcase oil should be changed and the oil filter replaced.

58 Start and run the engine at a fast idle and check for coolant and oil leaks.

59 Check the engine idle speed and ignition timing.

7.39 Before positioning the new pan gasket pieces, apply a bead of RTV-type sealant at the junction of the oil pan and block as shown

8 Camshaft and lifters — removal and installation

Removal

1 After marking the hoses to simplify installation and disconnecting them, remove the air cleaner.

2 Remove the intake manifold (see Section 4).

3 Remove the rocker arm covers (see Section 2).

4 Loosen the rocker arm nuts and rotate the rocker arms to the side.

5 Mark the pushrods if they are to be reused and remove them from the engine.

6 Remove the valve lifters from the engine using a special tool designed for this purpose. Sometimes they can be removed with a magnet if there is no varnish build up or wear on them. If they are stuck in their bores, you will have to obtain a special tool designed for grasping lifters internally and work them out.

Fig. 2D.16 Typical camshaft and related components — exploded view (Sec 8)

Fig. 2D.17 If your vehicle has a dual-sump pan, as shown, drain the oil from both plugs before removing the pan (Sec 9)

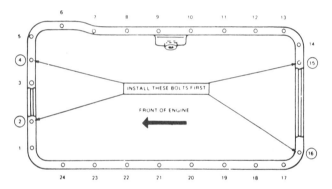

Fig. 2D.18 Oil pan bolt tightening sequence (Sec 9)

Fig. 2D.19 Typical V8 oil pump and inlet tube/screen assembly (Sec 10)

7   Remove the timing cover, chain and gears (see Section 7).
8   Remove the grille.
9   Remove the radiator (see Chapter 3).
10   Remove the retaining bolts securing the camshaft and thrust plate to the engine block.
11   Slowly withdraw the camshaft from the engine, being careful not to damage the bearings with the cam lobes.
12   See Chapter 2, Part E for camshaft and lifter inspection procedures.

Installation

13   Lubricate the camshaft journals with engine oil and apply engine assembly lube to the cam lobes.
14   Slide the camshaft into position, being careful not to scrape or nick the bearings.
15   Install the camshaft thrust plate. Tighten the thrust plate retaining bolts to the proper torque.
16   Check the camshaft endplay by pushing it toward the rear of the engine.
17   Install a dial indicator so that the stem is on the camshaft sprocket attaching bolt. Zero the dial indicator.
18   Position a large screwdriver between the camshaft gear and the block. **Note:** *Do not pry against aluminum or nylon camshaft sprockets when any type of valve train load is on the camshaft, as damage to the sprocket can result.*
19   Pull the camshaft forward with the screwdriver and release it.
20   Compare the dial indicator reading to the specifications listed in Part E of this Chapter.
21   If the endplay is excessive, check the spacer for correct installation before it is removed. If the spacer is installed correctly, replace the thrust plate. Notice that the thrust plate has a groove on it, which should face *IN* on all engines.
22   Check the timing chain deflection as described in Section 7.
23   Install the hydraulic valve lifters in their original bores if the old ones are being used. Make sure they are coated with engine assembly lube. Never use old lifters with a new camshaft.
24   The remainder of the installation procedure is the reverse of removal.

2D

9   Oil pan — removal and installation

Removal

1   Due to clearance limitations, we recommend that the engine be removed from the vehicle before attempting to remove the oil pan. See Section 13 for engine removal procedures.
2   Drain the oil from the pan. Note that some oil pans have two drain plugs, as shown in the accompanying illustration, and both must be removed.
3   With the engine removed and mounted on a suitable stand, remove the oil pan bolts.
4   Remove the oil pan from the engine.
5   Clean all old gasket material from the mating surfaces of the engine block and the pan.

Installation

6   Remove the rear main bearing cap oil seal.
7   Remove the timing cover oil seal.
8   Clean all mating surfaces and seal grooves.
9   Install new oil pan front cover oil seals.
10   Install a new rear main bearing cap oil seal.
11   Install new oil pan side gaskets on the block. Apply a thin coat of RTV-type gasket seal to both sides of the gaskets.
12   Make sure the tabs of the front and rear seal fit properly into the mating slots on the oil pan side seals. A small amount of RTV-type gasket sealant at each mating junction will help prevent leaks at these critical spots.
13   Attach the oil pan to the engine block and install the retaining bolts. Tighten the bolts to the specified torque, starting from the center and working out in each direction as shown in the accompanying illustration.

10   Oil pump — removal and installation

1   Remove the oil pan as described in Section 9.
2   Remove the bolts retaining the oil pump to the block.

Fig. 2D.20 Removing the front main oil seal on some engines requires the use of a special Ford tool (Sec 11)

Tool – T68P-6700-A

Fig. 2D.21 The front main oil seal may be installed as shown with the special Ford tool, or a large socket may be used to drive the seal into position (Sec 11)

3   Remove the oil pump assembly.
4   Clean the mating surfaces of the oil pump and the block.
5   Before installation, prime the pump by filling the inlet opening with oil and rotating the pump shaft until oil spurts out of the outlet.
6   Attach the oil pump to the engine block using the two retaining bolts.
7   Tighten the bolts to the proper torque.
8   Install the oil pan by referring to Section 9.

11   Crankshaft oil seals - replacement

Front seal
1   Remove the timing chain cover (see Section 1).
2   On all engines except 351M and 400, tap the front crankshaft seal out using a drive tool. **Note:** *The front oil seal should be replaced with a new one whenever the cover is removed.*
3   Clean the grooves in the front cover.
4   Install the new front oil seal using a special drive tool (or a large drift if the drive tool is not available). If you are using a large drift, be very careful not to damage the front seal. Make sure that the spring remains positioned inside the front seal.
5   On 351M/400 engines, remove the front seal using the special puller as shown in the accompanying illustration.
6   Clean the crankshaft front seal groove.
7   Install the new seal using the special drive tool or an appropriate size socket as shown in the accompanying illustration.

Rear seal – two-piece
8   The oil pan and oil pump must be removed to gain access to the seal (Section 9). See Chapter 2E for further information on the rear seal.
9   Loosen the main bearing cap bolts slightly to allow the crankshaft to drop no more than 1/32 inch.
10   Remove the rear main bearing cap and detach the oil seal from the cap. To remove the portion of the rear main seal housed in the block, install a small sheet metal screw in one end of the seal and pull on the screw to rotate the seal out of the groove. Exercise extreme

caution during this procedure to prevent scratching or damaging the crankshaft seal surfaces.
11   Carefully clean the seal grooves in the cap and block with a brush dipped in solvent.
12   Dip both new seal halves in clean engine oil.
13   For further installation procedures, see Chapter 2E.
14   Install the oil pan and oil pump.
15   The remainder of the installation procedure is the reverse of removal.

Rear seal – one-piece
16   The transmission ane flywheel or flexplate must be removed to gain access to the one-piece seal (refer to Chapter 7).
17   Refer to Chapter 2E, Section 20, to complete the procedure.

12   Engine mounts - replacement

1   Disconnect the negative cable from the battery.
2   Disconnect the throttle linkage from the carburetor on vehicles equipped with mechanical linkage.
3   Disconnect the fuel supply hose from the fuel tank line at the fuel pump. **Caution:** *Observe all precautions for working with flammable liquids (gasoline) when performing this operation.*
4   On vehicles equipped with an automatic transmission, remove the transmission cooler lines from the mounting clips located on the side of the engine block. Make sure that the lines are free from the engine, as the engine will have to be raised several inches to replace the mounts. Disconnect the clutch cross shaft on manual transmission equipped vehicles.
5   Disconnect the lower radiator hose from the radiator.
6   Disconnect the upper radiator hose from the radiator.
7   Disconnect the engine mount retaining nuts from the connecting studs at the insulator.
8   If the rear mount is being changed, make sure that the speedometer cable, driveshaft, and transmission linkage will not bind or contact the body as the transmission is being raised.
9   Raise the engine (or transmission) using a jack and a block of wood underneath the oil pan. Make sure that the engine mounts do not bind as the engine is raised off the insulator assembly.
10   Disconnect the engine mounts from the engine.
11   Install the new mounts on the engine, as shown in the accompanying illustration, making sure that the bolts are tightened to the proper torque.
12   Lower the engine back onto the insulators, making sure that the stud lines up with and falls into the hole provided in the engine mount insulator on the frame crossmember.
13   Attach the insulator retaining nut and lock washer. Tighten this nut to the proper torque (see accompanying illustration).
14   Assembly is the reverse of disassembly. Make certain that all linkages are attached securely and adjusted properly.

Fig. 2D.22 Typical engine front supports (Sec 12)

Fig. 2D.24 Engine rear support — Thunderbird only (Sec 12)

Fig. 2D.23 Typical engine rear support — all models except
Thunderbird (Sec 12)

2D

---

13   Engine — removal and installation

Note: *The engine must be removed with the transmission remaining in place in the vehicle. Also, due to the wide range of vehicle models and engines covered by this manual, the following instructions are general in nature and may include some steps not applicable to your vehicle.*

Removal

1   Remove the battery cables (negative first, then positive) from the battery.
2   Mark the position of the hood with a scribe or marking pen so it can be installed in the same position.
3   Remove the hood and cover the fenders for protection.
4   Remove the air cleaner and related emissions control components and supply hoses. Cover the carburetor inlet with a clean cloth.
5   Remove all vacuum lines from the intake manifold area. All lines and hoses should be clearly marked to prevent confusion when the engine is being installed.
6   Remove the fuel feed hose from the fuel pump. Use caution when performing this step as gasoline is flammable. All precautions pertaining to flammable liquids should be observed.
7   Plug the feed hose with a golf tee or a pencil to prevent fuel leakage.
8   Disconnect the wires at the rear of the engine and mark them clearly with numbered tape to simplify installation. In many cases there will be a large multi-wired connector. However, some vehicles will be equipped with individual wires leading to components such as the ignition coil and emissions control related items.
9   Remove the starter cable from the starter and position the cable out of the way.
10   Remove the spark plug wires and distributor cap as a unit.
11   Remove the choke cable from the carburetor.
12   Disconnect the transmission kickdown cable or linkage from the carburetor and the transmission bellhousing.
13   Disconnect the throttle linkage from the carburetor and the accelerator pedal (Chapter 3).
14   Remove the throttle linkage return spring.
15   Drain the engine oil and remove the oil filter.
16   Drain the coolant from the engine and radiator.
17   Remove the heater hoses from the water pump and intake manifold.
18   Secure the heater hoses out of the way.
19   Remove the radiator hoses from the engine.
20   Remove the radiator hoses from the radiator if there is not enough clearance for the radiator to be removed with the hoses still in place.
21   Remove the fan shroud from the radiator and slide it back over the fan assembly.
22   Remove the transmission cooler lines (if so equipped) from the bottom of the radiator.
23   Loosen the alternator adjusting bolt and remove the drivebelt from the pulleys.
24   Remove all other drivebelts attached to the water pump/fan drive pulley.
25   Remove the bolts retaining the fan and spacer (or the fan clutch assembly) to the water pump.
26   Remove the fan assembly and shroud by lifting them straight up and out of the engine compartment.
27   Remove the radiator to saddle retaining bolts and remove the radiator.
28   Remove the alternator retaining bolt and position the alternator and wiring out of the way. It is important to secure the alternator in place with a wire to prevent damage to the wiring connector at the rear of the alternator. Never allow the alternator to hang from the wiring.
29   In some cases the air conditioning system will not need to be discharged since the hoses leading to the compressor unit are long enough for it to be swung out of the way and secured to the fender well.
30   Disconnect the air conditioning hoses only if the system has been discharged. Remember that the system can only be discharged by a qualified specialist.
31   Remove the air conditioning compressor from the mounting brackets and secure it out of the way.
32   Remove the power steering pump belt.

33   Remove the power steering pump from the mounting bracket and position it out of the way. **Note:** *The following procedures must be performed with the vehicle raised. Make sure that it is supported securely on jackstands.*
34   Remove the starter (Chapter 5).
35   Remove the automatic transmission dipstick tube retaining bolt from the rear of the cylinder head (if applicable).
36   Remove the automatic transmission dipstick and tube.
37   Remove the lower bellhousing retaining bolts.
38   Remove the engine mount to frame insulator retaining nuts.
39   Support the transmission assembly securely.
40   Remove the flywheel inspection cover.
41   Remove the torque converter drain plug cover (if so equipped).
42   Remove the torque converter to flexplate retaining nuts. The crankshaft will have to be rotated 90° at a time to position each retaining nut for removal.
43   Remove the bolts holding the exhaust pipes to the exhaust manifold.
44   Remove the exhaust pipes from the exhaust manifold.
45   Remove the upper bellhousing retaining bolts.
46   Lower the vehicle and make sure the transmission is solidly supported.
47   Install a lifting sling or chain. There are several methods which can be used to accomplish this. Metal eye hooks can be attached with bolts positioned at diagonally opposite corners of the cylinder heads. Make sure that the bolts attaching the items are threaded well into the heads to prevent thread damage when the engine is lifted.
48   A sling can be fashioned from a short piece of chain connected to open-end hooks. A cable and bracket arrangement will also work well (photo).
49   Raise the engine high enough for the engine mount studs to clear the frame bracket insulators.
50   Double check all attachment points to ensure that all the retaining bolts holding the engine to the transmission or frame have been removed.
51   Separate the engine from the bellhousing or torque converter housing, making sure that the flywheel/clutch assembly pulls straight out of the housing without binding. You may need to adjust the engine height and angle for the two components to separate. A small wedge-type tool can be used between the housing and the engine block to separate them. However, if you feel any resistance make sure no retaining bolts are left in the engine. Do not force any parts during this removal procedure. If the engine is stuck to the transmission assembly, fasteners are probably still holding them together.
52   Pull the engine straight forward and away from the transmission.
53   Take care not to damage the transmission input shaft while performing this step.
54   When the input shaft or torque converter has completely cleared the clutch assembly or flexplate, raise the engine and remove it from the engine compartment. There should be no connections between the engine and the vehicle.
55   Place the engine on an engine stand for disassembly.

Installation
56   Lift the engine off the engine stand with a hoist. The chains should be positioned as they were during removal.
57   Lower the engine into place inside the engine compartment watching clearances closely. On manual transmissions, carefully guide the engine onto the transmission input shaft. The two components should be at the same angle with the shaft sliding easily into the engine.
58   Install the engine mount bolts and the bellhousing bolts.
59   Install the remaining engine components in the reverse order of removal.
60   Fill the cooling system with the proper coolant and water mixture (Chapter 1).
61   Fill the engine with the correct grade of engine oil (Chapter 1).
62   Connect the positive battery cable, followed by the negative battery cable. If sparks or arcing occur as the negative cable is connected to the battery, check that all electrical accessories are turned off (check the dome light first). If arcing still occurs, check that all electrical wiring

13.48   Lifting the engine from the vehicle will require a hoist, attached to the engine as shown (an assistant will be necessary to guide the engine past points of limited clearance)

is properly connected to the engine and transmission.
63   See Chapter 2, Part E, for initial engine start-up and break-in procedures.

14   Flywheel — removal, inspection and installation

Note: *These instructions are valid only if the engine has been removed from the vehicle. If the engine is still in the vehicle, the transmission, the bellhousing and clutch assembly must be removed to expose the flywheel (refer to Chapter 7). Automatic transmission equipped vehicles are equipped with a flexplate rather than a flywheel. It can be separated from the crankshaft by removing the mounting bolts. If the ring gear teeth are worn or damaged or if the flywheel or flexplate is damaged, replace it with a new one and tighten the mounting bolts to the specified torque.*

1   Mark the flywheel and the crankshaft end with a centerpunch to ensure installation in the same relative position.
2   To keep the crankshaft from turning, wedge a large screwdriver or pry bar between the ring gear teeth and the engine block (it must be positioned so that as the crankshaft moves, the tool bears against the block). Make sure that the tool is not pushing against the oil pan. Another method of preventing crankshaft rotation involves holding the front pulley retaining bolt with a large wrench or socket and breaker bar. This method may require a helper. **Caution:** *Support the flywheel before performing the following step as it could fall off and be damaged or cause injury.*
3   Remove the flywheel retaining bolts from the crankshaft flange.
4   Remove the flywheel from the crankshaft by pulling straight back on it.
5   Inspect the flywheel clutch disc mating surface for scoring, heat marks, cracks or warpage. If any of these conditions exist, the flywheel should be taken to an automotive machine shop to be resurfaced (or replaced with a new one). If the flywheel is cracked, it must be replaced with a new one.
6   Installation is the reverse of removal. The retaining bolts should be coated with a thread-locking compound and tightened in a criss-cross pattern to the prescribed torque.

Chapter 2 Part E
General engine overhaul procedures

Refer to Chapter 13 for specifications related to 1985 and later models

Contents

2E

Specifications

2.3L (140 ci) inline four-cylinder engines
Cylinder head

Valve seat width	
Intake	0.060 to 0.080 in
Exhaust	0.070 to 0.90 in
Valve seat angle	45°
Valve stem runout limit	0.0016 in
Valve arrangement (front to rear)	E-I-E-I-E-I-E-I
Lifter bore diameter	0.8430 to 0.9449 in
Valve stem-to-guide clearance	
Intake	0.0010 to 0.0027 in
Exhaust	0.0015 to 0.0032 in
Service limit	0.0055 in max.
Valve face runout limit	0.002 in max.
Valve face angle	44°
Valve stem diameter (standard)	
Intake	0.3416 to 0.3423 in
Exhaust	0.3411 to 0.3418 in
Valve stem diameter (0.015 oversize)	
Intake	0.3566 to 0.3573 in
Exhaust	0.3561 to 0.3568 in
Valve stem diameter (0.030 oversize)	
Intake	0.3716 to 0.3723 in
Exhaust	0.3711 to 0.3718 in
Valve springs	
1975 through 1977 compression pressure	
Intake	71 to 79 lbs @ 1.56 in
Exhaust	180 to 198 lbs @ 1.16 in
All others	
Intake	71 to 79 lbs @ 1.56 in
Exhaust	159 to 175 lbs @ 1.16 in
Free length (approximate)	1.89 in
Installed height	1.530 in to 1.590 in
Service limit	10% pressure loss @ specified length
Out-of-square limit	0.078 in

2.3L (140 ci) inline four-cylinder engines (continued)

Valve lifters
Diameter (standard)	0.8422 to 0.8427 in
Clearance to bore	0.0007 to 0.0027 in
Service limit	0.005 in max.
Collapsed tappet gap	
Allowable	0.035 to 0.055 in at cam
Desired	0.040 to 0.050 in at cam

Camshaft
Lobe lift	
1975 through 1983	
Intake	0.2437 in
Exhaust	0.2437 in
1984	
Intake	0.2381 in
Exhaust	0.2381 in
Allowable lobe lift loss	0.005 in max.
Theoretical valve lift @ zero lash	
Intake	0.3997 in
Exhaust	0.3997 in
Endplay	0.001 to 0.007 in
Service limit	0.009 in
Bearing clearance	0.001 to 0.003 in
Service limit	0.006 in
Journal diameter	
No. 1	1.7713 to 1.7720 in
No. 2	1.7713 to 1.7720 in
No. 3	1.7713 to 1.7720 in
No. 4	1.7713 to 1.7720 in
Runout limit	0.005 in
Out-of-round limit	0.0005 in
Front bearing location	0.000 to 0.010 in below front face of bearing tower

Cylinder block
Head gasket surface flatness	0.003 in for any 6 inch span to 0.006 overall
Cylinder bore	
Diameter	3.7795 to 3.7831 in
Out-of-round	0.0015 in
Out-of-round limit	0.005 in
Taper limit	0.0010 in

Crankshaft and flywheel
Main bearing journal diameter	2.399 to 2.3982 in
Out-of-round limit	0.0006 in max.
Taper limit	0.006 in per inch
Journal runout limit	0.002 in max.
Runout service limit	0.005 in
Connecting rod journal	
Diameter	2.0462 to 2.0472 in
Out-of-round limit	0.0006 in max.
Taper limit	0.0006 in per inch max.
Main bearing thrust face	
Runout limit	0.001 in max.
Crankshaft end play	0.004 to 0.008 in
Service limit	0.012 in
Auxiliary shaft end play	0.001 to 0.007 in
Connecting rod bearing oil clearance	
Desired	0.0008 to 0.0015 in
Allowable	0.0008 to 0.0026 in
Main bearing oil clearance	
Desired	0.0008 to 0.0015 in
Allowable	0.0008 to 0.0026 in
Auxiliary shaft bearing oil clearance	0.0006 to 0.0026 in

Connecting rods, pistons and rings
Connecting rod piston pin bore diameter	
1977 through 1981	0.9123 to 0.9126 in
1982 through 1984	0.9096 to 0.9012 in
Side clearance	
Standard	0.0035 to 0.0105 in
Service limit	0.014 in
Piston Diameter	
1975 through 1983	
Coded red	3.7780 to 3.7786 in

Coded blue	3.7792 to 3.7798 in
0.003 in oversize	3.7804 to 3.7810 in
Piston-to-bore clearance	0.0014 to 0.0022 in
Diameter (1984)	
Coded red	3.7764 to 3.7770 in
Coded blue	3.7776 to 3.7782 in
0.003 oversize	3.7788 to 3.7794 in
Piston-to-bore clearance	0.0030 to 0.0038 in
Pin bore diameter	0.9123 to 0.9126 in
Piston pin diameter	
Standard	0.9119 to 0.9124 in
0.001 oversize	0.9130 to 0.9133 in
0.002 oversize	0.9140 to 0.9143 in
Piston-to-pin clearance	0.002 to 0.004 in
Pin-to-rod clearance	Interference fit
Piston ring side clearance	
Compression (top)	0.002 to 0.004 in
Compression (bottom)	0.002 to 0.004 in
Oil ring	Snug fit
Service limit	0.006 in max.
Ring gap	
Compression (top)	0.010 to 0.020 in
Compression (bottom)	0.010 to 0.020 in
Oil (steel rail)	0.015 to 0.055 in

Oil pump

Relief valve spring tension	15.2 to 17.2 lbs @ 1.20 in
Driveshaft-to-housing bearing clearance	0.0015 to 0.0030 in
Relief valve-to-bore clearance	0.0015 to 0.0030 in
Rotor assembly end clearance (assembled)	0.004 in max.
Outer race-to-housing clearance	0.001 to 0.0013 in
Oil pressure (hot at 2000 rpm)	40 to 60 psi

Torque specifications   **Ft-lbs**

Auxiliary shaft gear bolt	28 to 40
Auxiliary shaft thrust plate bolt	6 to 9
Camshaft gear bolt	50 to 71
Camshaft thrust plate bolt	6 to 9
Connecting rod nut	
Step 1	25 to 30
Step 2	30 to 36
Crankshaft damper bolt	100 to 120
Flywheel-to-crankshaft bolt	56 to 64
Main bearing cap bolt	
Step 1	50 to 60
Step 2	80 to 90

3.3L (200 ci) inline six-cylinder engine
Cylinder head and valve train

Valve seat width	
Intake	0.060 to 0.080 in
Exhaust	0.070 to 0.090 in
Valve face runout limit	0.002 in max.
Valve seat angle	44°
Valve arrangement (front to rear)	E-I-I-E-I-E-E-I-E-I-I-E
Valve stem-to-guide clearance	
Intake	0.0008 to 0.0025 in
Exhaust	0.0010 to 0.0027 in
Service limit	0.0055 in
Valve stem diameter (standard)	
Intake	0.3100 to 0.3107 in
Exhaust	0.3098 to 0.3105 in
Valve stem diameter (0.015 in oversize)	
Intake	0.3250 to 0.3257 in
Exhaust	0.3248 to 0.3255 in
Valve stem diameter (0.030 in oversize)	
Intake	0.3400 to 0.3407 in
Exhaust	0.3398 to 0.3405 in
Valve spring pressure	
Intake	51 to 57 lbs @ 1.59 in
Exhaust	142 to 158 lbs @ 1.222 in
Free length (approximate)	1.79 in
Service limit	10% pressure loss @ spec length
Out-of-square limit	0.078 in

3.3L (200 ci) inline six-cylinder engines (continued)

Rocker arm
    Shaft diameter . . . . 0.7797 to 0.7807 in
    Bore diameter . . . . 0.7830 to 0.7845 in
    Pushrod runout . . . . 0.020 in
Valve lifter
    Diameter (standard) . . . . 0.8740 to 0.8745 in
    Clearance-in-bore . . . . 0.0007 to 0.0027 in
    Service limit . . . . 0.005 in max.
Allowable collapsed gap . . . . 0.085 to 0.209 in
Desired gap . . . . 0.110 to 0.184 in
Camshaft lobe lift
    Intake . . . . 0.245 in
    Exhaust . . . . 0.245 in
    Allowable lobe lift loss . . . . 0.005 in max.
Endplay . . . . 0.001 to 0.007 in
Service limit . . . . 0.009 in
Bearing oil clearance . . . . 0.001 to 0.003 in
Service limit . . . . 0.006 in
Journal diameter (all) . . . . 1.8095 to 1.8105 in
Runout limit . . . . 0.005 in
Front bearing location . . . . 0.110 to 0.130 in below front face of block
Camshaft bearing inside diameter (all) . . . . 1.8115 to 1.8125 in

Cylinder block
Head gasket surface flatness . . . . 0.003 in in any 6 inches; 0.006 in overall
Cylinder bore
    Diameter . . . . 3.6800 to 3.6848 in
    Out-of-round limit . . . . 0.0015 in
    Out-of-round service limit . . . . 0.005 in
    Taper service limit . . . . 0.010 in
Lifter bore diameter . . . . 0.8752 to 0.8767 in

Crankshaft and flywheel
Main bearing journal diameter . . . . 2.2482 to 2.2490 in
    Out-of-round limit . . . . 0.0006 in max.
    Taper limit . . . . 0.0006 in per inch
    Journal runout . . . . 0.002 in max.
    Runout limit . . . . 0.005 in
Connecting rod journal
    Diameter . . . . 2.1232 to 2.1240 in
    Out-of-round limit . . . . 0.0006 in max.
    Taper limit . . . . 0.006 in per inch
Main bearing thrust face
    Runout limit . . . . 0.001 in max.
    Crankshaft end play . . . . 0.004 to 0.008 in
    Service limit . . . . 0.012 in
Connecting rod bearing oil clearance
    Desired . . . . 0.0008 to 0.0015 in
    Allowable . . . . 0.0008 to 0.0024 in
Main bearing oil clearance
    Desired . . . . 0.0008 to 0.0015 in
    Allowable . . . . 0.0008 to 0.0024 in

Connecting rods, pistons and rings
Connecting rod piston pin bore diameter . . . . 0.9104 to 0.9112 in
Side clearance
    Standard . . . . 0.0035 in to 0.0105 in
    Service limit . . . . 0.014 in
Piston diameter
    Coded red . . . . 3.6784 to 3.6790 in
    Coded blue . . . . 3.6808 to 3.6814 in
Piston-to-bore clearance . . . . 0.0013 to 0.0021 in
Pin bore diameter . . . . 0.9124 to 0.9127 in
Piston pin length . . . . 3.010 to 3.040 in
Pin Diameter
    Standard . . . . 0.9119 to 0.9124 in
    0.001 in oversize . . . . 0.9130 to 0.9133 in
Pin-to-rod clearance . . . . Interference fit
Piston ring side clearance
    Compression (top) . . . . 0.002 to 0.004 in
    Compression (bottom) . . . . 0.002 to 0.004 in
    Oil ring . . . . Snug fit
    Service limit . . . . 0.006 in

Ring gap
    Compression (top) . . . .   0.008 to 0.016 in
    Compression (bottom) . . . .   0.008 to 0.016 in
    Oil ring (steel rail) . . . .   0.015 to 0.055 in

Torque specifications   **Ft-lbs**
Camshaft sprocket-to-camshaft . . . .   35 to 45
Camshaft thrust plate-to-block . . . .   12 to 18
Connecting rod nut . . . .   21 to 26
Damper or pulley-to-crankshaft . . . .   85 to 100
Flywheel-to-crankshaft . . . .   75 to 85
Main bearing cap bolts . . . .   60 to 70
Oil pan-to-cylinder block . . . .   7 to 9
Oil pump-to-cylinder block . . . .   10 to 15
Rocker arm support shaft-to-cylinder head . . . .   30 to 35
Spark plugs . . . .   10 to 15

3.8L (232 ci) V6 engine
Engine block
Cylinder bore
    Diameter . . . .   3.81 in
    Taper service limit . . . .   0.002 in
    Out of round service limit . . . .   0.002 in
Deck warpage limit . . . .   0.003 in per 6 in

Pistons and rings
Piston Diameter
    Coded red . . . .   3.8095 to 3.8101 in
    Coded blue . . . .   3.8107 to 3.8113 in
Piston-to-cylinder bore clearance . . . .   0.0014 to 0.0022 in
Piston ring-to-groove clearance
    Top compression . . . .   0.0016 to 0.0037 in
    Bottom compression . . . .   0.0016 to 0.0037 in
    Oil ring . . . .   Snug fit in groove
Piston ring end gap
    Top compression . . . .   0.01 to 0.02 in
    Bottom compression . . . .   0.01 to 0.02 in
    Oil ring . . . .   0.0150 to 0.0583 in
Piston pin diameter . . . .   0.9119 to 0.914 in
Piston pin-to-piston clearance . . . .   0.0002 to 0.0005 in
Piston pin-to-connecting rod clearance . . . .   Press fit at 1800 lbs

Crankshaft and flywheel
Main journal
    Diameter . . . .   2.5190 to 2.5198 in
    Taper limit . . . .   0.0003 in per 1 in
    Out-of-round limit . . . .   0.0003 in per 45° or 0.0006 in total
    Journal runout limit . . . .   0.002 in
Main bearing oil clearance
    Desired . . . .   0.0010 to 0.0014 in
    Allowable . . . .   0.0005 to 0.0023 in
Connecting rod journal
    Diameter . . . .   2.3103 to 2.3111 in
    Taper limit . . . .   0.0003 in per inch
    Out-of-round limit . . . .   0.0003 in per 45° or 0.0006 in total
Connecting rod bearing oil clearance
    Desired . . . .   0.0010 to 0.0014 in
    Allowable . . . .   0.0008 to 0.0027 in
Connecting rod side clearance
    Standard . . . .   0.0047 to 0.0114 in
    Service limit . . . .   0.014 in max
Crankshaft endplay . . . .   0.004 to 0.008 in
Flywheel clutch face runout limit . . . .   0.005 in TIR
Flywheel ring gear lateral runout
    Standard transmission . . . .   0.025 in TIR
    Automatic transmission . . . .   0.070 in TIR

Camshaft
Bearing journal diameter . . . .   2.0505 to 2.0515 in
Bearing oil clearance . . . .   0.001 to 0.003 in
Lobe lift
    Intake . . . .   0.240 in
    Exhaust . . . .   0.241 in
    Allowable lobe lift loss . . . .   0.005 in

2E

3.8L (232 ci) V6 engine (continued)

Camshaft drive — assembled gear face runout
Crankshaft .... 0.002 in
Camshaft .... 0.018 in

Cylinder heads and valve train
Head warpage limit .... 0.007 in
Valve seat angle.............................. 45°
Valve seat width (intake and exhaust) .... 0.006 to 0.08 in
Valve seat runout limit .... 0.003 in TIR
Valve face angle.............................. 44°
Valve face runout limit .... 0.002 in
Valve margin width .... 0.031 in min
Valve stem diameter (standard)
Intake .... 0.3416 to 0.3423 in
Exhaust.................................. 0.3411 to 0.3418 in
Valve guide diameter (intake and exhaust) .... 0.3433 to 0.3443 in
Valve stem-to-guide clearance
Intake .... 0.0010 to 0.0027 in
Exhaust.................................. 0.0015 to 0.0032 in
Valve spring free length .... 1.70 to 1.78 in
Valve spring pressure
Loaded (without damper) .... 215 lbs @ 1.40 in
Unloaded (without damper) .... 75 lbs @ 1.70 in
Service limit .... 10% loss of pressure
Collapsed lifter gap........................... 0.088 to 0.189 in
Lifter diameter .... 0.874 in
Lifter bore diameter .... 0.8752 to 0.8767 in
Lifter-to-bore clearance
Standard .... 0.0007 to 0.0027 in
Service limit .... 0.005 in

Torque specifications   **Ft-lbs**
Main bearing cap bolts .... 65 to 81
Camshaft sprocket-to-camshaft bolts .... 15 to 22
Connecting rod nuts .... 31 to 36
Cylinder head bolts
Step 1 47
Step 2 55
Step 3 63
Step 4 74
Step 5 .... Back off all bolts 2 turns
Step 6 .... Repeat steps 1 through 4
Rocker arm fulcrum-to-cylinder head bolt
Step 1 .... 5 to 11
Step 2 .... 18 to 25
Intake manifold-to-cylinder head bolts
Step 1 5
Step 2 10
Step 3 18
Rocker arm cover-to-cylinder head screws.............. 3 to 5
Spark plug-to-cylinder head...................... 17 to 22
Flywheel-to-crankshaft bolts .... 54 to 64
Distributor hold-down bolt .... 20 to 29
Crankshaft pulley-to-damper bolts .... 20 to 28
Crankshaft damper-to-crankshaft bolts .... 93 to 121

4.2L (255 ci), 5.0L (302 ci) and 5.8LW (351W) V8 engines

Engine block
Cylinder bore
Diameter
255 .... 3.6800 to 3.6835 in
302 .... 4.0004 to 4.0052 in
351W .... 4.0000 to 4.0048 in
Taper limit.................................. 0.0010 in
Out-of-round limit .... 0.005 in
Deck warpage limit............................ 0.003 in per 6 in or 0.006 in overall

Pistons and rings
Piston Diameter
255 coded red............................. 3.6784 to 3.6790 in
244 coded blue .... 2.6798 to 3.6804 in
302 coded red............................. 3.9978 to 3.9984 in
351W coded blue .... 4.003 in

Piston-to-bore clearance — selective fit	0.0018 to 0.0026 in
Piston ring-to-groove clearance	
Top compression	0.0019 to 0.0036 in
Bottom compression	0.002 to 0.004 in
Oil	Snug fit in groove
Service limit	0.002 in max increase in clearance
Piston ring end gap	
Top compression	0.010 to 0.020 in
Bottom compression	0.010 to 0.020 in
Oil (1975 through 1977)	0.015 to 0.055 in
Oil (1978 through 1984)	0.010 to 0.035 in
Piston pin diameter (standard)	0.9119 to 0.9124 in
Piston pin-to-piston clearance	
255 and 302	0.0002 to 0.0004 in
351W	0.0003 to 0.0005 in
Piston pin-to-connecting rod bushing clearance	Interference fit

Crankshaft and flywheel

Main journal	
Diameter	
255 and 302	2.2482 to 2.2490 in
351W	2.9994 to 3.0002 in
Taper limit — max per inch	0.0006 in
Out-of-round limit	0.0006 in
Runout limit	0.005 in
Main bearing oil clearance	
255 and 302 — No. 1 bearing	0.0001 to 0.0015 in
255 and 302 — all others	0.0005 to 0.0015 in
351W	0.0008 to 0.0026 in
Connecting rod journal diameter	
255 and 302	2.1228 to 2.1236 in
351W	2.3103 to 2.3111 in
Taper limit — max per inch	0.0006 in
Connecting rod bearing oil clearance	
Standard	0.0008 to 0.0015 in
Service limit	
255	0.0008 to 0.0024 in
302	0.0008 to 0.0025 in
Connecting rod side clearance	
Standard	0.010 to 0.020 in
Service limit	0.023 in
Crankshaft endplay	
Standard	0.004 to 0.008 in
Service limit	0.012 in

Camshaft

Bearing journal diameter	
No. 1	2.0805 to 2.0815 in
No. 2	2.0655 to 2.0665 in
No. 3	2.0505 to 2.0515 in
No. 4	2.0355 to 2.0365 in
No. 5	2.0205 to 2.0215 in
Bearing oil clearance	
Standard	0.001 to 0.003 in
Service limit	0.006 in
Front bearing location	0.005 to 0.020 in below front face of block
Lobe lift	
Intake	
255 and 302 (1975 through 1977)	0.2303 in
255 and 302 (1978 through 1984)	0.2375 in
351W (all)	0.2600 in
Exhaust	
255	
1981	0.2375 in
1982 through 1984	0.2474 in
302	
1980 and 1981	0.2470 in
1982 through 1984	0.2474 in
351W	0.2600 in
Maximum allowable lift loss	0.005 in
Endplay	
Standard	0.001 to 0.007 in
Service limit	0.009 in
Timing chain deflection limit	0.500 in

2E

4.2L (255 ci), 5.0L (302 ci) and 5.8L (351W) (continued)

Cylinder heads and valve train

Head warpage limit	0.003 in per 6 in or 0.006 in total
Valve seat angle	45°
Valve seat width	0.060 to 0.080 in
Valve seat runout limit	0.0015 in TIR
Valve face angle	44°
Valve face runout limit	0.002 in
Valve margin width	0.031 in min
Valve stem diameter	
Intake	0.3416 to 0.3423 in
Exhaust	0.3411 to 0.3418
Valve stem-to-guide clearance	
Intake	
Standard	0.0010 to 0.0027 in
Service limit	0.0055 in
Exhaust	
Standard	0.0015 to 0.0032 in
Service limit	0.0055 in
Valve spring free length	
255 and 302	
Intake	1.94 in
Exhaust	1.85 in
351W	
Intake	2.04 in
Exhaust	1.85 in
Valve spring pressure	
Intake (1st check)	74 to 82 lbs @ 1.78 in
Intake (2nd check)	
255	190 to 212 lbs @ 1.36 in
302	196 to 212 lbs @ 1.36 in
351W	190 to 210 lbs @ 1.36 in
Exhaust (1st check)	76 to 84 lbs @ 1.60 in
Exhaust (2nd check)	190 to 219 lbs @ 1.20 in
Service limit	10% loss of pressure
Valve spring installed height	
Intake	
255 and 302	1.6718 to 1.7031 in
351W	1.7656 to 1.7969 in
Exhaust	1.5781 to 1.6094 in
Valve spring out-of-square limit	0.078 in
Collapsed lifter gap clearance	
Allowable	
255 and 351W	0.100 to 0.200 in
302	0.071 to 0.193 in
Desired	
255 and 351W	0.125 to 0.175 in
302	0.096 to 0.165 in
Lifter diameter	0.8740 to 0.8745 in
Lifter bore diameter	0.8752 to 0.8767 in
Lifter-to-bore clearance	
Standard	0.0007 to 0.0027 in
Service limit	0.005 in
Pushrod runout limit	0.015 in TIR

Torque specifications — **Ft-lbs**

Camshaft sprocket gear-to-camshaft	40 to 45
Camshaft thrust plate-to-cylinder block	9 to 12
Connecting rod nuts	19 to 24
Timing cover bolts	12 to 18
Cylinder head bolts	
255 and 302	
1st step	55 to 65
2nd step	65 to 72
351W	
1st step	85
2nd step	95
3rd step	105 to 112
Damper-to-crankshaft	70 to 90
Flywheel-to-crankshaft	75 to 85
Main bearing cap bolts	60 to 70
Intake manifold-to-cylinder head	23 to 25
Exhaust manifold-to-cylinder head	18 to 24
Spark plugs	10 to 15
Rocker arm stud/bolt-to-cylinder head	18 to 25

5.8LM (351M) and 6.6l (400 ci) V8 engines
Engine block
Cylinder bore
    Diameter . . . .   4.0000 to 4.0048 in
    Taper limit . . . .   0.010 in
    Out-of-round limit . . . .   0.005 in
    Deck warpage limit . . . .   0.003 in per 6 in

Pistons and rings
Piston diameter
    Coded red . . . .   3.9982 to 3.9998 in
    Coded blue . . . .   3.9994 to 4.0000 in
Piston-to-cylinder bore clearance . . . .   0.0014 to 0.0022 in
Piston ring-to-groove clearance
    Top compression . . . .   0.0019 to 0.0036 in
    Bottom compression . . . .   0.002 to 0.004 in
    Oil . . . .   Snug fit in groove
    Service limit . . . .   0.002 in max increase in clearance
Piston ring end gap
    Top compression . . . .   0.010 to 0.020 in
    Bottom compression . . . .   0.010 to 0.020 in
    Oil (1975 and 1976) . . . .   0.015 to 0.055 in
Piston pin diameter (standard) . . . .   0.9749 to 0.9754 in
Piston pin-to-piston clearance . . . .   0.0003 to 0.0005 in
Piston pin-to-connecting rod bushing clearance . . . .   Interference fit

Crankshaft and flywheel
Main journal
    Diameter . . . .   2.9994 to 3.0002 in
    Taper limit — max per inch . . . .   0.0005 in
    Out-of-rounnd limit . . . .   0.0006 in
    Runout limit
        TIR maximum . . . .   0.002 in
        Service limit . . . .   0.005 in
Main bearing oil clearance
    Desired . . . .   0.0008 to 0.0015 in
    Allowable . . . .   0.0008 to 0.0026 in
Connecting rod journal
    Diameter . . . .   2.3103 to 2.3111 in
    Taper limit — max per inch . . . .   0.0006 in
    Out-of-round limit . . . .   0.0006 in
Connecting rod bearing oil clearance
    Desired . . . .   0.0008 to 0.0015 in
    Allowable . . . .   0.0008 to 0.0025 in
Connecting rod side clearance
    Standard . . . .   0.010 to 0.020 in
    Service limit . . . .   0.023 in
Crankshaft endplay
    Standard . . . .   0.004 to 0.008 in
    Service limit . . . .   0.012 in

Camshaft
Bearing journal diameter
    No. 1 . . . .   2.1238 to 2.1248 in
    No. 2 . . . .   2.0655 to 2.0665 in
    No. 3 . . . .   2.0505 to 2.0515 in
    No. 4 . . . .   2.0355 to 2.0365 in
    No. 5 . . . .   2.0205 to 2.0215 in
Bearing oil clearance
    Standard . . . .   0.001 to 0.003 in
    Service limit . . . .   0.006 in
Front bearing location . . . .   0.040 to 0.060 in below front face of block
Lobe lift
    Intake 351M (1975 and 1976) . . . .   0.235 in
    Exhaust 351M (1975 and 1976) . . . .   0.235 in
    Intake 400 (1975 and 1976) . . . .   0.2474 in
    Exhaust 400 (1975 and 1976) . . . .   0.250 in
    Intake (1977 through 1984) . . . .   0.250 in
    Exhaust (1977 through 1984) . . . .   0.250 in
    Maximum allowable lift loss . . . .   0.005 in

2E

5.8L (351 M) and 6.61L (400 ci) V8 engines (continued)

Endplay
    Standard .... 0.001 to 0.006 in
    Service limit .... 0.009 in
Timing chain defection limit .... 0.500 in

Cylinder heads and valve train

Head warpage limit .... 0.003 in per 6 in or 0.006 in overall
Valve seat angle.................................. 45º
Valve seat width
    Intake .... 0.060 to 0.080 in
    Exhaust.................................. 0.070 to 0.090 in
Valve seat runout limit .... 0.002 in TIR
Valve face angle.................................. 44º
Valve face runout limit .... 0.002 in TIR
Valve margin width .... 0.031 in min
Valve stem diameter
    Intake .... 0.3416 to 0.3423 in
    Exhaust.................................. 0.3411 to 0.3418 in
Valve guide diameter .... 0.3433 to 0.3443 in
Valve stem-to-guide clearance
    Intake
        Standard .... 0.0010 to 0.0027 in
        Service limit .... 0.005 in max
    Exhaust
        Standard .... 0.0015 to 0.0027 in
        Service limit .... 0.005 in max
Valve spring free length
    Intake .... 2.06 in
    Exhaust.................................. 1.93 in
Valve spring pressure
    Intake
        1st check .... 76 to 84 lbs @ 1.82 in
        2nd check .... 215 to 237 lbs @ 1.39 in
    Exhaust
        1st check .... 79 to 87 lbs @ 1.68 in
        2nd check .... 215 to 237 lbs @ 1.39 in
    Service limit .... 10% loss of pressure
Valve spring installed height
    Intake .... 1.8125 to 1.8438 in
    Exhaust.................................. 1.6875 to 1.7188 in
Valve spring out-of-square limit...................... 0.078 in
Collapsed lifter gap clearance
    Allowable .... 0.100 to 0.200 in
    Desired .... 0.125 to 0.175 in
Lifter diameter .... 0.8740 to 0.8745 in
Lifter bore diameter .... 0.8752 to 0.8767 in
Lifter-to-bore clearance
    Standard .... 0.007 to 0.027 in
    Service limit .... 0.005 in
Pushrod runout limit .... 0.015 in TIR

Torque specifications   Ft-lbs

Camshaft sprocket gear-to-camshaft .... 40 to 45
Camshaft thrust plate-to-cylinder block .... 9 to 12
Connecting rod nut................................ 40 to 45
Cylinder head bolts
    1st step 75
    2nd step .... 95 to 105
Damper-to-crankshaft.............................. 70 to 90
Main bearing cap bolts .... 95 to 105
Intake manifold-to-cylinder head
    3/8 in .... 22 to 32
    5/16 in .... 19 to 25
Exhaust manifold-to-cylinder head .... 18 to 24
Rocker arm stud/bolt-to-cylinder head .... 18 to 25
Spark plugs .... 10 to 15

7.5L (460 ci) V8 engine

Engine block

Cylinder bore
    Diameter .... 4.3600 to 4.3636 in
    Taper limit............................... 0.10 in
    Out-of-round limit .... 0.0015 in
Deck warpage limit................................ 0.003 in per 6 in or 0.006 in overall

Pistons and rings

Piston diameter	
Coded red	4.3585 to 4.3591 in
Coded blue	4.3597 to 4.3603 in
Piston-to-bore clearance — selective fit	0.0022 to 0.0030 in
Piston ring-to-groove clearance	
Compression — top and bottom	0.0025 to 0.0045
Oil	Snug fit in groove
Service limit	0.002 in max increase in clearance
Piston ring end gap	
Compression — top and bottom	0.010 to 0.020 in
Oil (1975 through 1977)	0.015 to 0.055 in
Oil (after 1977)	0.010 to 0.035 in
Piston pin diameter (standard)	1.0398 to 1.0403 in
Piston pin-to-piston clearance	0.0002 to 0.0004 in
Piston pin-to-connecting rod bushing clearance	Interference fit

Crankshaft and flywheel

Main journal	
Diameter	2.9994 to 3.0002 in
Taper limit — max per inch	0.0005 in
Out of round limit	0.0006 in
Runout limit	0.002 in
Main bearing oil clearance	
Standard	0.0008 to 0.0015 in
Service limit	0.0008 to 0.0026 in
Connecting rod journal	
Diameter	2.4992 to 2.5000 in
Taper limit — max per inch	0.0006 in
Out-of-round limit	0.0006 in
Connecting rod bearing oil clearance	
Desired	0.0008 to 0.0015 in
Allowable	0.0008 to 0.0025 in
Connecting rod side clearance	
Standard	0.010 to 0.020 in
Service limit	0.023 in
Crankshaft endplay	
Standard	0.004 to 0.008 in
Service limit	0.012 in

Camshaft

Bearing journal diameter (all)	2.1238 to 2.1248 in
Bearing oil clearance	
Standard	0.001 to 0.003 in
Service limit	0.006 in
Front bearing location	0.040 to 0.060 in below front face of block
Lobe lift	
Intake	0.252 in
Exhaust	0.278 in
Maximum allowable lift loss	0.005 in
Endplay	
Standard	0.001 to 0.006 in
Service limit	0.009 in
Timing chain deflection limit	0.500 in

Cylinder heads and valve train

Head warpage limit	0.003 in per 6 in or 0.006 in overall
Valve seat angle	45°
Valve seat width	0.060 to 0.080 in
Valve seat runout limit	0.002 in TIR
Valve face angle	44°
Valve face runout limit	0.002 in TIR
Valve margin width	0.03125 in min
Valve stem diameter	0.3416 to 0.3423 in
Valve guide diameter	0.3433 to 0.3443 in
Valve stem-to-guide clearance	
Standard	0.0010 to 0.0027 in
Service limit	0.0055 in
Valve spring free length	2.06 in
Valve spring pressure	
1st check	76 to 84 lbs @ 1.81 in
2nd check (1975 and 1976)	240 to 265 lbs @ 1.33 in
2nd check (1977 through 1984)	218 to 240 lbs @ 1.33 in
Service limit	10% loss of pressure
Valve spring installed height	1 1.7969 to 1.8281 in

2E

7.5L (460 ci) V8 engine (continued)

Valve spring out-of-square limit	0.078 in
Collapsed lifter gap clearance	
Allowable	0.075 to 0.175 in
Desired	0.100 to 0.150 in
Lifter diameter	0.8740 to 0.8745 in
Lifter bore diameter	0.8740 to 0.8745 in
Lifter-to-bore clearance	
Standard	0.0007 to 0.0027 in
Service limit	0.005 in
Pushrod runout limit	0.015 in TIR

Torque specifications	**Ft-lbs**
Camshaft sprocket gear-to-camshaft	40 to 45
Camshaft thrust plate-to-cylinder block	9 to 12
Connecting rod nut	45 to 50
Timing cover (5/16 in bolt)	15 to 21
Cylinder head bolts	
1st step	80
2nd step	110
3rd step	130 to 140
Damper-to-crankshaft	70 to 90
Main bearing cap bolts	95 to 105
Intake manifold-to-cylinder head	18 to 25
Spark plugs	5 to 10

1   General information

Included in this portion of Chapter 2 are the general overhaul procedures for the cylinder head and internal engine components. The information ranges from advice concerning preparation for an overhaul and the purchase of replacement parts to detailed, step-by-step procedures covering removal and installation of internal engine components and the inspection of parts.

The following Sections have been written based on the assumption that the engine has been removed from the vehicle. For information concerning in-vehicle engine repair, as well as removal and installation of the external components necessary for the overhaul, see Part A, B, C or D of Chapter 2 (depending on engine type) and Section 2 of this part.

The specifications included here in Part E are only those necessary for the inspection and overhaul procedures which follow. Refer to Part A, B, C or D for additional specifications related to the various engines covered in this manual.

2   Repair operations possible with the engine in the vehicle

Many major repair operations can be accomplished without removing the engine from the vehicle.

If possible clean the engine compartment and the exterior of the engine with some type of pressure washer before any work is begun. A clean engine will make the job easier and will help keep dirt out of the internal areas of the engine.

Remove the hood (Chapter 11) and cover the fenders to provide as much working room as possible and to prevent damage to the painted surfaces.

If oil or coolant leaks develop, indicating a need for gasket or seal replacement, the repairs can generally be made with the engine in the vehicle. The oil pan gasket, the cylinder head gasket, intake and exhaust manifold gaskets, timing cover gaskets and the front crankshaft oil seal are accessible with the engine in place.

Exterior engine components, such as the water pump, the starter motor, the alternator, the distributor, the fuel pump and the carburetor or TBI, as well as the intake and exhaust manifolds, are quite easily removed for repair with the engine in place.

Since the cylinder head can be removed without pulling the engine, valve component servicing can also be accomplished with the engine in the vehicle.

Replacement of, repairs to or inspection of the timing sprockets and chain or belt and the oil pump are all possible with the engine in place.

In extreme cases caused by a lack of necessary equipment, repair or replacement of piston rings, pistons, connecting rods and rod bearings is possible with the engine in the vehicle. However, this practice is not recommended because of the cleaning and preparation work that must be done to the components involved.

Detailed removal, inspection, repair and installation procedures for the above mentioned components can be found in the appropriate part of Chapter 2 or the other chapters in this manual.

3   Engine overhaul — general information

It is not always easy to determine when, or if, an engine should be completely overhauled, as a number of factors must be considered.

High mileage is not necessarily an indication that an overhaul is needed, while low mileage does not preclude the need for an overhaul. Frequency of servicing is the single most important consideration. An engine that has had regular and frequent oil and filter changes, as well as other required maintenance, will most likely give many thousands of miles of reliable service. Conversely, a neglected engine may require an overhaul very early in its life.

Excessive oil consumption is an indication that piston rings and/or valve guides are in need of attention (make sure that oil leaks are not responsible before deciding that the rings and guides are bad). Check the cylinder compression or have a leakdown test performed by an experienced mechanic to determine the extent of the work required.

If the engine is making obvious knocking or rumbling noises, the connecting rod and/or main bearings are probably at fault. Check the oil pressure with a gauge (installed in place of the oil pressure sending unit). If the pressure is extremely low, the bearings and/or oil pump are probably worn out.

Loss of power, rough running, excessive valve train noise and high fuel consumption may also point to the need for an overhaul, especially if they are all present at the same time. If a complete tune-up does not remedy the situation, major mechanical work is the only solution.

An engine overhaul generally involves restoring the internal parts to the specifications of a new engine. During an overhaul the piston rings are replaced and the cylinder walls are reconditioned through boring or honing. If the cylinders are bored new pistons will be required. The main and connecting rod bearings are replaced with new ones and, if necessary, the crankshaft may be ground undersize to restore the journals. The valves are generally serviced as well, since they are usually in less-than-perfect condition at this point. While the engine is being overhauled other components, such as the carburetor, distributor, starter and alternator can be rebuilt. The end result is a like-new engine that will give as many trouble-free miles as the original.

Before beginning the engine overhaul, read through the entire procedure to familiarize yourself with the scope and requirements of the job. Overhauling an engine is not difficult, but it is time consuming. Plan on the vehicle being tied up for a minimum of two weeks, especially if parts must be taken to an automotive machine shop for repair or reconditioning. Check on availability of parts and make sure that any necessary special tools and equipment are obtained in advance. Most work can be done with typical hand tools, although a number of precision measuring tools are required for inspecting parts to determine if they must be replaced. Often an automotive machine shop will handle the inspection of parts and offer advice concerning reconditioning and replacement. **Note:** *Always wait until the engine has been completely disassembled and all components have been inspected before deciding what service and repair operations must be performed by a machine shop.*

Since the condition of the block is the major factor to consider when determining whether to overhaul the original engine or buy a rebuilt one, never purchase parts or have machine work done on other components until the block has been thoroughly inspected.

As a final note, to ensure maximum life and minimum trouble from a rebuilt engine everything must be assembled with care in a spotlessly clean environment.

4   Engine rebuilding alternatives

The home mechanic has a number of options available when performing an engine overhaul. The decision to replace the engine block, piston/connecting rod assemblies and crankshaft depends on several factors, with the primary consideration being the condition of the block. Other considerations are cost, access to machine shop facilities, parts availability, time required to complete the project and experience.

Some of the rebuilding alternatives include:

Individual parts — If the inspection procedures reveal that the engine block and most engine components are in reusable condition, purchasing individual parts may be the most economical alternative. The block, crankshaft and piston/connecting rod assemblies should all be inspected carefully. Even if the block shows little wear, the cylinder bores should receive a finish hone.

Master kit (crankshaft kit) — This rebuild package usually contains of a reground crankshaft and a set of pistons and connecting rods. The pistons will already be installed on the connecting rods. These kits are commonly available for standard cylinder bores, as well as for engine blocks which have been bored to a regular oversize.

Short block — A short block consists of an engine block with a crankshaft and piston/connecting rod assemblies already installed. All new bearings are incorporated and all clearances will be correct. Your heads, valve train components, and external parts are then bolted to the short block.

Long block — A long block consists of a short block plus an oil pump, oil pan, cylinder head, rocker arm cover, valve train components, timing sprockets and chain or belt and timing chain or belt cover. All components are installed with new bearings, seals and gaskets incorporated throughout. The installation of manifolds and external parts is all that is necessary.

Give careful thought to which alternative is best for you and discuss the situation with local automotive machine shops or dealer parts and service departments before ordering or purchasing replacement parts.

5   Engine removal — methods and precautions

If it has been decided that an engine must be removed for overhaul or major repair work, certain preliminary steps should be taken.

Locating a suitable work area is extremely important. A shop is, of course, the most desirable place to work. Adequate work space, along with storage space for the vehicle, is very important. If a shop or garage is not available, at the very least a flat, level, clean work surface made of concrete or asphalt is required.

An engine hoist or A-frame will be necessary. Make sure that the equipment is rated in excess of the combined weight of the engine and its accessories. Safety is of primary importance, considering the potential hazards involved in lifting the engine out of the vehicle.

If the engine is being removed by a novice, a helper should be available. Advice and aid from someone more experienced would also be helpful. There are many instances when one person cannot simultaneously perform all of the operations required when lifting the engine out of the vehicle.

Plan the operation ahead of time. Arrange for all of the tools and equipment you will need prior to beginning the job. Some of the equipment necessary to perform engine removal and installation safely and with relative ease are (in addition to an engine hoist) a heavy duty floor jack, complete sets of wrenches and sockets as described in the front of this manual, wooden blocks and plenty of rags and cleaning solvent for mopping up the inevitable spills. If the hoist is to be rented, make sure that you arrange for it in advance and perform beforehand all of the operations possible without it. This will save you money and time.

Plan for the vehicle to be out of use for a considerable amount of time. A machine shop will be required to perform some of the work which the home mechanic cannot accomplish due to a lack of special equipment. These shops often have a busy schedule, so it would be wise to consult them before removing the engine in order to accurately estimate the amount of time required to rebuild or repair components that may need work.

Always use extreme caution when removing and installing the engine. Serious injury can result from careless actions. Plan ahead. Take your time and a job of this nature, although major, can be accomplished successfully.

6   Engine overhaul disassembly sequence

1   It is much easier to disassemble and work on the engine if it is mounted on a portable engine stand. These stands can often be rented for a reasonable fee from an equipment rental yard. Before the engine is mounted on a stand, the flywheel/flexplate should be removed from the engine (refer to Chapter 8).

2   If a stand is not available it is possible to disassemble the engine with it blocked up on a sturdy workbench or on the floor. Be extra careful not to tip or drop the engine when working without a stand.

3   If you are going to obtain a rebuilt engine, all external components must come off your engine to be transferred to the replacement engine (just as they will if you are doing a complete engine overhaul yourself). These include:

Alternator and brackets
Emissions control components
Distributor, spark plug wires and spark plugs
Thermostat and housing cover
Water pump
Carburetor/fuel injection components
Intake/exhaust manifolds
Oil filter
Fuel pump
Engine mounts
Flywheel/flexplate

Note: *When removing the external components from the engine pay close attention to details that may be helpful or important during installation. Note the installed position of gaskets, seals, spacers, pins, washers, bolts and other small items.*

4   If you are obtaining a short block (which consists of the engine block, crankshaft, pistons and connecting rods all assembled), then the cylinder head, oil pan and oil pump will have to be removed as well. See *Engine rebuilding alternatives* for additional information regarding the different possibilities to be considered.

5   If you are planning a complete overhaul, the engine must be disassembled and the internal components removed in the following order:

Rocker arm or camshaft cover
Cylinder head and pushrods (inline six, V6 and V8 only)
Cylinder head and camshaft (inline four-cylinder)
Valve lifters
Timing chain/belt cover
Timing chain/sprockets or belt
Camshaft (except inline four-cylinder)
Oil pan
Oil pump
Piston/connecting rod assemblies
Crankshaft

2E

6   Before beginning the disassembly and overhaul procedures, make sure the following items are available:

 Common hand tools
 Small cardboard boxes or plastic bags for storing parts
 Gasket scraper
 Ridge reamer
 Crankshaft damper puller
 Micrometers and/or dial caliper
 Telescoping gauges
 Dial indicator set
 Valve spring compressor
 Cylinder surfacing hone
 Piston ring groove cleaning tool
 Electric drill motor
 Tap and die set
 Wire brushes
 Cleaning solvent

7   Cylinder head — disassembly

Note: *New and rebuilt cylinder heads are commonly available for most engines at dealerships and auto parts stores. Due to the specialized tools necessary for some disassembly and inspection procedures it may be more practical and economical for the home mechanic to purchase a replacement head rather than taking the time to disassemble, inspect and recondition the original head.*

1   Cylinder head disassembly involves removal and disassembly of the intake and exhaust valves and their related components as shown in the accompanying illustration. If they are still in place, remove the nuts or bolts, fulcrums or rocker arm shaft, and separate the rocker arms from the cylinder head. Label the parts or store them separately so they can be reinstalled in their original locations.
2   Before the valves are removed, arrange to label and store them, along with their related components, so they can be kept separate and reinstalled in the same valve guides they are removed from.
3   Compress the valve spring on the first valve with a spring compressor and remove the keepers (photo). Carefully release the valve spring compressor and remove the retainer, the shield (if so equipped), the springs, the valve guide seal, any spring shims and the valve from the head. If the valve binds in the guide (won't pull through), push it back into the head and deburr the area around the keeper groove and the end of the valve stem with a fine file or whetstone.
4   Repeat the procedure for the remaining valves. Remember to keep together all the parts for each valve so they can be reinstalled in the same locations.
5   Once the valves have been removed and safely stored, the head should be thoroughly cleaned and inspected. If a complete engine overhaul is being done, finish the engine disassembly procedures before beginning the cylinder head cleaning and inspection process.

8   Cylinder head — cleaning and inspection

1   Thorough cleaning of the cylinder head and related valve train components, followed by a detailed inspection, will enable you to decide how much valve service work must be done during the engine overhaul.

Cleaning
2   Scrape away all traces of old gasket material and sealing compound from the head gasket, intake manifold and exhaust manifold sealing surfaces. On OHC engines work slowly and do not nick or gouge the soft aluminum of the head and intake manifold.
3   Remove any built-up scale around the coolant passages.
4   Run a stiff wire brush through the oil holes to remove any deposits that may have formed.
5   Run an appropriate size tap into each threaded hole to remove any corrosion and thread sealant that may be present. If compressed air is available, use it to clear the holes of debris produced by this operation.
6   Clean the exhaust and intake manifold stud threads in a similar manner with an appropriate size die. Clean the rocker arm pivot bolt or stud threads with a wire brush (except 2.3L four-cylinder engine).
7   Clean the cylinder head with solvent and dry it thoroughly. Compressed air will speed the drying process and ensure that all holes and

**Fig. 2E.1 Typical valve components — exploded view
(some engines may not be equipped with a retainer sleeve)
(Sec 7)**

recessed areas are clean. **Note:** *Decarbonizing chemicals are available and may prove very useful when cleaning cylinder heads and valve train components. They are very caustic and should be used with caution. Be sure to follow the instructions on the container.*
8   Clean the rocker arms, fulcrums or rocker arm shafts and pushrods with solvent and dry them thoroughly. Compressed air will speed the drying process and can be used to clean out the oil passages.
9   Clean all the valve springs, keepers, retainers, shields and spring shims with solvent and dry them thoroughly. Do the components from one valve at a time to avoid mixing up the parts.
10   Scrape off any heavy deposits that may have formed on the valves, then use a motorized wire brush to remove deposits from the valve heads and stems. Again, make sure the valves do not get mixed up. **Note:** *Do not use a motorized brush on aluminum cylinder heads.*

7.3   Use a valve spring compressor to compress the spring, then remove the keepers from the valve stem

Fig. 2E.2 A dial indicator can be used to determine the valve stem-to-guide clearance (Sec 8)

Inspection

Cylinder head

11 Inspect the head very carefully for cracks, evidence of coolant leakage or other damage. If cracks are found, a new cylinder head should be obtained.

12 Using a straightedge and feeler gauge, check the head gasket mating surface for warpage. If the warpage exceeds 0.006-inch over the length of the head, it must be resurfaced at a machine shop.

13 Examine the valve seats in each of the combustion chambers. If they are pitted, cracked or burned, the head will require valve service that is beyond the scope of the home mechanic.

14 A preliminary examination of the valve guides will indicate whether the heads can be reassembled with new seals, or whether a more complete study of the guides, with possible reconditioning or replacement being needed, is necessary.

15 A complete examination of the valve guides is a job best performed by an automotive machine shop, where precision measuring equipment is available. In addition to checking the valve stem to guide clearance, the shop will be able to check for a bell-mouth wear pattern in the guide.

16 Before taking your heads to a shop for a valve guide check, you can make a preliminary check with a dial indicator.

17 Remove the valve assembly (valve, valve spring, spring shims, retainer and keepers) from the head.

18 Reinsert the valve into the guide. If you have removed all the valves from the head, make sure the valve is the one that was originally installed in that guide. Don't mix up valve components.

19 Mount the dial indicator on the head so that the plunger rests against the valve stem, as shown in the accompanying illustration, as close to the top of the guide boss as possible.

20 Raise the valve until the head is between 1/16 and 1/8-inch off the seat.

21 Rock the valve stem back and forth in the guide, in line with the plunger of the dial indicator, and note the amount of lateral movement shown on the indicator.

22 Check the specifications for the valve stem-to-valve guide clearance for your engine. The specifications will give a minimum-maximum or a service limit figure. If the movement of the valve stem is more than the maximum or service limit figure given, the valve guides should be checked by a shop. If there is less than the maximum or service limit figure in lateral movement of the stem only new seals will be required.

23 Even if the valve guides show less than the maximum or service limit movement, if the valve seats and faces are going to be reground by a shop the guides should be checked and, if necessary, reconditioned.

24 On OHC engines inspect the camshaft bearing bores for wear, galling, gouges or discoloration, indicating overheating.

Rocker arm components (all engines except 2.3L four-cylinder)

25 Check the rocker arm faces (that contact the pushrod ends and valve stems) for pits, wear and rough spots. Check the pivot contact areas as well.

26 Inspect the pushrod ends for scuffing and excessive wear. Roll the pushrod on a flat surface, such as a piece of glass, to determine if it is bent.

27 Any damaged or excessively worn parts must be replaced with new ones.

Valves

28 Carefully inspect each valve face for cracks, pits and burned spots. Check the valve stem and neck for cracks. Rotate the valve and check for any obvious indication that it is bent. Check the end of the stem for pits and excessive wear. The presence of any of these conditions indicates the need for valve service by a properly equipped shop.

Valve components

29 Check each valve spring for wear (on the ends) and pits. Measure the free length (photo) and compare it to the specifications. Any springs that are shorter than specified have sagged and should not be reused. Stand the spring on a flat surface and check it for squareness (photo).

30 Check the spring retainers and keepers for obvious wear and cracks. Any questionable parts should be replaced with new ones, as extensive damage will occur in the event of failure during engine operation.

31 If the inspection process indicates that the valve components are in generally poor condition or worn beyond the limits specified, which is usually the case in an engine that is being overhauled, reassemble the valves in the cylinder head and refer to Section 9 for valve servicing recommendations.

32 If the inspection turns up no excessively worn parts, and if the valve faces and seats are in good condition, the valve train components can be reinstalled in the cylinder head without major servicing. Refer to the appropriate Section for cylinder head reassembly procedures.

2E

8.29A Measure the free length of each valve spring with a dial or vernier caliper

8.29B Check each valve spring for squareness

9   Valves — servicing

1   Because of the complex nature of the job and the special tools and equipment needed, servicing of the valves, the valve seats and the valve guides (commonly known as a *valve job*) is best left to a professional.

2   The home mechanic can remove and disassemble the head, do the initial cleaning and inspection, then reassemble and deliver the head to a dealer service department or a reputable automotive machine shop for the actual valve servicing.

3   The shop will remove the valves and springs, recondition or replace the valves and valve seats, recondition the valve guides, check and replace the valve springs, spring retainers and keepers (as necessary), replace the valve seals with new ones, reassemble the valve components and make sure the installed spring height is correct. The cylinder head gasket surface will also be resurfaced if it is warped.

4   After the valve job has been performed by a professional, the head will be in like-new condition. When the head is returned, be sure to clean it very thoroughly (before installation on the engine) to remove any metal particles and abrasive grit that may still be present from the valve service or head resurfacing operations. Use compressed air, if available, to blow out all the oil holes and passages.

10   Cylinder head — assembly

1   If the head was sent out for valve servicing, the valves and related components will already be in place.

2   If the head needs to be assembled, lay all the spring shims in the spring pockets from which they were removed, then lubricate and install one of the valves (use engine assembly lube or moly-based grease on the valve stem. Slip the plastic seal installation cap (included with the new seals) over the valve stem, then slide a new seal over the plastic cap until the seal jacket touches the top of the valve guide (see the accompanying illustration). Remove the plastic cap and push the seal onto the guide until it bottoms on the shoulder. Ford recommends a special tool for this procedure, but a deep socket or two screwdrivers will work if care is exercised. Repeat the procedure for the remaining valves.

3   Install the valve springs, the retainers and the keepers. When compressing the springs, do not let the retainers contact the valve guide seals. Make certain that the keepers are securely locked in their retaining grooves.

4   Double-check the installed valve spring height. If it was correct before disassembly, it should still be within the specified limits.

5   Install the rocker arms and tighten the bolts/nuts to the specified torque (where applicable). Be sure to lubricate the fulcrums with moly-based grease or engine assembly lube.

11   Piston/connecting rod assembly — removal

1   Using a ridge reamer, completely remove the ridge at the top of each cylinder (follow the manufacturer's instructions provided with the ridge reaming tool) (photo). Failure to remove the ridge before attempting to remove the piston/connecting rod assembly will result in broken pistons.

2   After the cylinder ridges have been removed, turn the engine upside-down on the engine stand, with the crankshaft at the top.

3   Before the connecting rods are removed, check the side clearance as follows: Mount a dial indicator with its stem in line with the crankshaft and touching the side of the number one connecting rod cap.

4   Push the connecting rod backward, as far as possible, and zero the dial indicator. Push the connecting rod all the way to the front and check the reading on the dial indicator. The distance that it moves is the side clearance. If the side clearance exceeds the service limit, a new connecting rod will be required. Repeat the procedure for the remaining connecting rods.

5   An alternative method is to slip feeler gauge blades between the connecting rod and the crankshaft throw until the play is removed (photo). The side clearance is equal to the thickness of the feeler gauge.

STEP #1 — WITH VALVES IN HEAD. PLACE PLASTIC INSTALLATION CAP OVER END OF VALVE STEM.
STEP #2 — START VALVE STEM SEAL CAREFULLY OVER CAP. PUSH SEAL DOWN UNTIL JACKET TOUCHES TOP OF GUIDE.
STEP #3 — REMOVE PLASTIC INSTALLATION CAP. USE INSTALLATION TOOL-T73P-6571-A OR SCREWDRIVERS TO BOTTOM SEAL ON VALVE GUIDE.

Fig. 2E.3 Some valve stem seals come with a plastic installation cap to prevent damage to the seal (be sure to remove the cap after installation of the seal) (Sec 10)

11.1   A ridge reamer is required to remove the ridge from the top of the cylinder (do this before removing the pistons)

11.5   Check the connecting rod side clearance with a feeler gauge as shown

6   Check the connecting rods and connecting rod caps for identification marks. If they are not plainly marked, identify each rod and cap, using a small punch to make the appropriate number of indentations to indicate the cylinders they are associated with (photo).

7   Loosen each of the connecting rod cap nuts approximately 1/2 turn. Remove the number one connecting rod cap and bearing insert. Do not drop the bearing insert out of the cap. Slip a short length of plastic or rubber hose over each connecting rod bolt to protect the crankshaft journal and cylinder wall when the piston is removed (photo). Push the connecting rod/piston assembly out through the top of the engine. Use a wooden shaft, such as the handle of a hammer, to push on the upper bearing insert in the connecting rod. If resistance is felt, double-check to make sure that all of the ridge was removed from the cylinder.

8   Repeat the procedure for the remaining cylinders. After removal, reassemble the connecting rod caps and bearing inserts in their respective connecting rods and install the cap nuts finger tight. Leaving the old bearing inserts in place until reassembly will help prevent the connecting rod bearing surfaces from being accidentally nicked or gouged.

12   Crankshaft — removal

1   Before the crankshaft is removed, check the endplay. Mount a dial indicator with the stem in line with the crankshaft and just touching one of the crank throws as shown in the accompanying illustration.

2   Push the crankshaft all the way to the rear and zero the dial indicator. Pry the crankshaft to the front as far as possible and check the reading on the dial indicator. The distance it moves is the endplay. If it is greater than specified, check the crankshaft thrust surfaces for wear. If no wear is apparent, new main bearings will correct the endplay.

3   If a dial indicator is not available, a feeler gauge can be used. Gently pry or push the crankshaft all the way to the front of the engine. Slip feeler gauge blades between the crankshaft and the front face of the thrust main bearing (photo) to determine the clearance.

4   Loosen each of the main bearing cap bolts 1/4-turn at a time, until they can be removed by hand. Check the main bearing caps to see if they are marked as to their locations. They are usually numbered

11.6   If your engine does not have numbers stamped on the rod bearing caps, mark them with a center punch before removal. During reassembly the rod/bearing assemblies must be installed in exactly the same positions

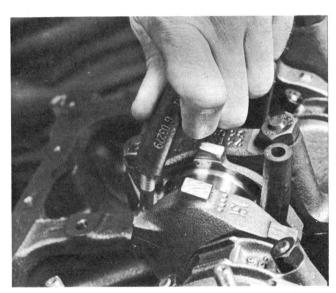

11.7   To prevent damage to the crankshaft journals and cylinder walls, slip sections of hose over the rod bolts before removing the pistons

Fig. 2E.4 Checking crankshaft end play with a dial indicator (Sec 12)

12.3   Checking crankshaft endplay with a feeler gauge

2E

consecutively from the front of the engine to the rear. If they are not, mark them with number stamping dies or a centerpunch (photo). Most main bearing caps have a cast-in arrow which points to the front of the engine (photo).

5   Gently tap the caps with a soft-faced hammer, then separate them from the engine block. If necessary, use the main bearing cap bolts as levers to remove the caps. Try not to drop the bearing insert if it comes out with the cap.

6   On OHC engines, the rear main bearing cap is recessed into the cylinder block. Rock the cap back and forth while pulling up on the crankshaft to remove it.

7   Carefully lift the crankshaft out of the engine. It is a good idea to have an assistant available, since the crankshaft is quite heavy. With the bearing inserts in place in the engine block and in the main bearing caps, return the caps to their respective locations on the engine block and tighten the bolts finger tight.

13   Engine block — cleaning

1   Remove the soft plugs from the engine block. Knock the plugs into the block (photo) using a hammer and punch, then grasp them with large pliers and pull them back through the holes (photo).

2   Using a gasket scraper, remove all traces of gasket material from the engine block. Be very careful not to nick or gouge the gasket sealing surfaces.

3   Remove the main bearing caps and separate the bearing inserts from the caps and the engine block. Tag the bearings according to which cylinder they removed from and whether they were in the cap or the block, then set them aside.

4   Remove the threaded oil gallery plugs from the front and back of the block.

5   If the engine is extremely dirty it should be taken to an automotive machine shop to be hot tanked. Any bearings left in the block (such as the camshaft bearings) will be damaged by the cleaning process, so plan on having new ones installed while the block is at the machine shop.

6   After the block is returned, clean all oil holes and oil galleries one more time. Brushes for cleaning oil holes and galleries are available at most auto parts stores, or rifle cleaning brushes can be substituted. Flush the passages with warm water until the water runs clear, dry the block thoroughly and wipe all machined surfaces with a light, rust preventative oil. If you have access to compressed air, use it to speed the drying process and to blow out all the oil holes and galleries.

7   If the block is not extremely dirty or sludged up, you can do an adequate cleaning job with warm soapy water and a stiff brush. Take plenty of time and do a thorough job. Regardless of the cleaning method used, be very sure to thoroughly clean all oil holes and galleries, dry the block completely and coat all machined surfaces with light oil.

8   The threaded holes in the block must be clean to ensure accurate torque readings during reassembly. Run the proper size tap into each of the holes to remove any rust, corrosion or thread sealant and to restore damaged threads. If possible, use compressed air to clear the

12.4   If the main caps are not identified by numbers and arrows to indicate position and direction of installation, mark them with a centerpunch

13.1A   A hammer and large punch can be used to drive the soft plugs into the block

13.1B   Use pliers to remove the soft plug from the block

13.10   A large socket on an extension can be used to drive the new soft plugs into their bores

holes of debris produced by this operation. Now is a good time to thoroughly clean the threads on the head bolts and the main bearing cap bolts as well.

9   Reinstall the main bearing caps and tighten the bolts finger tight.

10   After coating the sealing surfaces of the new soft plugs with gasket sealer, install them in the engine block (photo). Make sure they are driven in straight and seated properly or leakage could result. Special tools are available for this purpose, but equally good results can be obtained using a socket with an outside diameter that will just slip into the soft plug and a hammer.

11   If the engine is not going to be reassembled right away, cover it with a large plastic trash bag to keep it clean.

---

14   Engine block — inspection

1   Thoroughly clean the engine block as described in Section 13 and double-check to make sure that the ridge at the top of each cylinder has been completely removed.

2   Visually check the block for cracks, rust and corrosion. Check for stripped threads in the threaded holes.

3   Check the cylinder bores for scuffing and scoring.

4   Using the appropriate precision measuring tools, measure each cylinder's diameter at the top (just under the ridge), center and bottom of the cylinder bore, parallel to the crankshaft axis (photos). Next, measure each cylinder's diameter at the same three locations across the crankshaft axis. Compare the results to the specifications. If the cylinder walls are badly scuffed or scored, or if they are out-of-round

or tapered beyond the limits given in the specifications, have the engine block rebored and honed at an automotive machine shop. If a rebore is done, oversize pistons and rings will be required.

5   If the cylinders are in reasonably good condition and not worn to the outside of the limits they do not have to be rebored. Honing is all that is necessary.

6   Before honing the cylinders, install the main bearing caps (without the bearings) and tighten the bolts to the specified torque.

7   To hone the cylinders you will need a hone. Two types are available,

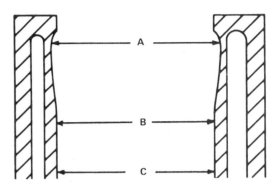

Fig. 2E.5 Measure the diameter of each cylinder just under the wear ridge (A), at the center (B), and at the bottom (C) (Sec 14)

14.4A   A telescoping gauge (snap-gauge) can be used to determine the cylinder bore diameter

14.4B   The gauge is then measured with a micrometer to determine the bore size

14.7A   Honing a cylinder with a 'bunch of grapes' hone

14.7B   Honing a cylinder with a stone-type hone

2E

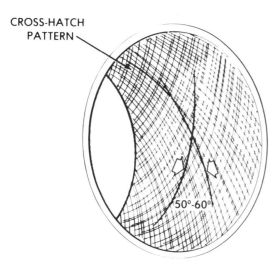

Fig. 2E.6 The cylinder hone should leave a smooth, cross-hatch pattern with the lines intersecting at a 60-degree angle (Sec 14)

Fig. 2E.7 A dial indicator can be mounted as shown to check the camshaft lobe lift (on 2.3L four-cylinder engines, lobe lift is taken directly from the face of the cam lobe) (Sec 15)

the traditional stone type and the 'bunch-of-grapes' type. Both will do a good job, and for the less-experienced mechanic the bunch-of-grapes type will probably be easier to use. You will also need plenty of light oil or honing oil, some rags and an electric drill motor. Mount the hone in the drill motor, compress the stones and slip the hone into the first cylinder (photos). Lubricate the cylinder thoroughly, turn on the drill and move the hone up and down in the cylinder at a pace which will produce a crosshatch pattern on the cylinder walls with the crosshatch lines intersecting at approximately a 60° angle, as shown in the accompanying illustration. Be sure to use plenty of lubricant and do not take off any more material than is absolutely necessary to produce the desired finish. Do not withdraw the hone from the cylinder while it is running. Instead, shut off the drill and continue moving the hone up and down in the cylinder until it comes to a complete stop, then withdraw the hone. Wipe the oil out of the cylinder and repeat the procedure on the remaining cylinders. Remember, do not remove too much material from the cylinder wall. If you do not have the tools or do not desire to perform the honing operation, most automotive machine shops will do it for a reasonable fee.

8   After the honing job is complete, chamfer the top edges of the cylinder bores with a small file so the rings will not catch as the pistons are installed.

9   The entire engine block must be thoroughly washed again with warm, soapy water to remove all traces of the abrasive grit produced during the honing operation. Be sure to run a brush through all oil holes and galleries and flush them with running water. After rinsing, dry the block and apply a coat of light rust preventative oil to all machined surfaces. Wrap the block in a plastic trash bag to keep it clean and set it aside until reassembly.

15   Camshaft, lifters and bearings — inspection and bearing replacement

Camshaft

1   Camshaft wear most often shows up as loss of lobe lift, which can be checked before the engine is disassembled.

2   Remove the rocker arm cover, then remove the nuts and separate the rocker arms and fulcrums or the rocker arm shaft from the cylinder head.

3   Beginning with the number one cylinder, mount a dial indicator with the stem resting on the end of, and directly in line with, the exhaust valve pushrod (OHV engine), as shown in the accompanying illustration, or directly on the cam lobe (OHC engine).

4   Rotate the crankshaft very slowly in the direction of normal rotation until the lifter or dial indicator stem is on the heel of the cam lobe. At this point the pushrod will be at its lowest position.

5   Zero the dial indicator, then very slowly rotate the crankshaft until the pushrod or lobe is at its highest position. Note and record the reading on the dial indicator, then compare it to the lobe lift specifications. Repeat the procedure for each of the remaining lobes.

7   If the lobe lift measurements are not as specified, a new camshaft should be installed.

8   After the camshaft has been removed from the engine, cleaned with solvent and dried, inspect the bearing journals for uneven wear, pitting or evidence of seizure. If the journals are damaged, the bearing inserts in the block or bores in the carrier are probably damaged as well. Both the camshaft and bearings will have to be replaced. Measure the inside diameter of each camshaft bearing and record the results (take two measurements, 90° apart, at each bearing).

9   Measure the bearing journals with a micrometer (photo) to determine if they are excessively worn or out-of-round. If they are more than 0.001-inch out-of-round, the camshaft should be replaced with a new one. Subtract the bearing journal diameter(s) from the corresponding bearing inside diameter measurement to obtain the clearance. If it is excessive, new bearings must be installed.

10 Check the camshaft lobes for heat discoloration, score marks, chipped areas, pitting or uneven wear. If the lobes are in good condition and if the lobe lift measurements are as specified, the camshaft can be reused.

Lifters

11 Clean the lifters with solvent and dry them thoroughly without mixing them up.

12 Check each lifter wall, pushrod seat and foot for scuffing, score marks or uneven wear. Each lifter foot (the surface that rides on the cam lobe) must be slightly convex, although this can be difficult to determine by eye. The lifter foot curve is in the arc of a 60-inch circle. If the base of the lifter is concave (photo), the lifters and camshaft must be replaced. If the lifter walls are damaged or worn (which is not very likely), inspect the lifter bores in the engine block as well. If the pushrod seats are worn, check the pushrod ends.

13 If new lifters are being installed, a new camshaft must also be installed. If a new camshaft is installed, then use new lifters as well. Never install used lifters unless the original camshaft is used and the lifters can be installed in their original locations.

Bearing replacement

14 Camshaft bearing replacement on OHV engines requires special tools and expertise that place it outside the scope of the home mechanic. Take the block to an automotive machine shop to ensure that the job is done correctly.

15 OHC engines do not have bearings, as the camshaft rides in the camshaft bores themselves. Consequently, the camshaft carrier must be replaced with a new one if the bores are worn or damaged.

15.9   The camshaft bearing journal diameter is subtracted from the bearing inside diameter to obtain the camshaft oil clearance, which must be as specified

15.12   If the bottom of any lifter is worn concave, scratched or galled, replace the entire set with new lifters

16.4   The piston ring grooves can be cleaned with a piece of broken ring

16.10   Check the ring side clearance with a feeler gauge

2E

16   Piston/connecting rod assembly — inspection

1   Before the inspection process can be carried out the piston and connecting rod assembly must be cleaned and the piston rings removed from the pistons. **Note:** *Always use new piston rings when the engine is reassembled.*

2   Remove the rings from the pistons. Do not nick or gouge the pistons in the process.

3   Scrape all traces of carbon from the top of the piston. A hand-held wire brush or a piece of fine emery cloth can be used once the majority of the deposits have been scraped away. Do not, under any circumstances, use a wire brush mounted in a drill motor to remove deposits from the pistons. The piston material is soft and will be eroded away by the wire brush.

4   Use a piece of broken ring to remove any carbon deposits from the ring grooves. Be very careful to remove only the carbon deposits. Do not remove any metal and do not nick or scratch the sides of the ring grooves (photo).

5   Once the deposits have been removed, clean the piston/rod assemblies with solvent and dry them thoroughly. Make sure that the oil return holes in the back sides of the ring grooves are clear.

6   If the pistons are not damaged or worn excessively, and if the engine block is not rebored, new pistons will not be necessary. Normal piston wear appears as even vertical wear on the piston thrust surfaces and slight looseness of the top ring in its groove. New piston rings should always be used when an engine is rebuilt.

7   Carefully inspect each piston for cracks around the skirt, at the pin bosses and at the ring lands.

8   Look for scoring and scuffing on the thrust faces of the skirt, holes in the piston crown and burned areas at the edge of the crown. If the skirt is scored or scuffed, the engine may have been suffering from overheating and/or abnormal combustion, which caused excessively high operating temperatures. The cooling and lubrication systems should be checked thoroughly. A hole in the piston crown is an indication that abnormal combustion (preignition) was occurring. Burned areas at the edge of the piston crown are usually evidence of spark knock (detonation). If any of the above problems exist, the causes must be corrected or the damage will occur again.

9   Corrosion of the piston (evidenced by pitting) indicates that coolant is leaking into the combustion chamber and/or the crankcase. Again, the cause must be corrected or the problem may persist in the rebuilt engine.

10   Measure the piston ring side clearance by laying a new ring in each ring groove and slipping a feeler gauge in between the ring and the edge of the ring groove (photo). Check the clearance at three or four locations around each groove. Be sure to use the correct ring for each groove. If the side clearance is greater than specified, new pistons rings

16.11   Measure the piston diameter at 90° to the piston pin hole

17.2   Measure the diameter of each crankshaft journal at several points to detect taper and out-of-round conditions

will have to be used.

11   Check the piston to bore clearance by measuring the bore (see Section 14) and the piston diameter. Make sure that the pistons and bores are correctly matched. Measure the piston across the skirt (photo). Subtract the piston diameter from the bore diameter to obtain the clearance. If it is greater than specified, the block will have to be rebored and new pistons and rings installed.

12   If the pistons must be removed from the connecting rods, such as when new pistons are installed, or if the piston pins have too much play in them, they should be taken to an automotive machine shop. While they are there have the connecting rods checked for bend and twist. Unless new pistons or connecting rods are to be installed, do not disassemble the pistons from the connecting rods.

13   Check the connecting rods for cracks or other damage. Remove the rod caps, lift out the old bearing inserts, wipe the rod and cap bearing surfaces clean and inspect them for nicks, gouges or scratches. After checking the rods, replace the old bearings, slip the caps into place and tighten the nuts finger tight.

17   Crankshaft — inspection

1   Clean the crankshaft with solvent and dry it thoroughly. Be sure to clean the oil holes with a stiff brush and flush them with solvent. Check the main and connecting rod bearing journals for uneven wear, scoring, pitting or cracks. Check the remainder of the crankshaft for cracks or damage.

2   Using a micrometer, measure the diameter of the main and connecting rod journals (photo) and compare the results to the specifications. By measuring the diameter at a number of points around the journal's circumference you will be able to determine whether or not the journal is out of round. Take measurements at each end of the journal, near the crank counterweights, to determine whether the journal is tapered.

3   If the crankshaft journals are damaged, tapered, out of round or worn beyond the limits given in the specifications, have the crankshaft reground by an automotive machine shop. Be sure to use the correct oversize bearing inserts if the crankshaft is reconditioned.

18   Main and connecting rod bearings — inspection

1   Even though the main and connecting rod bearings should be replaced with new ones during the engine overhaul, the old bearings should be retained for close examination. They will often reveal valuable

information about the condition of the engine.

2   Bearing failure occurs mainly because of lack of lubrication, the presence of dirt or other foreign particles, overloading the engine and corrosion. Regardless of the cause of bearing failure, it must be corrected before the engine is reassembled to prevent it from happening again.

3   When examining the bearings, remove them from the engine block, the main bearing caps, the connecting rods and the rod caps and lay them out on a clean surface in the same position as their location in the engine. This will enable you to match any bearing problems with the corresponding crankshaft journal.

4   Particulate contaminants get into the engine in a variety of ways. They may be left in the engine during assembly, or they may pass through filters or breathers. They may get into the oil, and from there into the bearings. Metal particles from machining operations and normal engine wear are often present. Abrasives are sometimes left in engine components after reconditioning, especially when parts are not thoroughly cleaned using the proper cleaning methods. Whatever the source, these foreign objects often end up embedded in the soft bearing material and are easily recognized. Large particles will not embed in the bearing and will score or gouge the bearing and shaft. The best prevention for this cause of bearing failure is to clean all parts thoroughly and keep everything spotlessly clean during engine assembly. Frequent and regular engine oil and filter changes are also recommended.

5   Lack of lubrication (or lubrication breakdown) has a number of interrelated causes. Excessive heat (which thins the oil), overloading (which squeezes the oil from the bearing face) and oil leakage or throwoff (from excessive bearing clearances, worn oil pump or high engine speeds) all contribute to lubrication breakdown. Blocked oil passages, which usually are the result of misaligned oil holes in a bearing shell, will also oil starve a bearing and destroy it. When lack of lubrication is the cause of bearing failure the bearing material is wiped or extruded from the steel backing of the bearing. Temperatures may increase to the point where the steel backing turns blue from overheating.

6   Driving habits can have a definite effect on bearing life. Full throttle, low speed operation (lugging the engine) puts very high loads on bearings, which tends to squeeze out the oil film. These loads cause the bearings to flex, which produces fine cracks in the bearing face (fatigue failure). Eventually the bearing material will loosen in pieces and tear away from the steel backing. Short trip driving leads to corrosion of bearings because insufficient engine heat is produced to drive off the condensed water and corrosive gases. These products collect in the engine oil, forming acid and sludge. As the oil is carried to the engine bearings the acid attacks and corrodes the bearing material. Incorrect bearing installation during engine assembly will lead to bearing failure

19.3A   Before checking piston ring end gap, the ring must be square in the cylinder bore. This is done by pushing the ring down with the top of a piston as shown

19.3B   With the ring square in the cylinder, measure the end gap with a feeler gauge

as well. Tight fitting bearings leave insufficient bearing oil clearance and will result in oil starvation. Dirt or foreign particles trapped behind a bearing insert result in high spots on the bearing, which can lead to failure.

19   Piston rings — installation

1   Before installing the new piston rings, the ring end gaps must be checked. It is assumed that the piston ring side clearance has been checked and verified correct (Section 16).
2   Lay out the piston/connecting rod assemblies and the new ring sets so the ring sets will be matched with the same piston and cylinder during both end gap measurement and engine assembly.
3   Insert the top (number one) ring into the cylinder and square it up with the cylinder walls by pushing it in with the top of the piston (photo). The ring should be near the lower limit of ring travel. To measure the end gap, slip a feeler gauge between the ends of the ring (photo). Compare the measurement to the specifications.
4   If the gap is larger or smaller than specified, double-check to make sure that you have the correct rings before proceeding.
5   If the gap is too small it must be enlarged or the ring ends may come in contact with each other during engine operation, which can cause serious damage to the engine. The end gap can be increased by filing the ring ends very carefully with a fine file. Mount the file in a vise equipped with soft jaws, slip the ring over the file with the ends contacting the file face and slowly move the ring to remove material from the ends. When performing this operation, file only from the outside in.
6   Excess end gap is not critical unless it is greater than 0.040-inch (1 mm). If the ring end gap is greater than 0.040-inch you have the wrong rings.
7   Repeat the procedure for each ring. Remember to keep rings, pistons and cylinders matched up.
8   Once the ring end gaps have been checked the rings can be installed on the pistons.
9   The oil control ring (lowest one on the piston) is installed first. It is composed of three separate components. Slip the spacer/expander into the groove, then install the upper side rail. Do not use a piston ring installation tool on the oil ring side rails, as they may be damaged. Instead, place one end of the side rail into the groove between the spacer/expander and the ring land, hold it firmly in place and slide a finger around the piston while pushing the rail into the groove. Install the lower side rail in the same manner.
10   After the three oil ring components have been installed, check to make sure that both the upper and lower side rails can be turned smoothly in the ring groove.

19.12   Installing the compression rings with a ring expander — the mark (arrow) must face up

11   The number two (middle) ring is installed next. It should be stamped with a mark so it can be readily distinguished from the top ring. **Note:** *Always follow the instructions printed on the ring package or box — different manufacturers may require different approaches.* Do not mix up the top and middle rings, as they have different cross sections.
12   Use a piston ring installation tool and make sure that the identification mark is facing the top of the piston, then slip the ring into the middle groove on the piston (photo). Do not expand the ring any more than is necessary to slide it over the piston.
13   Finally, install the number one (top) ring in the same manner. Make sure the identifying mark is facing up.
14   Repeat the procedure for the remaining pistons and rings.

20   Rear main oil seal – installation

Two-piece seal

1   Inspect the bearing cap and engine block mating surfaces and seal grooves for nicks, burrs and scratches. Remove any defects with a fine file or deburring tool.
2   Install one seal section in the block with the lip facing the front

Fig. 2E.8 Install the crankshaft rear oil seal as shown on all
V-type engines except early production 5.8LW (351W)
engines (if the original seal had a positioning pin, be sure to
remove the pin before installing the new seal) (Sec 20)

of the engine. Leave one end protruding from the block 3/8-inch and
make sure it is completely seated as shown in the accompanying
illustration.

3   See the accompanying illustration for split-type seal installation
on early production 2.3L and 5.8LW (351W) engines. Note the use
of sealant.

4   Repeat the procedure to install the remaining seal half in the rear
main bearing cap. In this case, leave the opposite end of the seal protruding from the cap the same distance the block seal is protruding
from the block.

5   During final installation of the crankshaft, after the main bearing
oil clearances have been checked with Plastigage as described in Section 21, apply a thin, even film of anaerobic-type gasket sealant to
the areas of the cap or block indicated in the accompanying illustration. **Caution:** *Do not get any sealant on the bearing face, crankshaft
journal or seal lip. Also, lubricate the seal lips with moly-based grease
or engine assembly lube.*

One-piece seal

6   Most late model engines covered in this manual use a one-piece
rear oil seal which must be pulled from its position at the rear of the

SEALER NOTE: CLEAN THE AREA WHERE SEALER
IS TO BE APPLIED BEFORE INSTALLING THE SEALS.
USE FORD SPOT REMOVER B7A-19521-A OR EQUIVALENT.
AFTER THE SEALS ARE IN PLACE, APPLY A 1/16 INCH
BEAD OF C3AZ-19562-A OR -B SEALER AS SHOWN.
SEALER MUST NOT CONTACT SEALS.

Fig. 2E.9 On some early 2.3L and 3.3L inline engines, a
split-type rear seal is used (note the use of sealant and the
position of the tab on the seal) (Sec 20)

crankshaft with a slide hammer and replaced with Ford tool No. T82L-
6701-A. See the accompanying illustration for instructions on the use
of this tool. A substitute seal installing tool can be fashioned from a
length of plastic or metal pipe and a few gentle blows of a hammer until the seal is firmly seated. Be sure to thoroughly lubricate the seal and
mating surfaces with clean engine oil before installation.

Fig. 2E.10 On early production 5.8LW (351W) engines, the crankshaft rear oil seal halves should be installed flush with
the faces of the block and bearing cap (apply RTV-type sealant as shown before final installation of the cap) (Sec 20)

LUBRICATE SEAL AND SEAL
MATING SURFACE WITH OIL.

FRONT OF ENGINE

CYLINDER BLOCK

SEAL INSTALLER
TOOL–T82L-6701-A

SEAL (INSTALL
WITH SPRING SIDE
TOWARD ENGINE)

Fig. 2E.11 Late model engines incorporate a one-piece crankshaft rear seal (note the Ford tool in this illustration) (Sec 20)

21 Crankshaft — installation and main bearing oil clearance check

1 Crankshaft installation is the first step in engine reassembly. It is assumed at this point that the engine block and crankshaft have been cleaned, inspected and repaired or reconditioned. **Note:** *Because of the variety of rear main bear oil seals used on OHV engines, refer to Chapter 2, Part A, Section 16 to determine if it is necessary to install the oil seal before proceeding.*

2 Remove the main bearing cap bolts and lift out the caps. Lay them out in the proper order to help ensure that they are installed correctly.

3 If they are still in place, remove the old bearing inserts from the block and main bearing caps.

4 Wipe the main bearing surfaces of the block and caps with a clean, lint free cloth. They must be kept absolutely clean. This includes keeping them free of oil. If anything, dust, oil, gasket sealer, or anything else, is trapped between the main bearing cap and the bearing insert it will cause a high-spot when the crankshaft is installed, which can quickly wipe the babbit material from the bearing. Oil between the cap and insert will also change the bearing clearance, and it can also act is a shield to prevent heat from being transfered from the bearing to the block, again destroying the bearing.

5 Clean the back sides of the new main bearing inserts and lay one bearing half in each main bearing saddle in the block. Lay the other bearing half from each bearing set in the corresponding main bearing cap. Make sure the tab on the bearing insert fits into the recess in the block or cap. Also, the oil holes in the block and cap must line up with the oil holes in the bearing insert. Do not hammer the bearing into place and do not nick or gouge the bearing faces. No lubrication should be used at this time.

6 The flanged thrust bearing must be installed in the number three cap and saddle.

7 Clean the faces of the bearings in the block and the crankshaft main bearing journals with a clean, lint free cloth. Check or clean the oil holes in the crankshaft, as any dirt here can go only one way — straight through the new bearings.

8 Once you are certain that the crankshaft is clean, carefully lay it in position (an assistant would be very helpful here) in the main bearings.

9 If you checked the main and rod journal sizes with a micrometer in Section 17, and are sure you have purchased the correct size bearing inserts, the following steps can be skipped. If, however, you were not able to check the journal sizes, or if you want to double-check to make sure you have the right size bearings, you can use Plastigauge to check actual bearing clearances.

10 Trim several pieces of the appropriate size Plastigage (so they are slightly shorter than the width of the main bearings) and place one piece on each crankshaft main bearing journal, parallel with the journal axis. Do not lay them across the oil holes.

11 Clean the faces of the bearings in the caps and install the caps in their respective positions (do not mix them up) with the arrows pointing toward the front of the engine. Do not disturb the Plastigage.

12 Starting with the center main and working out toward the ends, tighten the main bearing cap bolts, in three steps, to the specified torque. Do not rotate the crankshaft at any time during this operation.

13 Remove the bolts and carefully lift off the main bearing caps. Keep them in order. Do not disturb the Plastigage or rotate the crankshaft. If any of the main bearing caps are difficult to remove, tap them gently from side-to-side with a soft-faced hammer to loosen them.

14 Compare the width of the crushed Plastigage on each journal to the scale printed on the Plastigage container to obtain the main bearing oil clearance. Check the specifications to make sure it is correct.

15 If the clearance is not correct, double-check to make sure you have the right size bearing inserts. Also, make sure that no dirt or oil was between the bearing inserts and the main bearing caps or the block when the clearance was measured.

16 Carefully scrape all traces of the Plastigage material off the main bearing journals and the bearing faces. Do not nick or scratch the bearing faces.

17 Carefully lift the crankshaft out of the engine. Clean the bearing faces in the block, then apply a thin layer of moly-based grease or engine assembly lube to each of the bearing surfaces. Be sure to coat the thrust flange faces as well as the journal face of the thrust bearing.

18 Lubricate the rear main bearing oil seal (where it contacts the crankshaft) with moly-based grease or engine assembly lube.

19 Make sure the crankshaft journals are clean, then lay the crankshaft back in place in the block. Clean the faces of the bearings in the caps, then apply a thin layer of moly-based grease to each of the bearing faces. Install the caps in their respective positions with the arrows or tops of the number 1 on the caps pointing toward the front of the engine. Install the bolts.

20 Tighten all except the number three main bearing cap bolts to the specified torque. Tighten the number three cap bolts to 10 to 12 ft-lbs. Tap the end of the crankshaft, first rearward, then forward, using a lead or brass hammer to line up the rear main bearing and crankshaft thrust surfaces. Retighten all main bearing cap bolts to the specified torque.

21 On OHC engines, slightly tighten the main bearing cap bolts and tap the rear of the crankshaft with a plastic hammer. Tighten the bolts to the specified torque.

22 On all models, rotate the crankshaft a number of times by hand and check for any obvious binding.

23 Check the crankshaft end play with a feeler gauge or a dial indicator as described in Section 12.

22 Piston/connecting rod assembly — installation and bearing oil clearance check

1 Before installing the piston and connecting rod the cylinder walls must be perfectly clean, the top edge of each cylinder must be chamfered and the crankshaft must be in place.

2 Remove the connecting rod cap from the end of the number one connecting rod. Remove the old bearing inserts and wipe the bearing surfaces of the connecting rod and cap with a clean, lint free cloth (they must be kept spotlessly clean).

3 Clean the back side of the new upper bearing half, then lay it in place in the connecting rod. Make sure that the tab on the bearing fits into the recess in the rod. Do not hammer the bearing insert into place and be very careful not to nick or gouge the bearing face. Do not lubricate the bearing at this time.

4 Clean the back side of the other bearing half and install it in the rod cap. Again, make sure the tab on the bearing fits into the recess in the cap, and do not apply any lubricant. It is critically important that the mating surfaces of the bearing and connecting rod are perfectly

2E

clean and oil free when they are assembled.

5   Position the piston ring gaps as shown in the accompanying illustration, then slip sections of plastic or rubber hose over the connecting rod cap bolts.

6   Lubricate the piston and rings with clean engine oil and place a ring compressor over the piston. Leave the skirt protruding about 1/4-inch to guide the piston into the cylinder. The rings must be compressed flush with the piston body.

7   Rotate the crankshaft until the number one connecting rod journal is as far from the number one cylinder as possible (bottom dead center), and apply a uniform coat of engine oil to the cylinder wall.

8   With the notch or arrow on top of the piston facing to the front of the engine (photo), gently place the piston/connecting rod assembly into the number one cylinder bore and rest the bottom edge of the ring compressor on the engine block. Tap the top edge of the ring compressor to make sure it is contacting the block around its entire circumference.

9   Clean the number one connecting rod journal on the crankshaft and the bearing faces in the rod.

10   Carefully tap on the top of the piston with the end of a wooden hammer handle (photo) while guiding the end of the connecting rod into place on the crankshaft journal. The piston rings may try to pop out of the ring compressor just before entering the cylinder bore, so keep some downward pressure on the ring compressor. Work slowly,

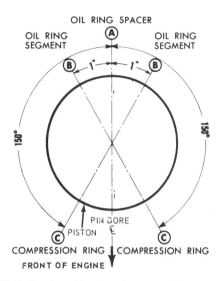

Fig. 2E.12 Before installing the pistons, position the piston ring end gaps as shown here (Sec 22)

22.8   An arrow or notch at one edge of the piston should point to the front of the engine after installation

22.10   The piston can be driven (gently) into the cylinder bore with the end of a wooden hammer handle

22.12   Plastigage must be placed parallel to the axis of the crankshaft before installing the caps to check clearance

22.14   Measuring the width of the Plastigage to determine oil clearance

and if any resistance is felt as the piston enters the cylinder, stop immediately. Find out what is hanging up and fix it before proceeding. Do not, for any reason, force the piston into the cylinder, as you will break a ring and/or the piston.

11 If you checked the rod journal diameter with a micrometer in Section 17 you know what size bearings will be needed. If, howver, you either weren't able to check the journal diameter, or if you want to double-check to make sure you have the right size bearings, you can use Plastigauge to check the bearing clearance.

12 Cut a piece of the the appropriate size Plastigage slightly shorter than the width of the connecting rod bearing and lay it in place on the number one connecting rod journal, parallel with the journal axis (it must not cross the oil hole in the journal) (photo).

13 Clean the connecting rod cap bearing face, remove the protective hoses from the connecting rod bolts and gently install the rod cap in place. Make sure the mating mark on the cap is on the same side as the mark on the connecting rod. Install the nuts and tighten them to the specified torque, working up to it in three steps. Do not rotate the crankshaft at any time during this operation.

14 Remove the rod cap, being very careful not to disturb the Plastigage. Compare the width of the crushed Plastigage to the scale printed on the Plastigage container to obtain the oil clearance (photo). Compare it to the specifications to make sure the clearance is correct. If the clearance is not correct, double-check to make sure that you have the correct size bearing inserts.

15 Carefully scrape all traces of the Plastigage material off the rod journal and/or bearing face (be very careful not to scratch the bearing — use your fingernail or a piece of hardwood). Make sure the bearing faces are perfectly clean, then apply a layer of moly-based grease or engine assembly lube to both of them. You will have to push the piston up into the cylinder to expose the face of the bearing insert in the connecting rod. Be sure to return the protective hoses to the rod bolts first.

16 Slide the connecting rod back into place on the journal, remove the protective hoses from the rod cap bolts, install the rod cap and tighten the nuts to the specified torque. Again, work up to the torque in three steps.

17 Repeat the entire procedure for the remaining piston and connecting rod assemblies. Keep the back sides of the bearing inserts and the inside of the connecting rod and cap perfectly clean when assembling them. Make sure you have the correct piston for the cylinder and that the notch or arrow on the piston faces to the front of the engine when the piston is installed. Use plenty of oil to lubricate the piston before installing the ring compressor. When installing the rod caps for the final time, be sure to lubricate the bearing faces adequately.

18 After the piston and connecting rod assemblies have been properly installed, rotate the crankshaft a number of times by hand and check for any obvious binding.

19 As a final step, the connecting rod end play must be checked. Refer to Section 11 for this procedure. Compare the measured end play to the specifications.

23   Valve adjustment

1 On V8 engines, the valve arrangement on the left bank is E-I-E-I-E-I-E-I and on the right bank is I-E-I-E-I-E-I-E. For the inline six engine, the valve arrangement is E-I-I-E-I-E-E-I-E-I-I-E. On V6 engines, the valve arrangement is I-E-I-E-I-E on the right bank and E-I-E-I-E-I on the left bank. On the 2.3L inline four-cylinder engine, the exhaust valves are on the left side of the cylinder head, numbered from one to four starting at the front. Intake valves are likewise numbered on the right side of the head.

2.3L inline four-cylinder engines

2 With the rocker arm cover removed, rotate the crankshaft so that the base circle of the camshaft lobe of the first valve to be checked is facing the cam follower.

3 Using special tool T74P-6565-A, compress the valve lash adjuster completely and hold it in this position.

4 Using a feeler gauge, make sure that the gap is as specified for the hydraulic lash adjuster.

5 If outside the allowable limit, either the cam follower is worn, the valve spring assembled height is incorrect, the camshaft is worn, or the lash adjuster is unserviceable.

All others

6 Normally these engines do not need valve adjustments because of the hydraulic lifters. If you have a running engine that has symptoms of valve clearance problems (such as excessive noise from a lifter), check for a defective part. Normally an engine will not need a valve adjustment unless a component malfunction has occurred. Hydraulic lifter failure and excessive rocker arm wear are two examples of likely component failure. Also, if major engine work is done, such as a valve job, which alters the relationship among valve train components, a means of compensating for the dimensional changes must be provided. Shorter and longer pushrods are available for this purpose (except 2.3L four-cylinder engine). To determine whether a shorter or longer pushrod is necessary, proceed as follows.

7 Bring the piston in the number one cylinder to top dead center (TDC) on the compression stroke. To do this, remove all of the spark plugs from the engine, then locate the number one cylinder spark plug wire and trace it back to the distributor. Make a mark on the distributor body directly below the terminal where the number one spark plug wire attaches to the distributor cap, then remove the cap and wires from the distributor. Using a wrench or socket over the large bolt at the front of the crankshaft, turn the engine over in a clockwise direction until the notch in the crankshaft pulley is aligned with the 0 on the timing mark tag, or until the pointer on the block is aligned with the zero mark on the pulley, depending upon how TDC on your particular engine is marked. At this point the rotor should be pointing at the mark you made on the distributor body. If it is not, turn the crankshaft one complete revolution (360°). The rotor should now be pointing at the mark on the distributor body. If not you have made the mark at the wrong plug wire connection.

8 Remove the rocker arm cover(s).

9 Make sure that the lifters are compressed (not pumped up with oil). This is accomplished during engine assembly by installing new lifters, or by compressing the lifters and relieving them of all internal oil pressure if they have been in service. A special tool is available for this procedure.

Fig. 2E.13 Checking the valve clearances (note the use of a tappet bleed down wrench. The 2.3L four-cylinder engine requires a different Ford tool for this adjustment) (Sec 23)

Inline six-cylinder engines

10 With the number one piston at TDC, position the lifter compressor tool on the intake rocker end and slowly apply pressure to bleed down the lifter until the plunger is completely bottomed. Hold the lifter in this position, as shown in the accompanying illustration, and check the available clearance between the rocker arm and the valve stem tip with a feeler gauge. Compare the measurements to the specifications. If the clearance is greater than specified, install a longer pushrod. If the clearance is less than specified, install a shorter pushrod.

2E

11 Repeat the procedure on the following valves:
No. 1 exhaust
No. 2 intake
No. 3 exhaust
No. 4 intake
No. 5 exhaust
12 Turn the crankshaft one complete turn (360°) and adjust the following valves:
No. 2 intake
No. 3 intake
No. 4 exhaust
No. 5 intake
No. 6 intake
No. 6 exhaust

V6 engines
13 Employing the lifter bleed down and measuring procedures outlined in Step 10, bring the engine to TDC for number one on the compression stroke and adjust the following valves:
No. 1 intake
No. 1 exhaust
No. 2 exhaust
No. 3 intake
No. 4 exhaust
No. 6 intake
14 Turn the crankshaft one complete turn (360°) and adjust the following valves:
No. 2 intake
No. 3 exhaust
No. 4 intake
No. 5 intake
No. 5 exhaust
No. 6 exhaust

255 and 302 cu in V8 engines
15 Employing the lifter bleed down and measuring procedures outlined in Step 10, bring the engine to TDC for number one on the compression stroke and adjust the following valves:
No. 1 intake
No. 1 exhaust
No. 4 exhaust
No. 5 exhaust
No. 7 intake
No. 8 intake
16 Turn the crankshaft 1/2 turn (180°) and adjust the following valves:
No. 2 exhaust
No. 4 intake
No. 5 intake
No. 6 exhaust
17 Turn the crankshaft 1/4 turn (90°), which will position you 90° before TDC on the exhaust stroke, and adjust the following valves:
No. 2 intake
No. 3 intake
No. 3 exhaust
No. 6 intake
No. 7 exhaust
No. 8 exhaust

351 and 400 V8 engines
18 Employing the lifter bleed down and measuring procedures outlined in Step 10, bring the engine to TDC for number one on the compression stroke and adjust the following valves:
No. 1 intake
No. 1 exhaust
No. 3 exhaust
No. 4 intake
No. 7 exhaust
No. 8 intake
19 Turn the crankshaft 1/2 turn (180°) and adjust the following valves:
No. 2 exhaust
No. 3 intake
No. 6 exhaust
No. 7 intake

20 Turn the crankshaft 1/4 turn (90°), which will position you 90° before top dead center on the exhaust stroke, and adjust the following valves:
No. 2 intake
No. 4 exhaust
No. 5 intake
No. 5 exhaust
No. 6 intake
No. 8 exhaust
21 After completion of the entire valve adjustment procedure, install the remaining engine components and run the engine. It may be necessary for an engine to run several minutes for the clearance in the valve train to be taken up completely by the hydraulic lifters, particularly if new lifters were installed.

24   Engine overhaul — reassembly sequence

1   Before beginning engine reassembly, make sure you have all the necessary new parts, gaskets and seals as well as the following items on hand:

Common hand tools
1/2-inch drive torque wrench
Piston ring installation tool
Piston ring compressor
Lengths of rubber to fit over connecting rod bolts
Plastigage
Feeler gauges
A fine-tooth file
Engine oil
Engine assembly lube or moly-based grease
RTV-type gasket sealant
Anaerobic-type gasket sealant
Thread locking compound

2   In order to save time and avoid problems, engine reassembly should be done in the following order.

Rear main oil seal (Except early model 2.3 and 3.3 L engines with
    one piece seals)
Crankshaft and main bearings
Piston rings
Piston/connecting rod assemblies
Oil pump
Oil pan
Camshaft (except 2.3L four-cylinder engine)
Timing chain/sprockets or gears
Timing chain/gear cover
Valve lifters (except 2.3L four-cylinder engine)
Cylinder head and pushrods (except 2.3L four-cylinder engine)
Cylinder head and camshaft (2.3L four-cylinder engine)
Intake and exhaust manifolds
Oil filter
Rocker arm/camshaft cover
Fuel pump
Water pump
Rear main oil seal (2.3L and 3.3L engines with one-piece seal only)
Flywheel/flexplate
Carburetor/fuel injection components
Thermostat and housing cover
Distributor, spark plug wires and spark plugs
Emissions control components
Alternator

25   Initial start-up and break-in after overhaul

1   Once the engine has been installed in the vehicle, double check the engine oil and coolant levels.
2   With the spark plugs out of the engine and the coil high tension lead grounded to the engine block, crank the engine over until oil pressure registers on the gauge (if so equipped) or until the oil light goes off.
3   Install the spark plugs, hook up the plug wires and the coil high tension lead.

4   Make sure the carburetor choke plate is closed, then start the engine. It may take a few moments for the gasoline to reach the carburetor, but the engine should start without a great deal of effort.

5   As soon as the engine starts it should be set at a fast idle (to ensure proper oil circulation) and allowed to warm up to normal operating temperature. While the engine is warming up make a thorough check for oil and coolant leaks.

6   Shut the engine off and recheck the engine oil and coolant levels. Restart the engine and check the ignition timing and the engine idle speed (refer to Chapter 1). Make any necessary adjustments.

7   Drive the vehicle to an area with minimum traffic, accelerate at full throttle from 30 to 50 mph, then allow the vehicle to slow to 30 mph with the throttle closed. Repeat the procedure 10 or 12 times. This will load the piston rings and cause them to seat properly against the cylinder walls. Check again for oil and coolant leaks.

8   Drive the vehicle gently for the first 500 miles (no sustained high speeds) and keep a constant check on the oil level. It is not unusual for an engine to use oil during the break-in period.

9   At 500 miles change the oil and filter and retorque the cylinder head bolts.

10   For the next few hundred miles drive the vehicle normally. Do not either pamper it or abuse it.

11   After 2000 miles, change the oil and filter again and consider the engine fully broken in.

2E

Chapter 3
Cooling, heating and air conditioning systems

Contents

Specifications

Coolant type	50/50 mixture of non-phosphate ethylene glycol antifreeze

Torque specifications	Ft-lbs
Fan-to-water pump bolts.	12 to 18
Radiator hose clamps	9 to 12
Water pump-to-engine bolts	
2.3L (140 ci) engine	14 to 21
3.3L (200 ci) engine	12 to 15
3.8L (232 ci) engine	7 to 9
4.2L (255 ci) engine	12 to 18
5.0L (302 ci) engine	12 to 18
5.8L (351 ci) engine	12 to 18
6.6L (400 ci) engine	12 to 18
7.5L (460 ci) engine	15 to 25
Transmission oil line fitting-to-radiator	12 to 18

1 General Information

Ford vehicles produced during the years covered by this manual have a cooling system consisting of either a vertical or a cross flow radiator, a thermostat for temperature control and an impeller-type water pump driven by a belt from the crankshaft pulley.

The radiator cooling fan is mounted on the front of the water pump. Certain vehicles incorporate an automatic clutch which disengages the fan at high speeds or when the outside temperature is low enough to maintain a low radiator temperature. Later models with the 2.3L four-cylinder engine may come equipped with an electric cooling fan.

The cooling system is pressurized by means of a spring-loaded radiator filler cap. Cooling efficiency is improved by raising the boiling point of the coolant through increased cooling system pressure. If the coolant temperature rises above the boiling point, the extra pressure in the system forces the radiator cap internal spring-loaded valve off its seat and exposes the overflow pipe or the coolant recovery bottle connecting tube to allow the displaced coolant a path of escape.

The cooling system functions as follows: cold water from the radiator circulates up the lower radiator hose to the water pump, where it is pumped into the cylinder block and around the water passages to cool the engine. The coolant then travels up into the cylinder head(s), around the combustion areas of the cylinders and valve seats, absorbing heat before it passes out through the thermostat. When the engine is running at the correct operating temperature, the water flow from the cylinder head(s) diverges to flow through the intake manifold, vehicle interior heater (when activated) and the radiator.

When the engine is cool (below normal operating temperature), the thermostat valve is closed, preventing the coolant from flowing into the radiator and restricting the flow to the engine. The restriction in the flow of coolant enables the engine to quickly warm to the correct operating temperature.

The coolant temperature is monitored by a sender mounted in either the cylinder head or the intake manifold. The sender, together with the gauge on the instrument panel, gives a continuous indication of coolant temperature.

Normal maintenance consists of checking the level of fluid in the radiator at regular intervals, inspecting the hoses and connections for signs of leakage or material deterioration, and checking the cooling fan drivebelt tension and condition (refer to Chapter 1 for details).

The heating system utilizes heat produced by the engine to warm the interior of the vehicle, via the flow of coolant through hoses attached to the heater and engine block. The system is manually controlled through dash mounted levers and switches. Air conditioning is an optional accessory, with all components contained in the engine compartment with the exception of the controls, which are also dash mounted. This system, like the water pump, is crankshaft driven by means of an accessory belt.

RADIATOR UPPER HOSE

THERMOSTAT HOUSING

Fig. 3.1 To locate the thermostat, trace the upper hose from the radiator (the thermostat shown is typical of inline four and six-cylinder engines) (Sec 3)

BOLT

STUD

WATER OUTLET CONNECTION

GASKET

THERMOSTAT OUTLET SIDE TO RADIATOR — UP —

Fig. 3.3 Thermostats on V6 and V8 engines are mounted in the top of the intake manifold (Sec 3)

2 Antifreeze — general information

Caution: *Do not allow antifreeze to come in contact with your skin or painted surfaces of the vehicle. Flush contacted areas immediately with plenty of water. Antifreeze can be fatal to children and pets. They like it because it is sweet. Wipe up garage floor and drip pan coolant spills immediately. Keep antifreeze containers covered and repair leaks in your cooling system immediately.*

The cooling system should be filled with a water/ethylene glycol-based antifreeze solution, which will prevent freezing down to at least -20°F. It also provides protection against corrosion and increases the coolant boiling point.

The cooling system should be drained, flushed and refilled at least every other year (see Chapter 1). The use of antifreeze solutions for periods of longer than two years is likely to cause damage and encourage the formation of rust and scale in the system.

Before adding antifreeze to the system, check all hose connections and retorque the cylinder head bolts, because antifreeze tends to leak through very minute openings.

The exact mixture of antifreeze to water which you should use depends on the relative weather conditions. The mixture should contain at least 50 percent antifreeze, but should never contain more than 70 percent antifreeze.

OUTLET CONNECTION

THERMOSTAT—OUTLET SIDE TO RADIATOR

SCREW AND WASHER TIGHTEN TO 19-29 N·m (14-21 LB-FT)

GASKET

GASKET

WATER PUMP

FRONT OF VEHICLE

Fig. 3.2 Thermostat and water pump assemblies — 2.3L four-cylinder engine — exploded view (Sec 3)

3 Thermostat — Replacement

Removal

1 Drain the radiator so that the coolant level is below the thermostat.

2.3L four-cylinder engine

2 Remove the hoses from the coolant outlet connection and the bypass outlet. Remove the thermostat housing, the thermostat and the gasket as shown in the accompanying illustration. Note that the outlet side of the thermostat faces away from the block.

Inline six-cylinder engine

3 Remove the coolant outlet elbow attaching bolts, then pull the elbow away from the cylinder head sufficiently to provide access to the thermostat.

4 Remove the thermostat and gasket, noting the top and bottom to assure proper installation.

V6 and V8 engines

5 Disconnect the bypass hoses at the water pump and intake manifold.

6 Remove the bypass tube, then remove the water outlet housing attaching bolts as shown in the accompanying illustration.

7 Bend the radiator upper hose upward and remove the thermostat and gasket, taking note of the top and bottom to assure proper installation.

Installation

2.3L four-cylinder engine

8 Clean both gasket mating surfaces, coat a new gasket with water-resistant sealer and position the gasket on the cylinder head. Install the thermostat in the housing and install the housing on the head. Reinstall the coolant hoses.

Inline six-cylinder engine

9 After cleaning the coolant outlet elbow and cylinder head gasket surfaces, coat a new gasket with water-resistant sealer and position the gasket on the cylinder head opening. **Note:** *The gasket must be positioned on the cylinder head before the thermostat is installed.*

10 The coolant elbow contains a locking recess into which the thermostat is turned and locked. Install the thermostat with the bridge section in the outlet elbow.

11 Turn the thermostat clockwise to lock it in position on the flats cast into the elbow.

3

5.4　Use of a flare-nut wrench as shown will prevent damage to the transmission cooler lines when removing them from the radiator

5.5　The cooling fan shroud is held in place by two bolts (A) as is the radiator support bracket (B). Both the shroud and the bracket must be removed before the radiator will come out

12　Position the elbow against the cylinder head and tighten the attaching bolts to the specified torque (see the *Torque specifications* in Chapter 2 for your particular engine).

V6 and V8 engines

13　After cleaning the water outlet gasket surfaces, coat a new water outlet gasket with water-resistant sealer.

14　Position the gasket on the intake manifold opening.

15　Install the thermostat in the intake manifold with the copper element toward the engine and the thermostat flange positioned in the recess.

16　Position the water outlet housing against the intake manifold and install and tighten the attaching bolts.

17　Install the water bypass line and tighten the hose connections.

All engines

18　Fill the cooling system with the proper amount and type of coolant.

19　Start and run the engine until it reaches normal operating temperature, then check the coolant level and look for leaks.

4　Thermostat — Check

1　The best way to check the operation of the thermostat is with it removed from the engine. In most cases, if the thermostat is suspect it is more economical to simply buy and install a replacement thermostat, as they are not very costly.

2　To check, first remove the thermostat as described in Section 3.

3　Inspect the thermostat for excessive corrosion and damage. Replace it with a new one if either of these conditions is noted.

4　Place the thermostat in hot water (25 degrees above the temperature stamped on the thermostat). When submerged in the water (which should be agitated thoroughly), the valve should open all the way.

5　Next, remove the thermostat using a piece of bent wire and place it in water which is 10 degrees below the temperature on the thermostat. At this temperature, the thermostat valve should close completely.

6　Reinstall the thermostat if it operates properly. If it does not, purchase a new thermostat of the same temperature rating.

5　Radiator — removal, servicing and installation

Note: *Refer to Chapter 1 for preliminary checks of the cooling system.*
Removal

1　Drain the radiator using the draincock located near the bottom of the radiator. See the information given in Chapter 1 pertaining to this.

Fig. 3.4　Typical cooling fan installation on 2.3L engines (Sec 5)

Fig. 3.5　Typical clutch-equipped fan assembly (Sec 5)

HOSE

HOSE REMOVED

CLAMP

1/8 INCH (3.2 mm)

BEAD

CLAMP

HOSE INSTALLED

Fig. 3.6 Check the condition of hoses (Chapter 1) before reconnecting them as shown (Sec 5)

2 Remove the lower radiator hose and clamp from the radiator. Be careful not to put excessive pressure on the outlet tube, as it can easily break away.

3 Remove the upper radiator hose from the radiator tank.

4 If equipped with an automatic transmission, remove the transmission cooler lines from the radiator, taking care not to twist the lines or damage the fittings. It is best to use a flare nut wrench for this job (photo). Plug the ends of the disconnected lines to prevent leakage and keep dirt from entering the system.

5 Remove the bolts which attach the fan shroud to the radiator support bracket. Remove the support bracket bolts (if applicable) (photo). Place the shroud over the fan, allowing space for radiator removal. In some cases the fan itself will have to be removed as shown in the accompanying illustrations. Once the fan is out of the way, the shroud, bracket and radiator can be lifted straight up together and out of the engine compartment.

Servicing

6 Inspect the radiator for signs of leakage, deterioration or rust. Inspect the cooling fins for distortion or damage. In most cases a radiator repair shop should be consulted for repairs.

7 With the radiator removed, brush accumulations of insects and leaves from the fins and examine and replace, if necessary, any hoses or clamps which have deteriorated.

8 The radiator can be flushed as described in Chapter 1.

9 Check the pressure rating of the radiator cap and have it tested by a service station.

10 If you are installing a new radiator, transfer the fittings from the old unit to the new one.

Installation

11 Installation is the reverse or removal. Take care to install the radiator into the vehicle with caution as the cooling fins along with the radiator itself are fragile and can be damaged easily by mishandling or contact with the fan or radiator support. Make sure that the radiator is mounted securely with the proper retaining bolts and that all hoses and clamps are in good condition.

12 After remounting all components related to the radiator, fill it with the proper type and amount of coolant.

13 Start the engine and allow it to reach normal operating temperature, then check for leaks.

---

6 Water pump — removal and installation

Note: See the appropriate part of Chapter 2 for exploded view drawings of your engine.

1 With the engine cold, drain the cooling system.

2 On some models it will be necessary to remove the air cleaner assembly and air intake duct to gain access to the water pump.

3 Remove the fan shroud retaining bolts.

4 Remove the fan/clutch retaining bolts from the nose of the water pump and remove the shroud, fan/clutch and spacer (if so equipped) (photo).

5 Loosen the accessory drivebelt idler, if equipped, and remove the drivebelt and water pump pulley. **Note:** In the Steps which follow, further references to drivebelt removal should be ignored if your vehicle is equipped with a serpentine drivebelt.

6 If equipped, loosen the power steering pump attaching bolts. Loosen the power steering pump drivebelt by releasing the adjustment bolt and allowing the power steering pump to move toward the engine. If the power steering pump bracket is retained at the water pump, the power steering pump should be completely removed and laid to one side to facilitate removal of the bracket.

7 If equipped with air conditioning, do not disconnect any of the hoses or lines. The following procedures can be performed by moving, not disconnecting, the compressor. Loosen the air conditioning compressor top bracket retaining bolts. Remove the bracket on engines that have it secured to the pump. Remove the air conditioner idler arm and assembly.

8 Remove the compressor and power steering pump drivebelt.

9 If equipped, remove the air pump pulley hub bolts and remove the bolt and pulley. Remove the air pump pivot bolt, bypass hose and air pump.

10 Loosen the alternator pivot bolt.

11 Remove the retaining bolt and spacer for the alternator.

12 Remove the adjustment arm bolt, pivot bolt and alternator drivebelt.

13 Remove the alternator bracket if it is retained at the water pump.

14 Disconnect the lower radiator hose from the water pump inlet.

15 Disconnect the heater hose from the water pump.

16 Disconnect the bypass hose from the water pump.

17 Remove the water pump retaining bolts and remove the water

6.4 Clutch driven fans may be removed by extracting the four attaching bolts (arrow)

6.17 After the belt-driven accessory brackets have been disconnected, the water pump may be removed

pump from the cylinder front cover or the engine block (depending on engine type). Take note of the installed positions of the various length bolts (photo).

18 Remove the separator plate from the water pump (460 engine only).

19 Remove the gasket(s) from the mating faces of the water pump and from the cylinder block.

20 Before installation, remove and clean all gasket material from the water pump, cylinder front cover, separator plate mating surfaces and/or cylinder block.

21 Position new gaskets on the water pump and coat them on both sides with water resistant sealer.

22 Install the water pump.

23 Install the retaining bolts finger-tight and make sure that all gaskets are in place and that the hoses line up in the correct position. It may be necessary to transfer some hose ports and/or fittings from the old pump if you are replacing it with a new one.

24 Tighten the retaining bolts to the proper torque.

25 Connect the radiator lower hose and clamp.

26 Connect the heater return hose and clamp.

27 Connect the bypass hose to the water pump.

28 If equipped, install the top air conditioning compressor bracket and idler pulley assembly.

29 Attach the remaining components to the water pump and engine in the reverse order of removal.

30 Adjust all of the belts for the alternator, air pump, power steering, air conditioning compressor and other drive accessories (if equipped).

31 Fill the cooling system with the proper coolant mixture.

32 Start the engine and make sure there are no leaks. Check the level frequently during the first few weeks of operation to ensure there are no leaks and that the level in the system is stable.

---

7 Water pump — check

1 A failure in the water pump can cause overheating and serious engine damage (the pump will not circulate coolant through the engine).

2 There are three ways to check the operation of the water pump while it is installed on the engine. If the pump is defective, it should be replaced with a new or rebuilt unit.

3 With the engine at normal operating temperature, squeeze the upper radiator hose. If the water pump is working properly, a coolant surge will be felt as the hose is released.

4 Water pumps are equipped with weep or vent holes. If a pump seal failure occurs, small amounts of coolant will leak from the weep hole. In most cases it will be necessary to use a flashlight from under the vehicle to see evidence of leakage from this point on the pump body.

5 If the water pump shaft bearings fail there may be a squealing sound emitted from the front of the engine while it is running. Shaft wear can be felt if the water pump pulley is forced up and down. Do not mistake drivebelt slippage (which also causes a squealing sound) for water pump failure.

---

8 Coolant temperature sending unit — check and replacement

Check

1 The water temperature indicating system consists of a sending unit which is screwed into the cylinder head or intake manifold (photo) and a corresponding temperature gauge mounted in the instrument panel. When the coolant temperature of the engine is low, the resistance of the sending unit is high and thus sends a restricted flow of current to the gauge. This causes the pointer to move only a short distance. As the temperature of the engine increases, the resistance at the sending unit decreases and thus causes an increased flow of current and movement of the gauge needle. **Note:** *Do not apply 12 volt current directly to the sending unit terminal at any time, as the voltage will damage the unit.*

2 Start the engine and allow it to run with a thermometer placed in the radiator neck until a minimum temperature of 180 °F is reached.

3 The gauge in the instrument panel should indicate within the normal band of the scale.

4 If the gauge does not indicate correctly, disconnect the gauge lead from the terminal at the sender unit.

8.1   The coolant temperature sending unit (arrow) is typically found on the intake manifold, though some may be mounted on the cylinder head

5 Connect the lead of a 12 volt test light or the positive lead of a voltmeter to the gauge lead that was disconnected.

6 Connect the other test lead to an engine ground.

7 With the ignition switch set to the On or Accessory position, a flashing light or fluctuating voltage should indicate that the instrument voltage regulator is operating and the gauge circuit is not grounded.

8 If the light stays on or the voltage reading is steady, the instrument voltage regulator is defective. If no voltage is indicated by the voltmeter or test light, check for an open circuit in the system.

9 If all of the above readings check correctly yet the gauge does not work properly, the sending unit should be replaced.

Replacement

10 Disconnect the cable from the negative battery terminal.

11 Disconnect the temperature sending unit wire at the sending unit.

12 Remove the temperature sending unit from the engine.

13 Prepare the new temperature sending unit for installation by applying electrically conductive thread sealing tape or spray on copper sealer to the threads.

14 Install the temperature sending unit.

15 Connect the wire to the sending unit.

16 Connect the cable at the negative battery terminal.

17 Start the engine and check that the temperature gauge is operating correctly.

---

9 Electrodrive cooling fan — general information

Caution: *Since the electric cooling fan is activated by temperature, it may start at any time, even when the ignition is off. Always disconnect the negative battery cable when working in the vicinity of the fan.*

The electric cooling fan is installed on late model 2.3L engines. The fan motor is activated by temperature switches in the radiator and the carburetor.

The fan operates whenever engine coolant temperatures reach 233 °F (112 °C) during normal driving. When the engine is shut off, the carburetor sensor activates the fan when the carburetor temperature reaches 155 °F (68 °C). A timer keeps the fan running for 20 minutes so that the fuel will not be vaporized, causing hard starting.

The fan motor is centrally mounted in the fan shroud and the fan is attached to the motor shaft by a retaining clip.

---

10 Electrodrive cooling fan — removal and installation

1 Disconnect the negative cable from the battery.

2 Unclip the fan motor wires from the shroud and unplug the connector at the motor pigtail connector.

Fig. 3.7 Electric cooling fan assembly —
exploded view (Sec 10)

Fig. 3.8 The fan can be separated from the fan motor by
removing the retainer clip as shown (Sec 10)

3   Remove the screws which mount the shroud to the radiator support and lift the shroud, complete with fan motor and fan, from the vehicle.
4   Set the shroud on a flat, clean area so that no dirt is transferred back into the engine compartment.
5   Remove the U-shaped retainer clip from the shaft and slide the fan from the motor shaft as shown in the accompanying illustration.
6   Remove the nuts which hold the fan motor to the shroud and lift the motor straight off the mounting studs.
7   Assembly and installation is the reverse of the removal.
8   The fan motor mounting studs are pressed into the shroud and will break out or strip if overtightened. Tighten the nuts evenly until all are snug. Use thread sealer to prevent the nuts from backing off.
9   Install the fan and retainer clips on the motor shaft. There is a key on the shaft to locate the fan.
10   Position the shroud on the radiator support brackets and install the four screws. Tighten the screws evenly.
11   Clip the wiring into position and reconnect the electrical plug.
12   Connect the battery cable.

11   Electrodrive cooling fan — testing the fan motor

1   There are three major components whose failure or improper operation will lead to overheating and hard hot starting. These components are the fan motor, the fan relay and the timer relay. To save time, the following test is divided into three sections. Perform the first test, then choose the symptom which best describes the remaining problem and complete that task. If problems persist, perform the entire test sequence, then seek the help of an authorized dealer if the problem is not solved.

Engine overheats and is hard to start
2   Unplug the motor connector. Using a jumper wire, connect the negative terminal to ground and the positive terminal to the positive terminal of the battery. If the motor does not run, replace it. If the motor does run, isolate the problem you are experiencing from the list below and perform the appropriate tests.

Engine overheats
3   Disconnect the timer relay plug. Turn the ignition on and connect the coolant temperature switch to ground. If the fan does not run, replace the coolant temperature switch. If the fan does run, continue the steps below.
4   Disconnect the coolant relay plug at the relay and check for power at point A from the battery and point B from the ignition. See the accompanying illustration for the location of the testing points. If power

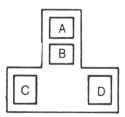

Fig. 3.9 Electric cooling fan coolant timer relay plug (Sec 11)

from these sources is not found, check the fusible link and the fuse and replace as necessary. Perform this test again. If power is found, continue. If power is not found, check the wires for continuity and the connectors for a tight fit. If power is found, continue.

5   Turn the ignition off. Check the wire from point D to the motor connector for continuity. Check the wire from point C to the coolant temperature switch connector. If continuity is not found, service the wiring and connectors as necessary. If continuity is found, replace the coolant relay, remove the testing equipment and restore all connections.

Hard hot starting

6   Unplug the coolant relay plug. Turn the ignition on and disconnect the carburetor temperature switch connector. Using a jumper wire, connect the temperature switch connector to ground. If the fan motor runs, replace the carburetor temperature switch. If the fan motor does not run, continue with the steps below.

7   Unplug the connector at the timer relay and check for current from point E to the battery and from point F to the ignition as shown in the accompanying illustration. If power is not found, check fusible link H and fuse 6 and replace parts as necessary. Repeat the test above. If power is not found, check and replace wiring as necessary. If power

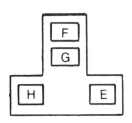

Fig. 3.10 Electric cooling fan coolant timer relay connector (Sec 11)

is found, continue the tasks below.

8   Turn the ignition off. Check the wiring and connectors from point G to the fan motor and from point H to the coolant temperature switch. If continuity is not found, replace wiring as necessary. If continuity is found, replace the timer relay, remove all test equipment and restore all connections.

12   Air conditioning system — servicing

Caution: *Before disconnecting any lines or attempting to remove any air conditioning system components, have the system evacuated by an air conditioning technician. Do not attempt to do this yourself. The refrigerant used in the system can cause serious injuries and respiratory irritation.*

1   Because of the special tools, equipment and skills required to service air conditioning systems, and the differences between the various systems that may be installed on these vehicles, air conditioner servicing cannot be covered in this manual.

2   Component removal, however, can usually be accomplished without special tools and equipment. The home mechanic may realize a substantial savings in repair costs if he removes components himself, takes them to a professional for repair, and/or replaces them with new ones (see **Caution** above).

3   Problems in the air conditioning system should be diagnosed, and the system refrigerant evacuated by an air conditioning technician before component removal and replacement is attempted.

4   Once the new or reconditioned component has been installed, the system should be charged and checked by an air conditioning technician.

5   Before removing air conditioning system components, get more than one estimate of repair costs from air conditioning service centers. You may find it to be cheaper and less trouble to let the entire operation be performed by someone else.

Fig. 3.11 Basic air conditioning system component layout (Sec 12)

13 Air conditioning compressor — removal and installation

Caution: *Before removing the compressor, the system must be evacuated by an air-conditioning technician. Do not attempt to do this yourself — the refrigerant in the system can cause serious injuries and respiratory irritation.*

1   After having the system evacuated, remove the compressor pivot and adjusting bolts.
2   Disconnect the wire.
3   Remove the drivebelt, routing the lower loop behind the vibration damper to gain additional slack, if necessary.
4   Remove the compressor from the mount.
5   Remove the fitting block (coupled hose assembly) bolt at the rear of the compressor.
6   Installation procedures are the reverse of those for removal. When installing the fitting block, use new O-rings and lubricate them with 500 viscosity refrigerant oil.
7   After the compressor is installed have the system recharged.

14 Air conditioning condenser — removal and installation

Caution: *Before removing the condenser the system must be evacuated by an air-conditioning technician. Do not attempt to do this yourself — the refrigerant used in the system can cause serious injuries and respiratory irritation.*

1   After having the system evacuated, disconnect the coupled hose and liquid line fittings.
2   Remove the screws retaining the top radiator shroud.
3   Remove the bolts holding the condenser to the top radiator support.
4   Carefully tilt the radiator to the rear and lift the condenser out of the bottom cradle supports.
5   If the condenser is being replaced with a new one, transfer the brackets and mounts from the old unit to the new one.
6   The installation procedures are the reverse of those for removal. When installing the hose and fittings, use new O-rings and lubricate them with 500 viscosity refrigerant oil.
7   After the condenser is installed have the system recharged.

3

Chapter 4   Fuel and exhaust systems

Refer to Chapter 13 for specifications and information related to 1985 and later models

Contents

Specifications

Fuel pump

Type	Cam-driven mechanical pump
	Single electric pump
	Dual electric pumps
Mechanical fuel pump static pressure	
2.3 and 3.3L engines	5.0 to 7.0 psi
3.8L, 5.0L and 6.6L engines	6.0 to 8.0 psi
7.5L engines	6.7 to 8.7 psi
Volume (at idle rpm)	1/2 liter (1 pint) in 20 seconds

Torque specifications	**Ft-lbs**
Carburetor-to-intake manifold	
1946 1V	12 to 15
5200/6500 2V	10 to 14
2150 2V	12 to 16
2700/7200VV	12 to 15
4350 4V	12 to 15
YFA 1V	10 to 14
Central fuel injection-to-intake manifold	10
CFI pressure regulator	2 to 4
Throttle body-to-main body	1 to 2
CFI injector retainer	2 to 5
Fuel line fittings	
Electric pumps	10 to 15
Mechanical pumps	15 to 18
Fuel pump-to-block bolts	
2.3L and 3.8L engines	14 to 21
5.0L and 5.8L engines	19 to 27
6.6L engine	
Nut	14 to 20
Bolt	10 to 15
7.5L engine	19 to 27

1   General information

The fuel system on all models consists of a fuel tank mounted to the chassis, a fuel pump and a carburetor or central fuel injection system, equipped with an air cleaner for filtering purposes. A combination of metal and rubber fuel hoses are used to connect these components. Some models are equipped with an electric fuel pump or dual electric fuel pumps.

The carburetor is a single, dual or four barrel, downdraft type, depending on the engine displacement and year of production.

The fuel system (especially the carburetor) is heavily interrelated with the emissions control system on all vehicles produced for sale in the United States. Certain modifying components of the emissions control system are described in Chapter 6. The exhaust system includes a catalytic converter, muffler, related emissions equipment and associated pipes and hardware. **Warning:** *Gasoline is extremely flam-mable, so extra precautions must be taken when working on any part of the fuel system. Do not smoke or allow open flames or bare light bulbs near the work area. Also, do not work in a garage if a natural gas appliance with a pilot light is present.*

2   Carburetor — servicing and overhaul

Warning: *Gasoline is extremely flammable, so extra precautions must be taken when working on any part of the fuel system. Do not smoke or allow open flames or bare light bulbs near the work area. Also, do not work in a garage if a natural gas appliance with a pilot light is present.*

1   A thorough road test and check of carburetor adjustments should be done before any major carburetor service. Specifications for some adjustments are listed on the Vehicle Emissions Control Information

HOT IDLE COMPENSATOR

AIR HORN

FAST IDLE ADJUSTING SCREW

CHOKE CAP CLAMP

ELECTRIC CHOKE

FEEDBACK MOTOR ASSEMBLY

CHOKE HOT AIR TUBE

CHOKE PULLDOWN VACUUM CONNECTION

FAST IDLE SPEED ADJUSTING SCREW

Fig. 4.1 Model 2150 21450 2V carburetor — right rear view (Sec 2)

4

AUTOMATIC CHOKE THERMOSTATIC HOUSING CAP

AIR HORN

FUEL BOWL VENT

TEMPERATURE COMPENSATED PUMP (TCP)

MAIN BODY

SOLE-VAC THROTTLE POSITIONER

SOLENOID ADJUST BRACKET

Fig. 4.2 Model 2150 2V carburetor — left front view (Sec 2)

Fig. 4.3 Model 2150 2V carburetor — exploded view (Sec 2)

Fig. 4.4 Model 7200VV/2700VV carburetor — right front view (Sec 2)

4

Fig. 4.5 Model 7200VV/2700VV carburetor — left front view (Sec 2)

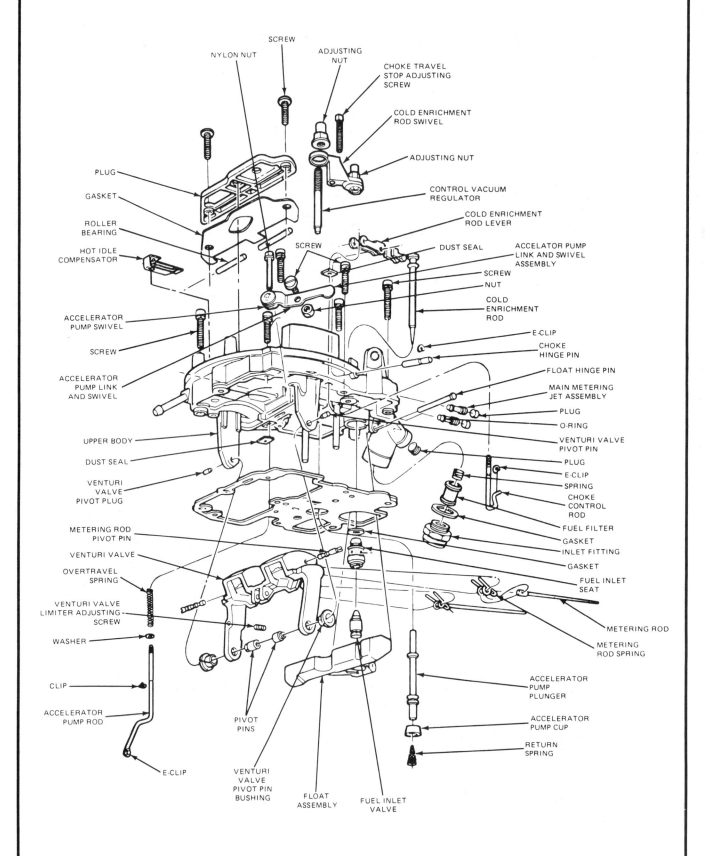

Fig. 4.6 Model 7200VV/2700VV carburetor air horn assembly — exploded view (Sec 2)

Fig. 4.7 Model 7200VV/2700VV carburetor main body — exploded view (Sec 2)

1 Throttle return control device
2 Throttle return control device bracket
3 Mounting screw
4 Adjusting screw (TSP on)
5 (Not applicable)
6 Screw (3) (breakaway)
7 Choke thermostatic housing retainer shroud
8 Choke thermostatic housing
9 Choke thermostatic housing gasket
10 Screw
11 Choke thermostatic lever
12 Choke shaft lever and pin assembly
13 Fast idle cam

13a Large E-clip
14 Fast idle intermediate lever
15 Screw (2)
16 Choke control diaphragm cover
17 Choke control diaphragm spring
18 Choke control diaphragm assembly
19 Choke control diaphragm rod
19a Clip
20 Choke housing bushing
21 Choke heat tube (if equipped)
22 Curb idle adjusting screw (TSP off)
23 Retaining nut
24 Fast idle adjusting lever
24a Nylon washer and bushing assembly
25 Fast idle lever
25a Large E-clip

26 Fast idle adjusting screw
27 Throttle plate screws (4)
28 Throttle plates
29 Venturi valve limiter stop pin
30 Throttle shaft assembly
31 Transmission kickdown adjusting screw
32 Venturi valve limiter lever and bushing assembly
33 E-clip
34 (Not applicable)
35 Throttle body
36 Fast idle cam adjusting screw
37 Transmission kickdown lever return spring (if equipped)
38 (Not applicable)
39 Screw (5)

Fig. 4.8 Model YFA 1V carburetor — right side view (Sec 2)

Fig. 4.9 Model YFA 1V carburetor — left side view (Sec 2)

Fig. 4.10 Model YFA 1V carburetor — exploded view (Sec 2)

4

PCV CONNECTION

VENTURI
VACUUM
(NOT USED)

SECONDARY
AIR VALVE

CHOKE PLATE

FAST IDLE
SPEED
ADJUSTMENT

Fig. 4.11 Model 4350 4V carburetor — top view (Sec 2)

"INTERNAL" FUEL BOWL VENTS

DELAYED CHOKE
PULLDOWN DIAPHRAGM

CHOKE PLATE

MECHANICAL FUEL
BOWL VENT VALVE

SOLENOID THROTTLE
POLITIONER

EGR CONNECTION

IDLE MIXTURE
ADJUSTMENT SCREWS

SPARK PORT

Fig. 4.12 Model 4350 4V carburetor — front view (Sec 2)

Fig. 4.13 Model 4350 4V carburetor — exploded view (Sec 2)

label found in the engine compartment.

2   Some performance complaints directed at the carburetor are actually a result of loose, misadjusted or malfunctioning engine or electrical components. Others develop when vacuum hoses leak, are disconnected or are incorrectly routed. The proper approach to analyzing carburetor problems should include a routine check as follows.

    a) Inspect all vacuum hoses and actuators for leaks and proper installation (see Chapter 5, Emissions control systems).

    b) Tighten the intake manifold nuts and carburetor mounting nuts evenly and securely.

    c) Perform a cylinder compression test.

    d) Clean or replace the spark plugs as necessary.

    e) Test the electrical resistance of the spark plug wires.

    f) Inspect the ignition primary wires and check the vacuum advance operation. Replace any defective parts.

    g) Check the ignition timing according to the instructions listed on the Emissions Control Information label.

    h) Set the carburetor idle mixture.

    i) Check the fuel pump pressure.

    j) Inspect the heat control valve in the air cleaner for proper operation.

    k) Remove the carburetor air filter element and blow out any dirt with compressed air. If the filter is extremely dirty replace it.

    l) Inspect the crankcase ventilation system.

3   Carburetor problems usually show up as flooding, hard starting, stalling, severe backfiring, poor acceleration and lack of response to idle mixture screw adjustments. A carburetor that is leaking fuel and/or covered with wet looking deposits needs attention.

4   Diagnosing carburetor problems may require that the engine be started and run with the air cleaner removed. While running the engine without the air cleaner backfires are possible. This situation is likely to occur if the carburetor is malfunctioning, but just the removal of the air cleaner can lean the air/fuel mixture enough to produce an engine backfire. Perform tests without the air cleaner for as short a time as possible. Do not position your face or any portions of your body directly over the carburetor during inspection or servicing procedures.

5   Once it is determined that the carburetor is in need of work or an overhaul, several alternatives should be considered. If you are going to attempt to overhaul the carburetor yourself, first obtain a good quality carburetor rebuild kit which will include all necessary gaskets, internal parts, instructions and a parts list. You will also need carburetor cleaning solvent and some means of blowing out the internal passages of the carburetor with air.

6   Due to the many configurations and variations of carburetors offered on the range of vehicles covered in this book, it is not feasible for us to do a step-by-step overhaul of each type. You will find a good, detailed instruction list with any quality carburetor overhaul kit and it will apply in a more specific manner to the carburetor you have.

7   An alternative to rebuilding is to obtain a new or rebuilt carburetor. These are readily available from dealers and auto parts stores for all engines covered in this manual. Make sure the exchange carburetor is identical to the original. Often a tag is attached to the top plate of the carburetor which will aid in determining the exact type of carburetor you have. When obtaining a rebuilt carburetor or a rebuild kit, take time to ascertain that the kit or carburetor matches your application exactly. Seemingly insignificant differences can make a considerable difference in the overall performance of your engine.

8   If you choose to overhaul your own carburetor, allow enough time to disassemble the carburetor carefully, soak the necessary parts in the cleaning solvent (usually for at least one-half day or according to the instructions listed on the carburetor cleaner) and reassemble it, which will usually take you much longer than disassembly. When you are disassembling a carburetor, take care to match each part with the illustration in your carburetor kit and lay the parts out in order on a clean work surface to help you reassemble the carburetor. Overhauls by amateurs sometimes result in a vehicle which runs poorly or not at all. To avoid this use care and patience when disassembling your carburetor so you can reassemble it correctly.

Fig. 4.14 Model 5200/6500 carburetor (Sec 2)

CURB IDLE SPEED
ADJUSTMENT SCREW

SOLENOID/KICKER
(TSP) (VOTM)

VACUUM CONNECTION
WHEN A/C EQUIPED

THROTTLE STOP
ADJUSTING SCREW

CURB IDLE
SPEED ADJUSTMENT
SCREW

CARBURETOR WITH SOLENOID KICKER & IDLE TRACKING SWITCH

CURB IDLE-ADJUSTMENT
POSITIONING ROD

NO THROTTLE STOP
ADJUSTING SCREW REQUIRED

IDLE TRACKING SWITCH

CARBURETOR WITH IDLE TRACKING SWITCH

LOOSEN LOCKNUT ROTATE
KICKER TO ADJUST
CURB IDLE SPEED

NO THROTTLE STOP
ADJUSTING SCREW REQUIRED

KICKER (VOTM)

VACUUM CONNECTION
WHEN A/C EQUIPPED

IDLE TRACKING SWITCH

CARBURETOR WITH KICKER (VOTM) & IDLE TRACKING SWITCH

CURB IDLE SPEED
ADJUSTMENT SCREW

SOLENOID (TSP)

THROTTLE STOP
ADJUSTING SCREW

IDLE TRACKING SWITCH

CARBURETOR WITH SOLENOID (TSP) & IDLE TRACKING SWITCH

4

Fig. 4.15 Model 5200 2V carburetor with throttle solenoid positioner (alternate throttle positioners shown) (Sec 2)

Fig. 4.16 Model 5200 carburetor — exploded view (model 6500 similar) (Sec 2)

Fig. 4.17 Model 1946 1V carburetor — throttle-side view (Sec 2)

4

Fig. 4.18 Model 1946 1V carburetor — choke-side view (Sec 2)

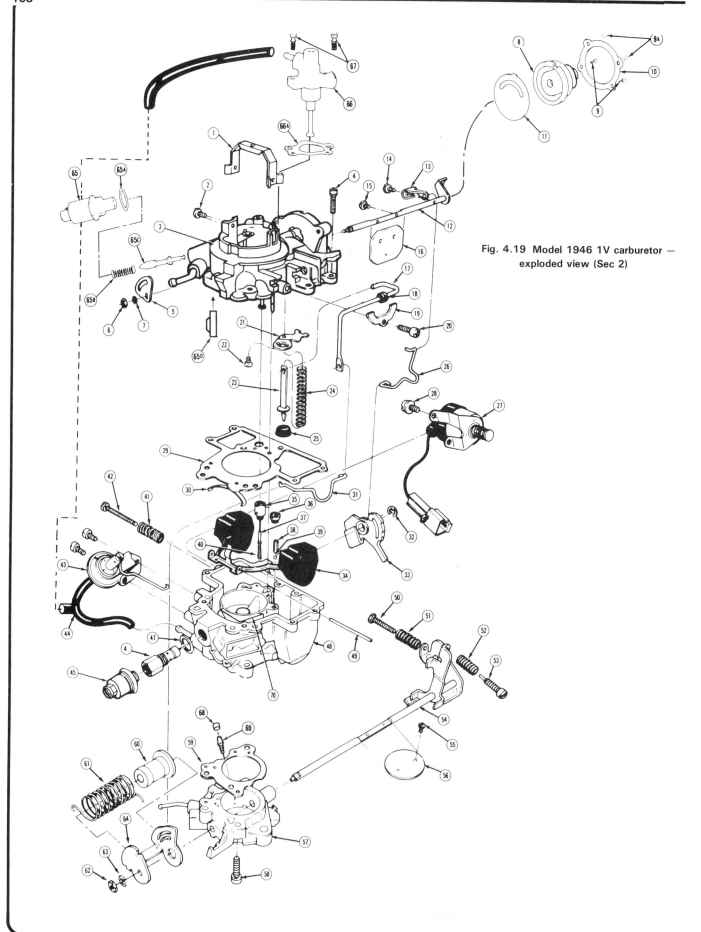

Fig. 4.19 Model 1946 1V carburetor — exploded view (Sec 2)

1 Air cleaner bracket
2 Air cleaner bracket screw (2)
3 Air horn
4 Screw and washer (8)
5 Choke pulldown lever
6 Choke shaft nut
7 Lockwasher
8 Choke bimetal assembly
9 Screw (2)
9A Rivet (2)
10 Choke cover retainer
11 Choke thermostatic housing locating disc
12 Choke shaft and lever assembly
13 Choke control lever
14 Screw
15 Screw
16 Choke plate
17 Accelerator pump operating rod
18 Accelerator pump rod grommet
19 Rod retaining clamp
20 Screw
21 Accelerator pump spring retaining plate
22 Screw
23 Accelerator pump piston stem
24 Accelerator pump spring
25 Accelerator pump piston cup
26 Fast idle cam link
27 Anti-diesel solenoid
28 Screw (2)
29 Air horn gasket
30 Float hinge retainer
31 Accelerator pump operating link
32 Retaining clip (fast idle cam)
33 Fast idle cam
34 Float assembly
35 Power valve body
36 Main metering jet
37 Power valve pin
38 Accelerator pump weight
39 Accelerator pump check ball
40 Power valve spring
41 Spring
42 Low idle (solenoid off) adjusting screw
43 Choke pulldown diaphragm assembly
44 Choke diaphragm vacuum hose
45 Fuel filter
46 Fuel inlet needle and seat assembly
47 Gasket
48 Main body assembly
49 Float hinge pin
50 Curb idle adjusting screw
51 Spring
52 Spring
53 Fast idle adjusting screw
54 Throttle shaft and lever assembly
55 Screw (2)
56 Throttle plate
56 Throttle plate
57 Throttle body assembly
58 Throttle body screw (3)
59 Throttle body gasket
60 Throttle return spring bushing
61 Throttle return spring
62 Nut
63 Lockwasher
64 Throttle return spring breacket
65 Bowl vent solenoid
65A Washer
65B Spring
65C Pintle
65D Seal
66 Power valve piston assembly
66A Gasket
67 Screw (2)
68 Idle mixture
69 Idle mixture needle concealment plug
70 Fuel bowl filter

Fig. 4.20 Typical caburetor identification tag/stamp (Sec 2)

3 Carburetor — removal and installation

There are a number of safety precautions to follow when working with gasoline. Refer to *Safety first* near the front of this manual.

1 Disconnect the negative cable at the battery. Remove the hose connections leading to the air cleaner and mark them with coded pieces of tape to simplify reassembly.
2 Remove the air cleaner assembly.
3 Use a small catch can and disconnect the fuel feed line from the carburetor. Plug the end of the hose to prevent further leakage.
4 Disconnect any electrical leads from the emissions control devices connected to the carburetor. Mark these connections so they can be installed in the proper position.
5 Remove any vacuum lines from the carburetor. Mark them for installation purposes.
6 Disconnect the kickdown lever or cable from the carburetor (if equipped).
7 Disconnect the throttle cable or linkage from the carburetor.
8 Disconnect any heater hoses that may be connected to the choke system.
9 Remove the carburetor retaining nuts from the studs.
10 Lift off the carburetor, spacer plate (if equipped), and gasket(s). Place a piece of cardboard over the intake manifold surface to keep anything from falling into the engine while the carburetor is off.
11 Before installation, carefully clean the mating surfaces of the intake manifold, spacer plate (if equipped), and the base of the carburetor of any old gasket material. These surfaces must be perfectly clean and smooth to prevent vacuum leaks.
12 Install a new gasket(s).
13 Install the carburetor and spacer plate (if equipped) over the studs on the intake manifold.
14 Install the retaining nuts and tighten them to the proper torque.

4 Carburetor — external adjustments

Note: *All carburetors on U.S. vehicles come equipped with adjustment limiters or limiter stops on the carburetor idle mixture screws. All adjustments are to be made only within the range provided by the limiter devices. In addition, the following procedures are intended for general use only. The information given on the Emissions Control Information label located under the hood is specific for your engine and should be followed.*

The instructions given below should be regarded only as temporary adjustments. The vehicle should be taken to a facility equipped with the necessary instruments for adjusting the idle mixture as soon as possible after the vehicle is running. At the same time the idle mixture

Fig. 4.21 Typical electrically-assisted carburetor choke system (2150 2V carburetor shown) (Sec 5)

Fig. 4.22 Automatic choke thermostatic spring housing 2150 2V carburetor (Sec 5)

Fig. 4.23 Automatic choke control assembly model 2700VV/7200VV carburetors (Sec 5)

is set, the idle speed should also be reset so your carburetor is operating within the range delineated on the Emissions Control Information label.

Idle speed (preliminary)
1   Set the fuel mixture screws to the full counterclockwise position allowed by the limiter caps.
2   Back off the idle speed adjusting screw until the throttle bore plates are seated in the throttle bore. Some vehicles are equipped with either a dashpot or a solenoid-type idle valve to hold the linkage open. Make sure these devices are not holding the idle up when making this adjustment.
3   Turn the idle adjusting screw inward until it contacts the throttle stop. Turn the screw an additional one and one half turns to establish a preliminary idle speed adjustment.

Idle speed (engine running)
4   Set the parking brake and block the wheels to prevent movement. If equipped with an automatic transmission, have an assistant apply the brakes as a further safety precaution during the following procedures.
5   Start the engine and allow it to reach normal operating temperature.
6   Make sure that the ignition timing is set as described in Chapter 1.
7   On vehicles with a manual shift transmissions the idle should be set with the transmission in Neutral. On vehicles with automatic transmissions the idle setting is made with the transmission in Drive.
8   Make sure the choke plate is fully opened.
9   Make sure the air conditioning is turned off.
10 Connect a tachometer according to the manufacturer's instructions.
11 Adjust the engine curb idle rpm to the specifications given on the Emissions Control Information label. Make sure the air cleaner is installed for this adjustment.
12 If so equipped, turn the solenoid assembly to obtain the specified curb idle rpm with the solenoid activated (see the Emission Control Information label for idle speed).
13 Set the automatic transmission to Neutral.
14 Disconnect the power to the solenoid lead wire at the connector.
15 Adjust the carburetor throttle stop screw to obtain 500 rpm in Neutral.
16 Connect the solenoid power wire and open the throttle slightly by hand. The solenoid plunger should hold the throttle lever in the extended position and move the rpm range up.

Fast idle adjustment
17 The fast idle adjusting screw is provided to maintain engine idle rpm while the choke is operating and the engine has a limited air supply when cold. As the choke plate moves through its range of travel from the closed to the open position, the fast idle cam rotates to allow slower idle speeds until the normal operating temperature and correct curb idle rpm is reached.
18 Before adjusting the fast idle make sure the curb idle speed is adjusted as previously described.

19 With the engine at normal operating temperature and the tachometer attached, manually rotate the fast idle cam until the fast idle adjusting screw rests on the specified step of the cam (see Emissions Control Information label for proper step).
20 Turn the fast idle adjusting screw inward or outward to obtain the specified fast idle rpm.

5   Automatic choke – inspection and adjustment

Note: *Choke checking procedures can be found in Chapter 1.*
1   Remove the air cleaner with the engine cold and not running.
2   Rotate the throttle (or have an assistant depress the gas pedal) to the open position and see if the choke plate shuts tightly in the opening of the upper body air horn. With the accelerator held open, make sure that the choke plate can be moved freely and that it is not hanging up due to deposits of varnish. If the choke plate has excessive deposits of varnish it will have to be either cleaned with a commercial spray-on carburetor cleaner or the carburetor will need to be dismantled and overhauled or replaced (see Section 2). A spray type carburetor cleaner will remove any surface varnish which may be causing sticky or erratic choke action. However, care must be used to prevent sediment from entering the throttle venturis.
3   Start the vehicle. If equipped with an electric choke, use a voltmeter to check that the electric assist on the side of the choke thermostat housing has voltage. Voltage should be constantly supplied to the temperature sensing switch as long as the engine is running. If no voltage is present, check the system circuit to determine the problem.

Fig. 4.24 Adjustment limiting choke cap YFA 1V carburetor   (Sec 5)

Fig. 4.25 Choke housing and electric choke components — 5200/6500 2V carburetors (Sec 5)

Fig. 4.26 Choke housing and cap adjustment — model 1946 1V carburetor (Sec 5)

4   Some automatic chokes come equipped with a thermostatic spring housing which controls the choke action. To adjust this type of housing, loosen the three screws which attach the thermostatic spring housing to the choke housing. The spring housing can now be turned to vary the setting on the choke. Set the spring housing to the specified mark (see Emissions Control label in the engine compartment) and tighten the retaining screws. Do not try to compensate for poor choke operation by varying the index setting from the specified spot. If the choke is not operating properly, the spring inside the housing may be worn or broken or other problems may exist in the choke system. If this situation exists the spring housing will have to be replaced.

5   Allow the vehicle to completely cool (at least four hours — preferably overnight) and check for proper operation as described in Chapter 1.

Fig. 4.27 Central Fuel Injection assembly — exploded view (Sec 6)

1 Fuel pressure regulator adjusting screw plug
2 Fuel pressure regulator
3 O-ring
4 Fuel pressure regulator gasket
5 Connector
6 Connector
7 Fuel charging main body
8 Plug
9 Injector assembly
10 O-ring
11 Fuel injector retaining screw
12 Fuel charging body gasket
13 Fuel injector retainer
14 Screw
15 Diagnostic valve
16 Fuel pressure relief valve cap
17 Fuel charging wiring assembly
18 Screw
19 Screw and washer
20 Ball
21 Control diaphragm cover
22 Control modulator spring

23 Pulldown diaphragm retainer
24 Pulldown control diaphragm
25 Pulldown control adjuster
26 Fast idle control rod
27 Fast idle cam
28 Choke housing shaft
29 Fast idle control rod positioner
30 Choke housing bushing
31 Thermostat housing gasket
32 Screw and washer
33 Choke thermostat lever
34 Thermostat housing
35 Retainer
36 Screw
37 Nut and washer
38 Fast idle cam adjuster lever
39 Screw
39 Fast idle pick-up lever return spring
40 Fast idle lever
41 Screw and washer
42 Throttle position sensor
43 Screw

44 Screw
45 Fuel charging throttle body
46 Screw
47 Throttle plate
48 Throttle control linkage bearing
49 E-clip
50 Pin
51 Throttle shaft
52 C-ring
53 Throttle control linkage bearing
54 Throttle return spring
55 Bushing
56 Transmission linkage lever
57 Screw
58 Transmission linkage lever pin
59 Throttle shaft spacer
60 Throttle lever ball
61 Throttle lever
62 Throttle positioner
63 Adjusting screw
64 Throttle positioner retaining spring
65 E-clip
66 Throttle positioner bracket
67 Screw

CONTROL DIAPHRAGM COVER

FUEL PRESSURE REGULATOR

FUEL PRESSURE RELIEF VALVE AND CAP

FUEL INLET FITTING

FUEL CHARGING MAIN BODY

FUEL INJECTORS

4

THERMOSTAT HOUSING ASSEMBLY

FUEL CHARGING THROTTLE BODY

THROTTLE POSITIONER ASSEMBLY

FAST IDLE SCREW

THROTTLE POSITION SENSOR

FUEL CHARGING WIRING ASSEMBLY

Fig. 4.28 Central Fuel Injection components — right front view (Sec 6)

THROTTLE POSITIONER ASSEMBLY

INJECTOR CONNECTORS

FUEL PRESSURE REGULATOR

FUEL PRESSURE RELIEF
VALVE AND CAP

FUEL INLET FITTING

FUEL CHARGING
MAIN BODY

IDLE SPEED SCREW

FUEL CHARGING
THROTTLE BODY

THROTTLE VALVE LEVER
ADJUSTING SCREW

EGR SOLENOID
FRESH AIR TUBE

FUEL RETURN
LINE FITTING

Fig. 4.29 Central Fuel Injection components — left rear view (Sec 6)

6 Central Fuel Injection (CFI) — general information

The Central Fuel Injection system incorporates two injectors mounted in a throttle body similar to that of a conventional carburetor. This produces greatly improved fuel metering in all running conditions and, since most of the control mechanism is electronic, reduces maintenance and minor repair problems. If a problem occurs with the electronic control module however, the only course of action the owner has (unless equipped with highly specialized equipment) is a trip to a specialist with the proper diagnostic equipment.

The Electronic Engine Control (EEC) module automatically adjusts the air/fuel mixture according to engine load and performance. A fuel pressure regulator mounted in the fuel charging assembly regulates the electric pump generated fuel pressure at a constant 39 psi. The injectors consist of a solenoid actuated pintle valve and a small inline fuel filter. They are energized by time modulated electronic pulses from the EEC. **Caution:** *Prior to any operation in which a fuel line will be disconnected, the high pressure in the system must first be relieved. Disconnect the negative battery cable to prevent sparks when fuel vapors are present.*

7 Central fuel injection (CFI) — idle speed adjustment

1   Place the transmission in Neutral or Park and firmly set the parking brake. Turn the air conditioning selector to the Off position.
2   Start the engine and let it run until it reaches normal operating temperature.
3   Shut the engine off, then restart it and run it at 2000 rpm for 60 seconds. If the vehicle is not equipped with a tachometer, attach an external one according to the manufacturer's instructions. Return the speed to idle and allow the engine to stabilize for 30 seconds. Bring the engine speed back to 2000 rpm and let it stabilize for approximately 10 seconds.
4   Place the transmission in Reverse. Check and adjust the curb idle speed within 60 seconds. If adjustment is required, loosen the saddle

bracket locking screw (see accompanying illustration). Turn the adjusting screw clockwise to increase the idle speed or counterclockwise to decrease the speed until the specified rpm is obtained (see the Emissions Control Information label for specified idle speed).
5   Tighten the saddle bracket locking screw and repeat the idle stabilization procedure in Step 3 to verify the final setting.

3.8L Central Fuel Injection — Curb idle speed check and throttle stop fast idle adjustments

6   Set the parking brake and block the wheels. If equipped with an automatic parking brake, always place the transmission in Reverse when checking curb idle. Make all adjustments at normal operating temperature with all accessories Off.
7   After engaging the transmission in Drive (or Reverse) and idling for 60 seconds, idle rpm should be within specification (refer to the Emission Control Information label for speeds).
8   If the engine curb idle speed is excessive and it is observed that the throttle lever is not in contact with the ISC motor, but held open by the throttle stop adjustment screw (TSAS), the ISC plunger must be retracted by performing the following procedure in the sequence described.
9   Shut the engine off and remove the air cleaner. In the engine compartment, locate the self-test connector and self-test input (STI) connector. These two connectors are located next to each other.
10   Connect a jumper wire between the STI connector and the signal return pin on the self test connector.
11   Turn the ignition to the Run position. Do not start the engine.
12   The ISC plunger will retract. Wait until the plunger is fully retracted (about ten seconds). **Note:** *If the plunger does not retract, it will have to be serviced by a qualified professional.*
13   Shut off the ignition.
14   Remove the jumper wire.
15   Using pliers, grasp the TSAS screw threads and turn the screw until it is removed from the CFI assembly. Install a new screw.
16   With the throttle plate closed, turn the new screw in until there is a 0.005-inch gap between the screw tip and the throttle lever surface which it contacts.

SADDLE BRACKET
LOCKING SCREW
FOR CURB IDLE

SADDLE BRACKET
ADJUSTING SCREW
CURB IDLE

Fig. 4.30 Central Fuel Injection — curb idle speed adjustment (Sec 7)

FAST IDLE SPEED
ADJUSTING SCREW

HIGH STEP

Fig. 4.31 Central Fuel Injection — fast idle speed adjustment (Sec 7)

17 Perform the fast idle adjustment by first removing the rubber dust cover from the ISC motor tip.
18 Push the tip back toward the motor to remove any lash, but without engaging the idle tracking switch.
19 Attempt to pass a 9/32-inch drill bit between the ISC motor tip and the throttle lever. **Note:** *be sure not to push back the idle tracking switch with the bit. It must pass through while making light contact with both surfaces.*
20 If the clearance between the ISC motor tip and the throttle lever is incorrect, loosen the ISC bracket lock screw and turn the ISC bracket adjusting screw until proper clearance is attained.
21 Tighten the lock screw and replace the rubber dust cover.
22 Reinstall the air cleaner.

5.0L Central Fuel Injection — fast idle adjustment

23 Place the transmission in Park or Neutral.
24 Bring the engine to normal operating temperature.
25 Disconnect the vacuum hose at the EGR valve and plug it. Disconnect and plug the canister purge line.
26 Disconnect and plug the vacuum hose at the fast idle pulldown motor. Turn the ignition off.
27 Set the fast idle lever on the high step of the fast idle cam as shown in the accompanying illustration.
28 With a tachometer, check and adjust the fast idle rpm between 20 and 60 seconds after restarting the engine. If the time limit is exceeded, repeat steps 26 and 27.
29 Remove the plug from the EGR hose and reconnect it. Remove the plug from the fast idle pulldown motor vacuum hose and reconnect it.
30 Reconnect the canister purge line.

---

8   Central Fuel Injection (CFI) — removal and installation

Warning: *Gasoline is extremely flammable, so extra precautions must be taken when working on any part of the fuel system. Do not smoke or allow open flames or bare light bulbs near the work area. Also, do not work in a garage if a natural gas appliance with a pilot light is present.*

Fuel pressure relief procedure

1 A Schrader-type diagnostic pressure valve is located on top of the fuel charging assembly. This valve is for monitoring fuel pressure, pressure relief prior to servicing, and for bleeding the fuel system of any air after servicing. A special Ford tool (No. T80L-9974-A) or equivalent is connected to this valve to relieve the pressure in the lines prior to performing any service procedures.

Removal

2 It is necessary to remove the CFI carburetor before cleaning the injector filter screens. It may also be financially advantageous to remove the CFI carburetor before taking it in for professional servicing or to exchange it for a rebuilt unit.
3 Disconnect the negative cable from the battery.
4 Remove the air cleaner. Disconnect the throttle cable and transmission throttle valve lever.
5 Disconnect all fuel, vacuum and electrical connections at the carburetor. Note the pressure relief procedure at the beginning of this Section.
6 Remove the carburetor to manifold retaining nuts. Remove the fuel charging assembly/carburetor from the vehicle. Remove the mounting gaskets from the intake manifold and spacer plate.

Installation

7 Making sure all gasket mating surfaces are clean, place new gaskets on either side of the spacer plate, then place the gasket/spacer assembly over the studs on the intake manifold.
8 Position the CFI carburetor over the four mounting studs and secure it with the attaching nuts. Tighten the nuts finger tight, then in three steps, tighten the nuts to the specified torque.
9 Reconnect the fuel line, electrical connectors, throttle cable and all emission system lines. Start the engine and check for leaks. Adjust the idle speed if necessary (see Section 7).

---

9   Central Fuel Injection (CFI) — injector filter screen cleaning

---

1 A dirty or clogged injector filter screen will normally first appear as decreased engine performance at high rpm and under heavy loads. Bear in mind that fuel injected models incorporate two additional fuel filters, one near the intake manifold and one mounted on the electric fuel pump inside the fuel tank. These filters are also suspect. If all filters

Fig. 4.32 Central Fuel Injection — injector cross-section and filter screen location (Sec 9)

Fig. 4.33 Removing the air cleaner mounting stud from the main fuel charging body (Sec 9)

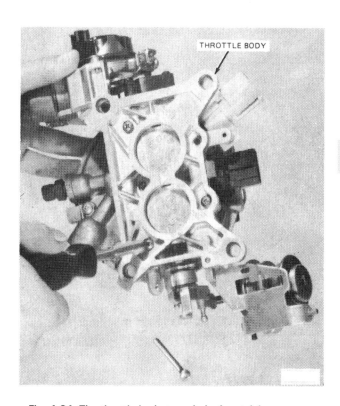

Fig. 4.34 The throttle body to main body retaining screws can be accessed through the bottom of the CFI assembly as shown (Sec 9)

Fig. 4.35 Removing the throttle body from the main body (Sec 9)

are clean, check the fuel pump(s) according to the procedure in this Chapter.

2   Remove the CFI carburetor from the intake manifold according to the procedure in Section 8.

3   Remove the center air cleaner mounting stud from the top of the main fuel charging body as shown in the accompanying illustration.

4   Invert the carburetor assembly and remove the four retaining screws as shown in the accompanying illustration. Separate the throttle body from the main body as shown in the accompanying illustration.

Fig. 4.36 Removing the CFI fuel charging assembly gasket
(replace it with a new one upon reassembly) (Sec 9)

Fig. 4.37 Removing the CFI pressure regulator retaining
screws (Sec 9)

Fig. 4.38 Removing the CFI Injector retainer (Sec 9)

Fig. 4.39 Identify the injectors as shown during removal to
avoid confusion during reassembly (Sec 9)

5   Carefully remove and discard the gasket as shown in the accompanying illustration. Do not damage the gasket surfaces.
6   Remove the three pressure regulator retaining screws as shown
in the accompanying illustration and the pressure regulator.
7   Disconnect the electrical connectors from the two injectors by pulling them directly out. Mark the connectors so they can be attached
to the same injectors when reassembled.
8   Remove the injector retainer screw and the injector retainer as
shown in the accompanying illustration.
9   Carefully remove each injector, noting by the mark on the injector
body whether it inserts at the choke or throttle side as shown in the
accompanying illustration.
10   Carefully remove the filter screens and replace them with new ones.
11   Reassembly of the injector unit is basically the reverse of
disassembly. Note that the injector retainer, pressure regulator, throttle
body and carburetor to manifold retaining bolts and screws must be
correctly tightened and all affected gaskets must be replaced with new
ones.

10   Throttle cable and kickdown rod — removal and installation

1   Pry the throttle cable retainer bushing from the top end of the accelerator pedal and remove the inner cable from the pedal assembly.
Note: *On later model vehicles the cable is retained by a Tinnerman type
fastener which must be pried off the end of the cable.*
2   Remove the circular retaining clip holding the inner cable to the
underside of the dash panel.
3   Remove the two screws retaining the outer cable to the dash panel.
4   Disconnect the control rod from the carburetor linkage.
5   Remove the screw or spring clip retaining the outer cable to the
engine bracket.
6   The complete cable assembly can now be removed.
7   To remove the kickdown rod (automatic transmission only), remove

Fig. 4.40 Typical fuel line routing — fuel-injected models
(Sec 11)

Fig. 4.41 Typical fuel line routing — non fuel-injected
models (Sec 11)

the C-type spring clips and pins at each end of the rod and remove the rod.

8   Install the throttle cable and kickdown rod by reversing the removal procedure.

---

11   Fuel lines and fittings — routing and replacement

Caution: *There are a number of safety precautions to follow when working with gasoline. Refer to 'Safety first' near the front of this manual.*

1   The fuel lines are either made of metal with short lengths of rubber hose connecting critical flex points, such as at the tank and fuel pump, or they are nylon high-pressure lines which use no rubber components. The fuel lines are retained to the body and frame with various clips and brackets. They generally will require no service; however, if they are allowed to come loose from their retaining brackets they can vibrate and eventually be worn through. If a fuel line must be replaced, have it done by a dealership or repair shop as it requires special tools to build the lines.

2   If a short section of metal fuel line is damaged, rubber fuel hose can be used to replace it if it is no longer than 12-inches. Cut a length of fuel quality rubber hose longer than the section to be replaced and use a tubing cutter to remove the damaged portion of the metal line. Install the rubber fuel line using two hose clamps and check to make sure no leaks are present. Do not use rubber tubing to repair nylon hose.

3   If new metal fuel lines are necessary, they must be cut, formed and flared out of fuel system tubing. If you have the equipment to do so, remove the old fuel line from the vehicle and duplicate the bends and length of the removed fuel line.

4   Install the new section of tubing and be careful to install new clamps and brackets where needed. Make sure the replacement tubing is of the same diameter, shape and quality as the original one. Make sure all flared ends conform to those on the original fuel line. Make sure metal fuel lines connected to fuel pumps or other fittings are of the double flare type. Remove all metal shavings from inside the tubing before installation.

5   Always check rubber hoses for signs of leakage or deterioration.

6   If a rubber hose is replaced, also replace the clamp and position it as shown in the accompanying illustration.

WHEN CLAMP IS SPECIFIED (ALL FUEL HOSES), INSTALL IN THIS AREA (BEYOND FIRST BEAD AND BEFORE HOSE END).

HOSE MUST BE INSTALLED WITHIN .06 IN OF SECOND BEAD ON FUEL AND VAPOR CONNECTIONS. FOR CONNECTIONS TO NIPPLES WITHOUT SECOND BEAD, MINIMUM ENGAGEMENT IS .67 IN.

Fig. 4.42 Proper method for repairing rubber-to-steel fuel
and vapor lines (Sec 11)

Fig. 4.43 Push connect fitting with hairpin clip (Sec 11)

CLIP

"O" RINGS

BODY

STEEL TUBE

SPACERS

Fig. 4.44 Push connect fitting with duck bill clip (Sec 11)

5/16 INCH 5-BARB CONNECTOR

CFI OR EFI NYLON TUBING

CFI OR EFI NYLON TUBING

ENGAGE ALL BARBS OF THE 5-BARB CONNECTOR

REPLACEMENT NYLON TUBING

5/16 INCH TUBING SPLICE—CFI, EFI

ENGAGE ONLY 2-BARBS INTO THE ORIGINAL TUBING

5/16 INCH 5-BARB CONNECTOR

NON-CFI NYLON TUBING

NON-CFI NYLON TUBING

ENGAGE ALL 5 BARBS INTO THE REPLACEMENT NYLON TUBING

REPLACEMENT NYLON TUBING

5/16 INCH TUBING SPLICE—NON-CFI, EFI

1/4 INCH 2-BARB CONNECTORS

ORIGINAL TUBING

ORIGINAL TUBING

ENGAGE ALL BARBS OF THE 2-BARB CONNECTOR

REPLACEMENT NYLON TUBING

1/4 INCH TUBING SPLICE

Fig. 4.45 Nylon tubing splicing combinations for fuel line repair (Sec 11)

STEEL TUBE ENDS

5/16 INCH CFI AND NON-CFI CONNECTOR

UNION

STEEL TO STEEL TUBE SPLICE

BULK NYLON—CFI

1/4 INCH NON-CFI CONNECTOR

NYLON TUBING 90 DEGREE CONNECTOR

NYLON TUBING STRAIGHT CONNECTOR

Fig. 4.46 Nylon fuel line service parts (Sec 11)

Plastic fuel tubing — general information

7   On fuel injected models and some others, Ford uses nylon fuel tubing made from material proven for use with fuels and resistant to most environmental conditions. This tubing must not be repaired using hose and hose clamps. The push-connect fittings cannot be repaired — they must be replaced, preferably by a Ford service department.

8   The plastic fuel lines can be damaged by torches, welding sparks, grinding and other operations which involve heat and high temperatures. If any service operation which involves heat is performed, locate all fuel system components (especially the plastic fuel lines) out of the way. It is recommended that the plastic fuel tubes be removed from the vehicle if a torch or high heat producing equipment is to be used for servicing the following areas:

  a) Exhaust or suspension components
  b) Floor pan under the vehicle and inside the passenger compartment on the right side
  c) Rocker panel on the right side
  d) Underbody frame rails and crossmembers on the right side
  e) The firewall or dash panel under the vehicle or inside the passenger compartment
  f) The front or rear wheel housings or fender aprons on the right side of the car

Push connectors — replacement

9   If a push connector on the plastic tubing has become damaged it can be replaced as follows with the Ford replacement part.

10   Relieve the fuel system pressure as outlined in Section 9.

11   Disconnect the damaged push connector. Be sure to bend the tab to the side before removing the retaining clip.

12   Select the proper size replacement push connector and nylon tube assembly.

13   Cut a section of the original nylon tube to the same length as the nylon tube attached to the new push connector.

14   Install a proper barbed connector (see accompanying illustrations) in the replacement nylon assembly. To make hand insertion of the barbed connectors into the nylon tubing easier, the tube end may be soaked in a cup of boiling water for one minute immediately before pushing the barbs into the nylon.

15   Check that the underbody clips are properly secured to the fuel tubes.

16   Start the engine and check for fuel leaks.

12   Mechanical fuel pumps — general information

Mechanical fuel pumps are bolted to the left side of the cylinder block or front cover on 2.3 liter engines and all V8 engines. On the 3.8 liter V6 engine it is located on the right side of the front cover. The pump is mechanically operated by an eccentric on the end of the camshaft. The pump rocker arm rides against the eccentric and provides the diaphragm pumping motion.

The pump cannot be disassembled for service and must be replaced if testing indicates it is not within performance specifications.

If a problem exists with the fuel pump it will not deliver adequate fuel to the carburetor during high engine speeds or under high loads. When the engine has a lean or fuel starved condition, the fuel pump is often suspect. Similar symptoms will be present if the fuel filter in or on the carburetor (or in the case of the electric fuel pump, inside the gas tank) is plugged or restricted, if the carburetor is lean or malfunctioning, if fuel lines and hoses are leaking, kinked or restricted or if the electrical system is shorting out or malfunctioning.

If the fuel pump is noisy, loosen the fuel pump mounting bolts and tighten them to specification. Replace the fuel pump gasket if necessary. Check for loose or missing fuel line attaching clips. Tighten the clips on the fuel lines if necessary.

Before removing a suspect fuel pump be sure there is adequate fuel in the tank and be sure the fuel filters are not plugged. Inspect all the fuel lines and rubber hoses and connections from the fuel pump to the fuel tank for fuel leaks. Tighten any loose connections and replace kinked, cracked or leaking fuel lines or hoses as required. Also inspect the fuel pump diaphragm crimp (the area where the stamped steel section is attached to the casting) and the breather holes in the casting for evidence of fuel or oil leakage. If the pump is leaking replace it.

13   Electric fuel pumps — general information

Some later models are equipped with an electric fuel pump system. Two systems are used. One system uses a single high-pressure, in-tank electric fuel pump. The pump is mounted with its inlet at the bottom of the sump. This design provides for satisfactory pump operation during extreme vehicle maneuvers and steep vehicle attitudes. The pump is protected at its inlet by a nylon pickup element to filter dirt and contaminates which could plug or damage the internal pump components. Models equipped with the in-tank electric fuel pump are also equipped with a fuel pump control relay which is controlled by the electronic engine control module (EEC).

The second type of system uses two electric fuel pumps. The first pump is a low pressure in-tank unit. The second pump is an externally mounted high pressure in-line unit. The fuel tank has an internal sump cavity in which the low pressure pump inlet rests. The function of the low pressure pump is to provide pressurized fuel to the inlet of the high pressure pump. This in-line high pressure pump is similar to the in-tank high pressure pump described above.

14   Fuel pump — removal and installation

Caution: *Use extreme caution when working around the fuel pump as the lines leading to and from the pump will be full of gasoline under pressure. It is a good idea to keep wet rags and a catch can available to try and keep the amounts of residual gasoline and spray to a minimum. Never smoke or use any type of electrical equipment around the fuel pump when removing or installing it. Use caution not to remove or install the fuel pump in an enclosed area and especially where an open flame is present, such as around a water heater. Further safety precautions can be found in* Safety first *near the front of this manual.*

Mechanical fuel pumps

1   Disconnect the negative cable at the battery and then remove the inlet line at the fuel pump.

2   Plug the end of the line to prevent leakage and possible contamination from dirt.

3   Remove the outlet pipe at the fuel pump and allow it to drain into a catch can.

4   Remove the two bolts and washers securing the fuel pump to the timing cover or cylinder block.

5   Remove the fuel pump and gasket (on some models a spacer plate may be positioned for heat insulation).

6   Clean the mating surfaces of the fuel pump, timing cover or cylinder block, and spacer (if so equipped). The mating surfaces must be perfectly smooth for a good gasket seal upon reinstallation.

7   Install a new gasket on the fuel pump mating surface, using an oil resistant sealer.

8   After cleaning the surfaces and applying the gasket, apply oil resistant sealer to the other side of the gasket and to the threads on the retaining bolts.

9   After installing the pump on the engine block, make sure the rocker

Fig. 4.47 Fuel pump — typically installed on 2.3L engines (Sec 14)

Fig. 4.48 Fuel pump — typical 3.3L engine model (Sec 14)

Fig. 4.49 Fuel pump — typical for V-6 and V-8 non fuel-injected engines (Sec 14)

Fig. 4.50 High-pressure in-tank electric fuel pump (Sec 14)

arm of the fuel pump is positioned correctly on the camshaft eccentric. It may be necessary to rotate the engine until the eccentric is at its low position to facilitate fuel pump installation.

10 Holding the fuel pump tightly against its mounting surface, install the retaining bolts and new lock washers.

11 Tighten the retaining bolts to the proper torque.

12 Remove the plug from the inlet line and connect the inlet line to the fuel pump.

13 Connect the outlet line to the fuel pump.

14 Connect the cable to the negative battery terminal.

15 Start the engine and check it for fuel and/or oil leaks.

Electric fuel pump

In-tank pump assembly

Caution: *Fuel supply lines will remain pressurized for a long period of time after the engine has been shut down. Relieve this pressure according to the procedure in Section 8 before servicing the fuel system.*

16 Place the vehicle on a hoist.

17 Depressurize the fuel system as previously described.

18 Remove the fuel from the tank by pumping it out through the filler hole.

19 Disconnect the supply line and return line fittings and vent line at the rear axle frame kickup.

20 Disconnect the electrical connector forward of the tank.

21 Disconnect and remove the fuel filler tube.

22 Remove the fuel tank support straps and move the fuel tank to a bench.

23 Remove any dirt that has accumulated around the fuel pump so

Fig. 4.51 High-pressure in-line electric fuel pump and fuel filter assembly (Sec 14)

Fig. 4.52 Low-pressure in-tank pump and sender assembly (viewed from the flange) (Sec 14)

that it will not enter the tank during the removal and installation procedure.
24   Disconnect the fuel supply line and return line fittings and the electrical connector.
25   Turn the fuel pump locking ring counterclockwise and remove the locking ring.
26   Remove the fuel pump and bracket assembly.
27   Remove the seal gasket. Discard the gasket and replace it with a new one during installation.
28   Clean the fuel pump mounting flange and fuel tank mounting surface and seal ring groove. Put a light coating of heavy grease onto a new seal ring to hold it in place during assembly and install it in the fuel ring groove.
29   Install the fuel pump and bracket assembly carefully to insure that the filter is not damaged. Be sure that the locating keys are in the keyways and that the seal ring remains in the groove.
30   Hold the pump assembly in place and install the locking ring finger tight. Be sure that all locking tabs are under the tank lock ring tabs.
31   Secure the fuel pump with the locking ring by rotating it clockwise until the ring rests against the stops.
32   The remaining installation is the reverse of the removal procedure.
33   Add a minimum of 38 liters (10 gallons) of fuel and check for leaks. If a pressure gauge is available, install it on the fuel charging assembly diagnostic valve. Turn the ignition key to the On position for three seconds, then turn the ignition key Off and back On for three more seconds repeatedly (five to ten times) until the pressure gauge shows at least 35 psi. Check for leaks at all fittings.

High pressure in-line pump assembly
34   Depressurize the fuel system as outlined and raise the vehicle with a hoist.
35   Disconnect the electrical connectors from the body harness and remove the inlet and outlet lines from the fuel pump.
36   The fuel pump may now be removed from the assembly by bending the tab out and sliding the pump out of the retaining ring.
37   Remove the electrical wiring harness from the assembly by inserting a screwdriver or knife between the connector and retaining clip and sliding the connector towards the pump inlet.
38   When installing, make sure the fittings on the pump have gaskets in place, that the gaskets are properly positioned and that the fittings have been tightened properly.
39   Check the wiring harness boots to make sure they are pushed into the pump terminals far enough to seal and check that the wire terminals are pushed onto the pump terminals fully.
40   Wrap the fuel pump retaining ring around the fuel pump. Locate the slot in the ring so that it faces the bracket base and push the pump and ring assembly into the bracket. Make sure the tab on the ring connects that tab of the bracket and that the bracket tabs do not contact the pump case. When the pump is fully inserted into the bracket and

Fig. 4.53 Testing a fuel pump for correct pressure and capacity (Sec 15)

the wiring harness comes out the bottom of the ring, bend the rear tab to prevent the pump from sliding out.
41   Connect the fuel lines to the pump assembly, then connect the electrical harness connector to the body electrical connector.
42   Start the vehicle and check for proper operation of the pump and for leaks.

---

15   Fuel pumps — testing

Mechanical fuel pump
To determine if the fuel pump is performing properly test the fuel pump for capacity and pressure with the fuel pump installed on the engine. If the engine is hot allow about 20 to 30 minutes to cool.

Capacity test
1   Remove the air cleaner.
2   Depressurize the fuel system (Section 8) and disconnect the fuel line at the carburetor or fuel filter.
3   Place a suitable non-breakable container (minimum 1/2 liter) at the end of the disconnected fuel line and crank the engine 10 revolutions. If little or no fuel flows from the fuel line during the tenth revolution, the fuel pump is inoperative. Replace the fuel pump.
4   If the fuel flow is adequate perform the following pressure test.

Pressure test
5   Connect a fuel pressure gauge (0 to 15 psi) to the carburetor end of the fuel line as shown in the accompanying illustration.
6   Start the engine and read the pressure after 10 seconds. Refer to the specifications for fuel pressure. If the pump pressure is too low or too high, install a new fuel pump.

Electric fuel pump
7   Make sure there is an adequate supply of fuel in the tank.
8   Check the inertia switch (which is located in the circuit just ahead of the fuel pump) to make sure it has not tripped.
9   Check the fuel pump output by disconnecting the fuel line where it enters the fuel filter, disconnecting the lead from the oil pressure switch and turning the ignition On. If fuel flows from the line into the
10   If no fuel flows from the line, check the power at the feed and output leads of the relay. If there is current at the feed lead but not at the output lead, replace the relay. If there is no current at the feed lead, trace the circuit back to its source checking all connectors and wires as you go. If there is current at the relay leads and the pump is not operating, check the current at the fuel pump. If there is no current, check all circuits between the relay and the pump. If there is current, the fuel pump must be replaced.

4

Fig. 4.54 Typical fuel tank installation (Sec 16)

16   Fuel tank — removal and installation

Removal

1   Fuel should be drained from the tank as completely as possible prior to tank removal. This is done by siphoning or pumping the fuel out through the fuel filler pipe. For some models the use of a small diameter hose might be necessary because of special components inside the fuel filler pipe. One quarter inch fuel hose is satisfactory for this.

2   Vehicles with fuel injected engines have reservoirs inside the fuel tank to maintain fuel near the fuel pickup during vehicle cornering maneuvers. These reservoirs could keep siphon tubes or hoses from reaching the bottom of the fuel tank. This situation can be overcome with a few repeated attempts using different hose positions.

3   Disconnect all fuel hoses and tubes.

4   On some models equipped with Central Fuel Injection, the plastic fuel tube connections are on top of the fuel tank and are not accessible. In these cases, the fuel lines must be disconnected with the tank partially removed from the vehicle.

5   On vehicles equipped with a metal retainer which fastens the filler pipe to the fuel tank, remove the screw attaching the retainer to the fuel tank flange.

6   Disconnect the electrical hookup to the fuel tank sender unit. On some vehicles the electrical connection is inaccessible on top of the tank and no intermediate connection point is provided. In these cases, partially remove the tank from the vehicle before disconnecting the fuel sender.

7   Place a safety support under the tank and remove the bolts or nuts from one end of the fuel tank straps. The straps are hinged at one end. Remove the bolts from the unhinged end then swing the straps out of the way. The fuel tank shield attached to the straps, if so equipped, should be left in place if possible to prevent it from being misplaced or incorrectly installed.

8   Partially remove the tank and disconnect the fuel lines and electrical connector from the fuel gauge sender. Refer to Section 11 for information on push-connect fittings.

9   Remove the fuel tank from the vehicle.

Installation

10 Before proceeding check the following items:
   a) Leak check the sender unit.
   b) Be sure the vapor separator valve is installed correctly in the tank top.
   c) Make all required fuel line, fuel return line, vapor vent and electrical connections which will be inaccessible after the tank is installed.
   d) Replace or reinstall all fuel tank shields.

Fig. 4.55 Restricted fuel tank filler opening — typical
(Sec 16)

11 Place the fuel tank in proper position in the vehicle. For most models, lubricate the fuel filler pipe with water-base tire mounting lubricant or dishwashing soap solution. Install the tank onto the filler pipe, then bring the tank into the installed position.

12 Wrap the fuel tank straps around the tank and start the attaching nuts or bolts. Align the tank with the straps. Be certain that the strap-mounted fuel tank shields are installed with the straps and are positioned correctly on the tank.

13 Check the hoses and wiring mounted on the tank top to be sure they are correctly routed and will not be pinched between the tank and vehicle body.

14 Tighten the fuel tank strap attaching nuts or bolts.

15 Reconnect the fuel hoses and lines which were disconnected. Be certain that the fuel supply, fuel return and vapor vent connections are made correctly. Trace the various lines to the engine to ensure proper connection.

16 If the vehicle is equipped with an electric fuel pump inside the tank, install the pump as outlined in Section 14.

17 Reconnect the electrical connections.

18 Replace the fuel drained from the tank, then start the engine.

19 Check all connections for leaks.

Fig. 4.56 Typical exhaust system compnents — V-6 and V-8 engines (Sec 19)

Fig. 4.57 Typical catalytic converter and heat shield assembly (Sec 19)

17   Fuel tank — cleaning and repair

1   With time it is likely that sediment will collect in the bottom of the fuel tank. Condensation, resulting in rust and other impurities, will usually be found in the fuel tank of any vehicle more than three or four years old.

2   When the tank is removed it should be vigorously flushed out with hot water and detergent and, if facilities are available, steam cleaned.

3   **Note:** *Never weld, solder or bring a bare light bulb close to an empty fuel tank. All repairs should be done by a professional due to the extremely hazardous conditions.*

18   Exhaust system — general information

Note: *Because of manufacturing changes, the exhaust system on your vehicle may differ from those shown in this manual. If problems arise,*

consult your dealer or qualified repair shop.

The exhaust system consists of an exhaust pipe, catalytic converter and muffler. Some models also use a resonator.

The exhaust system is serviced in four pieces: the rear section of the exhaust pipe, catalytic converter, muffler inlet pipe and muffler.

Due to the high temperatures of the exhaust system, do not work on the exhaust system until at least one hour after the vehicle has been run or driven.

19   Exhaust components — removal and installation

1   Refer to and perform the operations outlined in Chapter 1, *Exhaust system — inspection.*

2   If your inspection reveals the exhaust system, or portions of it, need to be replaced, first obtain the proper parts needed to repair the system. The components of the exhaust system can generally be split at their major divisions such as the exhaust pipe from the muffler or the muffler from the tailpipe. However, if corrosion is the cause for replacement, it will probably be necessary to replace the entire exhaust system.

3   Raise the vehicle and support it securely on jackstands.

4   Make sure the exhaust system is cool.

5   Apply some rust penetrant to the retainer bolts for the exhaust pipe flange.

6   Remove the exhaust pipe flange retaining nuts.

7   Remove the shields from the catalytic converter, if equipped.

8   Remove the clamps retaining the muffler or converter to the exhaust pipe(s).

9   Remove the hanger supporting the muffler and/or catalytic converter from the vehicle.

10 Remove the clamps retaining the rear of the muffler to the tailpipe.

11 Remove the sections necessary for replacement. It may be necessary to allow the axle to hang free from the rear frame in order to get the curved section of the tailpipe over the rear axle housing. Be sure to support the frame securely before removing the support from the axle.

12 Installation is the reverse of removal. Always use new gaskets and retaining nuts whenever the system is being replaced. It is also a good idea to use new hangers and retaining brackets when replacing the exhaust system.

13 Start the engine and check for exhaust leaks and rattles caused by misalignment.

Chapter 5   Engine electrical systems

Contents

Specifications

Ignition system

Type	Solid state Duraspark II or III, or EEC IV electronic ignition
Timing advance	Hybrid centrifugal and vacuum or electronically controlled
Static advance	See Emission Control Information label
Distributor direction of rotation	
V6 and V8 engines	Counterclockwise
Inline engines	Clockwise
Cylinder firing order	See Chapter 1
Spark plug type and gap	See Emission Control Information label
Spark plug wire resistance	Less than 5000 ohms per inch
Ignition timing	See Emission Control Information label
Ignition coil	12-volt

Charging system

Alternator brush length	
New	1/2-inch
Minimum	1/4-inch

Starting system

Starter brush length	
New	1/2-inch
Minimum	1/4 inch

Torque specifications	**Ft-lbs**
Alternator through bolt	3 to 4
Alternator brush holder screw	6 to 10
Diaphragm assembly to distributor base	2 to 3
Distributor holddown bolt	20
Spark plugs	
2.3L	5 to 10
3.3L	17 to 22
7.5L	5 to 10
All others	10 to 15
Starter motor through bolts	4 to 6
Starter motor mounting bolts	15 to 20
Stator lower plate-to-distributor base	1 to 3

1 General information

The engine electrical system includes the ignition, charging and starting components. They are considered separately from the rest of the electrical system (lighting, etc.) because of their proximity and importance to the engine.

Exercise caution when working around any of these components. They are easily damaged if tested, connected or stressed incorrectly. The alternator is driven by an engine drivebelt which could cause serious harm if your fingers or hands become entangled in it with the engine running. Both the starter and alternator are sources of direct battery voltage, which could arc or cause a fire if overloaded or shorted.

Never leave the ignition switch on for long periods of time with the engine not running. Do not disconnect battery cables while the engine is running. Be especially careful not to cross-connect battery cables from another source (such as another vehicle) when jumpstarting.

Don't ground either of the ignition coil terminals, even momentarily. When hooking up a test tachometer/dwell meter to the coil, make sure it is compatible with the type of ignition system on the vehicle and is hooked up as shown in the accompanying illustration.

Fig. 5.1 Correct tachometer-to-coil hookup (Sec 1)

Additional safety related information on the engine electrical system can be found in *Safety First* near the front of this manual. It should be referred to before beginning any operation included in this Chapter.

2 Ignition system — description and operation

Description

The ignition system on all vehicles covered in this manual will be either a Duraspark II or Duraspark III system, depending upon engine. Both systems are all-electronic and function in conjunction with one of three ignition modules. Testing of these ignition modules should be done by a Ford service department. If it is determined that the module requires replacement, make sure that you replace it with an exact duplicate of the original.

The Duraspark II system incorporates centrifugal and vacuum advance mechanisms in the distributor body. The spark advance in the Duraspark III system is dependent upon an Electronic Engine Control (EEC) system. The EEC controls spark advance in response to various engine sensors. On all Duraspark III systems (except V6) the distributor serves only to distribute the high voltage generated by the ignition coil.

The relationship of the distributor rotor to the cap is of special importance for proper high voltage distribution in the Duraspark III system incorporated on all engines except the V6. For this reason, the distributor is secured to the engine and the distributor rotor, rather than the distributor body, is adjustable (refer to Section 6 for this procedure).

The distributor used for the Duraspark III application on the V6 with EEC is a modified Duraspark II assembly. The centrifugal weights have been removed and very strong centrifugal springs are used to keep the sleeve and plate assembly stationary with respect to the distributor shaft. The diaphragm has been replaced by a special clip that prevents movement of the stator. Rotor alignment is not adjustable on this distributor and the only serviceable parts are the cap, rotor and adapter. If the distributor is found to be inoperative, the distributor housing and stator assembly must be replaced as a single unit.

The coil, coil high tension lead, distributor cap and spark plug wires are of standard design.

Operation

The Duraspark II ignition system consists of primary and secondary circuits. Included in the primary circuit are the battery, ignition switch,

5

Fig. 5.2 Duraspark II ignition system (Sec 2)

ballast resistor, coil primary winding, ignition module and distributor stator assembly. The secondary circuit consists of the coil secondary winding, distributor rotor, distributor cap, ignition wires and spark plugs.

   When the ignition switch is in the Run position, primary circuit current flows from the battery, through the ignition switch, the coil primary, the ignition module and back to the battery through the ignition system ground in the distributor. This current flow causes a magnetic field to be built up in the ignition coil. When the poles on the armature and stator assembly align, the ignition module turns the primary current off, collapsing the magnetic field in the ignition coil. The collapsing field induces a high voltage in the coil secondary winding and the coil wire conducts this high voltage to the distributor, where the cap and rotor distribute it to the appropriate spark plug. A timing circuit in the ignition module turns the primary current back on after a short time. High voltage is produced each time the magnetic field is built up and collapsed.

   The red ignition module wire provides operating voltage for the ignition module's electronic components in the Run mode. The white wire provides voltage for the ignition module during the Start mode, while

Fig. 5.3 Typical Duraspark distributor components (non-EED) — V8 engine shown (Sec 2)

Fig. 5.4 Duraspark III ignition system (Sec 2)

SPARK RETARD
INPUT

IGNITION MODULE

Fig. 5.5 Typical solid-state ignition module. Electrical leads
may vary (Sec 2)

the bypass provides increased voltage for the coil during the Start mode.

The Duraspark III system operates very similarly to the Duraspark II system. The only operational difference is that in the Duraspark III system for all engines except the V6, instead of the distributor stator assembly causing the ignition module to interrupt primary circuit current, a signal from the EEC microprocessor does this. In the Duraspark III for the V6, the stator assembly and armature act to send a signal to the EEC, which, in turn, signals the ignition module when and how to operate. In all other respects, system operation of the Duraspark II and III is the same.

The ballast resistor is actually a length of special wire, used to limit the primary ignition circuit current in the Run mode. It is part of the vehicle wiring harness inside the passenger compartment and under no circumstances should it be cut, spliced or replaced by any other type of wire.

3 Ignition system inspection and testing — general information

Note: *Initial checking procedures for many ignition components can be found in Chapter 1.*

Secondary ignition system problems and diagnosis are best handled with an automotive oscilloscope. An oscilloscope can pinpoint such problems as weak or fouled spark plugs, high resistance spark plug wires, a damaged or cracked distributor cap, worn rotor, leakage between spark plug wires and other similar problems.

Primary system ignition problems can also be determined with an oscilloscope. However, the main components sometimes require special test apparatus, procedures and operations.

A preliminary diagnosis of an ignition system can reveal such things as poor or disconnected wires and current leakage from the coil or the distributor.

With electronic ignition, the complexity of the design and testing procedures prevents in field diagnosis of many of the system's components by the home mechanic. If a preliminary overall visual check reveals no obvious problems, such as disconnected, broken or cracked components, the vehicle will have to be taken to a professional mechanic to have the components diagnosed.

4 Ignition system — check

Caution: *Because of the high voltage generated by the EEC system, extreme care should be taken whenever an operation is performed involving ignition components. This not only includes the distributor, coil,*

control module and spark plug wires, but related items that are connected to the system as well, such as the plug connections, tachometer and any test equipment. Before any work is performed the ignition should be turned off or the battery ground cable disconnected.

1   If the engine turns over but will not start, remove a spark plug wire from a spark plug and, using an insulated tool, hold the wire about 1/4-inch from a good ground. Have an assistant crank the engine.
2   If there is no spark, check another wire in the same manner. A few sparks, then no spark, should be considered as no spark.
3   If there is good spark, check the spark plugs (refer to Chapter 1) and/or the fuel system (refer to Chapter 4).
4   If there is a weak spark or no spark in a system with a remote coil, unplug the coil lead from the distributor, hold it about 1/4-inch from a good ground and check for spark as described above.
5   If there is no spark, have the system checked by a dealer or repair shop.
6   If there is a spark, check the distributor cap and/or rotor (refer to Chapter 1).
7   Further checks of the ignition system must be done by a dealer or repair shop.

5 Spark plugs — general information

Properly functioning spark plugs are necessary if the engine is to perform properly. At the intervals specified in Chapter 1 or your owner's manual, the spark plugs should be replaced with new ones. Removal and installation information can be found in Chapter 1.

It is important to replace spark plugs with new ones of the same heat range and type. A series of numbers and letters are included on the spark plug to help identify each variation.

The spark plug gap is very important. If it is too large or too small, the size of the spark and its efficiency will be seriously impaired. To set it, measure the gap with a feeler gauge, then bend the outer plug electrode until the correct gap is achieved.

The condition and appearance of the spark plugs can tell much about the condition and state of tune of the engine. If the insulator nose of the spark plug is clean and white, with no deposits, this is indicative of a weak mixture or too hot a plug (a hot plug transfers heat away from the electrode slowly — a cold plug transfers it away quickly). See Chapter 1 for color illustrations of spark plug conditions.

If the tip and insulator nose are covered with hard black deposits, this indicates that the mixture is too rich. Should the plug be black and oily, it is likely the rings and valve guides are worn as well as the mixture being too rich.

If the insulator nose is covered with light tan to greyish brown deposits, the mixture is correct and it is likely the engine is in good condition.

If there are any traces of long brown tapered stains on the outside of the white portion of the plug it will have to be replaced with a new one, as this indicates a faulty joint between the plug body and the insulator, allowing compression to leak past the insulator.

Always tighten a spark plug to the specified torque — no tighter.

6 Ignition coil — checking and replacement

Checking
1   The ignition coil cannot be satisfactorily tested without the proper electronic diagnostic equipment. If a fault is suspected in the coil, have it checked by a dealer or repair shop specializing in electrical repairs. The coil can be replaced with a new one using the following procedure.

Replacement
2   Disconnect the negative cable from the battery.
3   Using coded strips of tape, mark each of the wires at the coil to help return the wires to their original positions during reinstallation.
4   Remove the coil to distributor high tension lead.
5   Remove the connections at the coil. On electronic ignitions, these connections may be of the push-lock connector type. Separate them from the coil by releasing the tab at the bottom of the connector.
6   Remove the retaining bolt(s) holding the coil bracket to the engine.
7   Remove the coil from the coil bracket by loosening the clamp bolt.
8   Installation is the reverse of removal.

5

Fig. 5.6 Duraspark III distributor assembly — 3.8L engine
(Sec 7)

Fig. 5.7 Duraspark II distributor assembly — 2.3L engine
(Sec 7)

7   Distributor — removal and installation

Duraspark II for all engines and Duraspark III for V6

Removal

1   Disconnect the spring clips retaining the distributor cap to the adapter and position the cap and wires to one side.
2   Disconnect and plug the diaphragm assembly hose(s), if so equipped.
3   Disconnect the distributor connector from the wiring harness.
4   Rotate the engine to align the stator assembly pole and the armature pole.
5   Scribe a mark on the distributor body and engine to indicate the position of the distributor in the engine and the position of the rotor in the distributor.
6   Remove the distributor hold-down bolt and clamp.
7   Pull the distributor out of the engine. **Note:** *The engine should not be rotated while the distributor is out of the engine. If the engine is rotated refer to the installation procedure below.*

Installation if engine was rotated while distributor was removed

8   Rotate the engine until the number one piston is on the compression stroke (refer to Chapter 2E).
9   Align the timing marks for the correct initial timing, determined by referring to the Emissions Control Information label in the engine compartment.

10 Install the distributor in the engine with the rotor pointing at the number one cylinder terminal position on the cap and with the armature and stator assembly poles aligned.
11 Make sure the oil pump intermediate shaft properly engages the distributor shaft.
12 If the distributor will not seat properly in the engine it may be necessary to crank the engine after the distributor gear is partially engaged in order to properly mesh the distributor shaft with the oil pump intermediate shaft.
13 If it was necessary to crank the engine, again rotate the engine until the number one piston is on the compression stroke and align the timing marks for correct initial timing.
14 Rotate the distributor in the engine to align the armature and stator assembly poles and verify that the rotor is pointing at the number one cylinder cap terminal.
15 Install the distributor hold-down clamp and bolt, but do not tighten the bolt.

Installation if engine was not rotated while distributor was removed and original distributor is being reinstalled

16 Install the distributor in the engine with the rotor and distributor aligned with the previously scribed marks. The armature and stator assembly poles should also align when the distributor is fully seated in the engine.
17 If the distributor will not properly seat in the engine, crank the engine until the distributor shaft and oil pump intermediate shaft are properly meshed and the distributor is properly seated.
18 Install the distributor hold-down clamp and bolt, but do not tighten the bolt.

Fig. 5.8 Duraspark II distributor assembly — non-2.3L
engines (Sec 7)

Fig. 5.9 Typical Duraspark III distributor mounting system
(Sec 7)

**Installation if the engine was not rotated while the distributor was
removed and a new distributor is being installed**

19 Install the distributor in the engine with the rotor aligned with the
previously scribed mark on the block/manifold.

20 If necessary, crank the engine to seat the distributor.

21 Rotate the engine until the timing marks for the correct initial timing
(determined by referring to the Emissions Control Information label in
the engine compartment) are aligned and the rotor is pointing at the
number one cylinder cap terminal.

22 Rotate the distributor to align the armature and stator assembly
poles.

23 Install the distributor hold-down clamp and bolt, but do not tighten
the bolt.

Installation (all)

24 If, in Steps 10, 14, 16, or 22 above, the armature and stator
assembly poles cannot be aligned by rotating the distributor, pull the
distributor out of the engine enough to disengage the distributor gear
and rotate the distributor shaft to engage a different gear tooth, then
reinstall the distributor and repeat the steps in the appropriate installation procedure as necessary.

25 Connect the distributor connector to the wiring harness.

26 Install the distributor cap and ignition wires, making sure that the
wires are securely connected to the distributor cap and spark plugs.

27 Set the initial timing according to the Emissions Control Information label located in the engine compartment.

28 Tighten the distributor hold-down bolt to the specified torque.

29 Recheck the initial timing and adjust as necessary.

30 Connect the diaphragm assembly hose(s), if so equipped.

Duraspark III for all engines except V6

Removal

31 Disconnect the spring clips retaining the distributor cap to the
distributor cap adapter and position the cap and spark plug wires to
one side.

Fig. 5.10 Duraspark III distributor assembly — non-3.8L
engine (Sec 7)

32 Remove the rotor from the distributor shaft.
33 Rotate the engine until the number one piston is on the compression stroke (refer to Chapter 2E) and the sleeve and adapter alignment slots are in line.
34 Remove the distributor hold-down clamp and bolt. Remove the distributor. **Note:** *Do not rotate the engine with the distributor removed.*

Installation

35 Position the distributor in the engine so that the slot in the distributor base mounting flange is aligned with the hold-down bolt hole and the sleeve/adapter alignment slots are in line when the distributor is fully seated in the engine.
36 If the sleeve/adapter slots cannot be aligned, pull the distributor out of the engine enough to disengage the distributor gear and rotate the shaft to engage a different distributor gear tooth with the cam gear, then reinstall the distributor.
37 Install the distributor clamp and hold-down bolt and tighten the bolt to the specified torque.
38 Check the rotor alignment (refer to Section 9).
39 Install the distributor cap and wires, making sure that the wires are securely connected to the cap and spark plugs.

---

8 Duraspark II stator assembly — removal and installation

V8 engines

Removal

1 Remove the cable from the negative battery terminal.
2 Disconnect the spring clips retaining the distributor cap to the adapter and place the cap and wires aside.
3 Remove the rotor from the distributor shaft.
4 Disconnect the distributor connector from the wiring harness.
5 Disconnect the spring clips retaining the distributor cap adapter to the distributor body and remove the cap adapter.
6 Using a small gear puller or two screwdrivers, remove the armature from the sleeve and plate assembly.
7 Remove the E-clip retaining the diaphragm rod to the stator

assembly, then lift the diaphragm rod off the stator assembly pin.
8 Remove the screw retaining the ground strap at the stator assembly grommet.
9 Remove the wire retaining clip securing the stator assembly to the lower plate assembly.
10 Remove the grommet from the distributor base and lift the stator assembly off the lower plate.

Installation

11 If the lower plate assembly is to be reused, clean the bushing to remove any accumulated dirt and grease.
12 Install the stator assembly by reversing the removal procedure. Note when installing the armature that there are two locating notches in it. Install the armature on the sleeve and plate assembly employing the unused notch and a new roll pin.
13 Check the initial timing (refer to Chapter 1).

Six-cylinder engines

Removal

14 Disconnect the cable from the negative battery terminal.
15 Disconnect the spring clips retaining the distributor cap and place the cap and wires aside.
16 Remove the rotor from the distributor shaft.
17 Disconnect the distributor connector from the wiring harness.
18 Using a small gear puller or two screwdrivers as levers, remove the armature sleeve and plate assembly.
19 Remove the two screws retaining the lower plate assembly and stator assembly to the distributor base, noting that there are two different size screws employed.
20 Remove the lower plate assembly and stator assembly from the distributor.
21 Remove the E-clip, flat washer and wave washer securing the stator assembly to the lower plate assembly, then separate the stator assembly from the lower plate assembly. Note the installation of the wave washer.

Installation

22 Before installing the stator remove any accumulated dirt or grease from parts that are to be reused.

Fig. 5.11 Stator assembly replacement — Duraspark II distributor (four and eight cylinder engines) (Sec 8)

Fig. 5.12 Stator assembly replacement — Duraspark II distributor (four and six-cylinder engines only) (Sec 8)

23 Place the stator assembly on the lower plate assembly and install the wave washer (outer edges up), flat washer and E-clip.

24 Install the stator assembly/lower plate assembly on the distributor base, making sure to engage the pin on the stator assembly in the diaphragm rod.

25 Attach the lower plate assembly and stator assembly to the distributor base, making sure to install the different size screws in their proper locations.

26 When installing the armature, note that there are two notches in it. Install the armature on the sleeve and plate assembly employing the unused notch and a new roll pin.

27 Connect the distributor connector to the wiring harness.

28 Reinstall the rotor and distributor cap, making sure that the ignition wires are securely connected to the cap and spark plugs.

29 Connect the cable to the negative battery terminal.

30 Check the initial timing (refer to Chapter 1).

9 Duraspark III — rotor alignment (except V6 engine)

Note: *Refer to Fig. 5.6 to locate and identify pertinent components.*

1 Disconnect the spring clips retaining the distributor cap to the adapter and position the cap and wires to one side.

2 Remove the rotor from the sleeve assembly.

3 Rotate the engine until the number one piston is on the compression stroke (refer to Chapter 2E).

4 Slowly rotate the engine until a rotor alignment tool (Ford no. T79P-12200-A) can be inserted in the alignment slots in the sleeve assembly and adapter.

5 Read the timing mark on the crankshaft damper indicated by the timing pointer.

6 If the timing mark reading is 0°, plus or minus 4°, alignment is acceptable.

7 If the timing mark reading is beyond the acceptable limit make sure the number one piston is on the compression stroke.

8 Slowly rotate the engine until the timing pointer aligns with the 0° timing mark on the crankshaft damper.

9 Loosen the two sleeve assembly adjustment screws and insert the rotor alignment tool into the alignment slots in the sleeve assembly and adapter.

10 Tighten the sleeve assembly adjustment screws and remove the alignment tool.

11 Attach the rotor to the sleeve assembly.

12 Install the distributor cap and ignition wires, making sure that the ignition wires are securely connected to the cap and the spark plugs.

10 EEC IV electronic ignition system — general information

The EEC IV Thick Film Integrated (TFI) ignition system features a universal distributor design which is driven from the camshaft gear and uses no centrifugal or vacuum advance. The distributor is mounted on the engine in a die cast base incorporating an integrally mounted TFI IV ignition module. No distributor calibration is required and initial timing is not a normal adjustment. The high voltage distribution is accomplished through a conventional rotor, cap and ignition wires. These conventional distributor components can be cleaned, inspected and serviced in the same manner as the Duraspark distributors described in other Sections of this Chapter.

11 EEC IV Electronic ignition system distributor and TFI module — removal and installation

Distributor assembly

Note: *Service procedures other than those applied to conventional distributors must be done by a professional service department. However, it may be financially advantageous to remove and install the distributor assembly yourself.*

1 Disconnect the primary wiring connector from the distributor.

2 Using a screwdriver, remove the distributor cap and position it and the attached wires aside so they won't interfere with removal of the distributor.

3 Detach the distributor rotor by removing the two hold-down screws. Note the position of the polarizing square and circle in the shaft

Fig. 5.13 Rotor alignment — Duraspark III (Sec 9)

Fig. 5.14 EEC universal distributor — exploded view (Sec 11)

plate. This should be used as a reference during reinstallation. Some engines may be equipped with a security-type distributor hold-down bolt. If this is the case, a special tool is required (Ford tool no. T82L-12270-A). Other distributors use a conventional hold-down bolt and clamp. Remove the hold-down bolt and separate the distributor from the engine.

4 Before installing the distributor, rotate the shaft by hand to make sure it turns freely. Visually inspect for the presence of the base O-ring and replace this component if it is worn or damaged.

5 Position the polarizing square and circle in the shaft plate in the same location as they were when the distributor was removed. Install the distributor in the engine maintaining the same orientation of the TFI-4 module to the engine as when removed.

6 Install the distributor hold-down bolt and clamp and tighten the bolt so that the distributor can barely be rotated.

7 Install the distributor rotor.

8 Reconnect the vehicle wiring harness connector to the distributor and install the distributor cap with the attached wires. Check all spark plug wires to ensure that they are completely seated in the cap and on the plugs.

9 Check the ignition timing with a timing light (Chapter 1) and adjust it if necessary. Refer to the vehicle Emission Control Information label for specific timing information for your vehicle.

10 With the initial timing verified, tighten the distributor hold-down bolt to specification.

TFI IV ignition module

11 To remove the ignition module, first detach the distributor cap and position it and the attached wires aside.

12 Remove the TFI harness connector.

13 Remove the distributor from the engine.

14 Place the distributor on a workbench and remove the two TFI module mounting screws.

15 Slide the right side of the module down the distributor mounting flange and then back up the flange. Slide the left side of the module down the distributor mounting flange and then back up the flange. Continue alternating side-to-side until the module terminals are disengaged from the connector in the distributor base. With the terminals completely disengaged, slide the module down and pull it gently away from the mounting surface. **Caution:** *Do not attempt to lift the module from the mounting surface prior to moving the entire TFI module toward the distributor flange, as you will break the pins at the distributor module connector.*

Fig. 5.15 EEC Thick Film Ignition module — Type IV (Sec 11)

16 Place the TFI module on the distributor base mounting flange and carefully position it toward the distributor connector pins.

17 Install the two TFI module mounting screws.

18 Install the distributor in the engine.

19 Install the distributor cap and tighten the cap mounting screws.

20 Install the TFI harness connector.

21 Using an induction timing light, verify the engine timing according to specific recommendations on the vehicle Emission Control Information label.

12 Starting system — general information

The starting system consists of an electric starter motor with an integral positive engagement drive, the battery, a starter switch, a Neutral start switch (automatic transmission equipped vehicles only), a starter solenoid and wiring looms connecting these components.

When the ignition switch is turned to the Start position, the starter solenoid is energized through the starter control circuit. The solenoid then connects battery voltage to the starter motor.

Vehicles with automatic transmissions have a Neutral start switch in the starter control circuit which prevents operation of the starter if the selector lever is not in the N or P position.

When the starter is energized by the battery, current flows to the grounded field coil and operates the magnetic switch. This switch drives the starter drive plunger forward to engage the flywheel ring gear.

When the drive plunger reaches full travel, the field coil grounding contacts open and the starter motor contacts engage, turning the starter.

A holding coil is used to keep the starter drive shoe in the fully seated position while the starter is turning the engine.

When the battery voltage is released from the starter, a retracting spring withdraws the starter drive pinion from the flywheel and the motor contact is broken.

13 Starter motor — testing in vehicle

1 If the starter motor does not turn when the switch is operated, make sure that the shift lever is in Neutral or Park (automatic transmission) or that the clutch pedal is depressed (manual transmission).

2 Make sure that the battery is charged and that all cables, both at the battery and starter solenoid terminals, are secure.

3 If the motor spins but the engine is not cranked, the overrunning clutch in the starter motor is slipping and the starter motor must be removed from the engine and disassembled.

4 If, when the switch is actuated, the starter motor does not operate at all but the solenoid clicks, then the problem is in the main solenoid contacts or the starter motor itself.

5 If the solenoid plunger cannot be heard when the switch is actuated, the solenoid is defective or the solenoid circuit is open.

6 To check the solenoid, connect a jumper lead between the battery positive terminal and the terminal on the solenoid. If the starter motor now operates, the solenoid is OK and the problem is in the ignition or neutral start switches or in the wiring.

7 If the starter motor still does not operate, remove the starter assembly for disassembly, testing and repair.

8 If the starter motor cranks the engine at an abnormally slow speed, first make sure that the battery is charged and that all terminal connections are tight.

9 Run the engine until normal operating temperature is reached, then disconnect the coil wire from the distributor cap and ground it on the engine.

10 Connect a voltmeter positive lead to the starter motor terminal of the solenoid and then connect the negative lead to ground.

11 Actuate the ignition switch and take the voltmeter readings as soon as a steady figure is indicated. Do not allow the starter motor to turn for more than 30 seconds at a time. A reading of 9-volts or more, with the starter motor turning at normal cranking speed, is normal. If the reading is 9-volts or more but the cranking speed is slow, the motor is faulty. If the reading is less than 9-volts and the cranking speed is slow, the solenoid contacts are probably burned.

14 Starter — removal and installation

1 Disconnect the negative cable from the battery.

2 Disconnect the wire connecting the starter solenoid to the starter motor.

3 Remove the retaining bolts securing the starter to the bellhousing.

4 Pull the starter out of the bellhousing and lower it from the vehicle.

5 Installation is the reverse of removal. When inserting the starter into its opening of the bellhousing, make sure it fits squarely and the mating faces are flush. Tighten the retaining bolts to the proper torque.

Fig. 5.16 Typical starter — exploded view (Sec 12)

15 Starter brushes — replacement

Note: *The starter must be removed from the vehicle before the brushes can be replaced. Before attempting to replace the brushes in the starter, make sure the problem you are having is related to the brushes. Often, loose connections, poor battery condition or wiring problems are a more likely cause of no start or poor starting conditions. Check on the availability of internal replacement parts before proceeding.*

1 Remove the starter from the vehicle (Section 14).
2 Remove the two through-bolts from the starter frame.
3 Pull the brush endplate, along with the brush springs and brushes, from the holder.
4 Remove the ground brush retaining screws from the frame. Remove the brushes from the frame.
5 Cut the insulated brush leads from the field coils as close to the field connection point as possible.
6 Inspect the plastic brush holder for any signs of cracks or broken mounting pads. If these conditions exist, replace the plastic brush holder.
7 Place the new insulated field brush lead onto the field coil connection.
8 Crimp the clip provided with the brushes to hold the brush lead to the connection.
9 Using a low heat soldering gun (300 watts), solder the lead, the clip and the connection together using rosin core solder.
10 Install the ground brush leads to the frame with the retaining screws.
11 Install the brush holder and insert the brushes into the holder.
12 Install the brush springs. Make sure that the positive brush leads are positioned in their respective slots in the brush holder to prevent any chance of grounding the brushes.
13 Install the brush endplate. Make sure the endplate insulator is positioned correctly on the endplate.
14 Install the through-bolts in the starter frame.
15 A battery can be used to check the starter by connecting heavy cables, such as jumper cables, to the positive and negative battery posts.
16 Connect the ground lead to the starter.
17 Secure the starter in soft jaws of a vise or other similar clamping device.
18 Momentarily contact the starter connection with the positive cable from the battery.
19 The starter should spin and the solenoid drive should engage the gear in a forward position when this connection is completed.
20 If the starter operates correctly, install the starter in the vehicle as described in the previous Section.

16 Starter solenoid — removal and installation

1 Disconnect the negative cable from the battery, followed by the positive cable.
2 Disconnect the positive battery cable and feed cable from the terminal on the starter solenoid. Mark them to prevent mix-ups during installation.
3 Disconnect the starter feed wire from the opposite terminal on the starter solenoid. Mark the feed wire as above.
4 Disconnect the two starter solenoid triggering wires from the top posts on the solenoid. Make sure you mark or indicate the position of these wires as they can be cross-connected and damage the electrical system.
5 Remove the two starter solenoid to fender well retaining bolts.
6 Remove the starter solenoid.
7 Before installing the new or replacement solenoid, use a wire brush to carefully clean the mounting surface on the fender well for better grounding.
8 Attach the starter solenoid to the fender. **Note:** *Use care when tightening these bolts as they are self-threading and can easily be stripped in the mounting hole.*
9 Reconnect all wires to their original positions.

17 Charging system — general information and precautions

The charging system is made up of the alternator, voltage regulator and battery. These components work together to supply electrical power for the engine ignition, lights, radio, etc.

The alternator is turned by a drivebelt at the front of the engine. When the engine is operating, voltage is generated by the internal components of the alternator to be sent to the battery for storage.

The purpose of the voltage regulator is to limit the alternator voltage to a preset value. This prevents power surges, circuit overloads, etc., during peak voltage output.

The charging system does not ordinarily require periodic maintenance. The drivebelts, electrical wiring and connections should, however, be inspected at the intervals suggested in Chapter 1.

Take extreme care when making circuit connections to a vehicle equipped with an alternator and note the following: When making connections to the alternator from a battery, always match correct polarity. Before using electric arc welding equipment to repair any part of the vehicle, disconnect the wires from the alternator and the battery terminals. Never start the engine with a battery charger connected. Always disconnect both battery leads before using a battery charger.

18 Charging system — check

1   If a malfunction occurs in the charging circuit, do not immediately assume that the alternator is causing the problem. First check the following items:

The battery cables where they connect to the battery (make sure the connections are clean and tight).

The battery electrolyte specific gravity (if it is low, charge the battery).

Check the external alternator wiring and connections (they must be in good condition).

Check the drivebelt condition and tension (see Chapter 1).

Check the alternator mount bolts for tightness.

Run the engine and check the alternator for abnormal noise.

2   Using a voltmeter, check the battery voltage with the engine off. It should be approximately 12-volts.

3   Start the engine and check the battery voltage again. It should now be approximately 14 to 15-volts.

4   Due to the special equipment necessary to test or service the alternator is recommended that if a fault is suspected the vehicle be taken to a dealer or a shop with the proper equipment. Because of this the home mechanic should limit maintenance to checking connections and the inspection and replacement of the brushes.

5   The ammeter (ALT) gauge or alternator warning lamp on the instrument panel indicates charge or discharge (D) — current passing into or out of the battery. With the electrical equipment switched on and the engine idling the gauge needle may show a discharge condition. At fast idle or at normal driving speeds the needle should stay on the charge side of the gauge, with the charged state of the battery determining just how far over.

6   If the gauge does not show a change or (if equipped) the alternator lamp is on, there is a fault in the system. Before inspecting the brushes or replacing the alternator, the battery condition, belt tension and electrical cable connections should be checked.

19 Alternator — removal and installation

1   Disconnect the negative battery cable.

2   Carefully note the terminal connections at the rear or side of the alternator and disconnect them. Most connections will have a retaining nut and washer on them, however some connections may have a plastic snap-fit connector with a retaining clip. If a terminal is covered by a slip-on plastic cover, be careful when pulling the cover back so as not to damage the terminal or connector.

3   Loosen the alternator adjustment arm bolt.

4   Loosen the alternator pivot bolt.

5   Pivot the alternator to allow the drivebelt to be removed from the pulleys.

6   Remove the belt(s) from the pulley.

7   Remove the adjustment arm bolt and pivot the arm out of the way.

8   Remove the pivot bolt and spacer and carefully lift the alternator up and out of the engine compartment. Be careful not to drop or jar the alternator as it can be damaged. **Note:** *If purchasing a new or rebuilt alternator, take the original one with you to the dealer or parts store so the two can be compared side-by-side.*

9   Installation is the reverse of removal. Be careful when connecting all terminals at the rear or side of the alternator. Make sure they are clean and tight and that all terminal ends are tight on the wires. If you find any loose terminal ends, make sure you install new ones, as any arcing or shorting at the wires or terminals can damage the alternator.

20 Alternator brushes — replacement

Note: *Internal replacement parts for alternators may not be readily available in your area. Check into availability before proceeding.*

Rear terminal alternator

1   Remove the alternator as described in Section 19.

Fig. 5.17 Side terminal alternator (Sec 19)

Fig. 5.18 Rear terminal alternator (Sec 19)

WHITE BLACK

BLACK ORANGE

ORANGE BLUE

Fig. 5.19 Exploded view of rear terminal alternator (Sec 19)

2   Scribe a line across the length of the alternator housing to ensure correct reassembly.

3   Remove the housing through-bolts and the nuts and insulators from the rear housing. Make a careful note of all insulator locations.

4   Withdraw the rear housing section from the stator, rotor and front housing assembly.

Fig. 5.20 Brush holder assembly — rear terminal type (Sec 20)

5   Remove the brushes and springs from the brush holder assembly, which is located inside the rear housing.

6   Check the length of the brushes against the wear dimensions given in the specifications and replace the brushes with new ones if necessary.

7   Install the springs and brushes in the holder assembly and retain them in place by inserting a piece of stiff wire through the rear housing and brush terminal insulator as shown in the accompanying illustration. Make sure enough wire protrudes through the rear housing so it can be withdrawn at a later stage.

8   Attach the rear housing rotor and front housing assembly to the stator, making sure the scribed marks are aligned.

9   Install the housing through-bolts and rear end insulators and nuts but do not tighten the nuts at this time.

10 Carefully extract the piece of wire from the rear housing and make sure that the brushes are seated on the slip ring. Tighten the through-bolts and rear housing nuts.

11 Install the alternator as described in Section 19.

Side terminal alternator

12 Remove the alternator as described in Section 19 and scribe a mark on both end housings and the stator for ease of reassembly.

13 Remove the through-bolts and separate the front housing and rotor from the rear housing and stator. Be careful that you do not separate the rear housing and stator.

14 Use a soldering iron to unsolder and disengage the brush holder from the rear housing. Remove the brushes and springs from the brush holders.

15 Remove the two brush holder attaching screws and lift the brush holder from the rear housing.

16 Remove any sealing compound from the brush holder and rear housing.

Fig. 5.21 Exploded view of side terminal alternator (Sec 19)

17 Inspect the brushes for damage and check their dimensions against the specifications. If they are worn, replace them with new ones.

18 To reassemble, install the springs and brushes in the brush holders, inserting a piece of stiff wire to hold them in place as shown in the accompanying illustration.

19 Place the brush holder in position in the rear housing, using the wire to retract the brushes through the hole in the rear housing.

20 Install the brush holder attaching screws and push the holder toward the shaft opening as you tighten the screws. **Caution:** *The rectifier can be overheated and damaged if the soldering is not done quickly. Press the brush holder lead onto the rectifier lead and solder them in place.*

21 Place the rotor and front housing in position in the stator and rear housing. After aligning the scribe marks, install the through-bolts.

22 Turn the fan and pulley to check for binding in the alternator.

23 Withdraw the wire which is retracting the brushes and seal the hole with waterproof cement. **Note:** *Do not use RTV-type sealer on the hole.*

21 Regulator — removal and installation

1 Remove the negative cable from the battery.

2 Locate the voltage regulator. It will usually be positioned near the front of the vehicle.

3 Push the two tabs on either side of the quick release clip retaining the wiring loom to the regulator. Pull the quick release clip straight out from the side of the regulator.

4 Remove the two regulator retaining screws. Notice that one screw will locate the ground wire terminal.

5 Remove the regulator.

6 Installation is the reverse of removal. Make sure you get the wiring clip positioned firmly onto the regulator terminals and that both clips click into place.

22 Battery cables — check and replacement

1 Periodically inspect the entire length of each battery cable for damage, cracked or burned insulation and corrosion. Poor battery cable connections can cause starting problems and decreased engine performance.

2 Check the cable to terminal connections at the ends of the cables for cracks, loose wire strands and corrosion. The presence of white, fluffy deposits under the insulation at the cable terminal connection is a sign the cable is corroded and should be replaced. Check the terminals for distortion, missing mounting bolts or nuts and corrosion.

3 If only the positive cable is to be replaced, be sure to disconnect the negative cable from the battery first.

4 Disconnect and remove the cable from the vehicle. Make sure the replacement cable is the same length and diameter.

5 Clean the threads of the starter, solenoid or ground connection with a wire brush to remove rust and corrosion. Apply a light coat of petroleum jelly to the threads to ease installation and prevent future

Fig. 5.22 Brush holder assembly — side terminal type (Sec 20)

corrosion. Inspect the connections frequently to make sure they are clean and tight.

6 Attach the cable to the starter, solenoid or ground connection and tighten the mounting nut securely.

7 Before connecting the new cable to the battery, make sure it reaches the terminals without having to be stretched.

8 Connect the positive cable first, followed by the negative cable. Tighten the nuts and apply a thin coat of petroleum jelly to the terminal and cable connection.

23 Battery — removal and installation

1 The battery is located at the front of the engine compartment. It is held in place by a hold-down clamp near the bottom of the battery case.

2 Hydrogen gas is produced by the battery, so keep open flames and lighted cigarettes away from it at all times.

3 Always keep the battery in an upright position. Spilled electrolyte should be rinsed off immediately with large quantities of water. Always wear eye protection when working around a battery.

4 Always disconnect the negative (-) battery cable first, followed by the positive (+) cable.

5 After the cables are disconnected from the battery, remove the hold-down clamp.

6 Carefully lift the battery out of the engine compartment.

7 Installation is the reverse of removal. The cable clamps should be tight, but do not overtighten them as damage to the battery case could occur. The battery posts and cable ends should be cleaned prior to connection (see Chapter 1).

Chapter 6 Emissions control systems

Contents

1 General information

In order to meet U.S. federal anti-pollution laws, vehicles are equipped with a variety of emissions control systems, depending on the models and the states in which they are sold. Engine performance and longevity can be drastically affected by faulty or malfunctioning emissions systems.

The information in this Chapter describes the subsystems within the overall emissions control system and the maintenance operations for these subsystems that are within the reach of the home mechanic. The Emissions Control Information label, located in the engine compartment, contains information required to properly maintain the emissions control, ignition and fuel systems and for keeping the vehicle correctly tuned.

Due to the complexity of the subsystems, especially those governed by Electronic Engine Control (EEC), it is suggested that professional assistance be sought when you run into an emissions problem that cannot be readily diagnosed and repaired.

6

Fig. 6.1 Typical Emission Control Information decal found inside the engine compartment. This decal contains information necessary for the servicing the emissions systems (Sec 1)

2   Positive Crankcase Ventilation (PCV) system

General description

1   The positive crankcase ventilation system is a closed recirculation system which is designed to prevent engine crankcase fumes from escaping into the atmosphere through the engine oil filler cap. The crankcase control system regulates these blowby vapors by circulating them back into the intake manifold, where they are burned with the incoming fuel and air mixture.

2   The system consists of a replaceable PCV valve, a crankcase ventilation filter in the air cleaner and connecting hoses and gaskets.

3   The air source for the crankcase ventilation system is in the carburetor air cleaner. Air passes through a filter located in the air cleaner to a hose connecting the air cleaner to the oil filler cap, as shown in the accompanying illustrations. The oil filler cap is sealed at the opening to prevent the entrance of outside air. From the oil filler cap the air

Fig. 6.2 Schematic diagram of typical PCV system (Sec 2)

Fig. 6.3 Typical engine PCV layout. V-type engine shown, others similar (Sec 2)

flows into the rocker arm chamber, down past the pushrods and into the crankcase. The air then circulates from the crankcase up into another section of the rocker arm chamber. The air and crankcase gasses then pass through a one-way regulator valve (PCV valve) which controls the amount of flow as operating conditions vary. Some engines have a fixed orifice PCV valve that meters a steady flow of gas mixture regardless of the extent of engine blowby gasses. In either case, the air and gas mixture is routed to the intake manifold through the crankcase vent hose tube and fittings. This process goes on continuously while the engine is running.

Checking

4   Checking and replacement procedures for the PCV system are described in Chapter 1.

3   Fuel Evaporative Emissions Control system

General description

1   This system is designed to limit fuel vapors released to the atmosphere by trapping and storing fuel that evaporates from the fuel

Fig. 6.4 PCV valve installation. Make certain that the valve fits tightly in the rubber grommet (Sec 2)

tank (and in some cases, from the carburetor), which would normally enter the atmosphere, contributing to hydrocarbon (HC) emissions.

2   The serviceable parts of the system include a charcoal-filled canister, connection lines to the fuel tank and carburetor and the fuel tank filler cap.

3   Fuel vapors are vented from the fuel tank (and in some cases from the carburetor) for temporary storage in the canister, which is mounted on the right frame rail in the engine compartment as shown in the accompanying illustrations. The canister outlet is connected to the car-

buretor air cleaner so the stored vapors will be drawn into the engine and burned. The fuel tank filler cap vents air into the tank to replace the fuel being used, but does not vent fuel vapors to the outside air under normal conditions (unless tank pressure builds up to more than approximately two psi above normal atmospheric pressure).

Checking

4   The checking procedures for the fuel evaporative emissions control system are described in Chapter 1.

Fig. 6.5 Evaporative emissions canister and vent system on 2.3L engine (Sec 3)

6

Fig. 6.6 Evaporative emissions canister and vacuum hose routing (Sec 3)

PURGE VALVE

TO FUEL TANK

VIEW Z

FRONT OF VEHICLE

TO FUEL TANK

VIEW Z

Fig. 6.7 Typical evaporative emissions system on carbureted V-type engines (Sec 3)

4 Exhaust Gas Recirculation (EGR) system

General description

1   The EGR system is designed to reintroduce small amounts of exhaust gas into the combustion cycle, reducing the generation of nitrous oxide (NOx) emissions. The amount of exhaust gas reintroduced and the timing of the cycle is controlled by various factors such as engine speed, altitude, engine vacuum, exhaust system backpressure, coolant temperature and throttle opening. All EGR valves are vacuum actuated and the vacuum diagram for your particular vehicle is shown on the Emissions Control Information label in the engine compartment.

2   For the vehicles covered by this manual there are four basic types of EGR valves: the ported valve, the integral backpressure valve, the electronic sonic valve and the valve and transducer type EGR valve.

Ported valve

3   Two passages in the base connecting the exhaust system with the intake manifold are blocked by the ported EGR valve, which is opened by vacuum and closed by spring pressure. The valve may be of the poppet or tapered stem design and may have a base entry or side entry, the function being the same.

Integral backpressure valve

4   This poppet-type or tapered (pintle) valve cannot be opened by vacuum until the bleed hole is closed by exhaust backpressure. Once the valve opens it seeks a level dependent upon the exhaust backpressure flowing through the orifice. The higher the signal vacuum and exhaust backpressure, the more the valve opens. The valve body may be base entry or side entry.

EGR VALVE

EGR/PVS VALVE

TEE

(2V CARB.)

EGR PORT

VACUUM CHECK VALVE

TO DISTRIBUTOR

Fig. 6.8 Typical EGR vacuum system used on engines without Electronic Engine Control (EEC) (Sec 4)

Electronic sonic valve assembly

5   On vehicles equipped with an Electronic Engine Control (EEC) system, exhaust gas recirculation is controlled by the EEC through a system of engine sensors. The EGR valve in this system resembles and is operated in the same manner as a conventional ported design valve. However, it uses a tapered pintle valve for more exact control of the flow rate. A sensor on top of the valve tells how far the EGR valve is open and sends an electrical signal to the EEC, which is also receiving

Fig. 6.9 Base-entry, poppet-type EGR valve (left) and side-entry, tapered stem-type EGR valve (right) (Sec 4)

Fig. 6.10 Integral backpressure type EGR valve (Sec 4)

Fig. 6.11 EGR system used on engines equipped with
Electronic Engine Control (EEC) (Sec 4)

Fig. 6.12 Valve and transducer-type EGR valve. Transducer
to EGR valve feed nipple must point directly downward
during installation (Sec 4)

several other signals such as engine coolant temperature, rpm and throttle opening. The EEC signals the EGR control solenoids to maintain or alter the flow as required by the engine operating conditions. Source vacuum from the manifold is either bled off or applied to the diaphragm, depending on the EEC commands. A cooler is used to reduce the temperature of the exhaust gasses, helping the gasses to flow better, reducing the tendency of the engine to detonate and making the valve more durable.

6   The EGR valve operates only in the part-throttle mode. It remains closed in the cranking mode, the closed throttle mode and the wide open throttle mode.

Valve and transducer EGR valve

7   This valve consists of a modified EGR valve with a remote transducer. It operates similarly to the integral backpressure valve.

Checking

Ported valve and integral backpressure valve
8   Check that all vacuum lines are properly routed, all connections are secure and that the hoses are not crimped, cracked or broken. If deteriorated hoses are encountered, replace them with new ones.
9   Visually inspect the valve for rust or corrosion. If either is encountered clean the valve or replace it with a new one.
10 Using finger pressure, press in on the diaphragm at the bottom of the valve. If the valve sticks open or closed, or does not operate smoothly, clean the valve or replace it with a new one.

Electronic sonic valve assembly
11 If a malfunction is suspected in the electronic sonic valve or the EVP sensor to which it is attached, have the system checked at a Ford service department

Component replacement
12 When replacing any vacuum hoses, remove only one hose at a time and make sure that the replacement hose is of the same quality and size as the hose being replaced.
13 When replacing the EGR valve, label each hose as it is disconnected from the valve to ensure proper connection to the replacement valve.
14 The valve is easily removed from the intake manifold after disconnecting and labeling the attached hoses. Be sure to use a new gasket when installing the valve and check for leaks when the job is complete. Torque specifications can be found in Chapter 2. Refer to the appropriate part for your particular engine.

5   Spark control system

Note: *The information in this Section is applicable only to vehicles equipped with the Duraspark II ignition system. Because spark advance and retard functions on vehicles equipped with Duraspark III ignition systems are controlled by the Electronic Engine Control (EEC) microprocessor, checks and tests involving the spark control system on these vehicles must be performed by a Ford service department.*

General description
1   The spark control system is designed to reduce hydrocarbon and oxides of nitrogen (NOx) emissions by advancing the ignition timing when the engine is cold.
2   This systems is complex and has many valves, relays, amplifiers and other components built into it. Each vehicle will have a system peculiar to the model year, geographic region and gross vehicle weight rating. A schematic diagram located on the underside of the hood will detail the exact components and vacuum line routing of the particular system on your vehicle.
3   Various vacuum switches are used in the emissions system for modifying spark timing and engine idle. These vacuum switches have anywhere from two to four ports, depending on their function.

Ported Vacuum Switches (PVS)
4   A typical ported vacuum switch is situated in the cooling system

Fig. 6.13 Typical EGR valve installation (Sec 4)

Fig. 6.14 Typical distributor vent valve installation (Sec 5)

Fig. 6.15 Typical Cold Start Spark Advance (CSSA) system (Sec 5)

to increase idle rpm when the engine overheats. When the coolant is at normal temperature, the vacuum goes through the top and center ports of the PVS, providing the distributor with vacuum advance suitable for normal driving. When hot, the PVS center and bottom ports are connected so that the engine manifold vacuum allows the distributor to advance and increase idle.

Distributor vacuum vent valve
5   Some engines use a distributor vacuum vent valve both to prevent fuel from migrating into the distributor advance diaphragm and to act as a spark advance delay valve. During light acceleration, deceleration and idle, the vent valve dumps vacuum through a check valve. This keeps the distributor from advancing excessively for the load and evacuates the fuel in the spark port line.

Cold Start Spark Advance (CSSA)
6   The CSSA system is located in the distributor spark control system. When coolant temperature is below 128°F (53°C), it momentarily traps the spark port vacuum at the distributor advance diaphragm. The vacuum follows a path through the carburetor vacuum tap, the Distributor Retard Control Valve (DRCV), the CSSA ported vacuum switch and then the cooling vacuum switch to the distributor. At coolant temperatures above 128°F the CSSA PVS operates and the vacuum follows a path from the carburetor spark port through the cooling PVS to the distributor.

Cold Start Spark Hold (CSSH)
7   When the engine is cold the CSSH provides spark advance for improved cold engine acceleration. Below 128°F the CSSH ported vacuum switch is closed and the distributor vacuum is routed through a restrictor. Under cold starting conditions the high vacuum present advances the distributor. During cold acceleration, the vacuum is slowly bled off through the restrictor, slowing vacuum advance during initial acceleration.

Spark Delay Valve (SDV)
8   Spark delay valves are designed to slow the air flow in one direction while a check valve allows free flow in the opposite direction. This allows closer control of vacuum operated emission devices.

Checking
9   Visually check all vacuum hoses for cracks, splits or hardening. Remove the distributor cap and rotor. Apply a vacuum to the distributor advance port (and retard port, if so equipped) and see if the breaker or relay plate inside of the distributor moves. The plate should move opposite to the distributor direction of rotation when vacuum is applied to the advance port, and should move in the direction of rotation when vacuum is applied to the retard port (if so equipped).
10   Checking the temperature relays, delay valves or other modifiers of the spark timing system is beyond the scope of the average home mechanic. Consult an expert if you suspect that you have other problems within the spark advance system.

Component replacement
11   When replacing any vacuum hoses, remove only one hose at a time and make sure that the replacement hose is of the same quality and size as the hose being replaced.
12   If it is determined that a malfunction in the spark control system is due to a faulty distributor, refer to Chapter 5 for the replacement procedure.

6   Thermactor systems

General description
1   Thermactor systems are employed to reduce carbon monoxide and hydrocarbon emissions. Two types are found on vehicles covered by

Fig. 6.16 Schematic of a typical managed-air thermactor system with separate air control and air bypass valves (Sec 6)

Fig. 6.17 Schematic of a typical managed-air thermactor system with a combined bypass/control valve (Sec 6)

Fig. 6.18 Locations of thermactor valves on inline engines (Sec 6)

Fig. 6.19 Locations of thermactor valves on V-type engines (Sec 6)

Fig. 6.20 Typical thermactor air supply pump (Sec 6)

Fig. 6.21 Cross-section of typical air control valve in the thermactor system (Sec 6)

this manual, a conventional thermactor air injection system and a managed air thermactor system.

2 The conventional thermactor air injection system consists of an air supply pump, a bypass valve, a check valve, an air manifold and connecting hoses. The managed air thermactor system adds a second check valve and an air control valve to the system. The air control valve may be incorporated with the bypass valve into a single bypass/air control valve in some applications.

3 The thermactor air injection system functions by continuing combustion of unburned gasses after they leave the combustion chamber. This is done by injecting fresh air into the hot exhaust gasses leaving the exhaust ports. The fresh air mixes with hot exhaust gas to promote further oxidation of both hydrocarbons and carbon monoxide, thereby reducing their concentration and converting some of them into harmless carbon dioxide and water. During some modes of operation, such as extended idle, the thermactor air is dumped into the atmosphere by the bypass valve to prevent overheating of the exhaust system.

4 The managed air thermactor system serves the same function as the thermactor air injection system, but, through the addition of the air control valve, diverts thermactor air either upstream to the exhaust manifold check valve, or downstream to the added, rear section check

valve and on to the dual catalytic converter. The air is utilized in the converter to maintain feed gas oxygen contents at a high level. This system is configured in both electronic and non-electronic controlled versions.

Checking

Air supply pump

5 Check and adjust the drivebelt tension (refer to Chapter 1).

6 Disconnect the air supply hose at the air bypass valve inlet.

7 The pump is operating satisfactorily if air flow is felt at the pump outlet with the engine running at idle, increasing as the engine speed is increased.

8 If the air pump does not successfully pass the above tests, replace it with a new or rebuilt unit.

Air bypass valve

9 With the engine running at idle, disconnect the hose from the outlet valve.

10 Remove the vacuum line from the vacuum nipple and remove or bypass any restrictors or delay valves in the vacuum line.

11 Verify that vacuum is present in the vacuum line.

12 Reconnect the vacuum line to the vacuum nipple.

13 With engine running at 1500 rpm, air pump supply air should be felt or heard at the air bypass valve outlet.

14 With engine running at 1500 rpm, disconnect the vacuum line. Air at the valve outlet should be decreased or shut off and air pump supply air should be felt or heard at the silencer ports.

15 Reconnect all disconnected hoses.

16 If the normally closed air bypass valve does not successfully pass the above tests, check the air pump (refer to Steps 5 through 7).

17 If the air pump is operating satisfactorily, replace the air bypass valve with a new one.

Air supply control valve

18 With the engine running at 1500 rpm, disconnect the hose at the air supply control valve inlet and verify the presence of air flow through the hose.

19 Reconnect the hose to the valve inlet.

20 Disconnect the hoses at the vacuum nipple and at outlets A and B (refer to the accompanying illustration).

21 With the engine running at 1500 rpm, air flow should be felt at outlet B and there should be little or no air flow at outlet A.

22 With the engine running at 1500 rpm, connect a line from any manifold vacuum fitting to the vacuum nipple.

23 Air flow should be present at outlet A with little or no air flow at outlet B.

24 Restore all connections.

25 If all conditions above are not met, replace the air control valve with a new one.

Combination air bypass/air control valve

26 Disconnect the hoses from outlets A and B (refer to the accompanying illustration).

27 Disconnect the vacuum line at port D and plug the line.

28 With the engine running at 1500 rpm, verify that air flows from the bypass vents.

29 Unplug and reconnect the vacuum line to port D, then disconnect and plug the line attached to port S.

30 Verify that vacuum is present in the line to vacuum port D by momentarily disconnecting it.

31 Reconnect the vacuum line to port D.

32 With the engine running at 1500 rpm, verify that air is flowing out of outlet B with no air flow present at outlet A.

33 Attach a length of hose to port S.

34 With the engine running at 1500 rpm, apply vacuum by mouth or vacuum pump to the hose and verify that air is flowing out of outlet A.

35 Reconnect all hoses. Be sure to unplug the line to Port S before reconnecting it.

36 If all conditions above are not met, replace the combination valve with a new one.

Check valve

37 Disconnect the hoses from both ends of the check valve.

38 Blow through both ends of the check valve, verifying that air flows in one direction only.

39 If air flows in both directions or not at all, replace the check valve with a new one.

40 When reconnecting the valve, make sure it is installed in the proper direction.

Component replacement

41 The air bypass valve, air supply control valve, check valve and combination air bypass/air control valve may be replaced by disconnecting the hoses leading to them (be sure to label the hoses as they are disconnected to facilitate reconnection), replacing the faulty element with a new one and reconnecting the hoses to the proper ports. Make sure that the hoses are in good condition. If not, replace them with new ones.

42 To replace the air supply pump, first loosen the appropriate engine drivebelt(s) (refer to Chapter 1 for procedural assistance), then remove

Fig. 6.22 Details of typical combined air bypass/air control valve (Sec 6)

the faulty pump from the bracket, labeling all wires and hoses as they are removed to facilitate installation of the new unit.

43 After the new pump is installed, adjust the drivebelt(s) to the specified tension (refer to Chapter 1).

44 Torque specifications for thermactor component installation will be found in Chapter 2. Refer to the appropriate part for your particular engine.

7 Choke control system

General description

1 This system is installed to control emissions by precisely matching fuel supply to engine needs at all temperatures.

Fig. 6.23 Typical air cleaner and duct system (Sec 8)

2   Choke system modifiers include a full electric choke or electrically assisted heating coil and pull-down and pull-off assemblies. In addition, various control units which monitor engine temperature and choke position are mounted, along with their linkages, providing appropriate choke action relative to the engine's ability to run on lean fuel mixtures as it warms up.

3   All of the systems combine to modify choke opening by lessening the time the choke plate is closed, thus lessening the amount of unburned hydrocarbons produced.

Checking

4   Information on the Emissions Control Information label, located in the engine compartment, and instructions in carburetor rebuild kits applicable to your particular carburetor can be used to service and rebuild the choke modifying devices. Also, refer to the Chapter 1 and Chapter 4 for carburetor and choke inspection and adjustment procedures.

Component replacement

5   Due to the variety of carburetors used on vehicles covered in this manual and the differing choke control system components employed, it is not practical to list all the component replacement procedures. As is the case with general carburetor overhauls, the instructions accompanying the rebuild kit for your particular carburetor will fully explain these procedures.

---

8   Inlet air temperature control system

General description

1   The air cleaner temperature control system is used to keep the air entering the carburetor at a consistent temperature. The carburetor can then be calibrated much leaner for emissions reduction, improved warm-up and better driveability.

Fig. 6.24 Cold Weather Modulator (CWM) system operation (Sec 8)

6

2   Two air flow circuits are used. They are controlled by various intake manifold vacuum and temperature sensing valves. A vacuum motor operates a heat duct valve in the air cleaner.
3   When the under hood temperature is cold, air is drawn through the shroud which fits over the exhaust manifold, up through the heat riser tube and into the air cleaner. This provides warm air for the carburetor, resulting in better driveability and faster warm-up. As the under hood temperature rises, the duct valve is closed by the vacuum motor and the air is drawn through the cold air snorkel or duct. This provides a consistent intake air temperature.

Checking

General
4   Checking of this system should be done while the engine is cold.
5   Remove the clamp retaining the air hose to the metal duct and valve assembly. Start the engine and, looking through the duct and valve assembly, observe that the duct valve (heat control door) rotates to allow hot air from the heat riser tube to enter the air cleaner. As the engine warms up the vacuum motor should pull the valve open, closing off the heat riser tube and allowing ambient air to enter the duct.

Duct valve
6   If the duct valve does not perform as indicated, check that it is not rusted in an open or closed position by attempting to move it by hand. If it is rusted, it can usually be freed by cleaning and oiling. If it cannot be freed replace it with a new unit.

Vacuum motor
7   If the vacuum motor fails to perform as indicated, check carefully for a leak in the hose leading to it. If no leak is found, replace the vacuum motor with a new one.

Component replacement
8   Replacement of the valve assembly and vacuum motor is straightforward and is accomplished by unbolting the faulty component, removing the vacuum lines leading to it (where appropriate) and installing the new component.

---

9   Deceleration throttle control system

General description
1   This system reduces the hydrocarbon and carbon monoxide content of exhaust gasses by opening the throttle slightly during deceleration.
2   The system consists of a throttle positioner, a vacuum solenoid valve, a vacuum sensing switch and electrical links to an electronic speed sensor/governor module, although not all components are included in all systems.
3   On those models without a vacuum sensing switch, when the engine speed is higher than a predetermined rpm a signal is sent to the solenoid, which allows manifold vacuum to activate the throttle positioner.
4   On those models with a vacuum sensing switch, when the engine speed is higher than a predetermined rpm and manifold vacuum is at a certain value the vacuum switch sends a signal to the module, then to the solenoid, allowing manifold vacuum to activate the throttle positioner.

Checking

General
5   All of the following checks are to be made with the engine at full operating temperature and with all accessories off unless otherwise noted.
6   With the engine at idle, accelerate to 2000 rpm or more, then let the engine fall back to idle while watching to see if the vacuum diaphragm plunger extends and retracts. If the plunger performs as indicated, the system is functioning normally. If not, check the throttle positioner.

Throttle positioner
7   Remove the hose from the throttle positioner and, using a hand operated vacuum pump, apply suction to the diaphragm and trap it. If the diaphragm does not respond or will not hold vacuum, replace the throttle positioner with a new one.
8   Remove the vacuum pump from the diaphragm and see if the

VALVE CLOSED TO HEATED AIR

VALVE OPEN TO HEATED AIR

Fig. 6.25 Operation of the vacuum operated duct valve in the air inlet temperature control system (Sec 8)

diaphragm returns within five seconds. If not, replace the throttle positioner with a new one.

Vacuum solenoid valve
9   With the engine at idle, disconnect the vacuum supply hose from the solenoid valve and verify that the hose is supplying vacuum.
10   Disconnect the wires from the solenoid and apply battery voltage to first one terminal, then the other, without grounding the unused terminal, verifying that there is no increase in engine speed.
11   With battery voltage supplied to one terminal, ground the other terminal and verify that engine speed increases.
12   Remove the ground and verify that the engine returns to idle rpm.
13   If the solenoid fails to pass any of the above tests, replace it with a new one.

Vacuum sensing switch (if so equipped)
14   Disconnect the hose from the vacuum fitting on the switch.
15   Hook up a hand operated vacuum pump to the fitting.
16   Using an ohmmeter, verify that the switch is open (no continuity) while applying 19.4-in Hg vacuum or less to the switch.
17   Increase the vacuum to 20.6-in Hg or more and verify that the switch is closed (continuity).
18   If the switch fails to pass either of the above tests, replace it with a new one.

Electronic speed sensor/governor module (if so equipped)
19   If a fault is suspected in the module it must be checked by a Ford service department.

Component replacement
20   Replacement of the throttle positioner, solenoid valve and sensing switch is straightforward, accomplished by disconnecting the attached wires and/or hoses, removing the faulty component and replacing it with a new one.

Fig. 6.26 Operation of the deceleration throttle control system in which a vacuum switch is not used (Sec 9)

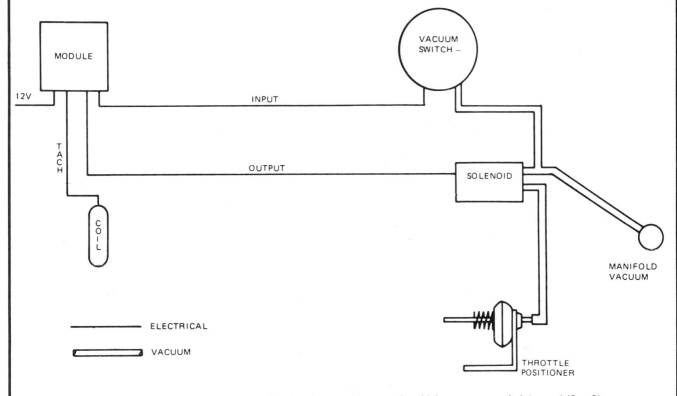

6

Fig. 6.27 Operation of the deceleration throttle control system in which a vacuum switch is used (Sec 9)

10   Exhaust control system

General description

1   This system is employed to eliminate any condensation of fuel on the cold surfaces of the intake system during cold engine operation and to provide better evaporation and distribution of the air/fuel mixture. The result is better driveability, faster warm-up and a reduction in the release of hydrocarbons to the atmosphere.

2   The component of this system is the exhaust heat control valve, which is controlled by either a thermostat or engine vacuum. It is mounted between the exhaust manifold and one branch of the exhaust pipe.

3   The valve operates by remaining closed when the engine is cold, routing hot exhaust gasses to the intake manifold area through the heat riser tube, then slowly opening as the engine temperature increases.

Checking

Bimetal thermostat valve

4   With the engine cold, manually rotate the valve shaft. It must move freely and return to the closed position as long as the engine is cold.

5   Start the engine and, as it warms up, make sure that the valve shaft rotates to the open position.

6   If the valve fails to operate as described, replace it with a new one.

Vacuum operated valve

7   Perform Step 4 above.

8   Warm up the engine to normal operating temperature.

9   Disconnect the vacuum line at the valve and verify that there is vacuum at the line. If not, check the vacuum line and vacuum source.

10   If the valve fails to operate when vacuum is applied, replace it with a new one.

Component replacement

11   The replacement of the exhaust heat control valve is straightforward, accomplished by unbolting the faulty valve, cleaning the mating surfaces on the exhaust manifold and exhaust pipe and installing a new valve.

Fig. 6.28 Typical temperature controlled exhaust heat control valve (Sec 10)

11   Catalytic converter

General description

1   The catalytic converter is designed to reduce hydrocarbon (HC) and carbon monoxide pollutants in the exhaust. The converter oxidizes these components and converts them to water and carbon dioxide.

2   The converter is located in the exhaust system and closely resembles a muffler. Some models have two converters, a light-off catalyst type, mounted just past the exhaust manifold pipe, and a con-

Fig. 6.29 Dual catalytic converter (Sec 11)

ventional oxidation catalyst or three-way catalyst type mounted farther downstream.

3   **Note:** *If large amounts of unburned gasoline enter the converter, it may overheat and cause a fire. Always observe the following precautions:*

Use only unleaded gasoline
Avoid prolonged idling
Do not prolong engine compression checks
Do not run the engine with a nearly empty fuel tank
Avoid coasting with the ignition turned Off

Checking

4   The catalytic converter requires little maintenance and servicing at regular intervals. However, the system should be inspected whenever the vehicle is raised on a lift or if the exhaust system is checked or serviced.

5   Check all connections in the exhaust pipe assembly for looseness or damage. Also check all the clamps for damage, cracks or missing fasteners. Check the rubber hangers for cracks.

6   The converter itself should be checked for damage or dents which could affect its performance. At the same time the converter is inspected, check the metal protector plate under it and the heat insulator above it for damage or loose fasteners.

Component replacement

7   Do not attempt to remove the catalytic converter until the complete exhaust system is cool. Raise the vehicle and support it securely on jackstands. Apply penetrating oil to the clamp bolts and allow it to soak in.

8   Remove the bolts and the rubber hangers, then separate the converter from the exhaust pipes. Remove the old gaskets if they are stuck to the pipes.

9   Installation of the converter is the reverse of removal. Use new exhaust pipe gaskets. Replace the rubber hangers with new ones if the originals are deteriorated. Start the engine and check carefully for exhaust leaks.

6

Chapter 7 Part A   Manual transmission

Contents

Specifications

Transmission type	4-speed synchomesh
Oil capacity	2.8 US quarts
Oil type	ESP-M2C83-C
Cluster gear-to-case endplay	0.006 to 0.018 in

Torque specifications — **Ft-lbs**

Input shaft bearing retainer-to-case bolt	30 to 36
Extension housing-to-case bolts	33 to 36
Access cover-to-case screw	8 to 10
Filler plug	24 to 27
Detent plug	12 to 14
Backup light switch	8 to 12
Gearshift lever bolts	17 to 25
Gearshift boot bolts	3 to 7

1   General information

The manual transmissions used on the models covered by this manual are equipped with four forward and one reverse gears.

All forward gears are engaged through blocker ring synchromesh units to obtain smooth, silent gear changes. All forward gears on the mainshaft are in constant mesh with their corresponding gears on the countershaft gear cluster and are helically cut for quiet running.

The countershaft reverse gear has straight cut spur teeth and drives the 1st/2nd gear synchronizer hub on the mainshaft through an interposed sliding idler gear.

Gears are engaged either by a single selector rail and forks or by levers in the side cover with forks. Control of the gears is from a floor mounted shift lever, which connects either with the single shift rail or the three selector levers and link rods.

Where close limits are required during assembly of the transmission, selective shims are used to eliminate excessive endfloat, or backlash, without the need of using matched assemblies.

2   Shift lever — removal and installation

Removal

1   Place the gearshift lever in Neutral.
2   Remove the attaching screws at the rear of the coin tray (if so equipped) and lift to release the tray from the front hold-down notch on the boot retainer. Lift the assembly over and away from the gearshift lever boot.
3   Remove the four capscrews attaching the boot to the floorplan

Fig. 7A.1 Manual transmission shift lever showing coin tray and shift lever boot (Sec 2)

Fig. 7A.2 Gearshift lever removal and installation (Sec 2)

Fig. 7A.3 Backup switch installation (Sec 3)

and move the boot upward and out of the way.

4   Remove the three lever attaching bolts. Remove the lever and the boot assembly from the extension housing.

5   Remove the gearshift knob and lock nut and slide the boot off the lever.

6   Remove the attaching screws from the step plate.

7   Remove the attaching screws from each kick pad and remove the pads. Lift the shift lever from the extension housing.

Installation

8   Make sure the shift lever insulator is in a straight downward position with the shift rail. Position the shift lever in the extension housing so that the forked ends engage in the insulator properly.

9   Install the three attaching bolts.

10 Slide the boot over the lever and install the attaching bolts.

11 Install the gearshift knob locking nut and the gearshift knob.

12 Position the coin tray over the shift lever boot and secure the tray to the front notch on the boot retaining ring. Attach the tray at the rear with the attaching screws.

3   Backup light switch — removal and installation

1   The backup light switch is mounted in the bottom of the transmission extension as shown in the accompanying illustration.

2   To remove the switch, disconnect the leads, unscrew and remove the switch, spring and plunger.

3   When refitting the switch, apply gasket sealant to the screw threads and refit the plunger, spring and switch.

4   Manual transmission — removal and installation

1   If the transmission is to be removed from the car without removing the engine, sufficient ground clearance is required. If an inspection pit or ramps are not available, jack the car as high as possible and support it securely on jackstands.

2   Disconnect the battery.

3   Unscrew the gear lever knob and remove the cover and rubber boot. If a package tray or center console is fitted, these must also be removed.

4   Remove the three bolts attaching the lever assembly to the transmission. Lift out the shift lever.

5   Place a drip tray beneath the transmission, remove the drain plug and, when the oil has drained, refit the plug and tighten it.

6   Put mating marks on the two faces of the rear axle U-joint flange. Remove the four bolts from the rear axle pinion flange and the two bolts from the driveshaft center bearing support and withdraw the driveshaft assembly from the extension housing. Tie a polyethylene bag around the end of the transmission extension to keep out dirt and to catch any oil which has not drained.

7   Pull back the rubber boot over the clutch release lever and loosen the adjuster so that the end of the clutch cable can be unhooked from the clutch release lever.

8   Remove the screw and lockplate securing the speedometer drive and disconnect the drive.

9   Remove the cover from the backup light switch. Note which way the leads are fitted and then remove them.

10 Detach the exhaust pipe from the exhaust manifold and tie the pipe out of the way so that the engine and transmission can be lowered.

11 Support the transmission and remove the bolt securing the transmission to the rear engine mounting and the four bolts securing the transmission crossmember to the floor. Remove the crossmember.

12 Lower the transmission slightly and support the engine at the oil pan. Use a block of wood between the jack or support and the pan to prevent damage to the pan. It may be necessary to slide the catalytic converter heat shield forward for clearance.

13 Remove the six bolts securing the clutch housing to the engine. Pull the transmission assembly to the rear to disengage the imput shaft from the clutch pilot bearing and clutch plate.

14 When the shaft is clear of the clutch remove the transmission assembly from beneath the car.

15 When installing, ensure that the two clutch housing guide bushings are fitted to the engine and that the clutch pilot bearing in the end of the crankshaft is in place and is serviceable. Tie the clutch lever to the clutch housing to prevent the release lever from slipping out while the transmission assembly is being fitted.

16 Apply molybdenum-based grease (Ford chassis lube) onto the end and splines of the input shaft and refit the transmission by reversing the removal procedure.

17 It is important when installing the transmission that it is exactly in line with the crankshaft, otherwise the input shaft will not enter the clutch drive plate and the crankshaft pilot bearing. If there is difficulty in mating the splines of the shaft and the clutch plate, select a gear to restrain the movement of the shaft and turn the transmission slightly until the splines enter. Do not attempt to force the transmission onto the engine. This may damage the splines and make fitting impossible.

18 After installation has been completed, refill the transmission with the specified gear oil (Chapter 1).

7A

Fig. 7A.4 Removing the shift rail detent plunger (Sec 5)

Fig. 7A.6 Driving out the interlock plate retaining pin
(Sec 5)

Fig. 7A.5 Driving out the access plug with a punch or drift
(Sec 5)

5   Manual transmission — disassembly

1   Remove the clutch release bearing and lever. Remove the clutch housing.
2   Remove the transmission cover and gasket.
3   Remove the threaded plug, spring and shift rail detent plunger located on the front of the transmission case as shown in the accompanying illustration.
4   At the rear of the transmission, drive out the access plug as shown in the accompanying illustration.
5   Drive out the interlock plate retaining pin as shown in the accompanying illustration and remove.
6   Remove the roll pin from the selector lever arm.
7   Remove the plug at the rear of the extension housing by tapping the front of the shift rail to displace it.
8   Pull the shift rail out of the back of the extension housing and case as shown in the accompanying illustration.
9   Remove the selector arm shift forks from the case.
10 Remove the extension housing attachment bolts and tap the housing with a plastic mallet to loosen it.
11 Rotate the loosened housing so that the countershaft is aligned with the cutaway in the extension housing flange.
12 Drive the countershaft rearward with a brass drift until it just clears the front of the case. Slide a dummy shaft in the case and gear until the countershaft gear can be lowered to the bottom of the case. Remove the countershaft.
13 Lift the extension housing and mainshaft assembly from the case as shown in the accompanying illustration.
14 Remove the four bolts securing the input shaft bearing retainer

Fig. 7A.7 Removing the shift rail (Sec 5)

Fig. 7A.8 Removing the extension housing and mainshaft (Sec 5)

to the front of the case. Remove the input shaft and bearing retainer assembly.

15 Remove the reverse idler shaft as shown in the accompanying illustration.

16 Remove the countershaft gear, bearing retaining washers, bearings and dummy shaft from the countershaft gear.

6 Output shaft — disassembly and assembly

1 Remove the 4th gear blocker ring from the output shaft.

2 Remove and discard the snap-ring from the forward end of the input shaft.

3 Remove and discard the 3rd/4th gear snap-ring.

4 Ease the hub and 3rd gear assembly forward by levering gently with a pair of needle nose pliers.

5 Remove the 3rd/4th gear synchronizer assembly and 3rd gear from the output shaft.

6 Remove the snap-ring and discard it. Remove the washer and slide the 2nd gear and blocker ring off the output shaft.

7 Scribe or paint alignment marks on the hub and synchronizer before disassembling. Pull the sleeve off the synchronizer before disassembling. Pull the sleeve off the hub and remove the inserts and springs to disassemble.

8 Remove the snap-ring retaining the output shaft bearing and press or tap the output shaft assembly out off the extension housing with a plastic hammer or mallet.

9 Remove the output shaft snap-ring and bearing.

10 Remove the speedometer gear with a press.

11 Press the 1st gear, spacer and bearing off the output shaft.

12 Since the 1st and 2nd speed synchronizer and hub are serviced

Fig. 7A.9 Removing the reverse idler gearshaft (Sec 5)

as a complete assembly with the shaft, do not attempt to separate them. If they are worn or damaged, the whole assembly must be replaced.

13 Before starting reassembly, clean all parts thoroughly and check their condition. Lubricate all parts with transmission oil before installing.

14 Reassemble the synchronizer sleeve and hub, making sure that the marks made in step 7 are lined up. Insert the hub inserts and fit the hub insert springs so that their open ends are staggered relative to each other.

15 Place the synchronizer blocker ring onto the cone of the 2nd gear and slide it onto the output shaft together with the 1st/2nd gear synchronizer hub. The gear on the hub should face forward.

16 Install the synchronizer blocker ring and snap-ring which holds the synchronizer in place.

7A

Fig. 7A.10 Output shaft and components (Sec 6)

Fig. 7A.11 Input shaft — exploded view (Sec 7)

Fig. 7A.12 Input shaft removal and installation (Sec 7)

17   Slide on 1st gear, so that the synchronizer cone lies just inside the synchronizer ring which has just been installed. Apply multipurpose grease to the cone surface of 1st gear and all shaft gear journals.
18   Install the spacer on the output shaft so that the large diameter is towards the rear.
19   A special Ford tool is required to determine which thickness snap-ring must be installed to eliminate shaft endplay. It is advisable to have your dealer perform this procedure.
20   Once the proper snap-ring is obtained, position it and the bearing on the end of the output shaft. Press the bearing into position. Install the selected snap-ring in the groove in the output shaft.
21   Install the synchronizer blocker ring to the cone of 3rd gear and install this assembly on the front of the output shaft. Install the 3rd/4th gear synchronizer hub with its wide boss toward the rear and retain it with a snap-ring.
22   The speedometer drive gear must also be installed with a press and a special tool, so this is another procedure best left to your dealer.

7   Input shaft — disassembly and assembly

1   It is not necessary to dismantle the input shaft unless a new bearing or a new shaft is being installed.
2   With a pair of snap-ring pliers, expand and remove the small snap-ring which secures the bearing to the input shaft.
3   With a soft head hammer, gently tap the bearing forward until it can be pulled from the shaft.
4   When fitting the bearing, be sure that the groove in the periphery of the outer bearing track is away from the gear, otherwise it will not

be possible to fit the large snap-ring which retains the bearing in place in the housing.
5   Either stand the input shaft upright on a bench and tap the bearing into place using a piece of tube of suitable diameter, or use the jaws of a vise to support the bearing and tap the rear of the input shaft with a soft-face hammer.
6   When the bearing is fully set, replace the old snap-ring with a new one.

8   Countershaft — disassembly and assembly

1   Remove the shim from each end of the countershaft and remove the 21 needle rollers from each end of the gear.
2   When reassembling, insert a shim into the bottom of the bore. Daub the bore with general purpose grease and insert the 21 needle rollers. When all the rollers are in place, smear grease over them to retain them and then secure the shim over the ends of the rollers with grease.

9   Transmission — inspection and overhaul

1   Carefully clean and examine all component parts for signs of excessive wear, damage, distortion or damage.
2   Examine the gears for excessive wear and broken or chipped teeth. It is not satisfactory to fit a new gear unless its mating gear is also replaced. If the condition of gears is bad, an exchange transmission should be fitted.
3   Examine the countershaft for wear on the ends which are in contact with the needle rollers, and if there is a wear step a new countershaft should be fitted.
4   The four synchronizer rings are certain to be worn and it is false economy not to replace them. New rings will improve the smoothness of gear changing.
5   The needle roller bearing between the nose of the mainshaft and the bore of the input shaft should be discarded and a new one fitted.
6   If there is excessive wear in the synchronizer units they must be replaced as a set. These units are expensive and, as the selector forks are also likely to need replacing, an exchange transmission may be a more satisfactory solution. If possible compare the synchronizer rings and selector forks with new ones before deciding what to do.
7   If the bearing in the extension is badly worn it is best to take the extension to a dealer to have the bearing pulled out and a new one fitted. The transmission needs to be assembled and the output shaft refitted for this to be done.
8   The oil seals in the extension housing and the front bearing retainer should be replaced. Drive out the old seal with a screwdriver and tap in a new seal with a hammer and piece of wood. Make sure that the seal has entered its bore squarely before attempting to tap it in.

Fig. 7A.13 Countershaft gear components (Sec 8)

Fig. 7A.14 Assembling the countershaft gear and bearings
(Sec 10)

10   Transmission — reassembly

1   When any bolt screws into a through-bore, sealing compound should be applied to the threads of the bolt before it is inserted.

2   Fit the reverse idler gear with the groove on the gear towards the rear. Insert the idler shaft and drive it in with a plastic hammer until the bottom of the step on the end of the shaft is flush with the end of the transmission. The milled flats should protrude slightly from the transmission face and should be aligned with a countershaft bore.

3   Fit the large thrust washer to the countershaft bore at the front of the transmission and the small thrust washer to the countershaft bore at the rear. The tabs on the washers should be towards the case and the washers should be greased to retain them in place.

4   Check that the needle rollers and end washers of the countershaft

Fig. 7A.15 Installing the countershaft gear (Sec 10)

gear are in place as shown in the accompanying illustration, then lower the gear cluster into the case carefully, making sure that the thrust washers are not displaced.

5   Push the input shaft, together with its ball bearing, into the front of the transmission until the snap-ring around the bearing bears against the front of the transmission case.

6   Fit the drive bearing retainer, using a new gasket, making sure that

Fig. 7A.16 Installing the bearing retainer seal (Sec 10)

Fig. 7A.17 Installing the output shaft in the extension housing (Sec 10)

Fig. 7A.18 Countershaft installation (Sec 10)

Fig. 7A.19 Extension housing plug installation (Sec 10)

the oil return bore of the gasket and bearing retainer are aligned. Apply sealing compound to the threads of the bolts, insert them and tighten to the torque setting given in the specifications.

7   Oil the new input shaft needle roller bearing and push it into the bore of the input shaft. Slide the top gear synchronizer blocker ring onto the cone of the input shaft.

8   Fit the extension housing gasket, then insert the assembled output shaft into the rear of the box and drive it in until the nose of the output shaft is fully engaged in the bore of the front driveshaft bearing.

9   Carefully turn the transmission upside-down, so that the countershaft gear cluster drops into engagement with the output shaft. Check that the gear and the two thrust washers are in line and then carefully push in the countershaft from the rear as shown in the accompanying illustration. If necessary tap the shaft in with a plastic head hammer, but take great care not to dislodge the thrust washers or needle rollers. When fully home, the bottom of the step on the idler shaft should be in line with the face of the box and the milled flats should be in line with the idler shaft bore.

10 Turn the transmission right side up and align the hole in the ball bearing support with the dowel on the extension housing. Fit the extension housing. Apply sealing compound to the threads of the bolts, insert them and tighten to the torque setting given in the specifications.

11 If a new extension housing bearing has been fitted, check that the notch or groove in it aligns with the oil return groove in the extension housing. If the new extension housing oil seal has not already been fitted, slide it over the extension shaft and carefully tap it in with a hammer and a block of wood.

12 Fit a new O-ring to the speedometer pinion assembly, refit the assembly and fit the snap-ring to secure it.

13 Insert the reverse gear interlock plunger, threaded plug and spring. Fit the bolt with a lock plate and insert the bolt. Tighten the bolt and bend the lock plates to secure it.

14 Insert the three selector forks into position in the transmission.

15 Slide the 1st/2nd gear selector rail through the right-hand bore in the case, then thread it through the 1st/2nd gear selector fork. Align the holes in the fork and rail and tap in the roll pin. Insert the plunger

into the case.

16 Fit the plunger into the 3rd/top gear selector rail, insert the rail through the center bore in the case and thread the rail through the 3rd/top gear selector fork. Fit the retaining clip to the groove in the selector rail. Align the holes in the selector fork and rail, insert the roll pin and tap it home.

17 Push the reverse gear selector rail through a left-hand bore in the housing, and then thread it through the reverse gear selector fork. Align the holes in the fork and rail, insert the roll pin and tap it home.

18 Fit the interlock plunger, apply sealing compound to the plug and screw in the plug.

19 Insert the reverse gear relay lever and secure it with a roll pin.

20 Insert the selector shaft through the selector housing cover and fit the cover using a new gasket. Insert the cover retaining bolts and screw them in finger tight.

21 Fit the selector shaft bracket.

22 Slide the selector finger onto the selector shaft. Engage the screw in the recess in the shaft and tighten the screw.

23 Drop the three detent balls into their bores in the case, grease the three springs and insert them into the recesses of the transmission cover. Fit a new cover gasket and position the cover onto it, insert the cover bolts and tighten them to the torque wrench setting given in the Specifications.

24 Check the play between the selector finger and 3rd/top gear selector rail.

25 Fit a new gasket to the extension housing cover. Position the cover, insert the fixing bolts and tighten them to the torque setting given in the Specifications. Apply sealer to a new extension housing plug and install a new plug as shown in the accompanying illustration.

26 Make sure that the oil drain plug is fitted and tightened, then fill the transmission to the correct level by pouring in 2.8 pints U.S. (1.3 liters) of oil to specification ESW-M2C83-C (SAE 80 EP).

7A

Chapter 7 Part B Automatic transmission

Refer to Chapter 13 for specifications related to 1985 and later models

Contents

Specifications

Transmission type . . . .   3-speed automatic
Fluid capacity . . . .   See Chapter 1 Specifications
Fluid type . . . .   See recommendation on transmission oil dipstick

C3 transmission

Torque specifications	Ft-lbs
Converter housing-to-case	27 to 39
Extension housing-to-case	27 to 39
Oil pump-to-converter housing	7 to 10
Flexplate-to-converter housing	27 to 49
Main control-to-case	7 to 9
Plate-to-valve body	7 to 9
Servo cover-to-case	7 to 9
Inner race-to-case	7 to 9
Oil pan	12 to 17
Governor-to-collector body	7 to 9
Converter housing-to-engine	28 to 38
Outer downshift lever nut	7 to 11
Inner manual lever nut	30 to 40
Neutral switch-to-case	12 to 15
Front band adjusting locknut	35 to 45
Oil cooler line-to-connetor	7 to 10
Converter drain plug	20 to 30
Flexplate-to-crankshaft	48 to 53
Filler tube-to-engine clip	28 to 38

C4 transmission

Torque specifications	Ft-lbs
Oil pan-to-case	12 to 16
Stator support-to-pump	12 to 20
Overrunning clutch race-to-case	13 to 20
Converter housing cover	12 to 16
Rear servo cover	12 to 20
Intermediate servo cover	16 to 22
Oil distributor sleeve	12 to 20
Extension housing-to-case	28 to 40
Front pump-to-case	28 to 38
Transmission-to-engine	40 to 50
Engine separator plate-to-converter housing	5 to 9
Downshift lever-to-shaft	12 to 16
Flexplate-to-converter	20 to 30
Band adjusting screws-to-case	35 to 45
Manual valve inner lever-to-shaft	30 to 40
Front pump pipe plug	6 to 12
Cooler line-to-transmission case	12 to 18

Filler tube-to-oil pan	32 to 42
End plates-to-body	2 to 4
Separator plate-to-lower body	3 to 5
Lower-to-upper body	3 to 5
Pump assembly-to-case	2 to 3

C5 transmission

Torque specifications	**Ft-lbs**
Oil cooler-to-transmission case	1 to 2
Oil pan-to-case	12 to 16
Converter housing cover-to-converter housing	17 to 21
Converter housing-to-case	28 to 40
Engine rear cover plate-to-transmission	12 to 16
Servo cover-to-case	12 to 20
Extension housing-to-case	28 to 40
Engine-to-transmission	40 to 50
Band adjusting screws-to-case	10
Drain plug-to-converter cover	12 to 17

C6 transmission

Torque specifications	**Ft-lbs**
Converter-to-flexplate	20 to 30
Oil pan-to-case	12 to 16
Servo cover-to-case	14 to 20
Extension housing-to-case	25 to 35
Converter cover-to-converter housing	30 to 60
Band adjustment screw locknut	35 to 45
Converter drain plug	14 to 29
Transmission-to-engine	40 to 50
Engine rear cover-to-converter	20 to 30

FMX Transmission

Torque specifications	**Ft-lbs**
Converter-to-flexplate	23 to 28
Converter housing-to-transmission case	40 to 50
Servo-to-transmission case	30 to 35
Oil pan-to-case	10 to 13
Converter cover-to-converter housing	12 to 16
Extension housing-to-transmission case	30 to 40
Converter drain plug	15 to 28
Band adjusting screw locknut	35 to 40
Oil filler tube-to-engine	20 to 25
Transmission-to-engine	40 to 50

A.O.D. Transmission

Torque specifications	**Ft-lbs**
Transmission-to-engine	40 to 50
Neutral start switch-to-case	7 to 8
Converter plug-to-converter	8 to 28
Cooler line-to-case	10 to 14
Extension housing-to-case	16 to 20
Oil pan-to-case	12 to 16

7B

1   General information

Due to the complexity of the automatic transmissions covered in this manual and to the specialized equipment necessary to perform most service operations, this Chapter addresses only those procedures concerning routine maintenance and adjustment. Except for removal and installation of the transmission assembly, major repair operations should be undertaken by a professional with the proper facilities.

Models covered in this manual may be equipped with any one of six automatic transmissions. Four of them, the C3, C4, C5 and C6, are of the same fundamental design but with varying power handling capabilities. The FMX automatic is installed with most midsize V8's. The Automatic Overdrive transmission (AOD) was introduced in 1980 and features an automatically engaged fourth speed. The AOD combines the convenience of automatic shifting with fuel saving features, an overdrive gear ratio and a mechanical no-slip feature.

Ford specifies a different grade transmission fluid than other manufac-

turers, and this must be used when refilling or adding fluid. The fluid specification for your vehicle can be found embossed on the transmission fluid dipstick or on the certification label on the left front door post.

2   General diagnosis

Automatic transmission malfunctions may be caused by four general conditions: poor engine performance, improper adjustments, hydraulic malfunctions and mechanical malfunctions. Diagnosis of these problems should always begin with the easily repaired items such as fluid level and condition, band adjustment and shift linkage adjustment. Next perform a road test to determine if the problem has been corrected or if more diagnosis is necessary. If the problem persists after the preliminary tests and corrections are completed additional diagnosis should be undertaken by a dealer or repair shop.

INTERLOCK AND PARKING MECHANISM

PARKING PAWL

GOVERNOR ASSEMBLY

VITON SEALS

OIL SEAL

THRUST WASHER NO. 11

OUTPUT SHAFT

GOVERNOR HUB

RETAINER

THROTTLE VALVE

NEUTRAL SWITCH

VACUUM DIAPHRAGM

THRUST WASHER NO. 10

BRAKE BAND

THRUST WASHER NO. 9

BRAKE DRUM

THRUST WASHER NO. 8

THRUST WASHER NO. 5

FRONT PLANET CARRIER

THRUST WASHER NO. 4

FORWARD CLUTCH

FRONT SERVO ASSEMBLY

FREE-WHEEL CLUTCH ASSEMBLY

REAR PLANET CARRIER

THRUST WASHER NO. 7

INPUT BELL HOUSING

SUN GEAR

THRUST WASHER NO.3

THRUST WASHER NO. 6 (NEEDLE BEARING)

COVER PLATE

CONTROL BLOCK

REAR SERVO ASSEMBLY

FILTER SCREEN

GASKET

FORWARD CLUTCH

THIRD AND REVERSE GEAR CLUTCH

THRUST WASHER NO. 2

BRAKE BAND

O-RING

PUMP

PUMP GEARS

GASKET

STEEL SEALS

THRUST WASHER NO. 1

SEPARATOR PLATE

TORQUE CONVERTER

INPUT SHAFT

STUDS

Fig. 7B.1 Ford C3 automatic transmission — exploded view (Sec 1)

Fig. 7B.2 Ford C4 automatic transmission — sectional view (Sec 1)

7B

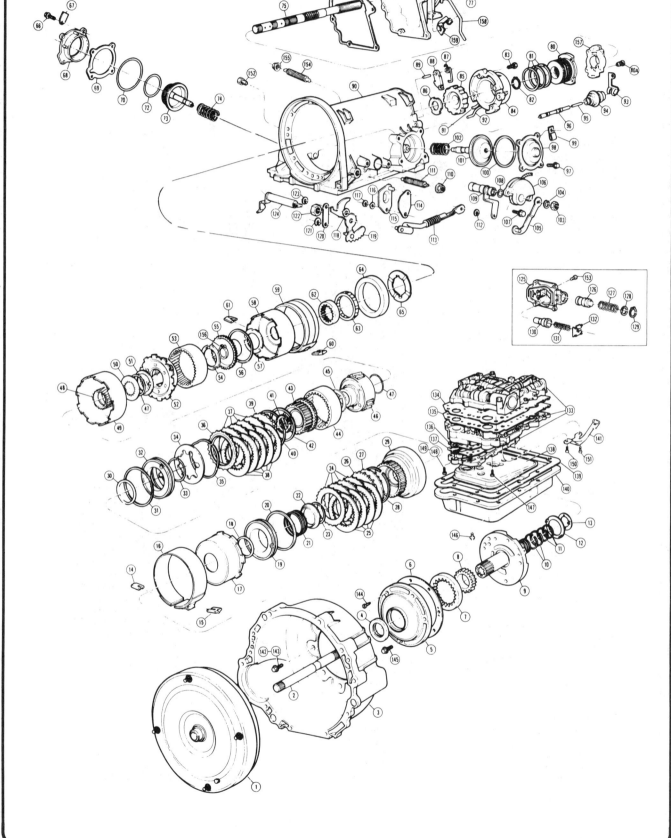

Fig. 7B.3 Ford C5 automatic transmission — exploded view (Sec 1)

1 Converter assembly
2 Imput shaft
3 Converter housing
4 Front pump seal assembly
5 Front pump body
6 Front pump gasket
7 Front pump driven gear
8 Front pump drive gear
9 Front pump stator support
10 Forward clutch cylinder seal
11 Reverse clutch cylinder seal
12 Thrust washer
13 Thrust washer
14 Intermediate brake strut
15 Intermediate brake strut
16 Intermediate band assembly
17 Intermediate brake drum assembly
18 Reverse clutch inner seal
19 High clutch piston assembly
20 High clutch outer seal
21 High clutch piston spring
22 Clutch piston spring retainer
23 Retaining ring
24 Clutch steel plate
25 Clutch friction plate
26 Clutch pressure plate
27 Pressure plate spring
28 Snap ring
29 Forward clutch cylinder
30 Clutch piston O-ring
31 Clutch outer seal
32 Forward clutch piston assembly
33 Piston spring ring
34 Piston disc spring
35 Wave ring
36 Foward clutch pressure plate
37 Clutch steel plate
38 Clutch friction plate
39 Clutch pressure plate
40 Retaining ring
41 Thrust washer
42 Retainer
43 Hub and bushing assembly
44 Output shaft ring gear
45 Thrust washer
46 Foward planetary assembly
47 Retainer
48 Sun gear
49 Input shell
50 Thrust washer
51 Thrust washer
52 Reverse planetary assembly
53 Output shaft ring gear
54 Thrust washer
55 Output shaft hub
56 Retaining ring

57 Thrust washer
58 Reverse brake drum assembly
59 Reverse band assembly
60 Reverse brake strut
61 Reverse band strut
62 Overrun clutch inner race
63 Spring and roller assembly
64 Overrun clutch outer race
65 Thrust washer
66 Washer-head bolt
67 Service tag
68 Intermediate band servo cover
69 Intermediate band servo gasket
70 Servo cover large seal
71 Delete
72 Servo piston small seal
73 Servo piston assembly
74 Servo piston spring
75 Output shaft assembly
76 Extension gasket
77 Extension assembly
78 Extension seal assembly
79 Washer-head bolts (6)
80 Governor oil collector body
80A Governor oil screen assembly
81 Governor seal ring
82 Retaining ring
83 Bolts (4)
84 Oil distributor sleeve
85 Output shaft parking gear
86 Thrust washer
87 Return spring
88 Parking pawl assembly
89 Straight pin
90 Case assembly
91 Oil distributor tube
92 Oil distributor tube
93 Clip
94 Diaphragm assembly
95 T.V. control rod
96 Throttle control valve
97 Bolts (4)
98 Reverse band servo cover
99 Wiring harness clip
100 Servo piston cover
101 Servo piston assembly
102 Servo piston spring
103 Hex nut
104 Washer
105 Downshift outer lever assembly
106 Neutral start switch
107 Screw and washer (2)
108 O-ring
109 Manual control lever assembly

110 Nut
111 Adjusting screw
112 Ring
113 Park lever actuating rod assembly
114 Park lever spacer
115 Park actuating lever assembly
116 Washer
117 Retaining ring
118 Park lever actuating rod roller
119 Manual valve detent inner lever
120 Lever link
121 Ring
122 Nut
123 Ring
124 Downshift detent inner lever
125 Governor valve body
126 Covernor primary valve
127 Governor primary valve spring
128 Washer
129 Retaining ring
130 Governor secondary valve
131 Governor secondary valve spring
132 Retainer
133 Main control assembly
134 Valve body plate
135 Valve body gasket
136 3-2 timing body plate
137 3-2 timing body gasket
138 Oil pan screen and grommet
139 Oil pan gasket
140 Oil pan assembly
141 Manual valve detent spring
142 Washer-head bolts (7)
143 Washer-head bolts (5)
144 Screws (2)
145 Washer-head bolts (7)
146 Washer-head bolts (11)
147 Screws (7)
148 Screw
149 Screws (2)
150 Screw
151 Screw
152 Plug
153 Washer head bolts (4)
154 Adjusting screw
155 Nut
156 Ring
157 Governor body assembly
158 Vent tube
159 Vent tube clamp

7B

Fig. 7B.4 Ford C6 automatic transmission — sectional view (Sec 1)

Fig. 7B.5 Typical Ford FMX automatic transmission — sectional view (Sec 1)

Fig. 7B.6 Typical cable-actuated manual floor shift linkage (Sec 3)

3   Shift linkage — check and adjustment

Floor shift linkage (all models)

1   Have an assistant position the shift selector in the Drive position and hold it in place during adjustment.

2   From under the car, loosen the manual shift lever retaining nut. Move the shift lever to the Drive position on the transmission itself (second detent position from the rear).

3   With both the selector lever and the manual lever in the Drive position tighten the attaching nut.

4   After adjustment check the operation of the selector in all positions.

Column shift linkage

5   Place the selector lever in the Drive position and hang a weight of at least 8 lbs. on it to ensure that the lever remains in position during adjustment.

6   Loosen the adjusting nut on the shift rod.

7   At the transmission make sure that the shift lever is in the Drive position (the second detent position from the full counterclockwise

7B

Fig. 7B.7 Typical rod-actuated manual floor shift linkage (Sec 3)

NOTE: 388122-S (302 ENG)
388714 (351 ENG)

Fig. 7B.8 Ford Automatic Overdrive (AOD) automatic transmission — exploded view (Sec 1)

1 Torque converter
2 Direct drive shaft
3 Front pump seal
4 Front pump O-ring
5 Front pump body
6 Front pump gasket
7 Front pump drive gear
8 Front pump driven gear
9 Front pump stator support
10 Intermediate clutch piston inner seal
11 Intermediate clutch piston outer seal
12 Front pump bushing
13 Intermediate clutch piston
14 Return springs and retainer
15 Intermediate clutch steel plates
16 Intermediate clutch friction plates
17 Intermediate clutch pressure plate
18 Thrust washer
19 Reverse clutch stator support seal rings
20 Forward clutch stator support seal rings
21 Overdrive band
22 Snap ring
23 Retining plate
24 Outer race
25 One-way clutch assembly
26 Reverse clutch drum
27 Reverse clutch piston seal
28 Reverse clutch piston
29 Reverse clutch piston seal
30 Thrust ring
31 Clutch piston return spring
32 Snap ring
33 Reverse clutch pressure plate
34 Reverse clutch friction plate
35 Reverse clutch steel plate
36 Reverse clutch pressure plate
37 Reverse clutch retaining ring
38 Thrust washer
39 Turbine shaft

40 Forward clutch cylinder and turbine shaft
41 Forward clutch piston outer seal
42 Forward clutch piston inner seal
43 Forward clutch piston
44 Forward clutch piston return spring
45 Return spring retainer
46 Snap ring
47 Waved plate
48 Forward clutch steel plate
49 Forward clutch friction plate
50 Forward clutch pressure plate
51 Snap ring
52 Needle bearing
53 Forward clutch hub
54 Needle bearing
55 Reverse sun gear and drive shell
56 Needle bearing
57 Forward sun gear
58 Retaining ring
59 Forward sun gear bushing
60 Center support planetary
61 Planetary cage spring and roller assembly
62 Planetary assembly
63 Reverse band
64 Direct clutch hub
65 Needle bearing
66 Snap ring
67 Thrust spacer
68 Direct clutch pressure plate
69 Direct clutch internal spline plates
70 Direct clutch external spline plates
71 Snap ring
72 Return spring and retainer
73 Direct clutch piston
74 Direct clutch inner piston seal
75 Direct clutch outer piston seal
76 Ring gear and park gear
77 Direct cylinder
78 Output shaft seal rings

79 Needle bearing
80 Output shaft
81 Output shaft seal outer
82 Output shaft hub
83 Snap ring
84 Snap ring
85 Rear case bushing
86 Needle bearing
87 Case assembly
88 Neutral start switch
89 Vent cap
90 Governor counterweight
91 Governor body assembly
92 Governor plug
93 Governor sleeve
94 Governor oil screen assembly
95 Governor valve spring
96 Governor valve
97 Governor body
98 Bolt
99 Clip
100 Bolt
101 Governor valve body cover
102 Snap ring
103 Extension housing bracket
104 Extension housing bushing
105 Extension housing
106 Extension housing seal
107 Bolt (6)
108 Pipe plug
109 Overdrive servo piston return spring
110 Overdrive servo piston
111 Overdrive servo piston seal
112 Overdrive servo cover seal rings
113 Overdrive servo cover
114 Snap ring
115 Reverse servo piston return spring
116 Reverse servo piston
117 Reverse servo cover
118 Snap ring
119 3-4 accumulator valve seal
120 3-4 accumulator valve

121 3-4 accumulator valve return spring
122 3-4 accumulator cover
123 3-4 accumulator cover seal
124 Snap ring
125 2-3 accumulator valve seal
126 2-3 accumulator valve
127 2-3 accumulator valve seal
128 2-3 accumulator valve return spring
129 2-3 accumulator cover
130 Snap ring
131 Park pawl shaft
132 Guide cup
133 Park pawl return spring
134 Manual lever
135 Grommet
136 Throttle lever oil seal
137 Nut and lockwasher
138 Outer throttle lever
139 Park pawl
140 Park pawl actuating rod
141 Inner manual lever
142 Roll pin
143 Detent spring
144 Nut
145 Inner throttle lever
146 Throttle torsion spring
147 Valve body reinforcement plate
148 Upper separator plate gasket
149 Separator plate
150 Lower separator plate gasket
151 Valve body
152 Oil pan filter and grommet
153 Oil pan gasket
154 Oil pan
155 Bolts (17)
156 Oil filter gasket
157 Bolts (8)
158 Bolts (17)
159 Bolts (3)
160 Governor drive ball
161 Anti-clunk spring
162 Grommet
163 Oil seal assembly

7B

Fig. 7B.9 Column-mounted manual shift linkage (AOD-type shown, others similar) (Sec 3)

Fig. 7B.10 Adjusting the neutral start switch as found on C3, C4, C5, and C6 automatic transmissions (Sec 5)

position). Align the slats on the slotted rod with those on the mounting stud.
8　Tighten the adjusting nut on the shift rod.
9　After adjustment check that the selector operates properly in all positions.

4 Kickdown rod — adjustment

Note: *This adjustment does not apply to FMX and Automatic Overdrive (AOD) transmissions.*
1　Disconnect the throttle and downshift return springs (if equipped).
2　Hold the carburetor throttle lever in the wide open position.
3　Hold the transmission downshift linkage in the full downshift position against the internal stop. Turn the adjustment screw on the carburetor downshift lever to obtain a 0.01 to 0.08 inch clearance between the tip of the screw and the throttle shaft lever tab.
4　Release the transmission and carburetor to their free positions. If the throttle and downshift return springs were removed, replace them at this time.
5　Road test the vehicle and readjust if necessary.

5 Neutral start switch — removal and installation

1　Jack up the car and support it firmly on jackstands.
2　Disconnect the downshift linkage rod from the transmission downshift lever.
3　Apply penetrating oil to the downshift lever shaft and nut and allow it to soak for a few minutes. Remove the transmission downshift lever retaining nut and lift away the lever.
4　Remove the neutral start switch securing bolts.
5　Disconnect the multi-wire connector from the switch. Remove the switch.
6　To install, place the switch on the transmission and install the bolts finger tight. Move the selector lever to Neutral position. Rotate the switch and fit a No. 43 drill bit into the gauge pin hole. The bit must be inserted a full 1/2 inch (12.3 mm). Tighten the switch securing bolts fully and remove the drill.
7　Installation is the reverse of the removal procedure. Check that the engine starts only when the selector is in the Neutral and Park positions. **Note:** *Some transmissions are equipped with a Neutral Start Switch which is not adjustable. In this case any fault will be due to a malfunctioning switch, wear on the internal actuating cam, or faulty wiring. If the switch is suspected of a fault it should be replaced with a new one. Always use a new O-ring seal and tighten to the specified torque.*

6 Transmission mounts — check and replacement

1　Raise the vehicle and support it securely on jackstands.
2　From underneath the vehicle, push up and pull down on the transmission extension housing. Observe the transmission mount for any signs of poor attachment or play due to degradation of the rubber insulator. If the transmission can be pushed upward but not pulled downward, it is a sign that the rubber is worn and the mount has bottomed out.
3　If the rubber insulator has separated from the plate, replace the mount.
4　Check that all the mounting bolts on the transmission and the engine mounts are securely fastened.

7 Extension housing oil seal — replacement

1　Raise the vehicle and support it securely on jackstands.
2　Remove the driveshaft (Chapter 8). Scribe marks on the driveshaft and yoke and the rear axle companion flange to assure proper positioning of the driveshaft during assembly.
3　Remove the oil seal from the end of the extension housing with a seal removing tool or a special Ford tool as shown in the accompanying illustration. If there is access, a thin blade screwdriver or chisel may also be used to remove the seal and the extension housing bushing which is behind the seal (photo).
4　Before installing the new seal inspect the sealing surface of the universal joint yoke for scoring. If scoring is found, replace the yoke.
5　Inspect the counterbore of the housing for burrs. Remove burrs with emery cloth or medium grit wet-and-dry sandpaper.
6　Install the new oil seal (photo) after coating the inside diameter of the seal with silicone sealant (photo) and the end of the rubber boot portion with grease.
7　Install the driveshaft using the scribe mark as a guide to assure correct balance. Lower the vehicle and check the oil level in the transmission. Add oil if necessary.

8 Automatic transmission — removal and installation

Note: *If the transmission is being removed for a major overhaul it is important to completely clean all the components including the converter, cooler, cooler lines and control valve body. Contaminants are a major cause for reccuring transmission troubles and must be removed from the system before the transmission is put back into service.*
1　If possible, raise the vehicle on a hoist or place it over an inspection

EXTENSION HOUSING

EXTENSION SEAL REMOVER
TOOL NO. T71P-7657-A

Fig. 7B.11 Removing the extension housing seal and
bushing with a seal remover designed for the task. In some
cases a screwdriver will suffice to pry out the seal if care is
taken not to damage the seal mating surfaces (Sec 7)

7.3   The extension housing seal may sustain some damage during
removal. Be extremely careful, however, not to damage the sealing
surface on the housing

7.6a   Installing the new extension housing seal. A large socket or
length of pipe of the proper diameter may also be helpful as installation
tools

7.6b   The outside perimeter of the new seal should receive a generous
bead of silicone sealant

8.4   The transmission converter drain plug can be aligned for access
by rotating the engine with the crankshaft pulley bolt (arrow)

8.5   The converter drain plug (arrow) must be at bottom center as
shown before removing it to drain fluid from the converter

7B

pit. Alternatively, raise the vehicle to obtain the maximum possible
amount of working room underneath. Support it securely on jackstands.
2   Place a large drain pan beneath the transmission oil pan. Working
from the rear, loosen the oil pan bolts and allow the fluid to drain.
Remove all the bolts except the two front ones to drain as much fluid
as possible, then temporarily install two bolts at the rear to hold the
pan in place.
3   Remove the torque converter drain plug access cover and adapter

plate bolts from the lower end of the converter housing.
4   Remove the flexplate to converter attaching nuts, turning the
engine as necessary to gain access by means of a socket on the
crankshaft pulley attaching bolt (photo). **Caution:** *Do not rotate the
engine backward.*
5   Rotate the engine until the converter drain plug is accessible, then
remove the plug, catching the fluid in the drain pan. Install and tighten
the drain plug afterward (photo).

8.18   The oil cooler lines should be removed with the aid of a flare-nut wrench. Do not use pliers.

8.19   Location of the transmission filler tube (C5 transmission shown)

6   Remove the driveshaft by referring to Chapter 8. Place a polyethylene bag over the end of the transmission to prevent dirt from entering.
7   Detach the speedometer cable from the extension housing by removing the hold-down bolt and withdrawing the cable and gear.
8   Disconnect the shift rod at the transmission manual lever and the kickdown rod at the transmission downshift lever. Remove the two bolts securing the bellcrank bracket to the converter housing.
9   Remove the three bolts retaining the starter to the engine and position the starter out of the way.
10 Disconnect the Neutral safety switch leads or wire connector.
11 Disconnect the vacuum lines from the vacuum modulator (C4 and C6 only).
12 Position a transmission jack beneath the transmission and raise it so that it just begins to lift the transmission weight.
13 Remove the nuts and bolts securing the rear mount and insulators to the crossmember.
14 If right and left gussets are installed between the crossmember and frame rails, remove the gusset attaching nuts and bolts and remove the gussets.
15 Remove the nuts and bolts securing the crossmember to the frame rails, raise the transmission slightly and remove the crossmember.
16 Disconnect the inlet pipe flange(s) from the exhaust manifold(s).
17 Support the rear of the engine using a jack and a block of wood.
18 Disconnect the oil cooler lines at the transmission and plug them

to prevent dirt from entering. Use a flare nut wrench to avoid rounding off the nuts (photo).
19 Remove the lower converter housing to engine bolts and the transmission filler tube (photo).
20 Make sure that the transmission is securely mounted on the jack, then remove the two upper converter housing to engine bolts.
21 Carefully move the transmission to the rear and down and away from the vehicle.
22 Installing the transmission is essentially the reverse of the removal procedure, but the following points should be noted:
   a) Rotate the converter to align the bolt drive lugs and drain plug with their holes in the flexplate.
   b) Do not allow the transmission to take a nose down attitude as the converter will move forward and disengage from the pump gear.
   c) When installing the flexplate to converter bolts, position the flexplate so the pilot hole is in the six o'clock position. First, install one bolt through the pilot hole and tighten it, followed by the remaining bolts. Do not attempt to install it in any other way.
   d) Adjust the kickdown rod and selector linkage as necessary.
   e) When the vehicle has been lowered to the ground, add sufficient fluid to bring the level up to the Max mark on the dipstick with the engine not running. Having done this, check and top off the fluid level as described in Chapter 1.

Chapter 8   Clutch and driveshaft

Contents

Specifications

Clutch
Type	Single dry plate, diaphragm spring
Actuation.....................................	Cable-actuated
Driveshaft type	One-piece with single or double cardan universal joints

Rear axle
Type	Integral-carrier, removable carrier or Traction-Lok limited slip
Ring gear size	6.75 in, 7.5 in or 8.5 in. See identification tag
Rear axle oil capacity	
6.75 in	2.5 US pints
7.5 in	3.5 US pints
8.5 in	4.0 US pints
Oil type	
Limited-slip differential	Ford ESW-M2 119-A or equivalent
Conventional differential	Ford ESW-M2C-154-A or equivalent

Torque specifications	Ft-lbs
Clutch pedal relay lever retaining nut	32 to 50
Flywheel housing-to-engine	
2.3L	28 to 38
3.3L, 4.2L and 5.0L	38 to 55
Pressure plate-to-flywheel	
2.3L	12 to 24
All others...................................	12 to 20
Universal joint-to-flange	70 to 95
Differential cover bolts	25 to 35
Oil filler plug	15 to 25
Driveshat-to-axle companion flange U-bolt	70 to 95
Rear axle shaft bearing retainer bolt nuts	20 to 40
Differential pinion shaft lock bolt	70 to 85
Brake backing plate bolts and nuts	20 to 40

8

---

1   Clutch — general information

The diaphragm single dry disc clutch, consisting of the clutch disc, pressure plate and clutch release bearing, is actuated by a pedal-operated linkage.

When the clutch pedal is in the up (released) position, the clutch disc is clamped between flywheel and the face of the pressure plate, thus transmitting the drive of the engine through the disc, which is splined to the transmission. Friction lining material is riveted to the clutch disc and the splined hub is spring cushioned to absorb transmission shocks.

When the clutch pedal is depressed, the clutch release lever moves the release bearing against the pressure plate diaphragm, which moves the pressure plate away from the clutch disc, disengaging the clutch

REAR FACE OF BLOCK & FLYWHEEL

3 REQUIRED

2 REQUIRED

INSTALLATION WITH SEAL OUTBOARD (TOWARD TRANSMISSION)

LUBRICATE LEVER CROWN & SPRING RETENTION CROWN SPRING MUST BE POSITIONED WITHIN BEARING GROOVE. SECTION A

SECTION A

CABLE ASSEMBLY

2.3 L ENGINE VIEW X

NOTE: DISC TO BE INSTALLED WITH SPRING RETAINER TOWARD REAR OF VEHICLE

LUBRICATE BALL & POCKET

LUBRICATE LEVER CROWN

UPPER TWO BOLTS DIRECTION

VIEW X

INSTALLED AFTER CABLE ASSEMBLY

LUBRICATE WITHIN $\frac{6.3}{25}$ OF REAR SHOULDER

Fig. 8.1 Typical clutch assembly used on vehicles in this manual. Note lubrication points and position of dowel pins and pilot bearing (Sec 1)

and disconnecting the drive to the transmission. Clutch pedal free play is adjusted automatically. The self adjusting mechanism consists of a spring loaded quadrant, spring-loaded pawl and spring-loaded clutch release cable, which preloads the clutch release lever bearing. As the clutch wears, the spring-loaded pawl at the top of the clutch pedal engages the gear quadrant as the pedal is depressed and pulls on the cable to adjust it.

2   Clutch pedal — removal and installation

1   Disconnect the negative cable from the battery.
2   Remove the clip holding the clutch cable to the pedal relay lever. Disconnect the clutch interlock switch on 1984 models.
3   Note the position of the preload spring, then remove it.

4   Remove the relay nut and lever.
5   Slide the pedal assembly from the pedal support bracket, then remove the entire assembly.
6   Inspect the pedal assembly, paying particular attention to the pedal pivot bushings. If they are cracked or galled, replace them.
7   Prior to installation, lightly coat the clutch pedal pivot with oil.
8   Slide the clutch pedal shaft through the pedal support bracket.
9   Install the clutch pedal relay lever over the corresponding 4-sided flats on the clutch pedal flats.
10 Install the preload spring.
11 Hold the pedal against the stop and install the clutch cable to the relay lever.
12 Attach the retaining clip.
13 Pump and release the pedal several times to insure adequate tension of the clutch cable.
14 Reconnect the negative battery cable.

Fig. 8.2 The clutch pedal on 1984 models must be disconnected from the clutch interlock switch before either can be removed (Sec 2)

Fig. 8.3 Self-adjusting clutch pedal assembly and linkage. 1981 version shown, other pre-1984 models are similar (Sec 2)

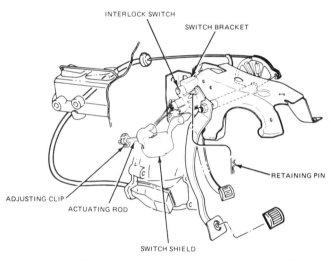

Fig. 8.4 Self-adjusting clutch pedal and linkage assembly, 1984 version (Sec 2)

Fig. 8.5 Clutch cable dash panel insulator (Sec 3)

Fig. 8.6 Self-adjusting clutch cable-to-clutch release lever installation (Sec 3)

3 Self-adjusting clutch cable — removal and installation

1   Pull the clutch cable as far back toward the driver's seat as it will go. Push the adjustment quadrant forward and unhook the cable from it. The quadrant will now rotate rearward.
2   From the engine compartment, remove the screw holding the cable assembly insulator to the dash panel as shown in the accompanying illustration. Pull the cable through the dash panel into the engine compartment.
3   From underneath the vehicle, remove the dust cover from the bellhousing and remove the rubber plug in the clutch release lever.
4   Slide the ball on the end of the cable assembly through the clutch release lever hole and remove the cable.
5   Remove the dash panel insulator and transfer it to the new clutch cable.
6   Insert the cable through the bellhousing hole into the clutch release lever hole. Slide the ball on the end of the cable assembly away from the hole in the clutch release lever and install the rubber plug as shown.
7   Attach the cable assembly to the bellhousing with the clip retainer and install the dust shield on the housing.
8   Push the cable assembly up into the engine compartment and then through the dash panel. Install the screw in the insulator.
9   Lift the clutch pedal to disengage the pawl and quadrant. Push the quadrant forward and hook the end of the cable over the rear of the quadrant.
10 Depress the clutch several times, which will adjust the cable.

4 Self-adjusting clutch mechanism — removal and installation

1   Disconnect the negative cable at the battery.
2   Referring to Chapter 10 remove the steering wheel.
3   Remove the steering column shrouds, if so equipped, and the left lower dash panel.
4   Disconnect the brake light switch and master cylinder pushrod at the brake pedal.
5   Push the clutch quadrant forward and disconnect the clutch cable. The quadrant should now rotate rearward.
6   Remove the brake pedal support bracket lateral brace bolt and disconnect all of the steering column electrical connectors.
7   Remove the nuts holding the steering column to the brake support

8

Fig. 8.7 Typical self-adjusting clutch quadrant and pawl assembly (Sec 5)

Fig. 8.8 Be sure to align the clutch disc, pressure plate and flywheel with a tool such as the clutch arbor used here (Sec 6)

bracket and lower the column to the floor.

8   Remove the booster nuts holding the brake pedal support bracket to the dash panel.

9   Remove the brake pedal support bracket bolts from the underside of the instrument panel and remove the bracket assembly from the car.

10   Remove the clutch pedal shaft nut and pedal and slide the self-adjusting mechanism out of the pedal support bracket.

11   Remove the bushings from the self-adjusting mechanism shaft and check them for wear, replacing them with new ones if necessary.

12   Installation is the reverse of removal. The self-adjusting mechanism shaft should be lubricated with lithium-base grease prior to installation. After installation the clutch pedal should be depressed several times to adjust the cable.

5   Self-adjusting clutch quadrant and pawl — removal and installation

1   Remove the self-adjusting mechanism.

2   Remove the hairpin clips holding the quadrant on the shaft assembly.

3   Remove the quadrant and spring and the pawl and spring.

4   Lubricate the pawl and quadrant pivot shafts with lithium grease.

5   Install the pawl, positioning the teeth towards the larger shaft with the spring hole at the end of the arm. The spring hole is not to be positioned beneath the arm.

6   Install the straight portion of the spring into the hole with the coil upwards.

7   Rotate the spring 180 degrees to the left, taking care that the straight portion stays in the hole. Slide the coiled portion over the boss.

8   Hook the bent portion of the spring under the arm and install the retaining clip on the opposite side of the spring.

9   Install the quadrant spring on the shaft with the bent portion inserted into the hole in the arm.

10   Slide the lubricated quadrant onto the shaft and align the projection at the bottom of the quadrant to a position beneath the arm of the shaft assembly. Push the pawl upwards so the bottom tooth of the pawl meshes with the bottom quadrant (as shown) and install the retaining pin.

11   With a pair of pliers, grasp the straight end of the quadrant spring and position it behind the ear of the quadrant.

12   Install the self-adjusting mechanism and the clutch pedal assembly.

6   Clutch — removal and installation

1   Remove the transmission as described in Chapter 7.

2   Disconnect the clutch release lever retaining spring from the release lever.

3   Disconnect the starter cable, then remove the starter.

4   Remove the bolts securing the engine rear plate to the front lower

part of the flywheel housing. Remove the flywheel housing lower cover (if so equipped).

5   Remove the flywheel housing securing bolts and move the housing back just far enough to clear the pressure plate, then move it to the right to free the pivot from the clutch equalizer bar. Take care not to disturb the linkage and assist spring.

6   Unscrew the pressure plate cover securing bolts one turn at a time, to prevent distortion of the cover assembly.

7   If the same pressure plate and cover assembly is to be reinstalled, mark the cover and flywheel so that the assembly can be installed in its original position.

8   Remove the clutch cover assembly and the clutch disc from the flywheel.

9   It is important that no oil or grease contaminates the clutch disc friction lining or the pressure plate and flywheel faces. It is advisable to handle the parts with clean hands and to wipe down the pressure plate and flywheel faces with a clean dry rag, acetone or alcohol before installing the clutch cover assembly.

10   Place the clutch disc and pressure plate assembly in position on the flywheel. If the same assembly is being reinstalled, align the matching marks made at removal and install the securing bolts. Tighten the bolts alternately a few turns at a time until the clutch disc is gripped lightly but can still be moved.

11   The clutch disc must now be centered so that when the transmission is installed, the input shaft splines will pass through the splines in the clutch disc hub and the nose of the imput shaft will engage the crankshaft pilot bearing.

12   Centering can be carried out by inserting an alignment tool into the clutch assembly as shown in the accompanying illustration and moving the clutch disc as necessary to obtain correct centering. Alternatively, if an old input shaft is available, this can be used as an arbor to center the disc.

13   After the clutch disc has been located correctly, tighten the securing bolts in an even and diagonal sequence to ensure the cover assembly is secured without distortion. Tighten the bolts to the specified torque.

14   Using a lithium-base grease, lightly lubricate the outside diameter of the transmission front bearing retainer, both sides of the release lever fork where it contacts the release bearing spring clips, and the release bearing surface that contacts the pressure plate release fingers. Fill the grease groove in the release bearing hub, then clean all excess grease from inside the bore.

15   Install the release bearing and hub on the release lever.

16   Install the felt washer on the pivot in the flywheel housing and

Fig. 8.9 Typical pilot bearing used on 2.3L engines. The seal must face away from the engine (Sec 8)

slip the pivot into the clutch equalizer shaft, taking care not to disturb the linkage. Locate the housing on the dowels in the cylinder block. Install the securing bolts and tighten them to the specified torque.

17 Install the starter motor and connect the cable.

18 Install the transmission as described in Chapter 7A.

19 Actuate the clutch pedal several times to adjust the cable tension.

7 Clutch — inspection and overhaul

1 Inspect the machined surfaces of the flywheel and pressure plate for scoring, ridges and burned marks. Minor defects can be removed by machining, but if any components are badly scored or burned they should be replaced with new ones.

2 Check the wear on the clutch fingers. If there is considerable difference in wear between the fingers, the excessively worn finger is binding, which means that the pressure plate assembly must be replaced with a new one. Check the pressure plate for warpage, using a steel rule.

3 Examine the clutch disc for worn or loose lining, distortion, loose nuts at the hub and broken springs. If any of these defects are found, replace the disc with a new or rebuilt unit.

4 Wipe all oil and dirt off the release bearing but do not clean it in solvent, as it is prelubricated. Inspect the bearing retainer for loose spring clips and rivets. Hold the bearing inner race and rotate the outer race. If it is noisy or rough, replace the bearing with a new one. Because of the nominal cost involved it is a good practice to install a new release bearing every time the clutch is replaced.

8 Clutch pilot bearing — removal and installation

1 A needle roller bearing is used as a clutch pilot bearing on all vehicles. On 2.3L models this is installed with the seal end toward the transmission as shown in the accompanying illustration. The bearings on all other models can be installed only in the proper position.

2 Remove the transmission (Chapter 7A), clutch, pressure plate and disc.

3 Pull the bearing from the crankshaft using a slide hammer or Ford tool T50T-100A or T59L-100B with puller attachment T58L-101-A.

4 To install the new bearing, coat the opening on the crankshaft with lithium grease. Apply only a small amount of grease, as the excess can find its way to the clutch, causing slippage.

5 With the bearing in position, tap it into the crankshaft. A socket and extension can be used to carefully tap the bearing squarely into place. Care must be taken when installing the bearing because it is easily damaged, which can lead to early failure.

6 Reinstall the clutch, pressure plate and transmission.

9 Driveshaft — general description

The driveshaft is a one-piece, tubular unit with a cardan-type universal joint installed at each end. The forward end of the front universal joint is splined and fits into the output shaft of the transmission. The rear universal joint connects to the differential through matching flanges

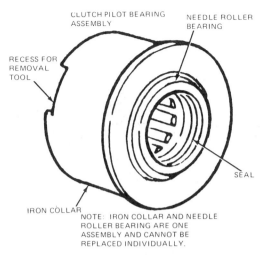

NOTE: IRON COLLAR AND NEEDLE ROLLER BEARING ARE ONE ASSEMBLY AND CANNOT BE REPLACED INDIVIDUALLY.

Fig. 8.10 Typical pilot bearing and adapter assembly used on non-2.3L engines (Sec 8)

Fig. 8.11 Typical driveshaft-to-axle U-joint connection. Note the use of scribe marks on the flanges to insure proper installation (Sec 10)

which are bolted together. The universal joints are replaceable components.

10 Driveshaft — removal and installation

1 Park the vehicle on a level surface.

2 Place the transmission in Park (automatic) or 1st gear (manual) and set the parking brake.

3 Raise the vehicle and support it firmly on jackstands.

4 Mark the flanges on the rear universal joint and the axle pinion as shown in the accompanying illustration prior to removal so that the balance of the unit will not be disturbed on reinstallation.

5 On the rear universal joint, remove the four bolts securing the driveshaft to the axle pinion. Support the driveshaft so that it doesn't fall.

6 Remove the driveshaft by lowering the rear carefully and pulling it rearward, sliding the front yoke from the transmission.

7 Plug the rear of the transmission and place a tray underneath to catch any fluid leakage.

8 Prior to reinstallation, check that the front yoke is free of dirt or grit and that the splines are not cracked, rounded or burred.

9 Inspect the transmission tail extension for cracks and make sure that the seal is in good condition.

10 Lubricate the driveshaft slip yoke splines with lithium grease, remove the plug from the transmission and insert the slip yoke into the transmission.

11 Making sure that the marks are aligned, install the bolts through the flanges of the rear universal joint and pinion and tighten them to specification.

12 Lower the vehicle and check the transmission fluid level before driving.

8

Fig. 8.13 Removable carrier conventional differential — sectional view (Sec 11)

- DRIVE PINION
- TAPERED ROLLER BEARINGS
- SEAL
- LEFT AXLE SHAFT
- PINION BEARING RETAINER
- BEARING SPACER
- PINION PILOT BEARING
- DIFFERENTIAL CASE
- DIFFERENTIAL PINION
- RING GEAR

Fig. 8.12 Typical removable-carrier axle assembly (Sec 11)

- DEFLECTOR
- FLANGE
- SEAL
- PINION FRONT BEARING
- PINION BEARING SPACER
- PINION RETAINER
- PINION REAR BEARING
- PINION REAR BEARING CUP
- PILOT BEARING RETAINER
- PILOT BEARING
- O-RING
- DRIVE PINION
- CARRIER HOUSING
- SHIM - 4663
- BEARING CAP
- ADJUSTING NUT
- THRUST WASHER
- DIFFERENTIAL PINION GEAR
- DIFFERENTIAL CASE COVER
- DRIVE GEAR ATTACHING BOLT
- FLAT WASHER (LIMITED SLIP ONLY)
- THRUST WASHER
- DIFFERENTIAL SIDE GEAR
- DIFFERENTIAL PINION SHAFT
- DIFFERENTIAL CASE
- RING GEAR
- DIFFERENTIAL BEARING
- DIFFERENTIAL BEARING CUP
- BEARING RETAINER
- AXLE SHAFT
- BEARING
- RETAINER RING
- GASKET
- SEAL
- AXLE HOUSING

Fig. 8.14 Typical integral-carrier axle and differential assembly. Note axle and bearing installation and C-clip axle retaining washers (Sec 11)

8

Fig. 8.15 Typical Integral-carrier differential assembly — sectional view (Sec 11)

Fig. 8.16 Traction-Lok differential with plate-type clutch — exploded view (Sec 11)

11 Rear axle — general information

On models covered in this manual, two basic types of rear axles are used: the removable carrier type and the integral carrier type. Integral carrier axles use C-locks on the inside end of the axleshafts to retain them. Removable carrier axles have no C-locks. All Traction-Lok (limited slip) axles are the removable carrier type. The axle type and ratio are stamped on a plate attached to a rear housing cover bolt. Always refer to this plate code and ratio when ordering parts.

Traction-Lok differentials may be of two types, the essential distinction being the clutch. Ford manufactured models use a multiple plate clutch, while the other, outside manufactured differential utilizes a brake cone type clutch design.

Fig. 8.17 Traction-Lok differential with plate-type clutch — sectional view (Sec 11)

Fig. 8.18 Traction-Lok differential with brake-cone-type clutch design — exploded view (Sec 11)

8

12 Rear axle oil — draining and refilling

1   Place the vehicle on a flat surface.
2   Place a suitable container under the differential, remove the drain plug and allow the oil to drain. Allow 15 minutes for complete drainage.
3   Refill the axle through the plug located on the upper side of the housing.
4   Tighten the fill plug and check for leaks.

13 Differential cover — removal and installation

1   The differential cover can be removed to inspect the differential for the cause of noise or vibration, missing or cracked gear teeth and metal flakes in the oil.
2   Drain the oil as described in Section 12.
3   Remove the bolts securing the differential cover to the axle housing.
4   After inspection, clean the cover and housing mating surfaces.
5   Apply a thin line of silicone sealant to the axle housing as shown.
6   Tighten the cover bolts in a criss-cross pattern to specifications.
7   Refill the axle with oil and take a test drive.
8   Check for leaks.

14 Differential pinion oil seal — removal and installation

1   Raise the vehicle and support it securely on jackstands.
2   Remove the rear wheels and brake drums.

Fig. 8.19 Apply silicone sealant to the face of the axle housing as shown before installing the cover (Sec 13)

Fig. 8.20 Mark the relative positions of the pinion shaft and flange before removal (Sec 14)

Fig. 8.21 Loosen the pinon nut while holding the flange from turning (Sec 14)

Fig. 8.22 If a seal removing tool such as this is not available, the differential pinion seal may be removed carefully by tapping it out with a hammer and chisel (Sec 14)

Fig. 8.23 Tapping a new pinion seal into place (Sec 14)

3   Mark the driveshaft and axle pinion flange for ease of realignment during reassembly. Remove the driveshaft.
4   Mark the relationship between the pinion and flange as shown.
5   Hold the flange to keep it from turning and remove the pinion nut. Remove the differential flange as shown.
6   Pry out the old seal with a slide hammer and reversed jaws or other appropriate tool as shown. It may also be removed with a hammer and cold chisel or screwdriver (photo).
7   Clean the oil seal mounting surface.
8   Tap the new seal into place, taking care to insert it squarely as shown in the accompanying illustration.
9   Inspect the splines on the pinion shaft for burrs and nicks. Remove any rough areas with a crocus cloth. Wipe the splines clean.
10 Install the differential flange, aligning it with the marks made during removal.
11 Tighten the pinion nut while allowing the assembly some movement to seat properly.
12 Reinstall the driveshaft, brake drums and wheels.
13 Check the differential oil level and fill as necessary.
14 Lower the car and take a test drive to check for leaks.

15   Axleshafts — removal and installation

Removable carrier axle
Note: *Bearings must be installed and removed from the axleshaft with an arbor press. If you do not have access to one, we do not advise any attempt to repair or work on the axleshaft and bearing assembly.*

14.7   The differential pinion oil seal may be driven out with a hammer and chisel, making certain not to damage the mating surface on the housing

1   Remove the wheel, tire and brake drum. On cars equipped with rear disc brakes, remove the caliper and disc (Chapter 9).
2   Remove the nuts holding the retainer plate to the backing plate as shown in the accompanying illustration.
3   Disconnect the brake line.
4   Remove the retainer and install the nuts finger tight to prevent the brake backing plate from dislodging.
5   Using a slide hammer, extract the axleshaft and bearing assembly.
6   To remove the bearing, nick the bearing retainer in four places using a chisel. It is not necessary to cut the retainer but only to distort it sufficiently to allow the bearing retainer to be slid off the shaft.
7   Remove the bearing with the press and install a new one by pressing it into position. Similarly press on the new retainer. Do not attempt to press the bearing and the retainer on at the same time.
8   Assemble the axleshaft and bearing in the housing, making certain that the bearing is properly seated. Install the retainer, brake drum, wheel and tire. Bleed the brakes (Chapter 9). On disc brake equipped cars, install the disc and caliper.

Integral carrier axles
9   Raise and support the rear of the car. Remove the wheels and tires from the brake drums. On disc brake equipped models, remove the caliper and disc (Chapter 9).
10 Drain the lubricant from the rear axle as described in Section 12.
11 Remove the clips securing the brake drums to the axleshaft lug nut studs and remove the drums.
12 Remove the differential housing cover and gasket.
13 Position jackstands under the frame and lower the axle housing. This will give access to the inside of the differential. Through the open-

Fig. 8.24 The wheel bearing retaining nuts are accessible through the holes in the axle flange (Sec 15)

Fig. 8.25 Integral-carrier differential pinion shaft and lock-bolt (Sec 15)

Fig. 8.26 Removing or installing the axleshaft C-locks on the removable carrier conventional differential (Sec 15)

Fig. 8.27 Axle seal removal (Sec 15)

Fig. 8.29 Be careful not to damage the seal when installing
the axle (Sec 15)

Fig. 8.28 Installing a new axle seal using a special tool or
an appropriately-sized socket (Sec 15)

16   Universal joints — check

1   Wear in the universal joints is characterized by vibration in the driveline, clunking noises when starting from a standstill and metallic squeaking and grating sounds. Another symptom of universal joint or driveline bearing problems is a harmonic rumbling at highway cruising speeds.
2   To make a simple check of universal joint condition, park the vehicle on a level surface with the transmission in gear (manual transmission) or Park. Block the wheels and engage the parking brake.
3   From underneath the car, hold the axle pinion flange with one hand while moving the driveshaft with the other. If there is noticeable looseness in the universal joint, the joint is worn and should be replaced with a new one.
4   Repeat this check at the front of the driveshaft, paying particular attention to the universal joint condition and wear or looseness in the sliding spline section of the yoke.

17   Universal joints — overhaul

1   Remove the driveshaft.
2   Position the driveshaft assembly in a sturdy vise and remove the snap-rings retaining the bearings in the slip yoke and in the driveshaft (photo).
3   Using a large punch or press, drive one of the bearings toward the center of the joint. This will force the opposite bearing out (photo). Grasp each bearing with a pair of pliers and pull it from the driveshaft yoke as it is being pressed out of the universal joint assembly (photo). Drive or press the spider in the opposite direction so that the opposite bearing is accessible to be removed with a pair of pliers. Use this procedure to remove all the bearings from the universal joints.
4   When the bearings have been removed, lift the spider from the yoke and thoroughly clean all dirt and debris from the yokes on both ends of the driveshaft.
5   We recommend the use of a press when installing new bearings in the universal joint yokes. However, if a press is not available the bearings can be driven into position, with extreme care taken to prevent damage or misalignment.
6   Start a new bearing into the yoke at the rear of the driveshaft, position a new spider in the rear of the yoke and press or drive in the new bearing about 1/4-inch below the outer surface of the yoke. Install a new snap-ring.
7   Repeat the procedure on the opposite side of the yoke. Press or drive the bearing until the opposite bearing, which has just been installed, contacts the inner surface of the snap-ring.
8   Install a new snap-ring on the second bearing.
9   Reposition the driveshaft so that the opposite end is accessible

ing in the rear of the differential, remove the side gear pinion shaft lock bolt and the side gear pinion shaft as shown in the accompanying illustration. Push the axleshafts inward and remove the C-locks from the inner end of the axleshafts as shown. Remove the axleshafts with a slide hammer, making certain the seal is not damaged by the splines on the axleshafts.
14   Remove the bearing and oil seal from the housing as shown.
15   Inspect the axleshaft housing and axleshafts for burrs, deformities or other irregularities. Replace any worn or damaged parts. Slight pitting and wear on the axleshaft is considered normal.
16   Coat the wheel bearing rollers with axle lubricant and install the bearings in the housing until they seat firmly against the shoulder. Wipe all lubricant from the oil seal bore before installing a new seal.
17   Note that the oil seals are marked *Right* and *Left*. Do not interchange the seals from side to side.
18   Slide the axleshafts into place as shown, being careful not to damage the seal with the splines. Engage the splines with the differential side gears. Install the C-locks on the inner end of the axleshafts and seat the C-locks in the counterbore of the differential side gears.
19   Rotate the pinion gears until the differential pinion shaft can be installed. Install the differential pinion shaft lock bolt.
20   Install the brake drum on the axleshaft flange. On cars with rear disc brakes install the disc and caliper.
21   Install the wheel and tire.
22   Clean the gasket surface of the housing and install a new cover gasket and the housing cover. On some models it is only necessary to use a sealant instead of a gasket. Raise the rear axle so it is in the running position and add lubricant to bring the lubricant level to the bottom of the filler plug hole. Tighten the filler plug and check for leaks.
23   Road test the vehicle.

Fig. 8.30 Typical single cardan type driveshaft and U-joints (Sec 17)

17.2 The universal joint snap rings can be removed with small pliers

17.3A The universal joint bearing cups can be pressed out with a vise and different size sockets

NOTE: POSITION ZERK FITTINGS SO THEY POINT AWAY FROM THE CENTER YOKE AS SHOWN.

Fig. 8.31 Typical location of U-joint lubrication nipples (Sec 17)

17.3B The bearing cup can be extracted with locking pliers

for bearing replacement. Install the new bearings, spider and snap-rings in the same manner as described previously.

10 Position the slip yoke on the spider and install new bearings and snap-rings.

11 Check both reassembled joints for freedom of movement. If any part has been misaligned and binds, this can sometimes be remedied

by tapping sharply on the side of the yoke with a brass hammer. This should firmly seat the needle bearings and provide the desired freedom of movement. Exercise care to firmly support the shaft during this operation and under no circumstances apply direct blows to the bearings themselves. Do not install the driveshaft into the vehicle if there is any binding in the universal joints.

8

Fig. 8.32 Driveshaft and U-joints -- double cardan type (Versailles shown, others are similar) (Sec 17)

Fig. 8.33 Typical driveshaft and U-joint assembly used on some later models (Sec 17)

Chapter 9 Brakes

Refer to Chapter 13 for specifications related to 1985 and later models

Contents

Specifications

General

Brake fluid type	DOT type 3
Master cylinder bore diameter	
Disc/drum	1.0 in
4-wheel disc	1.125 in

Drum brakes

Drum diameter	
1975 sedans	10.0 in
1975 - 81 station wagons	11.03 in
1976 - 81 sedans	11.03 in
1982 sedans	9.0 in
1982 station wagons	10.0 in
1983 - 84 sedans	10.0 in
1983 - 84 station wagons	11.03 in
Drum wear limit	Specified on drum
Out-of-round limit	0.007 in
Brake lining wear limit	1/32 in above rivet heads

Wheel cylinders

Bore diameter	
Sedans	0.8125 in
Station wagons	0.9375 in
Maximum allowable hone	0.003 in

Disc brakes

Pad lining service limit	1/8 in from shoe surface
Lining to disc clearance	0.010 in max
Disc thickness	
Front	
Standard	0.870 in
Service	0.810 in
Rear	
Standard	0.945 in
Service	0.895 in
Maximum runout	
Front	0.003 in
Rear	0.004 in

9

Brake specifications (continued)

Torque specifications	Ft-lbs
Drum brake wheel cylinder-to-backing plate	10 to 20
Drum brake backing plate-to-axle housing	20 to 40
Drum brake wheel cylinder bleeder screw	8 to 15
Disc brake caliper bleeder screw	6 to 15
Brake pedal pivot shaft nut	15 to 25
Brake booster-to-firewall	15 to 25
Master cylinder-to-firewall	13 to 25
Master cylinder-to-booster	13 to 25
Pressure differential valve bracket	7 to 11
Front brake anchor plate-to-spindle bolt	
Upper	90 to 120
Lower	55 to 75
Rear disc brake anchor plate-to-axle	90 to 120
Rear caliper end retainer	75 to 95
Caliper key retaining screws	12 to 16
Rear disc parking brake retainer screw	16 to 22
Brake hose-to-caliper	10 to 15
Parking brake control mounting screws	12 to 24

1 General information

All vehicles covered in this manual are equipped with hydraulically operated front and rear brake systems. All front brakes are disk-type while the rear brake systems may be either drum brakes or disk-type brakes. A quick visual inspection will tell you what type of brakes you have at the rear of your vehicle. The hydraulic system consists of a dual master cylinder and two-way brake control valve assembly. The master cylinder has two hydraulic supply reservoirs. The reservoir that is nearest to the dash panel furnishes brake fluid to the front wheel brakes while the other cylinder, closest to the radiator, is used to supply fluid to the rear brakes. If unequal hydraulic pressure occurs between the front and rear brakes, the pressure differential valve will sense the condition, activate the brake warning lamp switch and turn on the warning lamp at the instrument panel. The pressure to the rear brakes is controlled by the proportioning valve which is one of the two functions of the two-way brake control valve assembly on later models.

After completing any operation involving the disassembly of any part of the brake system, always test drive the vehicle to check for proper braking performance before resuming normal driving. When testing the brakes, perform the tests on a clean, dry, flat surface. Conditions other than these can lead to inaccurate test results. Test the brakes at various speeds with both light and heavy pedal pressure. The vehicle should stop evenly without pulling to either side. Avoid locking the brakes because this slides the tires and diminishes braking efficiency and control.

Tires, vehicle load and front end alignment are factors which also affect braking performance.

Torque values given in the specifications are for dry, unlubricated fasteners.

2 Hydraulic brake hoses and lines — inspection and replacement

1   About every six months, with the vehicle raised and placed securely on jackstands, the flexible hoses which connect the steel brake lines with front and rear brake assemblies should be inspected for cracks, chafing of the outer cover, leaks, blisters and other damage. These are important and vulnerable parts of the brake system and inspection should be complete.
2   If a section of the brake tubing becomes damaged, the entire section should be replaced with tubing of the same type, size, shape and length. Copper tubing should never be used in a hydraulic system. When bending brake tubing to fit under body or rear axle contours, be careful not to kink or crack the tubing.

Steel hydraulic brake lines
3   When it becomes necessary to replace steel lines use only double wall steel tubing. The outside diameter of the tubing is used for sizing.

4   Auto parts stores and brake supply houses carry various lengths of prefabricated brake line. Depending upon the type of tubing used, these sections can either be bent by hand to the desired shape or can be bent with a tubing bender.
5   If prefabricated lines are not available, obtain the recommended steel tubing and fittings to match the line to be replaced. Determine the correct length by measuring the old brake line, then cutting the new tubing to length, leaving about 1/2 inch extra for flaring the ends. All brake tubing should be double-flared to provide good, leak-proof connections. Clean the brake tubing by flushing with clean brake fluid before installation. Install the fittings onto the cut tubing and flare the ends using an ISO flaring tool.
6   Tube flaring and bending can usually be performed by a local auto parts store if the proper equipment is not available.
7   When installing the brake line, leave at least 3/4 inch clearance between the line and any moving parts.

Flexible brake hose
8   When installing a new front brake hose, position the hose to avoid contact with other chassis parts. Install the hose on the caliper. Engage the other end of the hose in the bracket on the frame. Install the retaining clip and connect the steel brake line tube to the hose.
9   A rear brake hose should be installed so that it does not touch adjacent chassis parts or body. Position the hose junction block on the axle and attach it with a bolt and lockwasher. Connect the hose to the caliper or wheel cylinder, then engage the other end in the bracket. Install the retaining clips. Install the steel lines to the junction block, thread them into the hose fitting and tighten them with a tubing wrench.

3 Hydraulic system — bleeding

1   Removal of all the air from the braking system is essential for the correct operation of the system. Before undertaking this task check the level of fluid in the reservoir and top-up if necessary.
2   Check all brake line unions and connections for possible leakage, and at the same time check the condition of the rubber hoses, which may be cracked or worn.
3   If the condition of a caliper or wheel cylinder is in doubt, check for signs of fluid leakage.
4   If there is any possibility that incorrect fluid has been used in the system, drain all the fluid and flush with methylated spirits. Replace all piston seals and cups, as they will be affected and could possibly fail under pressure.
5   You will need a clean jar, a 12-inch (30 cm) length of rubber tubing which fits tightly over the bleed valve and the correct grade of brake fluid.
6   The primary (front) and secondary (rear) hydraulic brake systems are bled separately. Always bleed the longest line first.
7   To bleed the secondary system (rear), clean the area around the

FRONT INLET

METERING ROD

FRONT OUTLET

METERING VALVE

PUSH IN HERE WHEN BLEEDING FRONT SYSTEM

ROD COVER

FRONT OUTLET

Fig. 9.1 On vehicles equipped with a metering valve as part of the pressure differential/control valve body, it is necessary to press in on the metering rod cover while bleeding the front hydraulic system (Sec 3)

bleed valves and start at the right rear wheel cylinder. Remove the rubber cap over the end of the bleed valve and fit the end of the rubber tube over the bleed nipple.

8   Place the end of the rubber tube in the jar, which should contain sufficient brake fluid to keep the end of the tube submerged during the operation.

9   Open the bleed valve approximately 3/4 turn and have an assistant depress the brake pedal slowly through its full travel. Hold the brake pedal fully depressed.

10 Close the bleed valve and allow the pedal to return to the released position.

11 Continue this sequence until no more air bubbles issue from the bleed tube. Give the brake pedal two more strokes to ensure that the line is completely free of air, and then tighten the bleed valve. Be sure

that the rubber tube remains submerged until the valve is closed.

12 At regular intervals during the bleeding sequence, make sure that the reservoir is kept topped-up, otherwise air will enter again at this point. Do not re-use fluid bled from the system.

13 Repeat the procedure on the left rear brake line.

14 To bleed the primary system (front), start with the right front side and finish with the left front cylinder. The procedure is identical to that previously described. **Note:** *Some models have a bleed valve incorporated in the master cylinder. Where this is the case, the master cylinder should be bled before the brake lines. The bleeding procedure is identical to that already described. Do not use the secondary piston stop screw, which is located on the bottom of some master cylinders, for bleeding. This could damage the secondary piston on the stop screw. 1984 models may have a metering valve incorporated into the pressure differential valve. If this is so for your vehicle, it will be necessary to push in and hold the bleeder rod, as shown in the accompanying illustration, while bleeding the primary (front) hydraulic system.*

15 Top-up the master cylinder to within 1/4-inch of the top of the reservoir, check that the gasket is correctly located in the cover and then install the cover.

4 Parking brake — adjustment

Note: *If new parking brake cables have been installed, apply approximately 100 pounds of pedal effort several times to the parking brake foot pedal prior to adjustment. Check the operation of the parking brake with the vehicle on a hoist and the parking brake released. If there is any slack in the cables or if the rear brakes drag, adjust accordingly.*

1   Fully release the parking brake.

2   Place the transmission in the Neutral position.

3   Raise the vehicle and support it securely on jackstands.

4   Tighten the adjusting nut on the cable equalizer until the rear wheels just begin to drag on the shoes (drum brakes) or the calipers just start to move (disc brakes) as shown in the accompanying illustration.

5   Loosen the nut on drum brake systems just enough so that the shoes no longer drag. On disc brake systems, loosen the nut so that the levers on the calipers just return to the stop position. The stop position is determined by inserting a 1/4-inch pin into the socket of the caliper housings. If the lever can be moved rearward, it is too tight and must be readjusted.

6   Lower the vehicle and check the parking brake operation.

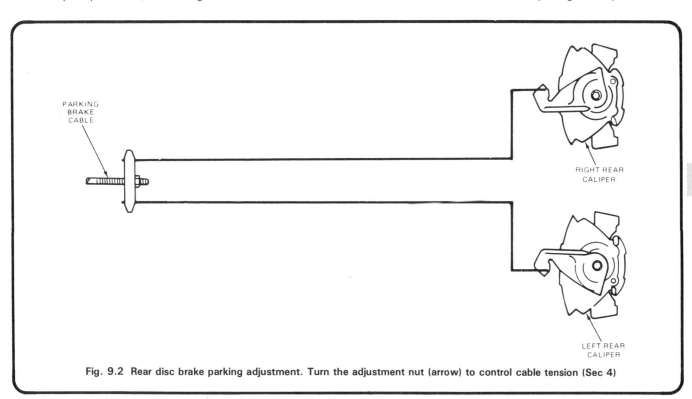

PARKING BRAKE CABLE

RIGHT REAR CALIPER

LEFT REAR CALIPER

9

Fig. 9.2 Rear disc brake parking adjustment. Turn the adjustment nut (arrow) to control cable tension (Sec 4)

FRAME REF.

VIEW Y

NOTE:
L.H. CABLE
TO GO OVER
R.H. CABLE

LOWER SUSPENSION
ARM REF.

VIEW X
R.H. SHOWN – L.H. TYPICAL
(MUST BE MOUNTED ON
INBOARD SURFACE)

VIEW R

VIEW W

VIEW U

VIEW X

VIEW Y

VIEW Z

VIEW T.B.D.

MAXIMUM EFFECTIVE FORCE USED
TO INSERT END FITTING IN BACKING
PLATE 100 LBS. TO AVOID PERMANENT
DAMAGE TO CONDUIT.

PRONGS MUST BE
SECURELY
LOCKED IN PLACE

VIEW U
CABLE WITHIN BRAKE DRUM
L.H. SHOWN – R.H. TYPICAL

COWL REF.

VIEW T

VIEW V

THIS SEAL MUST
PASS THRU HOLE
IN DASH.

SOUND
DEADENER
REF.

VIEW Z
MANUAL RELEASE

VIEW V

BACK UP LIGHT
SWITCH REF.

STEERING
COLUMN
REF.

VIEW Z
AUTOMATIC RELEASE

SOUND DEADENER
REF.

VIEW T.B.D.

UPPER ARM

VIEW R

NO. 4 CROSSMEMBER

CABLE LOCATER
SLEEVE

VIEW W

Fig. 9.3 Typical parking brake system for vehicles with rear drum brakes (Sec 4 and 7)

Fig. 9.4 Typical stoplight switch installation (Sec 5)

5 Stoplight switch — removal and installation

1 The stoplight switch is located on a flange or a bracket protruding from the brake pedal support. The switch assembly is installed on the pin of the brake pedal arm so that it straddles the master cylinder push rod. The switch assembly is a slip fit on the pedal arm pin. The switch assembly moves with the pedal arm whenever the brake pedal is depressed. If the brake lights are inoperative, and it has been determined that the bulbs are not burned out, replace the switch as follows:
2 Disconnect the wires from the switch.
3 Remove the hairpin retainer. Slide the stoplight switch pushrod and the nylon washers and bushing away from the pedal and remove the switch.
4 Position the switch, pushrod, bushing and washers on the brake pedal pin and install the hairpin retainer.
5 Assemble the lead connector to the switch and install the wires in the retaining clip.

6 Brake pedal — removal and installation

1 Disconnect the negative cable at the battery.
2 Disconnect the stoplight switch wire from the switch.
3 Remove the clutch cable from the pedal on manual transmission vehicles.
4 Loosen the brake booster nuts approximately 1/4 inch and remove the pushrod retainer and washer.
5 Slide the stoplight switch out along the brake pedal to clear the pin. Lower the stoplight switch to remove.

Fig. 9.5 Typical brake pedal assembly and installation (Sec 6)

Fig. 9.6 Typical rear disc brake lever and cable installation (Sec 7)

Fig. 9.7 Front disc brake caliper — sectional view (Sec 8)

6   Remove the black stoplight switch bushing from the push rod.
7   Loosen the pedal support attaching nuts at the dash panel. Note the location of the pivot location and washers before removing the pedal. Remove the pivot bolt and the pedal.
8   Installation is the reverse of removal. However, during installation, coat the pivot points with motor oil to prolong bearing life and ease of operation.
9   Check for proper operation before driving.

7 Parking brake cables — replacement

Note: *After replacing cables adjust the parking brake.*

Front cable
1   Raise the vehicle, support it securely on jackstands, and loosen the adjuster nut.
2   Disconnect the cable from the equalizer lever assembly and remove the clip retaining the cable to the body.
3   From inside the vehicle, disconnect the cable from the control assembly.
4   Remove the cable from inside the vehicle.
5   To install, insert the cable through the floor pan holes and attach it to the control assembly inside the vehicle.
6   From underneath the vehicle, fasten the cable to the body bracket and attach it to the equalizer lever assembly.

Intermediate cable
7   From under the vehicle, remove the cable adjusting nut.
8   Disconnect the intermediate cable ends at the left rear and at the transverse cable.
9   Remove the cable and equalizer lever assembly, keeping track of the order in which the cotter pin, washer and spring were removed for ease of reassembly.
10   Install the equalizer assembly onto the pin, holding it in place while installing the spring, washer and cotter pin.
11   Connect the cable ends to the left rear and the transverse cable.
12   Install the cable adjusting nut.

Transverse cable
13   Remove the cable adjusting nut.
14   Disconnect the cable ends at the right rear of the transverse cable and the intermediate cable.
15   Remove any retaining clips or brackets and remove the cable.
16   With the cable held in position, install the retaining clips or brackets holding the cable to the body.
17   Reconnect the cable ends.
18   Reinstall the adjusting nut.

8.4   To release the caliper for brake pad access on early models, knock out the caliper retaining key and spring

8 Front disc brake caliper and pad — removal and installation

1   Raise the vehicle and support it securely on jackstands.
2   Remove the front wheels.

Caliper removal — early models
3   Remove the retaining screw from the caliper retaining key.
4   Use a hammer and a punch or rod to carefully tap the caliper retaining key and spring out of the anchor plate (photo).
5   After disconnecting the hydraulic line from the back of the caliper (photo), press the caliper inward and outward against the action of the springs then lift the caliper assembly away from the anchor plate (photo).

Caliper removal — later models
6   Later models have calipers retained by two locating pins. Once these pins are removed, the caliper can be removed for servicing following the same procedures as for earlier types.

Pad replacement
7   Suspend the caliper from the upper suspension arm with a wire, being careful not to twist or stretch the brake hose.
8   Remove the inner brake pad from the anchor plate, noting the position of the anti-rattle clip. Tap lightly on the outer pad to remove it

8.5a Before the caliper can be removed it must be disconnected from the brake line

8.5b Removing the caliper from the disc

CALIPER LOCATING PINS (2)
TIGHTEN TO 40-54 N·m
(30-40 LB·FT)

SPINDLE-ANCHOR PLATE

BLEED SCREW

INLET
PORT

SHIELD

CALIPER ASSEMBLY

CALIPER ASSEMBLY INSTALLED
LH SIDE SHOWN

Fig. 9.8 Later model front disc brake assembly. Note the position of and torque value for the caliper locating pins (Sec 8)

8.8 A hammer is often of assistance when trying to remove a sticky pad

ALL VEHICLES, EXCEPT CONTINENTAL

INNER SHOE
INSTALLED

RH INNER SHOE INSTALLATION

Fig. 9.9 Typical installation of front disc brake pads. Note warning concerning the outer shoe torque buttons (Sec 8)

RH OUTER SHOE INSTALLATION

OUTER
SHOE
INSTALLED
TO CALIPER

WEAR
INDICATOR

OUTER
SHOE

TORQUE
BUTTONS

WARNING: OUTER SHOE TORQUE BUTTONS
MUST BE SOLIDLY SEATED IN CALIPER
HOLES OR TEMPORARY LOSS OF BRAKES
MAY OCCUR.

9

CALIPER ASSEMBLY

PISTON SEAL

PISTON

DUST BOOT

INNER SHOE

OUTER SHOE

INSULATOR

PLASTIC SLEEVE

LOCATING PIN

CLIP

WEAR INDICATOR

Fig. 9.10 Typical late model front disc brake caliper assembly (Sec 9)

(photo). If the pads are to be reused, mark them so they will be re-installed in the original positions.

9   Clean the caliper, anchor plate and disc and inspect them for wear, damage, corrosion and leakage.

10 If the pad lining is worn to within 1/8-inch (3.175 mm) of the backing plate, replace the front pads with new ones.

11 If new pads are to be installed, a C-clamp and a block of wood measuring 1-3/4 by 3/4 by 3/4-inch will be necessary to push the caliper piston into its bore.

12 Remove the C-clamp and install the inner and outer brake pads.

13 Prior to installing the caliper, lightly lubricate the V grooves where the caliper slides into the anchor plate.

14 Remove the supporting wire and position the caliper in the anchor plate.

15 Use a bar or large screwdriver to hold the caliper against the upper edge of the anchor plate.

16 Carefully insert the caliper spring.

17 Remove the screwdriver or bar and lightly tap the caliper key into place.

18 Install the caliper key retaining screw.

19 Press on the brake pedal several times to seat the pads and centralize the caliper.

20 Install the wheels, lower the vehicle and take it for a test drive.

9 Front disc brake caliper — overhaul

1   Remove the caliper as previously described. Disconnect the hydraulic line and plug the hose to prevent contamination.

2   Remove the rubber dust boot.

3   Fit a rag or shop cloth next to the piston bore and strike the caliper sharply on a block of wood to dislodge the piston, with the cloth catching it. Several attempts may be necessary before the piston comes out.

4   Remove the rubber piston seal from the cylinder bore.

5   Thoroughly wash all parts in clean hydraulic fluid. Replace all the rubber seals with new ones during reassembly, lubricating them first with brake fluid.

6   Inspect the piston and bore for signs of wear, score marks or other damage as shown in the accompanying illustration. A new caliper will

be necessary if any of these are evident.

7   To reassemble, place the new caliper seal into its groove in the cylinder bore, making sure that it does not become twisted.

8   Install a new dust boot, ensuring that the flange seats correctly in the outer groove of the caliper bore.

CRACKS, CHIPS, GOUGES MAY NOT ENTER PISTON SEAL GROOVE.

CRACKS, CHIPS, GOUGES MAY BE 1/2-INCH LONG AND MAY GO INWARD ALMOST TO PISTON SEAL GROOVE.

NO CRACKS, CHIPS, GOUGES, OR ANY OTHER SURFACE DAMAGE ON GROUND SEAL SURFACE (PISTON O.D.) ARE ACCEPTABLE.

CRACKS COMPLETELY ACROSS PISTON FACE, NOT ACCEPTABLE; BUT CRACKS PARTIALLY ACROSS ARE.

BOTTOM OF DUST BOOT GROOVE.

Fig. 9.11 Check the disc brake caliper piston for irregularities as shown (Sec 9)

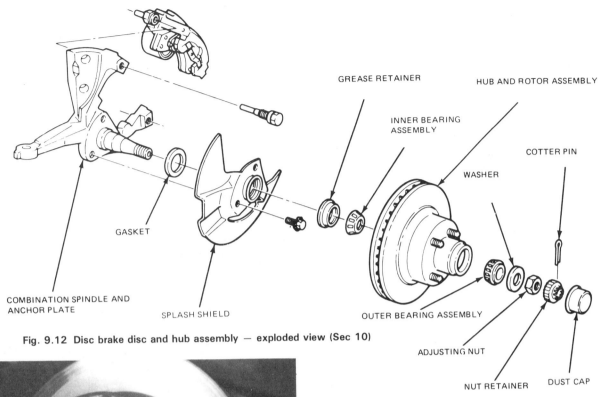

GREASE RETAINER

HUB AND ROTOR ASSEMBLY

INNER BEARING
ASSEMBLY

COTTER PIN

WASHER

GASKET

COMBINATION SPINDLE AND
ANCHOR PLATE

SPLASH SHIELD

OUTER BEARING ASSEMBLY

ADJUSTING NUT

NUT RETAINER   DUST CAP

Fig. 9.12 Disc brake disc and hub assembly — exploded view (Sec 10)

10.2   Removing the grease cap from the hub

9   Carefully insert the piston into the bore. When it is about three-quarters of the way in, spread the dust boot over the piston. Seat the dust boot in the piston groove and push the piston fully into the bore.
10   Reassembly is now complete and the unit is ready for installation.
11   After installation, bleed the hydraulic system.

10   Front brake disc and hub — removal and installation

1   Remove the caliper and anchor plate assembly. To save extra work and time, if the caliper and anchor plate do not require attention, it is not necessary to disconnect the brake hose from the caliper. Suspend the assembly with string or wire from the upper suspension arm.
2   Remove the grease cap from the wheel spindle (photo).
3   Withdraw the cotter pin (photo) and nut locking cap (photo) from

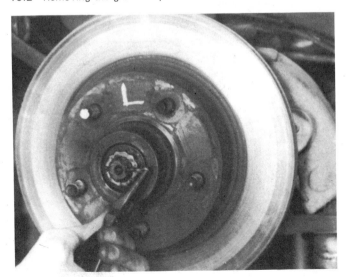

10.3a   Removing the cotter pin from the spindle

10.3b   The nut locking cap locks the wheel bearing tightness at the proper level

9

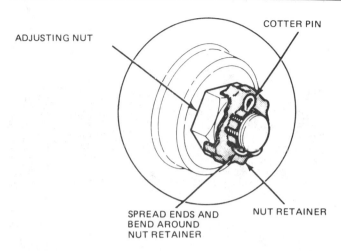

Fig. 9.13 Front wheel bearing adjustment nut and retainer assembly. Tighten the nut while rotating the hub then back off the nut and retighten it finger-tight before installing the retainer and cotter pin (Sec 10)

the wheel bearing adjusting nut.

4   Remove the wheel bearing adjusting nut from the spindle.

5   Grip the hub and disc assembly and pull it outwards far enough to loosen the washer and outer wheel bearing.

6   Push the hub and disc back onto the spindle and remove the washer and outer wheel bearing from the spindle (photo).

7   Grip the hub and disc assembly and pull it from the spindle (photo).

8   Carefully pry out the grease seal (photo) and lift the inner tapered bearing from the back of the hub assembly.

9   Clean the hub and wash the bearings with solvent, making sure that no grease or oil is allowed to get onto the brake disc. Clean any grease from the rotor with denatured alcohol or an approved brake cleaner.

10   Thoroughly clean the disc and inspect for signs of deep scoring or excessive corrosion. If these are evident the disc may be turned but the minimum thickness of the disc must not be less than the figure printed on the brake disc. It is desirable however, to fit a new disc if at all possible. A new disc should be cleaned to remove its protective coating, using brake cleaner. Notice that the discs have curved cooling fins. The disc must be installed so that the fins are pointing in the same direction as they were in the factory installation. Generally, earlier models point toward the front of the vehicle. No accurate generalization can be made regarding this, however, so be sure to make a note of it during removal.

11   To reassemble, first work a suitable grease well into the bearings.

12   To reassemble the hub, fit the inner bearing (photo) and then gently tap the grease seal into the hub (photo). A new seal should always be fitted. Lubricate the lips of the new seal with grease (photo).

13   Place the hub and disc assembly on the spindle, keeping the assembly centered to prevent damage to the inner grease seal.

14   Place the outer wheel bearing and flat washer on the spindle.

15   Screw the wheel bearing adjusting nut onto the spindle. Check the bearing preload as described in Chapter 1. Always use a new cotter pin.

16   Detach the caliper and anchor plate from the upper suspension arm remount it on the spindle. Be careful not to stretch or twist the brake flexible hose.

---

11   Rear disc brake caliper and pad — removal and installation

1   Raise the vehicle and support it securely on jackstands.

2   Remove the rear wheels.

3   Disconnect the parking brake cable at the lever.

4   If the caliper is to be removed from the vehicle, disconnect the brake hose and plug it.

5   Remove the caliper key retaining screw as shown in the accompanying illustration.

6   Remove the caliper retaining key and support spring, using a hammer and drift to carefully drive the key out as shown in the accompanying illustration.

10.6   Removing the washer and outer bearing cone for inspection and repacking

10.7   After removing the hub and rotor measure the thickness of the rotor with a micrometer or calipers and compare it to the figure printed on the disc

10.8   Don't scratch the surface on the hub when removing the seal. Always replace the seal with a new one

10.12a When the bearing has been cleaned, inspected and repacked with grease, reinstall it into the hub

10.12b Lightly tap the new seal into place with a soft hammer or hammer and wood block

7 The caliper can now be removed by first pushing the caliper downward against the anchor plate and then rotating the upper end out of the anchor plate.

8 If the caliper cannot be removed easily it will be necessary to loosen the caliper and retainer 1/2-turn, which will allow the piston to be forced back into its bore. Before loosening the retainer remove the parking brake lever and scribe a line across the end retainer and caliper housing to make sure the retainer is not loosened more than 1/2-turn. If the retainer is moved more than 1/2-turn the thrust screw and retainer seal may be broken, allowing fluid leakage.

9 The piston can now be forced back into its bore and the caliper moved. After removal, hang the caliper out of the way with a piece of wire, taking care not to twist or stretch the brake hose.

10 Remove the inner pad from the anchor plate and tap lightly on the outer pad to ease removal. If the pads are to be reinstalled, mark them so that they can be installed in their original locations. If the anti-rattle clip comes loose, reposition it as shown in the accompanying illustration.

11 Clean and inspect the caliper, anchor plate and disc for corrosion, wear and fluid leakage. If the disc or pads are worn beyond specifications they must be replaced with new ones. If the pads on one wheel require replacement, the pads on the other wheel must also be replaced to maintain equal braking action.

10.12c Lubricate the installed seal with bearing grease before reinstalling the hub

9

①

Fig. 9.14 Removing the rear disc brake caliper key retaining screw (Sec 11)

②

Fig. 9.15 A few sharp taps with a hammer and punch should drive out the caliper key (Sec 11)

LOOP TO INSIDE AWAY FROM ROTOR

Fig. 9.16 Anti-rattle clip installation (Sec 11)

Fig. 9.17 Adjusting the rear disc brake piston depth. A
C-clamp will also work for this operation (Sec 11)

Fig. 9.18 Sectional view of rear caliper housing (Sec 12)

12 If the end retainer has been loosened 1/2-turn the caliper should
be installed without the pads. Tighten the end retainer to specification and install the parking brake lever to its keyed spline. Install the
parking brake lever downward and rearward.
13 Remove the caliper.
14 Reinstall the brake pads. If installing new pads it will be necessary
to screw the piston back into the caliper bore using Ford tool
T75P-2588-B or equivalent to provide sufficient clearance. Remove
the brake rotor. Install the caliper, without pads, using the key only.
Referring to the accompanying figure, hold the shaft and turn the tool
handle counterclockwise until the tool seats firmly against the piston.
Loosen the handle 1/4 turn. Hold the handle and turn the tool shaft
clockwise until the piston is fully bottomed in its bore. The piston will
continue to turn even when bottomed, so check to make sure there
is no further inward movement. Remove the caliper and reinstall the
rotor.
15 With the anti-rattle clip in place in the lower inner pad support,

position the inner pad on the anchor plate.
16 Install the outer pad so that the lower flange ends are against the
caliper leg abutments and the upper flanges are over the caliper leg
shoulders.
17 Lightly lubricate the areas where the caliper and anchor plate will
slide on one another.
18 Place the caliper housing lower V groove on the anchor plate lower
abutment surface.
19 Being careful not to damage the piston dust boot, rotate the caliper
into position over the disc.
20 Seat the inner pad against the brake disc by pulling the caliper outward. The clearance between the outer pad lining and the disc must
be 1/16-inch or less.
21 If the gap is greater than 1/16-inch, remove the caliper and adjust
the piston outward following the procedure in Step 16.
22 Hold the caliper in place against the anchor plate and install the

Fig. 9.19 Rear disc brake caliper assembly — exploded
view (Sec 12)

Fig. 9.20 Rear caliper with end retainer removed (Sec 12)

Fig. 9.21 Removing the anti-rotation screw (Sec 12)

Fig. 9.22 Removing the thrust screw from the rear disc brake caliper (Sec 12)

Fig. 9.23 Pushing the rear caliper piston out with a special Ford tool (Sec 12)

Fig. 9.24 Checking the parking brake adjuster operation (Sec 12)

Fig 9.25 Filling the rear caliper with brake fluid (Sec 12)

caliper support spring and key so that the key's semi-circular slot is over the retaining screw threaded hole in the anchor plate.

23 Install the key retaining screw and tighten to specification.

24 If the brake hose has been disconnected, remove the plug and reinstall it. It will be necessary to bleed the brakes as described in Section 3.

25 Connect and adjust the parking brake cable.

26 Install the wheels, lower the vehicle and take it for a test drive to check for proper braking action.

12 Rear disc brake caliper — overhaul

1 Remove the brake caliper as previously described.

2 Remove the caliper end retainer as shown in the accompanying illustration and lift out the operating shaft, thrust bearing and balls.

3 Use a magnet or tweezers to remove the thrust screw anti-rotation pin as shown in the accompanying illustration. If the pins are difficult to remove, it will be necessary to use Ford tool T75P-2588-B or equivalent to push the piston back into the housing. Adjust the piston so that it protrudes about one inch. Push the piston back into the caliper housing and rotate the tool shaft counterclockwise until the thrust screw is clear of the anti-rotation pin.

4 Remove the thrust screw by turning it counterclockwise with a 1/4-inch Allen wrench, or on earlier models, a 1/4-inch square socket drive as shown in the accompanying illustration.

5 Use Ford tool T75P-2588-A or equivalent to push the piston out as shown in the accompanying illustration.

6 Remove the piston seal, boot, thrust screw O-ring seal and end-ring lip seal.

7 Clean the metal parts with isopropyl alcohol and dry with compressed air if possible.

8 Inspect the caliper for pitting, scoring or worn parts. If any of these conditions are found, or the chrome plating on the bore is worn, the components must be replaced with new parts.

9 Check the adjuster operation by assembling the thrust screw and pulling the two apart about 1/4-inch as shown in the accompanying illustration. The brass drive ring must remain stationary during this operation, causing the nut to rotate. The piston/adjuster assembly must be replaced with a new one if this does not occur.

10 Inspect the parking brake lever for damage and replace if necessary.

11 Lubricate the new caliper piston seal with clean brake fluid and seat it fully into the cylinder bore, being careful not to twist it.

12 Install the new dust boot by seating it squarely in the caliper bore outer groove.

13 Lubricate the piston/adjuster assembly with clean brake fluid and install it in the cylinder bore, spreading the dust boot over the seal as it is installed. Make sure the dust boot is seated in the piston groove.

14 Place the caliper securely in a vise and fill the piston adjuster assembly to the bottom edge of the thrust screw with clean brake fluid as shown in the accompanying illustration.

9

Fig. 9.26 Bottoming the rear caliper piston (Sec 12)

15 Lubricate a new thrust screw O-ring seal with clean brake fluid and install it in the thrust screw groove.
16 Install the thrust screw into the piston adjuster assembly with a 1/4-inch Allen wrench (1/4-inch square socket on early models) until the screw tip surface is flush with the bottom of the threaded bore. Be careful not to cut the O-ring. Set the thrust screw so that the notches on the screw and caliper housing are aligned. Install the anti-rotation pin.
17 Place the three balls in their sockets in the thrust screw, apply liberal amounts of silicone grease on the parking brake mechanism components and install the operating shaft on the balls.
18 Cover the thrust bearing with a coat of silicone grease and install it.
19 Install a new O-ring and lip seal onto the end retainer.
20 Lightly lubricate the O-ring seal and lip seal with silicone grease and install the end retainer in the caliper. Hold the shaft firmly during installation to prevent the balls from being dislodged. Reseat the lip seal if necessary and tighten the end retainer.
21 Install the parking brake lever and tighten the retaining screw to specification.
22 With the caliper in a vise, use tool T75P-2588-B or equivalent to bottom the piston as shown in the illustration.
23 Install the caliper as previously described.

---

13 Rear drum brake shoes — adjustment

Automatic adjusters are fitted to the rear drum brakes and these operate when the car is backed-up and stopped. Should car use be

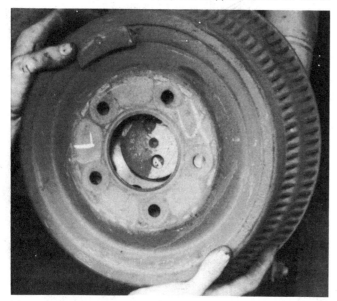

14.5/1 Remove the brake drum

Fig. 9.27 Rear drum brakes may be adjusted by turning the star adjuster as shown (Sec 13)

such that it is not backed-up very often and the pedal movement has increased, it will be necessary to adjust the brakes as follows:
1   Drive the car rearwards and apply the brake pedal firmly. Now drive it forwards, and again apply the brake pedal firmly.
2   Repeat the cycle until a desirable pedal movement is obtained. Should this not happen it will be necessary to remove the drum and hub assembly and inspect the adjuster mechanism as described in Section 14.

---

14 Rear drum brake shoes — replacement

1   Whenever you are working on the brake system, be aware that asbestos dust is present. It has been proven to be harmful to your health, so be careful not to inhale any of it.
2   Raise the vehicle and place it securely on jackstands.
3   Release the parking brake handle.
4   Remove the wheel and tire assembly. **Note:** *All four rear shoes should be replaced at the same time, but to avoid mixing up parts, work on only one brake assembly at a time.*
5   Refer to the accompanying photographs and perform the brake shoe replacement procedure. **Note:** *If the brake drum cannot be easily pulled off the axle and shoe assembly, make sure that the parking brake*

14.5/2 Remove the primary and secondary shoe-to-anchor springs with a spring removal tool.

14.1 Components of a typical drum brake assembly

1	Secondary brake shoe return spring	5	Adjustment pawl	9	Wheel cylinder
2	Automatic adjuster cable	6	Adjusting screw and wheel assembly	10	Primary brake shoe return spring
3	Hold-down spring and pin	7	Primary brake shoe	11	Anchor pin
4	Secondary brake shoe	8	Adjusting pawl return spring	12	Shoe guide

14.5/3 Unhook the adjusting cable eye from the anchor pin

14.5/4 Remove the shoe guide

9

14.5/5   Remove all the shoe retaining springs and pins

14.5/6   While separating the shoes, extract the adjustment screw and wheel

14.5/7   Remove the primary shoe and the parking brake strut and spring assembly

14.5/8   Take out the adjuster pawl . . .

14.5/9   . . . and remove the secondary shoe from the backing plate

14.5/10   Separate the parking brake cable and spring from the actuating lever

14.5/11 Remove the E-clip retaining the parking brake lever to the shoe. This step completes the shoe removal procedure. Check all springs for tension and cracking and replace them as necessary. Also check the wheel cylnder for leakage. If the wheel cylinder is leaking it should be replaced with a new or remanufactured unit

14.5/12 Install the parking brake lever onto the new brake shoe with the attaching pin and E-clip

14.5/13 Disassemble, clean and lubricate the adjusting screw and wheel assembly

14.5/14 Lightly coat the shoe guide pads, wheel cylinder ends and anchor pin with multipurpose grease

14.5/15 Further reassembly is essentially the reverse of disassembly. Pay particular attention to the slots on the wheel cylinder plungers (A) and the parking brake strut (B), making sure they are correctly positioned on the brake shoes

14.5/16 The shoe retaining pins and springs should be securely seated

9

14.5/17   The long end of the adjusting screw should point toward the front of the vehicle

14.5/18   Install the self-adjusting pawl first . . .

14.5/19   . . . followed by the guide and adjuster cable

14.5/20   Connect the adjuster spring to the pawl and test for operation by turning the axle forward and backward. The adjuster should exhibit a ratchet action, turning the adjustment wheel in a downward direction.

is completely released, then squirt some penetrating oil around the center hub area. Allow the oil to soak in and try to pull the drum off again. If the drum still cannot be pulled off, the brake shoes will have to be retracted. Insert a small screwdriver through the slot in the backing plate and pull the lever off the adjusting screw wheel while turning the adjusting wheel with another small screwdriver as shown in the accompanying illustration, moving the shoes away from the drum. The drum may now be pulled off.

6   Before reinstalling the drum it should be checked for cracks, score marks, deep scratches and hard spots, which will appear as small discolored areas. If the hard spots cannot be removed with fine emery cloth or if any of the other conditions listed exist, the drum must be taken to an automotive machine shop to have it turned. If the drum will not clean up before the maximum drum diameter is reached in the machining operation, the drum will have to be replaced with a new one. **Note:** *The maximum diameter is indicated on each brake drum.*

7   Install the brake drum and install the wheel stud lock washers.

8   Mount the wheels and tires.

9   Make a number of forward and reverse stops to adjust the brakes until a satisfactory pedal action is obtained.

15   Master cylinder — removal, installation and overhaul

Removal and installation

1   Unscrew the brake lines from the primary and secondary outlet ports of the master cylinder (photo). Plug the ends of the lines to prevent

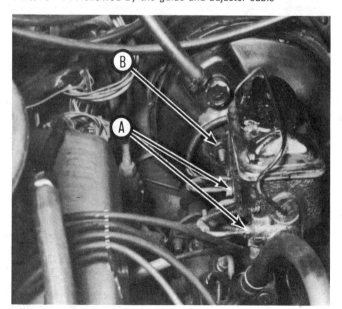

15.1   The brake master cylinder can be removed after disconnecting the hydraulic lines (A) and removing the two attaching bolts (B)

Fig. 9.28 Brake master cylinder — exploded view (Sec 15)

contamination. Take suitable precautions to catch the hydraulic fluid as the unions are detached from the master cylinder body.

2   Remove the two bolts securing the master cylinder to the firewall or servo unit.

3   Pull the master cylinder forward and lift it upward from the car. Do not allow brake fluid to contact any paint, as it acts as a solvent.

4   Installation is the reverse of the removal procedure. It will be necessary to bleed the hydraulic system as described in Section 2.

5   If a replacement master cylinder is to be fitted, it will be necessary to lubricate the seals before fitting to the car, as they have a protective coating when originally assembled. Remove the blanking plugs from the hydraulic line union seats. Inject some clean hydraulic fluid into the master cylinder and operate the pushrod several times so that the fluid spreads over all the internal working surfaces.

Fig. 9.29 Removing a snap-ring with snap-ring pliers (Sec 15)

Overhaul

6   Clean the exterior of the master cylinder and wipe dry with a lint free rag. Remove the filler cover and gasket from the top of the reservoir and pour out any remaining hydraulic fluid.

7   Remove the secondary piston stop bolt from the bottom of the master cylinder body.

8   Remove the bleed screw.

9   Depress the primary piston and remove the snap-ring from the groove at the rear of the master cylinder bore as shown in the accompanying illustration.

10   Remove the pushrod and the primary piston assembly.

11   Do not remove the screw that retains the primary return spring retainer, return spring, primary cup and protector on the primary position. This is factory set and must not be disturbed.

12   Remove the secondary piston assembly.

13   Do not remove the outlet seats, outlet check valves and outlet check valve springs from the master cylinder body.

14   Examine the bore of the cylinder carefully for scoring or ridges. If the bore is smooth a new seal can be fitted. If, however, there is any doubt of the condition of the bore then a new master cylinder must be fitted. Minor scratches or scoring in the bore can be removed using a honing tool.

15   If the seals are swollen or very loose on the pistons, suspect oil contamination in the system. Oil will swell these rubber seals and if one is found to be swollen it is reasonable to assume that all seals in the braking system need attention.

16   Thoroughly clean all parts in clean hydraulic fluid or methylated spirits.

17   All components should be assembled wet after dipping them in fresh brake fluid.

18   Insert the complete secondary piston and return spring assembly into the master cylinder bore, easing the seals into the bore, taking care that they do not roll over.

19   Insert the primary piston assembly into the master cylinder bore.

20   Depress the primary piston and fit the snap-ring into the cylinder bore groove.

21   Refit the pushrod, boot and retainer onto the pushrod and fit the assembly into the end of the primary piston. Check that the retainer is correctly seated and holding the pushrod securely.

22   Place the inner end of the pushrod boot in the master cylinder body retaining groove.

9

Fig. 9.30　Drum brake wheel cylinder — exploded view (Sec 16)

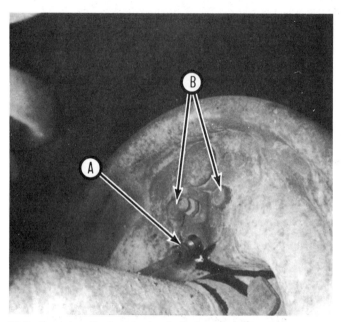

16.2　Rear drum brake wheel cylinder hydraulic line (A) and attaching bolts (B)

16.3　Removing the rear drum brake wheel cylinder from the brake backing plate

23　Fit the secondary piston stop bolt and O-ring into the bottom of the master cylinder body.

24　Reinstall the diaphragm into the filler cover, making sure it is correctly seated, and replace the cover.

16　Rear drum brake wheel cylinder — removal and installation

Note: *Due to the wide availability of reconditioned and aftermarket brake components, it has become easier and comparable in cost to replace a damaged or worn wheel cylinder than it is to rebuild it yourself. Therefore, overhaul of wheel cylinders is not covered in this manual. Be sure to take your old wheel cylinder with you to the parts dealer for positive identification.*

1　Remove the brake shoes.

2　On the back side of the brake backing plate, loosen the brake line fitting at the wheel cylinder (photo). Do not try to pull the brake tube from the wheel cylinder as this could bend it, making installation difficult.

3　Remove the two bolts securing the wheel cylinder to the brake backing plate and remove the cylinder (photo).

4　Plug the brake line to stop hydraulic fluid leakage.

5　Installation is the reverse of removal. After reinstallation it will be necessary to bleed the hydraulic system.

17　Power brake booster — removal and installation

A vacuum booster is part of the brake circuit, in series with a master cylinder, to provide assistance to the driver when the brake pedal is depressed. This reduces the effort required by the driver to operate the brakes under all braking conditions. The unit utilizes a vacuum obtained from the intake manifold and is comprised of a booster diaphragm and check valve.

Under normal operating conditions the vacuum booster will give trouble-free service for a very long time. If, however, it is suspected that the unit is faulty it must be exchanged for a new unit. No attempt should be made to repair the old unit, as it is not a serviceable item.

1　Remove the stoplight switch and actuating rod from the brake pedal as described in Section 6.

2　Working under the hood, remove the air cleaner from the carburetor and the vacuum hose from the servo unit.

3　Remove the master cylinder as described in Section 18.

4　From inside the vehicle, remove the nuts securing the servo unit to the firewall.

5　From inside the engine compartment, move the servo unit forward until the actuating rod is clear of the firewall, rotate it and lift it upward until it is clear of the engine compartment.

6　Installation is the reverse of removal. After installation, bleed the brakes as described in Section 3.

Fig. 9.31 Typical power brake vacuum booster and mounting — exploded view (Sec 17)

Fig. 9.32 Hydraulic system pressure differential/control valve without metering valve (1975 to 83) (Sec 18)

Fig. 9.33 Hydraulic system pressure differential/control valve with metering valve (1984) (Sec 18)

18 Pressure differential valve assembly — removal and installation

The pressure differential valve senses an unbalanced hydraulic pressure condition existing between the front and rear brake systems. When there is a pressure loss in either system during brake application, the piston will move off-center, causing the brake warning lamp to light. The warning lamp will shut off when the brake system is accurately serviced, properly bled and the brakes are applied to center the piston.

The brake warning lamp switch is mounted on top of the control valve body. Under normal conditions, when the differential valve piston is centrally located, the spring-loaded warning switch plunger fits into the piston's tapered groove leaving the contacts of the warning switch open.

1984 vehicles have a metering valve designed into the differential valve assembly. This valve limits the pressure to the front brakes until a predetermined front hydraulic pressure has been reached. It is found in the forward end of the control valve central bore, as shown in the accompanying illustration. The bleeder rod must be depressed manually when bleeding the front brakes.

1   Disconnect the brake warning light connector from the warning light switch.

9

2   Disconnect the unions from the valve assembly. Plug the ends of the lines to prevent loss of hydraulic fluid.
3   Remove the two nuts and bolts securing the valve bracket to the underside of the fender apron. Remove the assembly from the vehicle.
4   To install the assembly, position the brake control valve assembly at the fender apron holes and install the two assembly mount nuts.
5   Reconnect all brake lines to the control valve assembly.
6   Connect the brake warning lamp switch wiring harness connector to the brake warning lamp switch. Verify this connection by turning the ignition switch to the Start position. The lamp should come on.
7   Bleed the brake system and centralize the pressure differential valve.

19 Pressure differential valve — centralization

1   After any repair or bleeding operations it is possible that the brake warning light will come on due to the pressure differential valve remaining in an off-center position.
2   To centralize the valve, first turn the ignition switch to the ON position.
3   Depress the brake pedal several times and the piston will center itself, causing the warning light to go out.
4   Turn the ignition Off.
5   Test for a firm resistance at the brake pedal.

Chapter 10 Suspension and steering systems

Refer to Chapter 13 for specifications and information related to 1985 and later models

Contents

Specifications

Front suspension
    Type . . . . Independent with coil springs on the upper A-arms (Type A) or independent with coil springs on the lower A-arms (Type B) or single arm modified MacPherson strut (Strut)

Rear suspension
    Type . . . . Coil springs suspended by four arms or leaf springs

Steering
    Type . . . . Ford or Saginaw integral power steering or Ford non-integral power steering, or gear-worm and recirculating-ball manual steering

Power steering pump
    1975 — 1978
        6.6L and 7.5L engines . . . . Saginaw
        Others . . . . Ford-Thompson
    1979 — 1984
        All models . . . . Ford Model CII

Torque specifications

	Ft-lbs
Type A front suspension (coil spring on upper A-arm)	
Shock absorber-to-spring seat	8 to 12
Shock absorber upper attachment	10 to 16
Shock absorber upper bracket	32 to 48
Upper suspension arm-to-body	
1975 thru 1977	85 to 100
1978 thru 1984	110 to 130
Spring seat-to-upper arm	24 to 40
Balljoint-to-spindle	75 to 95
Srut-to-lower arm	90 to 115
Lower arm-to-underbody	85 to 100
Stabilizer bar mounting bracket	6 to 12
Strut-to-underbody nut	70 to 80
Sway bar-to-lower arm	6 to 12

10

Torque specifications (continued)

Type B front suspension (coil spring on lower A-arm)

Lower A-arm to No. 2 crossmember.................	95 to 110
Upper arm-to-frame...........................	120 to 140
Stabilizer bar-to-lower arm....................	9 to 12
Balljoint-to-spindle..........................	80 to 120
Strut-to-lower arm...........................	80 to 115
Stabilizer bar-to-frame.......................	14 to 26
Shock absorber upper attachment	22 to 30
Shock absorber-to-lower arm	12 to 18
Brake splash guard-to-spindle	9 to 14
Caliper-to-spindle	
Upper bolt	110 to 140
Lower bolt	90 to 120
Strut-to-frame	95 to 105

Strut (Modified MacPherson Strut) front suspension

Lower arm-to-No. 2 crossmember	150 to 180
Stabilizer bar mounting clamp	20 to 25
Stabilizer bar-to-lower arm	9 to 12
Spindle-to-shock strut	150 to 180
Shock strut-to-upper mount	55 to 92
Balljoint-to-spindle..........................	100 to 120
Shock upper mount-to-body	62 to 75
Steering gear-to-No. 2 crossmember	90 to 100
Tie rod end-to-spindle	35 to 47

Rear suspension — leaf spring type

Spring shackle..............................	14 to 22
Shock absorber	
Upper mount	45 to 65
Lower mount	14 to 26
Axle U-bolt nut	30 to 45
Spring front hanger bolt......................	80 to 120

Rear suspension — coil spring type

Shock absorber upper attachment	20 to 26
Shock absorber lower attachment	55 to 70
Upper arm-to-frame	100 to 130
Track bar-to-axle track bar stud	75 to 85
Track bar stud-to-axle	140 to 150
Track bar-to-frame	50 to 70
Lower arm-to-frame	100 to 105
Lower arm-to-axle	90 to 100
Stabilizer bar bracket	18 to 20
Stabilizer bar-to-rear link	16 to 20
Stabilizer bar-to-lower arm	50 to 55

Steering system

Pitman arm-to-sector shaft	200 to 225
Steering gear-to-frame	
Recirculating-ball type	60 to 65
Rack-and-pinion type	80 to 100
Steering shaft flexible coupling nut	20 to 30
Steering wheel attaching nut	30 to 40
Steering column stud nuts	20 to 37
Steering column adjustment bracket nuts	20 to 37
Steering power cylinder-to-center link	43 to 47
Power cylinder to bracket	18 to 24
Steering gear-to-frame	55 to 75
Pitman arm-to-steering gear	170 to 230
Pressure hose-to-gear	16 to 25
Return hose-to-gear	25 to 34
Hose clamps...............................	2 to 4
Pump pivot bolts	25 to 40
Belt adjustment nuts	30 to 40
Pump bracket-to-engine	45 to 65
Tie-rod end-to-spindle arm	35 to 47

1   General information

The front suspension on models covered in this manual may be either the single-arm type or double-arm type. The single arm type is a modified MacPherson strut, made up of a shock absorber/strut assembly, coil spring and lower A-arm. Each front wheel rotates on a spindle, the upper end of which is mounted to the lower strut and the lower end to the A-arm. The lower end of the spindle is attached with a balljoint. The upper end of the strut is attached to the body structure through an insulator bushing. The coil spring mounts between the front frame crossmember and the lower A-arm. To control body roll a front stabilizer bar is fitted.

On the double arm front suspensions, the coil spring may rest either on the upper arm on earlier models, or the lower arm on later models. The front wheels on these also rotate on a spindle, but the upper and lower ends of the spindle attach to upper and lower balljoints, which are mounted to each of the A-arms. The upper arm pivots on a bushing and shaft assembly bolted to the frame. The lower

Fig. 10.1 Front shock absorber lower attachment (Sec 2)

SHOCK ABSORBER
INSULATOR
SPRING PIVOT PLATE
INSULATOR
UPPER ARM ASSEMBLY
RETAINING NUTS
WASHER

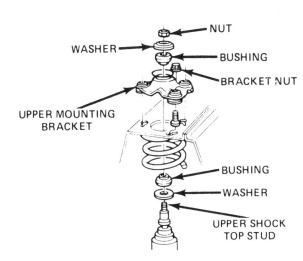

NUT
WASHER
BUSHING
BRACKET NUT
UPPER MOUNTING BRACKET
BUSHING
WASHER
UPPER SHOCK TOP STUD

Fig. 10.2 Typical front shock absorber upper attachments (Sec 2)

2.4 Front shock absorber lower mount (Type B suspension shown)

arm pivots on the number two crossmember. The shock absorber is bolted to the A-arm. On later models the arm and strut assembly has been replaced by a new lower A-arm. The upper balljoint incorporates a new low-friction design and the lower balljoint has a built-in wear indicator. The front stabilizer bar is standard on all models.

The MacPherson struts are non-serviceable and must be replaced as a unit. The balljoints and lower suspension arm bushings are not separately serviced and must be replaced as an assembly. Caster and camber angles on the MacPherson strut type suspension are set at the factory and cannot be adjusted in the field. Toe-in should be adjusted by an alignment shop. Later models may be equipped with optional gas-charged shock absorbers.

The rear suspension may be either of the coil spring or leaf spring type. The rear axle housing rests on the spring assembly suspended from hangers integral with the body. Coil spring models locate the axle assembly by four pressed steel arms. Rubber insulated shock absorbers are fitted on each side. Later models may have optional gas charged rear shock absorbers.

Most vehicles covered in this manual come equipped with power steering. Some may have manual steering. Steering gears are manufactured either by Ford or Saginaw, and are either the integral or non-integral type. On pre-1979 models the power steering pumps may be either the Saginaw type or the Ford-Thompson type. From 1979 through 1984 the Ford type CII power steering pump is used.

2 Front shock absorber — removal and installation

Note: *This procedure does not apply to the modified strut suspension. See Section 10.*

1   Remove the shock absorber upper attaching nuts.
2   On type A suspensions, with the spring on the upper A-arm, place wood blocks under the upper suspension arm to support it. On type B suspensions, with the spring on the lower A-arm, support the lower arm.
3   Raise the vehicle and support it securely.
4   Remove the nuts attaching the lower end of the shock absorber (photo).
5   The shock absorber can now be removed from the vehicle.
6   Remove the bracket and insulators from the spring assembly.
7   Transfer the mounting hardware and insulators on the new shock absorber.
8   Insert the shock absorber into the spring tower, seating the studs into the pivot plate holes.
9   Install the attaching nuts and brackets.
10 Remove the supports and lower the vehicle.

10

3.3   Checking balljoint axial movement by applying force with a pry bar

NEW
OK

WORN IF FLUSH OR
BELOW SURFACE
OF COVER

BALL JOINT COVER

NEW
OK

CHECKING SURFACE

WORN IF FLUSH OR
BELOW SURFACE
OF COVER

BALL JOINT COVER

NEW
OK

CHECKING SURFACE

WORN IF FLUSH OR
BELOW SURFACE
OF COVER

Fig. 10.5 Later models incorporate balljoint wear indicators.
Balljoints should be replaced if the indicator is flush with or
below the surface as shown (Sec 3)

MAXIMUM TOLERANCE

Fig. 10.3 Measuring lower balljoint radial play. Note jacking
point for suspensions with the spring on the lower arm
(Sec 3)

MAXIMUM
TOLERANCE

F 1500- B

Fig. 10.4 Measuring upper balljoint radial play. Note jacking
point for suspensions with the spring on the upper arm
(Sec 3)

3   Balljoints — checking

1   For vehicles with springs on the upper A-arm (Type A) place the jack on the frame or crossmember. For those with springs on the lower A-arm (Type B) jack from the lower control arm. In each case, use jackstands since you will be doing some vigorous shaking of the vehicle.
2   With the car properly supported, two checks will be made, one for radial play (side-to-side), and the other for axial play (up and down).

Axial movement check
3   Axial movement is up and down movement. Check axial movement by jacking up the front end and using a short pry bar under the tire to move the wheel up and down (photo).

Radial movement check
4   Radial movement is in and out play. Check for it by jacking up the

Fig. 10.6 Typical Type A front suspension layout (Sec 4)

front end and moving the tire toward and away from the car by grasping the top and bottom of the wheel by hand.

5   Replace the lower balljoint when axial movement exceeds .05 inches or radial movement exceeds .025 inches. Replace the upper balljoints when the stub shows any looseness. **Note:** *Balljoints on some Ford vehicles are pressed in. It is inadvisable for these to be replaced anywhere but in a shop specially equipped with an arbor press to do the job. On all vehicles removing the tapered balljoint stud from the hole can be extremely difficult. It is suggested that unless you have considerable patience and determination, that the vehicle be taken to a professional for balljoint replacement.*

4   Type A and B suspensions sway bar and insulators — removal and installation

1   Raise the vehicle and support it securely on jackstands.
2   Disconnect the links at both ends of the sway bar (photo).
3   Unbolt both of the attachment brackets and remove the bar assembly.
4   Lubricate the insulators and contacting parts of the sway bar with rubber lubricant. Slide the new insulators into place on the bar.
5   Install the brackets and tighten the bolts.
6   Reconnect the sway bar end links.
7   Lower the vehicle.

4.2   The sway bar can be removed by first disconnecting the link (A) and then detaching the insulator brackets (B)

10

Fig. 10.7 Sway bar end link components (Sec 5)

Fig. 10.8 Proper location of front spring upper end (Sec 6)

5 Type A suspension sway bar link bushings — removal and installation

1   Raise the vehicle and support it securely on jackstands.
2   Remove the nuts from the sway bar end link bolt and remove the bolt.
3   Assemble the cup-type washer and the new insulator bushing.
4   Install the end link through the sway bar end and install the spacer, cup washers and new bushings.
5   Install the bolt with the head at the top and tighten to specification.
6   Lower the vehicle.

6 Type A suspension front coil spring — removal and installation

1   Install wood blocks under the upper suspension arm.
2   Remove the front shock absorbers.
3   Raise the vehicle and support it securely on jackstands.
4   Remove the front wheels, brake caliper and disc as described in Chapter 9.
5   Use a spring compressor tool to compress the spring.
6   Remove the two nuts attaching the upper suspension arm to the spring tower and swing it away from the tower.
7   Slowly release the spring compressor tension and remove the tool from the spring. Remove the spring.
8   To install, position the upper insulator on the spring and secure it with tape.
9   Place the spring in position in the spring tower and compress it with the tool.
10 Swing the upper suspension arm into position, install the bolts and nuts and tighten to specification.
11 Slowly release the compressor tool tension and guide the spring into position in the upper spring seat. The tail end must be within 1/2-inch (13 mm) of the tab on the spring.
12 Remove the spring compressor.
13 Install the brake caliper, disc and shock absorber.
14 Remove the blocks from the upper suspension arm, install the wheels and lower the vehicle.

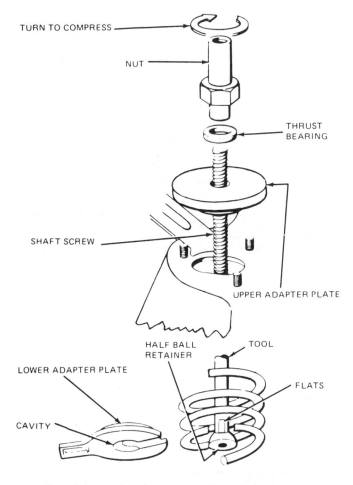

Fig. 10.9 Suspension spring compressor tool. Follow manufacturer's instructions for your particular spring compressor (Sec 6)

7 Type A suspension lower arm — removal and installation

Note: *Upper and lower suspension arms must be replaced as a unit.*

1   Place wood blocks under the suspension arm.
2   Raise the vehicle, support it securely and remove the front wheel.
3   Disconnect and remove the sway bar links.
4   Unbolt the lower strut at the lower arm.
5   Remove the nuts and bolts attaching the strut to the lower arm.
6   Remove the cotter pin and loosen the lower balljoint stud nut two turns.
7   Install a suitable balljoint removal tool between the ends of the upper and lower balljoint studs.

Fig. 10.10 Type A suspension upper arm assembly (Sec 8)

8 Turn the tool adaptor screw until the stud is under compression. Loosen the spindle near the lower stud by tapping sharply with a hammer. Do not use the tool alone to try to loosen the stud.
9 Remove the balljoint stud and lower the arm.
10 Remove the cam bolt, nut and lock washer and lower the arm.
11 To install, place the lower arm in position to the bracket and loosely install the cam bolt, washer and nut.
12 Raise the arm and guide the balljoint into the spindle bore, installing the stud nut loosely.
13 Reconnect the sway bar.
14 Install the lower strut to the arm and tighten the bolts to specification.
15 Tighten the lower balljoint stud to specification and then tighten it until the next slot is aligned with the cotter pin hole and install the cotter pin.
16 Hold the head of the lower pivot bolt with a wrench and tighten the nut to specification.
17 Remove the wood blocks and jackstands, install the front wheel and lower the vehicle.
18 Have the front end alignment checked.

8 Type A suspension upper arm — removal and installation

Note: *Upper and lower suspension arms should be replaced as a set.*
1 Position blocks under the upper suspension arm. Raise the vehicle, support it securely and remove the front wheel.
2 Remove the shock absorbers.
3 Compress the spring with a spring compressor tool.
4 Place a jackstand under the lower arm, remove the cotter pin from the upper balljoint stud and loosen the nut two turns.
5 Seat a suitable balljoint remover tool between the ends of the upper and lower balljoint studs.
6 Turn the tool until the studs are under pressure.
7 Remove the nut and lift the stud from the spindle.
8 From inside the engine compartment, remove the upper inner shaft attaching nuts and remove the upper arm.
9 Clean the grease and loose dirt from the upper arm suspension parts.
10 To install, place the upper arm and spring seat assembly in position on the spring tower and install the attaching nuts.
11 Install the upper balljoint stud in the top of the spindle and tighten the nut to specification. Tighten the nut further so that the cotter pin holes line up, and install the cotter pin.
12 Release and remove the spring compressor tool.
13 Remove the wood blocks from the upper suspension arm and lower the vehicle.
14 Check the front end alignment.

Fig. 10.11 Front suspension balljoints and steering knuckles may be separated with the aid of a screw-type puller, which is preferable to the wedge or pickle-fork type of puller (Sec 9)

9 Type A suspension spindle — removal and installation

1 Place wood blocks under the front suspension arm.
2 Raise the vehicle, support it securely and remove the front wheel.
3 Remove the front hub and brake assembly as described in Chapter 9.
4 Disconnect the tie rod end, using a pickle fork type wedge tool or a bearing puller.
5 Remove the balljoint stud cotter pins and loosen the nuts two turns.
6 Install a suitable balljoint removal tool between the upper and lower balljoint studs and turn the tool so that considerable pressure is exerted at the studs.
7 Strike the spindle sharply with a hammer near the studs to break them loose.
8 Place a jack under the lower suspension arm.
9 Remove the balljoint stud nuts and lower the jack to remove the spindle.
10 To install, place the spindle onto the lower stud and install the nut to specification. Tighten the nut further if necessary to install the cotter pin.
11 Use the jack to raise the lower arm, guiding the upper balljoint stud into the spindle. Install the nut and remove the jack.
12 Reconnect the tie rod end and install the nut and cotter pin.

10 Type B suspension front spring — removal and installation

Removal
1 Raise the vehicle and support it securely on jackstands.
2 Disconnect the lower end of the shock absorber from the lower arm. It may be necessary to use a pry bar.
3 Place a jack under the lower arm to support it.
4 Install a suitable spring compressor to relieve tension on the spring. When this has been done and you are certain that the compressor is securely in place, remove the bolts which attach the strut and jounce bumper to the lower arm. If equipped, disconnect the lower end of

10

APRON

VIEW Z

ASSEMBLE FLUSH TO
1.4" OUT FROM END
OF SPRING

**Fig. 10.12 Modified MacPherson strut suspension —
exploded view (Sec 16)**

the sway bar stud from the lower arm.

5   Remove the nut and bolt that secures the inner end of the arm to the crossmember.

6   Carefully and very slowly, lower the jack. When the pressure has been completely relieved the jack may be released and the spring and compressor removed as a unit.

Installation

7   Place the spring upper insulator on the spring and secure it with

tape. Position the spring on the lower arm so that the lower end properly engages the seat. The end of the spring must be no more than 1/2-inch from the end of the depression in the arm.

8   Compress the spring with the spring compressor and raise the lower arm carefully while guiding the inner end to align with the bolt hole in the crossmember. Insert the attaching bolt in the crossmember and through the lower arm. Loosely attach the nut on the lower arm inner pivot bolt.

9   Secure the lower end of the shock absorber to the lower arm with the two attaching bolts and lower the jack.

SHOCK STRUT
INSULATOR

INTEGRAL SPINDLE & BRAKE
ANCHOR PLATE DESIGN

NO. 2 CROSSMEMBER

SHOCK
STRUT

STANDARD FRONT
STABILIZER BAR

LOWER "A" ARM ASSEMBLY

Fig. 10.13 Modified MacPherson strut suspension (Sec 16)

UPPER PLATE

LOWER PLATE

Fig. 10.14 Spring compressor installed showing upper and
lower place locations (Sec 16)

Fig. 10.15 Spring compressor inserted through control arm
(Sec 16)

10

11.7a   Although the wedge or pickle-fork will separate the balljoint successfully, it usually will cause damage to the rubber seal. A screw-type puller is recommended

11.7b   By first applying tension to the balljoint with a screw-type puller, then rapping it with a soft hammer, the balljoint can be separated with the grease seal intact

10   Replace the strut and jounce bumper with the attaching bolts.
11   Connect the sway bar to the lower arm using a new nut and bolt with the washer and insulators.
12   Remove the jackstands and lower the vehicle.
13   After the vehicle has been lowered to the floor and is at curb height, torque the lower arm inner pivot nut to specification.

11   Type B suspension front wheel spindle — removal and installation

Removal

1   Raise the vehicle and support it securely on jackstands.
2   Remove the disc brake caliper from the rotor (Chapter 9) and wire it to the underbody to prevent damage to the brake hose.
3   Remove the grease cap from the hub, then remove the cotter pin, nut lock, adjusting nut, washer and outer bearing cone and roller assembly.
4   Pull the hub and rotor assembly off the wheel spindle.
5   Remove the caliper shield.
6   Disconnect the spindle connecting rod end from the spindle arm. Remove the cotter pins from both balljoint stud nuts and loosen the nuts two turns. Do not remove the nuts from the studs at this time.
7   Using a wedge (photo) or screw-type balljoint puller (photo), break the balljoint studs loose in the spindle. Insert the spring compressor and compress the spring. As an added precaution, chain the spring to the upper A-arm to prevent it from flying loose.
8   Remove the upper and lower balljoint stud nuts. Lower the lower A-arm and remove the spindle.

Installation

9   Position the spindle on the lower balljoint stud and install the stud nut. Torque the nut to specification and install a new cotter pin.
10   Raise the lower arm and guide the upper balljoint stud into the spindle. Install the stud nut. Torque the nut to specification and install a new cotter pin. Carefully release the tension on the spring compressor and remove the chain if attached.
11   Connect the spindle connecting rod end to the spindle arm and install the attaching nut. Install a new cotter pin.
12   Replace the caliper splash shield.
13   Install the hub and rotor.
14   Position the caliper to the rotor and spindle and install the attaching bolts.
15   Install the wheel and tire on the hub and adjust the wheel bearing.
16   If the spindle is being replaced due to damage, check and adjust the caster, camber and toe-in as required.

12   Type B suspension lower arm — removal and installation

Removal

1   Raise the front of the vehicle and position support it securely on jackstands. Remove the wheel and tire.
2   Remove the front spring as described in the previous Section.
3   Remove the nut and bolt attaching the lower arm to the number two crossmember and remove the arm.

Installation

4   Position the lower arm to the number two crossmember and loosely attach the nut on the lower arm pivot bolt. Do not tighten the nut at this time.
5   Install the front spring as described in the previous Section. Do not tighten the lower arm pivot nut until the vehicle has been lowered to the floor and is at curb height.
6   If the lower arm is being replaced due to damage, check the caster, camber and toe-in and have them adjusted as required.

13   Type B suspension — upper arm removal and installation

Removal

1   Raise the vehicle, support it securely on jackstands and remove the wheel cover, wheel and tire from the hub.
2   Remove the cotter pin from the upper balljoint stud and loosen the upper balljoint stud nut one or two turns.
3   Install a wedge puller on the balljoint and tap the spindle near the upper stud with a hammer to loosen the stud in the spindle.
4   Insert a spring compressor tool in the spring and compress the spring. Place a floor jack under the lower arm. As an additional safety precaution wrap a chain around one coil of the spring and through the A-arm to prevent the spring from flying loose.
5   Remove the nuts from the upper balljoint stud (photo).
6   Remove the upper arm inner shaft attaching bolts. Remove the upper arm inner shaft as an assembly.

Installation

7   Position the upper arm inner shaft on the frame bracket and install the two attaching bolts and washer to a snug fit.
8   Connect the upper balljoint stud to the spindle and install the attaching nut. Torque the nut to specification and continue to tighten the nut until the cotter pin hole in the stud is in line with the nut slots, then install a new cotter pin.
9   Install the wheel and tire on the hub and adjust the wheel bearings as outlined in Chapter 1.

13.5 Upper balljoint stud bracket (A) (factory unit has rivets which must be drilled-out instead of bolts), and upper arm inner shaft attaching bolts (B)

10 Remove the jackstands and lower the vehicle.
11 Adjust caster, camber and toe-in as required.

14 Strut suspension sway bar link insulators — removal and installation

1 Raise the vehicle and support it on jackstands.
2 Remove the nut, washer and insulator from the top of the stabilizer bar bolt.
3 Remove the bolt, washers and spacers. Note their location for reinstallation.
4 Inspect the insulators for cracks or breakage and replace as necessary.
5 Install the stabilizer bar insulators by reversing the above procedure.
6 Tighten the attaching nut to specification.

15 Strut suspension sway bar — removal and installation

1 Raise the vehicle and support it on jackstands.
2 Loosen the bolt securing the sway bar to the sway bar link.
3 Loosen the bolts at the sway bar insulator attaching clamps.
4 When all tension has been removed from the sway bar bolts, complete their removal and lift out the sway bar.
5 Check the plastic bushings for grooves or cracks. Replace as necessary.
6 Installation is the reverse of removal with the following precautions:
7 Coat any rubber/metal junction with a rubber lubricant to avoid galling.
8 Torque the attaching brackets and stabilizer link bolts to specifications.

16 Strut suspension front coil spring — removal and installation

Note: *Extreme caution should be exercised during this procedure, as injury could result if the tension is suddenly released from the compressed spring.*

1 Raise the vehicle and support on jackstands.
2 Remove the front wheel(s).
3 Disconnect the stabilizer link from the lower A-arm.
4 Disconnect the steering coupler bolts.
5 Disconnect the tie-rod from the steering spindle, using a pickle fork tool or bearing puller.
6 Using a spring compressor, compress the spring. When installing the compressor, turn the end plates so as to hold as much of the spring as possible.

Fig. 10.16 Marking the spring compressor endplate position (Sec 16)

Fig. 10.17 Installing the new spring (Sec 16)

Fig. 10.18 Lower spring pigtail must be covering hole B and clearing hole A as shown (Sec 16)

7 Tighten the spring compressor until the spring is loose in the seat.
8 With an assistant's help, support the inboard end of the suspension arm and remove the two bolts securing it to the crossmember. A hydraulic jack is the safest method of providing support.
9 Carefully lower the jack to remove the spring.
10 If a new spring is to be installed, mark with chalk the spring compressor end plate position on the old spring so that the new spring can be marked and installed in the same position. Measure the distance between the marks so that the new spring can be compressed the same amount prior to installation. Carefully remove the compressor to relieve the spring tension.
11 Installation is the reverse of removal, with the following precautions:
12 Check that the spring is fully seated onto the spring perch before releasing the compressor. The lower end of the coil spring must be

Fig. 10.19 Modified MacPherson strut shock — sectional view (Sec 17)

located between the two holes in the lower spring pocket.
13 Torque the lower A-arm bolts and the tie-rod nut to specifications.
14 Check the front suspension for binding and loose bolts before driving the car.

---

17   Strut suspension strut — removal and installation

1   Raise the vehicle and support it on jackstands.
2   Insert the ignition key and turn to the unlock position to allow free movement of the front wheels.
3   Inside the engine compartment, on the top of the inner fender, loosen the strut mount nut. Use a screwdriver on the shaft to keep the strut from turning.
4   Remove the wheel assembly.
5   Remove the brake caliper, rotor and dust shield.
6   Remove the two lower nuts and bolts securing the strut to the spindle. Remove the upper strut nut. Lift the strut up to compress the rod, then pull down to remove it.

Fig. 10.20 Strut suspension upper mount — typical (Sec 17)

Fig. 10.21 Four-bar link coil rear suspension (Sec 19)

7 The struts cannot be rebuilt. Should there be evidence of leakage, or rust on the shaft or cracks, they must be replaced.
8 Installation is the reverse of removal.
9 Torque the strut upper nuts to specification.
10 Torque the lower strut mount bolts to specification.

18 Strut suspension spindle — removal and installation

1 Raise the vehicle and support it on jackstands.
2 Remove the wheel assembly, rotor, brake caliper and dust shield.
3 Remove the tie-rod end.
4 Remove the cotter pin from the balljoint nut.
5 Loosen the nut two turns, but do not remove the nut at this time.
6 Strike the side of the A-arm to relieve the stud pressure.
7 Position a floor jack under the A-arm and compress the spring until working clearance is obtained.
8 Remove the two nuts and bolts securing the spindle to the strut and the loosened balljoint nut. Remove the spindle.
9 Installation is the reverse of the removal sequence.
10 Place the spindle on the balljoint stud and install the nut finger tight.
11 Position the strut to the spindle and install the two bolts and nuts.
12 Tighten the balljoint nut.
13 Remove the floor jack.

14 Install the stabilizer link.
15 Attach the tie-rod and torque the nut to specification. Install the cotter pin.
16 Install the brake caliper, dust shield, rotor and wheel assembly.
17 Remove jackstands.

19 Rear suspension — general information

Coil spring type

Vehicles with coil springs in the rear are equipped with a four bar link suspension. The rear axle is suspended from the vehicle by two short upper arms to control lateral sway and two lower arms which control longitudinal axle movement.

The coil springs are connected between the lower suspension arm and the frame. The springs mount to an upper seat welded to the frame and a lower seat on the lower suspension arm. The shock absorbers are mounted between the upper shock tower in the fender well and the two lower shock brackets welded to the axle tube.

Leaf spring type

The rear suspension consists of leaf springs mounted to the rear axle by U-bolts. The shock absorbers are attached at the top to brackets on the chassis. The lower ends bolt to studs on the U-bolt plates.

STABILIZER BAR

VIEW A

VIEW A

Fig. 10.22 Typical stabilizer bar installation (Sec 19)

10

23-37 N·m
(17-27 LB·FT)

VIEW X

95-135 N·m
(70-100 LB·FT)

75-95 N·m
(55-70 LB·FT)

108-142 N·m
(80-105 LB·FT)

FRONT OF
VEHICLE

VIEW B

95-135 N·m
(70-100 LB·FT)

VIEW Y

108-142 N·m
(80-104 LB·FT)

Fig. 10.23 Rear suspension without stabilizer bar — exploded view (Sec 19)

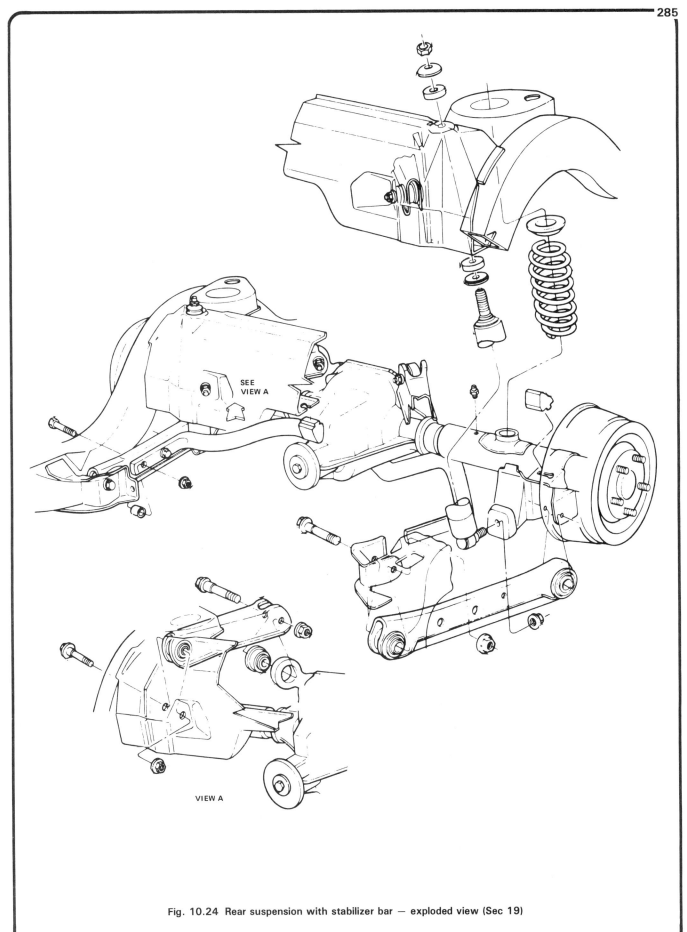

SEE
VIEW A

VIEW A

10

Fig. 10.24 Rear suspension with stabilizer bar — exploded view (Sec 19)

VIEW T

VIEW U

VIEW V

INSERT FROM
DRIVESHAFT SIDE ONLY

INSTALLATION
14-22 FT-LBS
(19-29 N·m)

INSTALLATION
14-22 FT-LBS
(19-29 N·m)

VIEW X

VIEW X

MODEL "H" AND MODEL "K"

VIEW U

VIEW T

VIEW V

VIEW W

VIEW Z

HD

70-110 FT-LB
(95-149 N·m)

VIEW Z
MODEL "H" AND MODEL "K"

Fig. 10.25 Typical leaf spring suspension (Versailles shown) (Sec 19)

20 Rear shock absorber — removal and installation

Coil spring type

Note: *Some later models may incorporate a Torx-type bolt which requires a special wrench.*

1 Raise the rear of the vehicle, support it securely on jackstands and remove the rear wheels.
2 Remove the shock absorber nuts from the lower end (photo) and compress the shock.
3 Remove the upper nut and withdraw the shock absorber from the vehicle.
4 Install the new shock absorber on the upper mounting and install the nuts finger tight.
5 Extend the shock absorber and attach it to the lower mount. Install all necessary washers and bushings before tightening the nuts.
6 Install the wheels and lower the vehicle.

Leaf spring type

7 Remove the lower end of the shock absorber from the spring plate.
8 Remove the top end of the shock from the upper mounting bracket. Compress the shock absorber and remove it.
9 Transfer all washers and bushings to the new shock absorber and install it in the reverse order of removal.

21 Rear suspension leaf spring — removal and installation

1 Raise the vehicle and support it securely on jackstands.
2 Remove the rear wheels.
3 Place a jack under the axle housing and raise it sufficiently to remove the weight from the spring.
4 Disconnect the lower end of the shock absorber and compress it upward and out of the way.

Fig. 10.26 Leaf spring suspension shackle components
(Sec 21)

Fig. 10.27 Leaf spring front hanger components (Sec 21)

20.2 Upper (A) and lower (B) rear shock absorber mounting bolts

5 Remove the nuts from the U-bolts and remove the U-bolts and spring plate.
6 Remove the rear shackle assembly.
7 Remove the front spring hanger bolt and remove the spring.
8 If the bushings in the spring eyes are distorted or worn and in need of replacement, it is recommended that this be left to your dealer or a properly equipped shop.
9 To install, place the spring in position under the axle and install the shackle assembly, with the nuts finger tight.
10 Place the spring front eye in the hanger and insert the bolt, tightening the nut finger tight.
11 Lower the jack so that the axle rests on the spring.
12 Install the U-bolts and plate.
13 Reconnect the shock absorber lower end.
14 Lower the axle until the spring is at its approximate ride height and tighten the front hanger nut and rear shackle bolts to specification.
15 Install the rear wheels and lower the jack.

22 Rear suspension coil spring — removal and installation

Note: *Springs must always be replaced in pairs.*
1 Raise the vehicle and support it securely on jackstands under the frame so that the rear suspension is fully extended. Remove the rear wheels.
2 Remove the rear stabilizer bar, if equipped.
3 Support the axle under the differential so that the shock absorbers are compressed about one inch.
4 With a jack under the lower suspension arm pivot bolt, remove the bolt and nut.
5 Slowly lower the jack to relieve the spring pressure. Remove the spring and insulator (if equipped).
6 To install, place the upper and lower spring insulators (if equipped) in position. Tape in place if necessary. Position the spring on the lower suspension arm spring seat so that the pigtail on the lower arm is at the rear and pointing toward the left side of the vehicle.
7 Raise the jack slowly until the spring is compressed and the pivot bolt holes are in alignment.
8 Install the pivot bolt and nut with the nut facing outwards. The manufacturer recommends using new bolts and nuts. Do not tighten the nuts until the vehicle weight is lowered onto the suspension.
9 Install the rear sway bar, if equipped.
10 Remove the support from the pivot point and axle and install the rear wheels.
11 Lower the vehicle so that its weight is resting on the suspension and tighten lower suspension arm pivot bolts.

10

23   Shock absorbers — inspection

1   The most common test of the shock absorber's damping is simply to bounce the corners of the vehicle several times and observe whether or not the car stops bouncing once the input is stopped. A slight rebound and settling indicates good damping, but if the vehicle continues to bounce several times, the shock absorbers must be replaced.

2   If your shock absorbers stand up to the bounce test, visually inspect the shock body for signs of fluid leakage, punctures or deep dents in the metal of the body. Replace any shock absorber which is leaking or damaged, in spite of proper damping indicated in the bounce test.

3   When you have removed a shock absorber, pull the piston rod out and push it back in several times to check for smooth operation throughout the travel of the piston rod. Replace the shock absorber if it gives any signs of hard or soft spots in the piston travel.

4   When you install a new shock absorber, pump the piston rod fully in and out several times to lubricate the seals and fill the hydraulic sections of the unit.

MacPherson strut type shock absorbers

5   Since these shocks constantly carry a side load, their dampening force is much higher on the vehicle than in the removed state. Therefore, the above bench test may reveal very little resistance compared to a conventional shock. This is a normal and acceptable condition.

6   Strut-type shocks should be replaced as a set if oil leakage is evident, usually indicated by a large amount of oily dirt. A thin, consistent oil film is normal.

24   Power steering — general description

1   The power steering systems available on models in this manual have a crankshaft driven pump which generates hydraulic power for a servo assisted steering gear.

2   The power steering pump incorporates an integral fluid reservoir.

3   Owing to the complexity of the power steering system it is recommended that repair or overhaul is entrusted to a specialist in this type of work.

25   Power steering pump — removal and installation

1   Disconnect the fluid return hose from the pump and drain the fluid from the pump reservoir. Disconnect the pressure hose from the pump. Plug the lines to prevent contamination.

2   Loosen the pump mounting bolts and move the pump toward the engine block to relieve tension on the drivebelt. After removing the belt, remove the pump from the car.

3   Installation is the reverse of the above procedure. Position the pump loosely on the bracket and tighten the adjusting bolt after installing the drivebelt and adjusting it to the correct tension.

4   Reinstall the pressure and return lines and fill the reservoir with an approved fluid. Start the engine and turn the steering wheel from lock to lock several times to distribute the fluid, then recheck the fluid level and top-off if necessary.

26   Steering gear – removal and installation

Recirculating – ball type
Manual steering

1   Raise the vehicle and support it securely on jackstands. Disconnect the negative cable at the battery.

2   Disconnect the flexible coupling in the steering shaft.

3   Remove the nut and lockwasher from the
Pitman arm and use a suitable puller to remove the Pitman arm.

4   Remove the steering gear attaching bolts and remove the steering gear. The steering gear can be rebuilt, but due to its complexity and the requirement for special tools, repair is best left to your dealer or a qualified shop.

5   To install, place the steering gear in position with the flexible coupling on the steering shaft, install the attaching bolts and tighten to specification.

6   Install the Pitman arm, washer and nut, tightening to specification.

7   Install the flexible coupling nuts and tighten to specification.

8   Reconnect the battery negative cable.

Fig. 10.28 Typical non-integral power steering system (Sec 24)

Fig. 10.29 Typical power steering pump installation (1984 shown) (Sec 25)

Fig. 10.30a Steering gear and linkage assembly (Sec 26)

RUBBER INSULATOR

NO. 2 CROSSMEMBER

INSULATOR WASHER

ROD END

BELLOWS

GRIP THE ROD IN THIS AREA
ONLY FOR SETTING TOE. DO
NOT GRIP ON THE TIE ROD
THREADS.

Fig. 10.30b Installation details of the rack-and-pinion
type steering gear (Sec 26)

10

Fig. 10.31   Ford integral power steering gear (Sec 26)

Power steering

9   Tag the pressure and return lines on the steering gear for future identification.

10   Disconnect the lines from the steering gear. Plug the lines and ports in the gear to prevent contamination.

11   Remove the bolts which secure the flexible coupling to the steering gear and column.

12   Raise the vehicle and remove the sector shaft attaching nut.

13   Remove the Pitman arm from the sector shaft, being careful not to damage the seal (photo).

14   Support the steering gear and remove the steering gear attaching bolts.

15   Remove the clamp bolt that holds the flexible coupling to the steering gear. Work the gear free of the flex coupling and remove the gear.

16   To install, slide the flex coupling into place on the steering shaft assembly. Turn the steering wheel so that the spokes are in a horizontal position.

17   Center the steering gear input shaft and slide the steering gear input shaft into the flex coupling and into place on the frame side rail. Install the attaching bolts.

18   Be sure that wheels are in the straight ahead position, then install the Pitman arm on the sector shaft. Install and tighten the sector shaft and attaching bolts.

19   Move the flex coupling into place on the input and steering col-umn shaft. Install the attaching bolts.

20   Connect the pressure and return lines to the steering gear. Tighten the line. Fill the reservoir as described in Chapter I. Turn the steering wheel from stop to stop to distribute the fluid.

21   Recheck the fluid level and add fluid if necessary.

22   Start the engine and turn the steering wheel from left to right and inspect for fluid leaks.

Rack-and-pinion type
Removal

23   Raise the front of the vehicle and support it securely on jack-stands. Apply the parking brake.

24   Place a drain plug under the steering gear (power steering only). Remove the power steering pressure and return lines and cap the ends to prevent excessive fluid loss and contamination.

25   Mark the relationship of the intermediate shaft flexible coupling to the steering gear input shaft. Remove the pinch bolt.

26   Separate the tie-rod-ends from the spindle arms.

27   Support the steering gear and remove the steering gear-to-frame mounting nuts and bolts. Lower the unit, separate the intermediate shaft from the steering gear input shaft and remove the steering gear from the vehicle.

Installation

28   Raise the steering gear into position and connect the intermediate shaft, aligning the marks.

29   Install the mounting bolts and washers and tighten the nuts to the specified torque.

30   Connect the tie-rod ends to the spindle arms. Tighten the nuts to the specified torque.

31   Install the intermediate shaft pinch bolt and tighten it to the specified torque.

32   Connect the power steering pressure and return hoses to the steering gear and fill the power steering pump reservoir with the recommended fluid (Chapter 1).

33   Lower the vehicle and bleed the steering system as outlined in Section 27.

---

27   Power steering – bleeding

The power steering system will only need bleeding in the event of air being introduced into the system, such as when lines have been disconnected or where a leakage has occured. To bleed the system:

1   Open the hood and check the fluid level in the fluid reservoir. Top up if necessary using the specified type of fluid.

2   If fluid is added, wait two minutes then run the engine at approximately 1500 rpm. Slowly turn the steering wheel from lock to lock, while checking and refilling the fluid until the level remains steady and no more bubbles appear in the reservoir. Do not hold the steering wheel in the far right or left positions.

26.13   Power steering gear Pitman arm-to-sector shaft attaching nut

Fig. 10.32   The steering wheel can be removed with a puller after removing the steering pad and retaining nut (Sec 28)

28.3   Mark the steering wheel hub and shaft to facilitate proper alignment when reinstalling the wheel

28.4   Removing the steering wheel with a puller

WHEEL LOCATING NOTCH

GROOVE ON STEEL HUB ON STEERING WHEEL MUST BE IN LINE WITH MARK ON TOP END OF STEERING SHAFT TO LINE UP STEERING WHEEL SPOKES PROPERLY — STANDARD AND OPTIONAL WHEEL.

Fig. 10.33 Steering wheel locating notch — later models only (Sec 28)

Fig. 10.34 Typical steering column assembly (Sec 29)

28   Steering wheel — removal and installation

1   Disconnect the negative cable at the battery.
2   Pull out on the steering wheel hub cover (2- and 3-spoke) or push the emblem out from behind (4-spoke).
3   After marking the hub and shaft for alignment (photo), remove and discard the steering wheel attaching nut.
4   Remove the steering wheel with a suitable puller. Do not strike the end of the steering column with a hammer or use a knock-off type of puller, as this will damage the collapsible steering column bearing (photo).
5   When reinstalling align the marks on the steering shaft with those on the wheel. Later models have an alignment notch.
6   Install a new steering wheel nut and tighten to specification.
7   Align the hub cover pins or springs with their holes or slots in the steering wheel and push into place.

29   Steering column — removal and installation

1   Disconnect the negative cable at the battery.
2   Remove the steering wheel.
3   Disconnect the flexible coupling at the steering input flange and disengage the safety strap assembly.
4   Remove the steering column trim shrouds.
5   On column shift models, disconnect the transmission shift rod from the selector lever. Using the proper tool, remove the grommet and replace it with a new one at reassembly.
6   Remove the steering column cover and hood release (if equipped) which is located directly under the column.
7   Disconnect all of the steering column switches and mark their positions for ease of reassembly.
8   Remove the screws attaching the dust boot to the dash panel.
9   Remove the nuts holding the column to the brake pedal support.
10 Lower the column to clear the mounting bolts. On column shift models, reach between the steering column and the instrument panel and lift the shift cable off the cleat on the shift lever. The column can now be pulled out so the U-joint assembly passes through the dash panel clearance hole.
11 When reinstalling the safety strap and bolt assemblies to the steering gear input shaft, make sure that the straps are positioned to prevent metal-to-metal contact. Also, the flexible coupling must not be distorted

10

UPPER

CYLINDER ASSY.

LUBRICATE END OF LOCK
CYLINDER

LEVER ASSY.

PRESS ENTIRE
SURFACE IN PLACE WITH
STICKY SIDE AGAINST
SWITCHES & THIS HOLE
OVER TURN SIGNAL
HANDLE SHANK.

LUBRICATE END OF
LEVER WITH ESB-M1C41-A
OR EQUIVALENT

GPD RELEASE
CABLE CLAMP

LOWER

SCREW

Fig. 10.35 Typical steering column shroud and control components (Sec 29)

when the bolts are tightened. By prying the shaft up or down with a suitable pry bar the insulator can be adjusted so that it is installed flat.
12 The rest of reinstallation is a reversal of removal. Be sure to install the dust boot over the steering shaft before inserting the shaft through the dash panel.

---

30 Ignition lock cylinder — replacement

1975 through 1981 models

1 Disconnect the negative cable at the battery.
2 On cars with fixed steering columns remove the trim pad from the steering wheel, then remove the steering wheel.
3 Insert a stiff length of wire into the hole in the lock cylinder housing. On cars with a tilt steering wheel this hole can be found on the outside of the steering column near the flasher button. It is not necessary to remove the steering wheel on tilt-type steering columns.
4 Place the gear shift lever in Park on cars with automatic transmission and in Reverse on cars with manual transmissions. Turn the ignition key to the On position.
5 Push in with the wire to release the lock cylinder. Remove the lock cylinder and wire.
6 Insert the new cylinder into the housing and turn it to the Off posi-

tion. This will lock the cylinder into place.
7 Reinstall the steering wheel and pad and connect the negative battery cable.

1982 through 1984 models

8 Remove the steering column assembly and the shift cane assembly on column shift equipped vehicles.
9 Remove the two screws attaching the turn signal switch to the lock cylinder housing and remove the switch. Remove the washer/wiper switch by removing the two screws. On fixed column vehicles remove the upper steering shaft bearing.
10 Remove the two bolts connecting the lock cylinder housing to the outer tube flange bracket. Turn the ignition key to the Start position and pull the actuator interlock out of the clearance hole in the tube. Lift the casting off the upper steering shaft and remove the ignition lock drive gear.
11 On vehicles with a tilt column remove the steering wheel and the upper conical spring bearing plate and C-clip ring. Move the tilt column to the uppermost position to unload the spring and remove the tilt pivot pins. Remove the upper casting from the lock cylinder housing and remove the bolt and nut attaching the lower U-joint shaft assembly to the steering column shaft. Remove the steering shaft assembly from the column by pulling the assembly out of the top end of the column.

LOCKING BUTTON
SNAP RETAINER

IGNITION SWITCH
ACTUATOR AND
STEERING WHEEL
LOCK PIN ASSEMBLY

T-BOLT RETAINING
NUTS (2) REQUIRED

TURN SIGNAL SWITCH

ROD TO IGNITION
SWITCH

MOUNTING SCREWS
(3) REQUIRED

HAZARD
WARNING
SWITCH

WIRE LOOM

SNAP RING
RETAINER

FLANGE CASTING

DRIVE GEAR

BEARING

MOUNTING SCREW

SNAP RING

KEY WARNING
BUZZER
TERMINAL

LOCK CYLINDER

Fig. 10.37 Lock cylinder assembly — 1982 and later (Sec 30)

Fig. 10.37 Lock cylinder assembly — 1982 and later
(Sec 30)

Remove the two bolts that connect the lock cylinder housing to the outer tube flange bracket. Turn the ignition key to the Start position and remove the ignition lock drive gear.

12 To install the lock cylinder housing on fixed column vehicles first install the ignition lock drive gear and actuator. Install the upper steering shaft bearing and sleeve and the retainer plate. Place the lock cylinder housing onto the steering column flange bracket in the same manner as it was removed. Turn the ignition key to the Start position to locate the actuator interlock through the clearance hole in the outer tube. Install and tighten the two bolts holding the lock cylinder housing to the bracket. Install the steering wheel attaching nut until the steering shaft is drawn up into the bearing enough to allow the installation of the snap ring. Remove the attaching bolt and install the snap ring in the groove on the upper shaft.

13 Install the turn signal switch and the washer/wiper switch.

14 Install the shift cane on column shift vehicles and install the steering column. On tilt column models installation is the reverse of removal. When installing the conical spring onto the upper shaft, compress the spring until it snaps into the upper groove. When reinstalling the lower U-joint shaft assembly into the lower steering column shaft, insert the attaching bolt through the column lower tube with the head of the bolt against the concave portion of the tube.

15 Install the steering column and the steering wheel.

---

31 Ignition switch — replacement

1975 through 1978

1 Disconnect the negative cable from the battery.

2 Remove the steering column shroud and detach the steering column from the brake support bracket.

3 Disconnect the switch wiring at the multiple plug and remove the two nuts that retain the switch to the steering column.

4 On models with column mounted gearshift levers, detach the switch plunger from the actuator rod and remove the switch. On models with console mounted gearshift levers the pin connecting the plunger to the actuator should be removed before removing the switch.

5 To reinstall the switch, place the lock mechanism at the top of the column with the switch in the Lock position. Place the automatic shift lever in Park and manual shift lever in Reverse. Turn the switch to Lock and remove the key. New switches are held in lock by plastic pins. To lock previously installed switches, pull the switch plunger out as far as you can then push it back to the first position. Insert a stiff,

10

small diameter wire in the locking hole at the top of the switch.

6   Connect the switch plunger to the switch actuator rod and position the switch on the column. Install the attaching nuts finger tight.

7   Move the switch up and down in various positions to locate the mid position of the rod and then tighten the nuts. After this has been done remove the locking pins or wire and attach the steering column to the brake support bracket.

8   Install the shroud.

1979 through 1984

9   Disconnect the negative battery cable and remove the upper shroud below the steering wheel by unsnapping the retaining clips. On tilt column models it is necessary to remove the attaching screws.

10 Disconnect the ignition switch connector and drill out the bolts holding the switch to the lock cylinder using a 1/8 inch drill.

11 An Easy-out tool can be used to remove the drilled out bolts.

12 Disengage the switch from the actuator pin.

13 Adjust the new ignition switch by sliding the carrier to the Lock position. Insert a small drill bit through the switch housing and into the carrier to restrict movement of the carrier. A new replacement comes with an adjusting pin already installed.

14 Turn the ignition to the Lock position and install the ignition switch on the actuator pin.

15 Install new break-off type bolts and tighten them until the heads break off.

16 Remove the drill bit or adjusting pin and connect all electrical connections and the negative battery cable.

17 Install the steering column shroud.

Chapter 11 Body

Contents

1 General information

As with other parts of the vehicle, proper maintenance of body components plays an important part in retention of the vehicle's market value. It is far less costly to handle small problems before they grow into larger ones. Information in this Chapter will tell you all you need to know to keep seals sealing, body panels aligned and general appearance up to par.

The vehicle body is of unitized, welded construction. Major body components which are particularly vulnerable in accidents are removable. It is often cheaper and less time consuming to replace an entire panel than it is to attempt a restoration of the old one. However, this must be decided on a case-by-case basis.

2 Body — maintenance

1   The condition of your vehicle's body is very important, because it is on this that the resale value will mainly depend. It is much more difficult to repair a neglected or damaged body than it is to repair mechanical components. The hidden areas of the body, such as the fender wells and the engine compartment, are equally important, although they obviously do not require as frequent attention as the rest of the body.

2   Once a year, or every 12000 miles, it is a good idea to have the underside of the body steam cleaned. All traces of dirt and oil will be removed and the underside can then be inspected carefully for rust, damaged brake lines, frayed electrical wiring, damaged cables and other problems. The front suspension components should be greased after completion of the cleaning and inspection.

3   At the same time, clean the engine and the engine compartment, using either a steam cleaner or a water soluble degreaser.

4   The fender wells should be given particular attention, as undercoating can peel away and stones and dirt thrown up by the tires can cause the paint to chip and flake, allowing rust to set in. If rust is found, clean down to the bare metal and apply an anti-rust paint.

5   The body should be washed once a week (or when dirty). Wet the vehicle thoroughly to soften the dirt, then wash it down with a soft sponge and plenty of clean, soapy water. If the dirt is not washed off very carefully it will, in time, wear down the paint.

6   Spots of tar or asphalt coating thrown up from the road should be removed with a cloth soaked in solvent.

7   Once every six months give the body and chrome trim a thorough wax coating. If a chrome cleaner is used to remove rust from any plated parts, remember that the cleaner also removes part of the chrome, so use it sparingly.

11

3   Roof covering and vinyl trim — maintenance

Under no circumstances try to clean any external vinyl trim or roof covering with detergents, caustic soap or petroleum based cleaners. Plain soap and water is all that is required, with a soft brush to clean dirt that may be ingrained. Wash the covering as frequently as the rest of the vehicle.

After cleaning, application of a high quality rubber and vinyl protectant will help prevent oxidation and cracking. This protectant can also be applied to all interior and exterior vinyl components, as well as to vacuum lines and rubber hoses, which often fail as a result of chemical degradation.

4   Upholstery and carpets — maintenance

1   Every three months remove the carpets or mats and clean the interior of the vehicle (more frequently if necessary). Vacuum the upholstery and carpets to remove loose dirt and dust.
2   If the upholstery is soiled, apply upholstery cleaner with a damp sponge and wipe it off with a clean, dry cloth.

5   Body repair — minor damage

See color photo sequence on pages 298 and 299

Repair of minor scratches

If the scratch is very superficial and does not penetrate to the metal of the body, repair is simple. Lightly rub the scratched area with a fine rubbing compound to remove loose paint and built-up wax. Rinse the area with clean water.

Apply touch-up paint to the scratch, using a small brush. Continue to apply thin layers of paint until the surface of the paint in the scratch is level with the surrounding paint. Allow the new paint at least two weeks to harden, then blend it into the surrounding paint by rubbing with a very fine rubbing compound. Finally, apply a coat of wax to the scratch area.

If the scratch has penetrated the paint and exposed the metal of the body, causing the metal to rust, a different repair technique is required. Remove all loose rust from the bottom of the scratch with a pocket knife, then apply rust-inhibiting paint to prevent the formation of rust in the future. Using a rubber or nylon applicator, coat the scratched area with glaze-type filler. If required, the filler can be mixed with thinner to provide a very thin paste, which is ideal for filling narrow scratches. Before the glaze filler in the scratch hardens, wrap a piece of smooth cotton cloth around the tip of a finger. Dip the cloth in thinner and then quickly wipe it along the surface of the scratch. This will ensure that the surface of the filler is slightly hollow. The scratch can now be painted over as described earlier in this section.

Repair of dents

When repairing dents, the first job is to pull the dent out until the affected area is as close as possible to its original shape. There is no point in trying to restore the original shape completely, as the metal in the damaged area will have stretched on impact and cannot be restored to its original contours. It is better to bring the level of the dent up to a point which is about 1/8-inch below the level of the surrounding metal. In cases where the dent is very shallow it is not worth trying to pull it out at all.

If the back side of the dent is accessible, it can be hammered out gently from behind using a soft-faced hammer. While doing this, hold a block of wood firmly against the opposite side of the metal to absorb the hammer blows and prevent the metal from being stretched.

If the dent is in a section of the body which has double layers, or some other factor that makes it inaccessible from behind, a different technique is required. Drill several small holes through the metal inside the damaged area, particularly in the deeper sections. Screw long, self-tapping screws into the holes just enough for them to get a good grip in the metal. Now the dent can be pulled out by pulling on the protruding heads of the screws with locking pliers.

The next stage of repair is the removal of paint from the damaged area and from an inch or so of the surrounding metal. This is easily done with a wire brush or sanding disk in a drill motor, although it can

be done just as effectively by hand with sandpaper. To complete the preparation for filling, score the surface of the bare metal with a screwdriver or the tang of a file (or drill small holes in the affected area). This will provide a very good grip for the filler material. To complete the repair, see the Section on filling and painting.

Repair of rust holes or gashes

Remove all paint from the affected area and from an inch or so of the surrounding metal, using a sanding disk or wire brush mounted in a drill motor. If these are not available, a few sheets of sandpaper will do the job just as effectively. With the paint removed you will be able to determine the severity of the corrosion and decide whether to replace the whole panel, if possible, or repair the affected area. New body panels are not as expensive as most people think and it is often quicker to install a new panel than to repair large areas of rust.

Remove all trim pieces from the affected area (except those which will act as a guide to the original shape of the damaged body, i.e. headlight shells, etc.). Using metal snips or a hacksaw blade, remove all loose metal and any other metal that is badly affected by rust. Hammer the edges of the hole in to create a slight depression for the filler material.

Wire brush the affected area to remove the powdery rust from the surface of the metal. If the back of the rusted area is accessible, treat it with rust-inhibiting paint.

Before filling is done, block the hole in some way. This can be done with sheet metal riveted or screwed into place, or by stuffing the hole with wire mesh.

Once the hole is blocked off, the affected area can be filled and painted (see the following sub-section on filling and painting).

Filling and painting

Many types of body fillers are available, but generally speaking, body repair kits which contain filler paste and a tube of resin hardener are best for this type of repair work. A wide, flexible plastic or nylon applicator will be necessary for imparting a smooth and contoured finish to the surface of the filler material.

Mix a small amount of filler on a clean piece of wood or cardboard (use the hardener sparingly). Follow the manufacturer's instructions on the package; otherwise the filler will set incorrectly.

Using the applicator, apply the filler paste to the prepared area. Draw the applicator across the surface of the filler to achieve the desired contour and to level the filler surface. As soon as a contour that approximates the original is achieved, stop working the paste. If you continue, the paste will begin to stick to the applicator. Continue to add thin layers of filler paste at 20 minute intervals until the level of the filler is just above the surrounding metal.

Once the filler has hardened the excess can be removed with a body file. From then on, progressively finer grades of sandpaper should be used, starting with a 180-grit paper and finishing with 600-grit wet-or-dry paper. Always wrap the sandpaper around a flat rubber or wooden block, otherwise the surface of the filler will not be completely flat. During the sanding of the filler surface, the wet-or-dry paper should be periodically rinsed in water. This will ensure that a very smooth finish is produced in the final stage.

At this point the repair area should be surrounded by a ring of bare metal, which in turn should be encircled by the finely feathered edge of good paint. Rinse the repair area with clean water until all of the dust produced by the sanding operation is gone.

Spray the entire area with a light coat of primer. This will reveal any imperfections in the surface of the filler. Repair the imperfections with fresh filler paste or glaze filler and once more smooth the surface with sandpaper. Repeat this spray-and-repair procedure until you are satisfied that the surface of the filler and the feathered edge of the paint are perfect. Rinse the area with clean water and allow it to dry completely.

The repair area is now ready for painting. Spray painting must be carried out in a warm, dry, windless and dust-free atmosphere. These conditions can be created if you have access to a large indoor work area, but if you are forced to work in the open, you will have to pick the day very carefully. If you are working indoors, dousing the floor in the work area with water will help settle the dust which would otherwise be in the air. If the repair area is confined to one body panel, mask off the surrounding panels. This will help minimize the effects of a slight mismatch in paint color. Trim pieces such as chrome strips, door handles, etc., will also need to be masked off or removed. Use masking tape and several thicknesses of newspaper for the masking operations.

Before spraying, shake the paint can thoroughly, then spray a test area until the spray painting technique is mastered. Cover the repair area with a thick coat of primer. The thickness should be built up using several thin layers of primer rather than one thick one. Using 600-grit wet-or-dry sandpaper, rub down the surface of the primer until it is very smooth. While doing this, the work area should be thoroughly rinsed with water and the wet-or-dry sandpaper periodically rinsed as well. Allow the primer to dry before spraying additional coats.

Spray on the top coat, again building up the thickness by using several thin layers of paint. Begin spraying in the center of the repair area and then, using a circular motion, work out until the whole repair area and about two inches of the surrounding original paint is covered. Remove all masking material 10 to 15 minutes after spraying on the

final coat of paint. Allow the new paint at least two weeks to harden, then use a very fine rubbing compound to blend the edges of the new paint into the existing paint. Finally, apply a coat of wax.

6 Body repair — major damage

1   Major damage must be repaired by an auto body shop equipped to perform unibody repairs. These shops have available the specialized equipment required to do the job properly.

2   If the damage is extensive, the underbody must be checked for

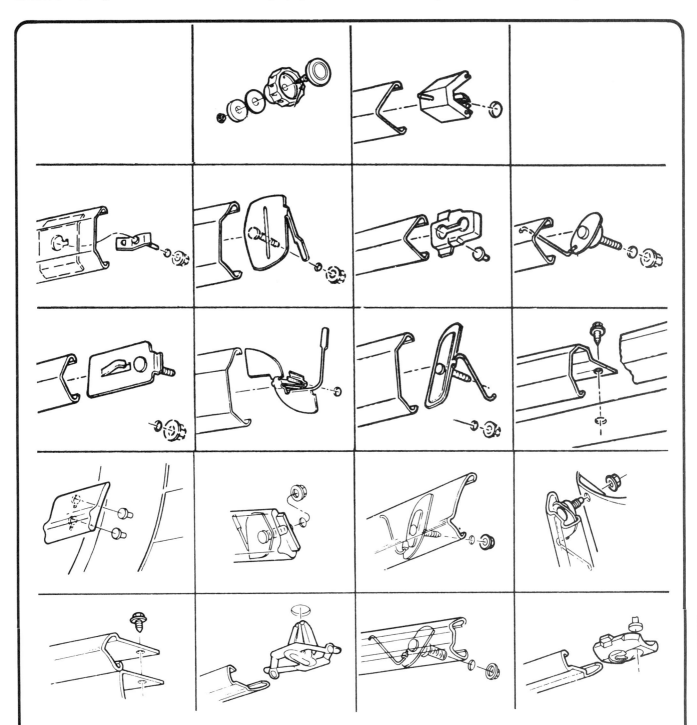

Fig. 11.1 Typical Ford exterior trim attachments. New clips are available should you destroy them while removing the trim prior to performing body repairs. Note that some versions require access from behind (Sec 5)

11

These photos illustrate a method of repairing simple dents. They are intended to supplement *Body repair - minor damage* in this Chapter and should not be used as the sole instructions for body repair on these vehicles.

1   If you can't access the backside of the body panel to hammer out the dent, pull it out with a slide-hammer-type dent puller. In the deepest portion of the dent or along the crease line, drill or punch hole(s) at least one inch apart . . .

2   . . . then screw the slide-hammer into the hole and operate it. Tap with a hammer near the edge of the dent to help 'pop' the metal back to its original shape. When you're finished, the dent area should be close to its original contour and about 1/8-inch below the surface of the surrounding metal

3   Using coarse-grit sandpaper, remove the paint down to the bare metal. Hand sanding works fine, but the disc sander shown here makes the job faster. Use finer (about 320-grit) sandpaper to feather-edge the paint at least one inch around the dent area

4   When the paint is removed, touch will probably be more helpful than sight for telling if the metal is straight. Hammer down the high spots or raise the low spots as necessary. Clean the repair area with wax/silicone remover

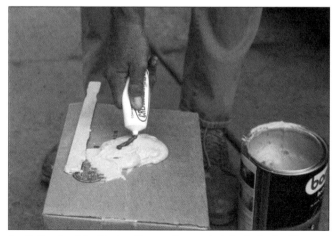

5   Following label instructions, mix up a batch of plastic filler and hardener. The ratio of filler to hardener is critical, and, if you mix it incorrectly, it will either not cure properly or cure too quickly (you won't have time to file and sand it into shape)

6   Working quickly so the filler doesn't harden, use a plastic applicator to press the body filler firmly into the metal, assuring it bonds completely. Work the filler until it matches the original contour and is slightly above the surrounding metal

7 Let the filler harden until you can just dent it with your fingernail. Use a body file or Surform tool (shown here) to rough-shape the filler

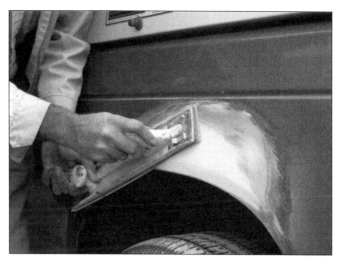

8 Use coarse-grit sandpaper and a sanding board or block to work the filler down until it's smooth and even. Work down to finer grits of sandpaper - always using a board or block - ending up with 360 or 400 grit

9 You shouldn't be able to feel any ridge at the transition from the filler to the bare metal or from the bare metal to the old paint. As soon as the repair is flat and uniform, remove the dust and mask off the adjacent panels or trim pieces

10 Apply several layers of primer to the area. Don't spray the primer on too heavy, so it sags or runs, and make sure each coat is dry before you spray on the next one. A professional-type spray gun is being used here, but aerosol spray primer is available inexpensively from auto parts stores

11 The primer will help reveal imperfections or scratches. Fill these with glazing compound. Follow the label instructions and sand it with 360 or 400-grit sandpaper until it's smooth. Repeat the glazing, sanding and respraying until the primer reveals a perfectly smooth surface

12 Finish sand the primer with very fine sandpaper (400 or 600-grit) to remove the primer overspray. Clean the area with water and allow it to dry. Use a tack rag to remove any dust, then apply the finish coat. Don't attempt to rub out or wax the repair area until the paint has dried completely (at least two weeks)

proper alignment or the vehicle's handling characteristics may be adversely affected and other components may wear at an accelerated rate.

3   Due to the fact that on many models major body components (hood, fenders, etc.) are separate and replaceable units, any seriously damaged components should be replaced rather than repaired. Sometimes these components can be found in a wrecking yard that specializes in used vehicle components (often at considerable savings over the cost of new parts).

7   Hinges and locks — maintenance

Every 3000 miles or three months, the door, hood and rear hatch hinges should be lubricated with a few drops of oil and the locks treated with dry graphite lubricant. The door and rear hatch striker plates should also be given a thin coat of grease to reduce wear and ensure free movement.

8   Doors — alignment

1   The door hinge bolt holes are elongated or enlarged so that the hinge and door alignment can be accomplished.
2   Loosen the hinge bolts just enough so that the door can be moved with a padded pry bar.
3   After the door has been adjusted, tighten the hinge bolts and check the door fit.
4   Repeat this operation until the proper fit is obtained.
5   After the alignment is made, check the striker plate for proper closing.

9   Door latch striker — removal, installation and adjustment

1   Use a pair of locking pliers to unscrew the door latch striker stud.
2   The striker stud may be adjusted vertically and laterally as well as fore-and-aft.
3   The latch striker must not be used to compensate for door misalignment.
4   The door latch striker can be shimmed to obtain the correct clearance between the latch and striker.
5   The clearance can be checked by cleaning the latch jams and striker area and applying a thin layer of dark grease to the striker. Close and open the door, noting the pattern of the grease.
6   Move the striker assembly laterally to provide a flush fit at the door and pillar or quarter panel.
7   Tighten the striker stud after adjustment.

10   Door latch assembly — removal and installation

Front door
1   Remove the door trim and water shield.
2   Disconnect the rod ends from the latch. Because of its configuration, the remote link and latch-to-lock rod cannot be removed.
3   Remove the lock cylinder rod from the cylinder lever.
4   Remove the screws attaching the latch assembly to the door and remove the latch.
5   Remove the remote link and latch-to-cylinder rods.
6   Lock the cylinder rod by installing the remote link and latch.
7   Position the latch in the door and install the attaching screws.
8   Connect the latch-to-cylinder rod to the lock cylinder lever.
9   Connect the remaining rods and check the latch operation.
10   Reinstall the water shield and trim panel.

Rear door
11   Remove the trim panel and water shield.
12   Disconnect the rear door latch actuating rod from the latch assembly.
13   Remove the screw which attaches the door latch bellcrank and remove the bellcrank.
14   Remove the screws retaining the door latch and remove the latch.

Fig. 11.2 Front door adjustment and lubrication points (Sec 8)

Fig. 11.3 Rear door adjustment and lubrication points (Sec 8)

Fig. 11.4 Door latch striker adjustment (Sec 9)

Fig. 11.5 Door latch remote control assembly (Sec 13)

Fig. 11.6 Door latch remote control — close-up view
(Sec 13)

15 To install, place the latch assembly in position and install the attaching screws.
16 Connect the door latch actuating rod.
17 Assemble the door latch bellcrank to the push button rod control
link and install the bellcrank to the door inner panel.
18 Check the operation of the latch assembly.
19 Install the door water shield and trim.

11 Door hinges — removal and installation

1 Remove the door.
2 Mark the location of the hinge on the door, remove the bolts and
lift away the hinges.
3 Repeat this procedure for the body mounted hinges.
4 Installation is a reversal of removal. If new hinges are installed it
will probably be necessary to align the door as described elsewhere
in this Chapter.

12 Doors — removal and installation

1 Use a pencil or scribe to mark the hinge location for ease of
reinstallation.
2 With an assistant supporting the weight of the door, remove the
upper and lower hinge retaining bolts. Lift the door away and stand
it on an old blanket.
3 Installation is a reversal of removal, using the marks scribed around
the hinges in Step 1 as a guide. If it is necessary to realign the door,
refer to the appropriate Section in this Chapter.

13 Door latch remote control — removal and installation

1 Remove the door trim panel and water shield.
2 Remove the three attaching nuts and disengage the control
assembly.
3 To disengage the assembly from the diamond shaped slot in the
inner door panel, squeeze the remote rod clip and then free the rod.
Remove the assembly from the door panel.
4 To install, place the remote control on the rod and push the
assembly into the door panel. Install the attaching nuts.
5 Squeeze the rod clip and install it into the diamond shaped hole.
6 Check the mechanism for proper operation.
7 Install the water shield and door trim panel.

11

Fig. 11.7 Typical door trim panel installation (Sec 14)

Fig. 11.8 Door outside handle and latch mechanism. Ford shown — Mercury similar (Sec 15)

Fig. 11.9 Door weatherstrip installation should begin at point A (Sec 16)

14 Door trim panel — removal and installation

1 Remove the door handle and cup.
2 Remove the window crank.
3 Remove the armrest.
4 Use a screwdriver to pry the panel away from the door and remove the panel.
5 Carefully peel the water shield away from the door inner panel.
6 To install, position the water shield against the inner panel so that the adhesive on the back aligns with the adhesive on the door and press into place.
7 The rest of installation is the reverse of removal.

15 Door outside handle — removal and installation

1 Remove the door trim and water shield.
2 Disconnect the door latch activating rod from the door outside handle.
3 Prop the door handle open with a piece of 1/2-inch by 4-inch wood to expose the two blind rivets which retain the handle.
4 Use a drift punch to punch out the center of each rivet. Drill out the remainder of the rivet with a 1/4-inch drill, taking care not to enlarge the hole.
5 Remove the door handle.
6 To install, place the handle in position with the wood underneath and the holes aligned.
7 Install 2-1/4 by 1/2-inch blind oval head rivets or 2-1/4 by 20 by 3/4-inch weld studs with nuts and washers.
8 Remove the wood block and check the door handle operation.
9 Install the trim panel and water shield.

16 Weatherstripping — removal and installation

1 Remove the old weatherstripping by pulling it away from the door

to break it loose from the adhesive.
2 Clean out the old adhesive.
3 Apply new adhesive.
4 Press the new weatherstripping into position until it is secure.
5 Note that the new weatherstripping should be cut longer than necessary and then compressed to insure a proper seal.

17 Hood — removal and installation

1 Raise the hood.
2 Place protective pads along the edges of the engine compartment to prevent damage to the painted surfaces.
3 Scribe or paint lines around the mounting brackets so the hood can be installed in the same position.
4 Apply white paint around the bracket-to-hood bolts so they can be aligned quickly and accurately during installation.
5 With an assistant supporting the weight, remove the bracket bolts and detach the hood from the vehicle.
6 Installation is the reverse of removal. Be sure to align the brackets and bolts with the marks made prior to removal.

18 Hood hinges — removal and installation

1 Open the hood and support it in the open position.
2 Remove the hood.
3 Scribe around the hinge housing with a pencil or scribe for ease of installation.
4 Remove the bolts securing the hinge to the body and remove the hinge.
5 Installation is the reverse of removal.

Fig. 11.10 Typical hood hinge and support components
(Sec 17)

Fig. 11.11 Hood latch and cable assembly (Sec 19)

11

Fig. 11.12 Luggage compartment latch and lock assembly — earlier version (Sec 23)

19   Hood latch — removal, installation and adjustment

1   Open the hood and support it in the open position.
2   Remove the hood latch cable retainer plate and disengage the cable from the hood latch assembly.
3   Remove the latch attaching screws and remove the latch.
4   Installation is the reverse of removal. Do not fully tighten the latch screws until adjustment is made.
5   The hood latch can be adjusted from side-to-side to align it with the hood latch hook. It can also be adjusted up and down to obtain a flush fit between the hood and fenders.
6   Move the hood latch from side-to-side until it is properly aligned with the opening in the hood inner panel.
7   Loosen the hood bumper lock nuts and lower the bumpers.
8   Move the latch up and down until the proper fit is obtained when the hood is pulled up. Tighten the hood latch screws.
9   Raise the hood bumpers to eliminate any hood looseness and then tighten the bumper lock nuts.

20   Hood latch control cable — removal and installation

1   Prop the hood securely in the open position.
2   Remove the hood latch cable retainer screws, plate and cable clip.
3   Disengage the cable and ferrule from the latch assembly.
4   Remove the cable retaining clips.
5   From inside the vehicle, remove the bracket and screws and carefully pull the cable assembly through the retaining wall.
6   To install, insert the cable assembly through the retaining wall and seat the grommet securely.
7   Install the cable mounting bracket and screws.
8   Route the cable and install the retaining clips.
9   Install the cable clip and hood latch retaining plate.
10 Prior to closing the hood, check the cable release for proper operation.

21   Trunk lid — removal and installation

1   Support the trunk lid in the open position.

Fig. 11.13 Luggage compartment latch and lock assembly — later version (Sec 23)

2   Remove the screws securing the hinges to the trunk lid.
3   With the help of an assistant, lift the trunk lid from the vehicle.
4   Installation is the reverse of removal. It may be necessary to adjust the position of the trunk lid after installation.

22   Trunk lid — adjustment

1   The trunk lid can be moved fore-and-aft by loosening the hinge to lid securing screws.
2   The up-and-down adjustment is obtained by adding or subtracting shims between the hinge and lid.

23   Trunk lid latch and lock — removal and installation

1   Open the trunk lid and scribe around any component which could affect adjustment for ease of installation.

Fig. 11.14 Torsion bar loading and adjustment (Sec 24)

Fig. 11.15 Station wagon liftgate latch and lock assembly (Sec 25)

2   Remove the lock cylinder retainer screws, rivets and retainer.
3   Remove the latch attaching screws and latch.

24   Trunk lid torsion bar — adjustment

1   The trunk lid should open when the latch is released. If not, the torsion bar tension should be increased. If the lid opens with too much force, the torsion bar tension is excessive and must be decreased.
2   Prop the trunk lid open with a long piece of wood during torsion bar adjustment.
3   Grasp the torsion bar near the adjustment slot with a suitable tool, such as locking pliers, and move it to the appropriate slot to increase or decrease tension. **Caution:** *Be extremely careful. The torsion bar is under considerable pressure.*
4   After adjusting one torsion bar, check the trunk lid operation before adjusting the other bar.
5   After adjustment, the difference between the right or left side torsion bar ends should not be more than one slot.

25   Station wagon liftgate latch and lock — removal and installation

1   Open the liftgate and support it.

2   Remove the trim panel.
3   Remove the license plate holder.
4   Remove the latch and cover assembly.
5   Remove the retainer which holds the lock cylinder in place and remove the lock cylinder.
6   Installation is the reverse of removal. It may be necessary to adjust the components after installation for proper action.

26   Station wagon liftgate — adjustment

1   Remove the upper rear interior garnish molding and loosen the hinges slightly to gain access to the header roof panel attaching nut and washer.
2   Adjust the hinge as necessary to obtain proper closing and fit and reinstall the headliner and garnish molding.

27   Station wagon gas cylinder liftgate assist rod — removal and installation

1   Open the liftgate and support it.
2   Use a small screwdriver to push the locking wedge out of the ball socket or unsnap the locking spring of the lift assembly, depending on design.

11

Fig. 11.16 Station wagon liftgate hinge adjustments are
made at the header roof panel (Sec 26)

3   Detach the opposite end of the rod in the same manner.
4   Remove the assist rod.
5   To install, place the rod in position on the ball socket and push
the locking wedge or ball socket at first one end, then the other.
6   Close the liftgate and check for proper operation.

28 Door window glass — adjustment

1   Remove the door trim panel and water shield.
2   For fore-and-aft adjustment, loosen the run and bracket assembly
upper attaching screws and adjust the glass as necessary. Tighten the
screws.
3   For in and out adjustment, lower the glass two inches, then loosen
the lower guide screws. Move the top of the glass in or out until the
proper position in the run is obtained and tighten the screws.
4   Install the water shield and trim panel.

Fig. 11.17 Station wagon liftgate assist rod and gas
cylinder assemblies (Sec 27)

GLASS

VIEW A

VIEW C

VIEW B

RIVET

REGULATOR
ASSEMBLY

NUT AND WASHER
ASSEMBLY

RUN AND
BRACKET ASSEMBLY

RUN ASSEMBLY

GLASS

VIEW A

RETAINER
ASSEMBLY

GLASS

SPACER

RIVET

BRACKET
ASSEMBLY

VIEW B

.10" APPROX. DIM.
INSIDE & OUTSIDE

WEATHERSTRIP
ASSEMBLY

VIEW D

INNER & OUTER BELT
W/STRIPS MUST BE
DRIVEN DOWN UNTIL
THE ATTACHING CLIPS
FULLY SEAT THEM—
SELVES ON THE BOT-
TOM OF THE SLOTS.

VIEW D

WEATHERSTRIP
ASSEMBLY

WEATHERSTRIP
ASSEMBLY

VIEW C

R2667-C

Fig. 11.18 Front door window mechanism — models without vent windows (Sec 29)

VIEW A

SCREW

VENT

SECTION B

SECTION C

BRACKET

SECTION D

VIEW F

.10

APPROX. DIM.
INSIDE & OUTSIDE

SECTION E

F

REGULATOR
ASSY.

BRACKET

RIVET

REGULATOR

A

B

C

E

D

NUT AND WASHER
ASSY.

RUN AND BRACKET
ASSY.

Fig. 11.19 Front door window mechanism — models with vent windows (Sec 29)

11

29   Front door window glass — removal and installation

1   Remove the door trim panel and water shield.
2   Remove the screws attaching the glass stabilizers and remove the stabilizers.
3   Use a drift punch to remove the center pins retaining the glass. Drill out the remainder of the rivets using a 1/4-inch drill bit.
4   Push out the rivets and remove the glass.
5   To install, snap the plastic retainer and spacer assembly onto the glass with the metal retainer on the outside.
6   Place the glass in position to the bracket and install three 1/4-inch rivets to fasten the glass to the bracket. As an alternative, 1/4-inch by 1-inch bolts with nuts can be used in place of rivets.
7   Install the glass stabilizer and adjust the assembly.
8   Install the water shield and trim.

30   Windshield, stationary quarter window and rear glass — removal and installation

   The windshield, stationary quarter window and rear glass on all models are sealed in place with a special butyl compound. Removal of the existing sealant requires the use of an electric knife specially made for the operation, and glass replacement is a complex operation.
   In view of this, it is not recommended that stationary glass removal be attempted by the home mechanic. If replacement is necessary due to breakage or leakage, the work should be referred to your dealer or a qualified glass or body shop.

31   Front door window regulator — removal and installation

1   With the glass in the full up position, remove the door trim panel and water shield.
2   If equipped with power windows, disconnect the negative cable at the battery and remove the motor.
3   Use a drift punch to remove the centers from the regulator rivets and then drill out the remainder with a 1/4-inch drill bit.
4   Remove the regulator arm from the glass bracket.
5   Remove the regulator from the door.
6   If equipped with power windows, place the complete regulator assembly in a vise and drill a 5/16-inch hole through both the regulator sector gear and plate. Install a 1/4-inch bolt with nut so that the sector gear can't move when the motor and drive assembly are removed. Remove the motor assembly and install it on the new regulator, using a T-bar tool to release the counter balance spring.
7   Prior to assembly, lubricate the window mechanism with polyethylene grease.
8   Install the regulator mounting nut and retainer assemblies and the motor support bracket (if equipped).
9   Place the regulator in position on the door and insert the roller into the glass bracket channel.
10   Install the regulator to the inner panel, using 1/4-inch by 1-inch screws with washers or 1/4-inch blind rivets.
11   Connect the motor wires on power window equipped models.
12   Check the window mechanism for proper operation.
13   Install the water shield and door trim panel.

32   Rear door window glass — removal and installation

1   Remove the door trim and water shield.
2   Remove the three screws at the weatherstripping belt line.
3   Support the glass and remove the center of the attaching rivets with a punch, drilling out the remainder with a 1/4-inch drill bit.
4   Remove the glass support and remove the glass.
5   Install the nylon glass protectors.
6   Place the glass in the door and install the glass bracket to the glass, using 1/4-inch by 1-inch bolts with nuts.
7   Install the down stop bracket to the inner panel, using 1/4-inch hex head bolts.
8   Adjust the stabilizers and glass to fit properly in the opening.

Fig. 11.20 Rear door with stationary vent glass — sectional view (Sec 32)

9   Install the belt line weatherstripping.
10 Install the water shield and door trim panel.

33   Rear door window regulator — removal and installation

1   Remove the door trim panel and water shield.
2   Support the window glass in the full up position. On power window equipped models, disconnect the negative cable at the battery and the motor wires.
3   Drive out the center pin of the regulator retaining rivets with a punch and then drill out the remainder of the rivet with a 1/4-inch drill bit.
4   Disengage the regulator arm from the glass bracket and remove the regulator assembly from the door.
5   On power window equipped models, place the regulator in a vise, remove the motor and drive and install them on the new regulator.
6   Lubricate the window mechanism with polyethylene grease prior to installation.
7   Install the regulator through the access hole in the inner panel.
8   Place the regulator through the access hole in the inner panel.
9   Install 3-1/4 by 1/2-inch bolts with nuts and washers to attach the regulator to the inner panel.
10 Check the window mechanism for proper operation.
11 Install the water shield and door trim panel.
12 Reconnect the battery negative cable on power window equipped models.

34   Console — removal and installation

1   Open the console and remove the attaching screws.
2   Disconnect any wiring connectors and remove the console

Fig. 11.21 Rear window door glass installation (Sec 32)

Fig. 11.22 Floor console assembly (Sec 34)

11

Fig. 11.23 Instrument panel trim pad installation (Sec 35)

Fig. 11.24 Instrument panel pad and components (Sec 35)

assembly from the vehicle.

3   Installation is a reversal of removal, taking care to connect the wiring connectors.

35   Instrument panel trim pad — removal and installation

1   Remove the screws from each defroster opening.

2   Along the lower edge of the pad, remove the retaining screws.

3   Pull the pad and upper finish panel toward the rear and withdraw them from the instrument panel.

4   To install, place the pad and upper finish panel in position on the instrument panel, align the screw holes and install the screws.

36   Front and rear bumpers — removal and installation

1   Scribe around the bumper isolator attaching bolts for ease of instal-

lation. Remove the bolts and, with the help of an assistant, remove the bumper, making sure to note the number and order of removal of the spacers.

2   If the bumper is to be replaced, transfer the bumper guards, pads and license plate bracket to the new bumper. To avoid damage to the license plate bracket tabs, squeeze them together during removal. On rear bumpers, remove the two license plate light screws and remove the lights. On some models it may be necessary to remove the rear stone deflectors.

3   To install, with an assistant holding the bumper in place to the isolators, install the bolts and tighten to specification.

37   Radiator grille — removal and installation

1   Remove the attaching screws and withdraw the grille assembly from the vehicle.

2   To install, position the grille to the opening and reinstall the screws.

Fig. 11.25 Stone deflector installation — rear shown, front similar (Sec 36)

Fig. 11.26 Front bumper components (Sec 36)

11

ISOLATOR
AND BRACKET

SCREW AND
WASHER

SPACER (USE
AS REQ'D.)

REINFORCEMENT
ASSY.

SHIELD

DRIVE PIN

BRACKET

BOLT

NUT

U-NUT

REAR BUMPER

PAD

NUT

BOLT
ASSEMBLY

BRACKET

GUARD ASSEMBLY

PAD

Fig. 11.27 Rear bumper components (Sec 36)

SCREW AND WASHER

HOUSING
ASSEMBLY

HOOD BUMPER

HOOD BUMPER

SCREW

NUT

SUPPORT

SCREW

NUT

HEADLAMP
DOOR

SCREW

GRILLE
ASSEMBLY

GRILLE
ASSEMBLY

PANEL
ASSEMBLY

SCREW

SCREW

Fig. 11.28 Radiator grille components (Sec 37)

Chapter 12   Chassis electrical system

Refer to Chapter 13 for information related to 1985 and later models

Contents

1   General information

This Chapter covers service and repair procedures for electrical components not included in Chapter 5, *Engine Electrical System*. Look in this Chapter for information concerning wiring, lighting and electrically driven accessories.

Electrical systems on vehicles covered in this manual are of the 12-volt negative ground type. The vehicle's electrical components draw power from a lead/acid battery, the charge of which is maintained by the alternator. **Warning:** *When servicing any electrical component or performing major non-electrical procedures, disconnect the negative cable at the battery to prevent electrical short-circuiting and fires.*

2   Electrical troubleshooting — general information

A typical electrical circuit consists of the component, any switches, relays, motors, etc. related to that component and the wiring and connectors that connect the component to both the battery and the chassis. To aid in locating a problem in any electrical circuit, representative wiring diagrams are included at the end of this manual.

Before tackling any troublesome electrical circuit, first study the appropriate diagrams to get a complete understanding of what makes up that individual circuit. Trouble spots, for instance, can often be narrowed down by noting if other components related to that circuit are operating properly or not. If several components or circuits fail at one time, chances are the problem lies in the fuse or ground connection, as several circuits often are routed through the same fuse and ground connections.

Electrical problems often stem from simple causes, such as loose or corroded connections, a blown fuse or a melted fusible link. Prior to any electrical troubleshooting always visually check the condition of the fuses, wires and connections in the problem circuit.

If testing instruments are going to be utilized, use the diagrams to plan ahead of time where you will make the necessary connections in order to accurately pinpoint the trouble spot.

The basic tools needed for electrical troubleshooting include a circuit tester or voltmeter (a 12-volt bulb with a set of test leads can also be used), a continuity tester (which includes a bulb, battery and set of test leads) and a jumper wire, preferably with a circuit breaker incorporated, which can be used to bypass electrical components.

Voltage checks should be performed if a circuit is not functioning properly. Connect one lead of a circuit tester to either the negative battery terminal or a known good ground. Connect the other lead to the circuit being tested, preferably near to the battery or fuse. If the bulb of the tester goes on, voltage is reaching that point, which means the part of the circuit between that point and the battery is problem free. Continue checking along the entire circuit in the same fashion. When you reach a point where no voltage is present, the problem lies between there and the last good test point. Most of the time the problem is due to a loose connection. Keep in mind that some circuits receive voltage only when the ignition key is in the Accessory or Run position.

A method of finding shorts in a circuit is to remove the fuse and connect a test light or voltmeter in its place. With the component being energized by that circuit shut off, there should be no load in the circuit. Move the wiring harness from side-to-side while watching the test light. If the bulb goes on, there is a short to ground somewhere in that area, probably where insulation has rubbed off of a wire. The same test can be performed on other components of the circuit, including the switch.

A ground check should be done to see if a component is grounded properly. Disconnect the battery and connect one lead of a self-powered test light, such as a continuity tester, to a known good ground. Connect the other lead to the wire or ground connection being tested. If the bulb goes on, the ground is good. If the bulb does not go on, the ground is not good.

A continuity check is performed to see if a circuit, section of circuit or individual component is passing electricity properly. Disconnect the battery and connect one lead of a self-powered test light to the battery side of the circuit. Connect the other lead of the test light to a good ground. If the bulb goes on, there is continuity, which means the circuit is passing electricity properly. Switches can be checked in the same way.

Remember that all electrical circuits are composed of electricity running from the battery, through the wires, switches, relays, etc. to the electrical component (light bulb, motor, etc.). From there it is run to the body or frame (ground) where it is passed back to the battery. Any electrical problem is an interruption in the flow of electricity to and from the battery.

12

Fig. 12.1 Typical fuse panel layout (Sec 3)

Fig. 12.2 Be sure the replacement fusible link is the proper gauge before splicing it into the circuit (Sec 4)

3 Fuses — general information

The electrical circuits of the vehicle are protected by a combination of fuses, circuit breakers and fusible links. The fuse block is located on the underside of the instrument panel on the driver's side as shown in the accompanying illustration. Each of the fuses is designed to protect a specific circuit, and the various circuits are identified on the fuse panel.

Miniaturized fuses are employed in the fuse block. These compact fuses, with blade terminal design, allow fingertip removal and replacement.

If an electrical component has failed, your first check should be the fuse. A fuse which has *blown* is easily identified by inspecting the element inside the plastic body. Also, the blade terminal tips are exposed in the fuse body, allowing for continuity checks.

It is important that the correct fuse be installed. The different electrical circuits need varying amounts of protection, indicated by the amperage rating on the fuse body.

At no time should the fuse be bypassed with pieces of metal or foil. Serious damage to the electrical system could result.

If the replacement fuse immediately fails, do not replace it again until the cause of the problem is isolated and corrected. In most cases, this will be a short circuit in the wiring caused by a broken or deteriorated wire.

4 Fusible links — general information

In addition to fuses, the wiring is protected by fusible links. These links are used in circuits which are not ordinarily fused, such as the ignition circuit.

Although the fusible links appear to be a heavier gauge than the wire they are protecting, the appearance is due to the thick insulation. All fusible links are four wire gauges smaller than the wire they are designed to protect.

The location of the fusible links may be determined by referring to the wiring diagrams at the end of this manual.

The fusible links cannot be repaired, but a new link of the same size wire can be put in its place. The procedure is as follows:

a) Disconnect the battery ground cable.
b) Cut the damaged fusible link out of the wiring.
c) Strip the insulation approximately 1/2-inch.
d) Position the wire from the harness on the new fusible link and crimp it into place.
e) Use rosin core solder at each end of the new link to obtain a good solder joint.

f) Use plenty of electrical tape around the soldered joints. No wires should be exposed.
g) Connect the battery ground cable. Test the circuit for proper operation.

5 Circuit breakers — general information

A circuit breaker is used to protect the windshield wiper/washer wiring and is located on the fuse panel. An electrical overload in the system will cause the wipers or washer to go on and off, or in some cases to remain off. If this happens, check the entire circuit immediately. Once the overload condition is corrected, the circuit breaker will function normally.

Circuit breakers are sometimes used with accessories such as power windows, power door locks and the rear window defogger.

The circuit breakers may be found by referring to the wiring diagrams at the end of this manual.

6 Battery — removal and installation

1   The battery is located at the front of the engine compartment. It is held in place by a holddown bracket across the top of the battery.
2   As hydrogen gas is produced by the battery, keep open flames or lighted cigarettes away from the battery at all times.
3   Avoid spilling any of the electrolyte battery fluid on the vehicle or yourself. Always keep the battery in an upright position. Any spilled electrolyte should be immediately flushed with large amounts of water. Wear eye protection when working with a battery to prevent eye damage from splashed fluid.
4   Always disconnect the negative (-) battery cable first, followed by the positive (+) cable.
5   After the cables are disconnected from the battery, remove the holddown assembly.
6   Carefully lift the battery from the tray and out of the engine compartment.
7   Installation is the reverse of removal. However, make sure that the holddown assembly is securely tightened. Do not over-tighten, as this may damage the battery. The battery posts and cable ends should be cleaned prior to connection.

7 Battery charging

1   In winter, when heavy demand is placed upon the battery, such as when starting from cold, and much electrical equipment is continually in use, it is a good idea to occasionally have the battery fully charged from an external source at the rate of 3.5 to 4 amps.
2   Continue to charge the battery at this rate until no further rise in

Fig. 12.3 Horn test (Sec 8)

specific gravity is noted over a four hour period.
3   Alternatively, a trickle charging at the rate of 1.5 amps can be safely used overnight.
4   Special rapid boost charges which are claimed to restore the power of the battery in one to two hours are most dangerous, as they can cause serious damage to the battery plates. This type of charge should be used only in an emergency.

8   Horn — fault testing

1   If the horn proves inoperable, first check the fuse. A blown fuse can be readily identified at the fuse panel in the left side of the instrument panel.
2   If the fuse is in good condition, disconnect the electrical lead at the horn. Run jumper wires from the battery positive and negative terminals to the horn terminals as shown in the accompanying illustration.
3   If the horn does not work and there is no evidence of spark at the battery terminal, turn the adjusting screw 1/4 to 3/8 of a turn counterclockwise.
4   If the horn does not sound after adjustment, replace it with a new unit.

9   Headlight sealed beam unit — removal and installation

Removal
1   Remove the headlamp screws, door and retaining ring. Make sure that the retaining screws and not the adjusting screws are removed.

Fig. 12.4 Typical rectangular headlight and sidemarker installation (Sec 9)

Fig. 12.5 Typical round headlight and sidemarker installation (Sec 9)

12

Fig. 12.6 Headlight switch — all pre-1982 models (Sec 11)

2   Pull the headlight forward and support it as you disconnect the wiring plug.

Installation
3   Install the plug to the new headlamp and position it by locating the glass tabs at the back in the slots in the receptacle.
4   Install the headlight retaining ring, screws and door.
5   Check the headlight alignment.

---

10   Headlights — alignment

1   Any adjustments which affect the aim of the headlights should be considered temporary only. After adjustment, always have the beams readjusted by a facility with the proper aligning equipment as soon as possible. In some states, these facilities must be state authorized. Check with your local motor vehicle department concerning the laws in your area. If optical beam setting equipment is not available the following procedure may be used:
2   Position the car on level ground 10 feet (3 meters) in front of a dark wall or board. The wall or board must be at a right angle to the centerline of the car.
3   Draw a vertical line on the board or wall in line with the centerline of the car.
4   Bounce the car on its suspension to ensure correct settlement of the springs then measure the height between the ground and the center of the headlights.
5   Draw a horizontal line across the board or wall at this measured height. On this horizontal line mark a cross on either side of the vertical centerline, the distance between the center of the light unit and the center of the car.
6   Remove the headlight rims and switch the headlights onto high beam.
7   By careful adjusting of the horizontal and vertical adjusting screws on each light, align the centers of each beam onto the crosses which were previously marked on the horizontal line.
8   Bounce the car on its suspension again and check that the beams return to the correct position. At the same time check the operation of the dimmer switch. Replace the headlight rims.
9   This is a temporary, emergency operation until the headlights can be adjusted using the proper equipment.

---

11   Headlight switch — removal and installation

1   Disconnect the negative cable at the battery.
2   Pull the control knob to the On position.
3   Reach under the instrument panel and press the release button on the switch. With the release button pushed in, pull the control knob out of the switch. Remove the autolamp control bezel, if equipped.
4   Unscrew the bezel nut which retains the switch to the instrument panel.
5   Detach the switch, disconnect the electrical connector and remove the switch.
6   To reinstall, connect the electrical plug, place the switch in position

Fig. 12.7 Headlight switch with autolamp delay — typical on 1982 and later vehicles (Sec 11)

on the instrument panel and install the bezel nut.
7   Insert the knob and shaft into the switch, rotating it slightly until a clock is heard.
8   Connect the battery ground cable and check the switch for proper operation.

---

12   Turn signal and hazard flasher — removal and replacement

1   The turn signal and hazard flasher are found on the main fuse panel, which is located in the lower left of the instrument panel.
2   The turn signal flasher unit plugs into the fuse panel and is retained by a spring clip.
3   To remove, grip firmly and pull straight out, taking care not to bend the connector tabs.
4   The hazard warning flasher is located on the opposite side of the fuse panel and is removed in the same way.
5   Replacement is the reverse of removal.

---

13   Instrument cluster (conventional) — removal and installation

1   Disconnect the negative cable at the battery.
2   Remove the steering column shroud.
3   Remove the cluster trim cover.
4   Remove the screw retaining the cable to the steering column and detach the cable loop from the shift cane (column shift models only). Remove the plastic clamp from around the steering column.
5   Remove the screws retaining the instrument cluster to the instrument panel and pull the cluster away from the panel. Disconnect the speedometer cable as described in Section 21.
6   Disconnect the cluster electrical plug from the receptacle in the printed circuit.
7   Lift the cluster away from the dash panel.
8   When installing, apply a 3/16-inch ball of silicone grease in the speedometer head drive hole.
9   Connect the electrical feed plug to the printed circuit.
10   After aligning the speedometer connector with the adapter, push the cable onto the speedometer with a twisting motion until the catch is engaged.
11   Place the cluster in position in the instrument panel and engage the locating pins.
12   Install the instrument cluster retaining screws.
13   Install the plastic cable clamp (if equipped) around the steering column, engaging the clamp locator pin in the slot in the column tube. Start the clamp screw into the retaining clip but do not tighten it fully. Place the loop on the cable over the pin on the shift lever. With the transmission selector in the *Drive* position, rotate the cable clamp

Fig. 12.8 Steering column cover removal (Sec 13)

Fig. 12.9 Later model instrument cluster trim panel removal (Sec 13)

around the column tube until the indicator pointer is centered on the D. Tighten the clamp screw and move the lever through all shift positions, checking the pointer location.

14 Connect the battery negative cable.

14 Instrument cluster (electronic) — removal and installation

1 Disconnect the negative cable at the battery.
2 Remove the lower instrument panel trim cover screws and lift out the cover.
3 Remove the steering column cover.
4 Remove the six screws which attach the instrument cluster trim

panel.
5 If the vehicle is equipped with a column shift, remove the attaching screw from the transmission indicator cable bracket and detach the cable bracket from the steering column pin.
6 Gently pull the cluster away from the instrument panel.
7 Disconnect the speedometer cable at the speedometer head. In most cases, this will be a quick-connect fitting.
8 Disconnect the cluster feed plug and ground wire from the backplate and remove the cluster. **Note:** *It is not necessary to completely remove the cluster from the vehicle for bulb servicing.*
9 Installation is the reverse of removal. Lubricate the speedometer head drive shaft with silicone lubricant prior to assembly.
10 Check the alignment of the transmission selector indicators before tightening the cable clamp on the steering column.

12

Fig. 12.10 Conventional instrument panel and trim panel installation (Sec 13)

Fig. 12.11 Typical electronic instrument cluster removal (Sec 14)

Fig. 12.12 Standard instrument panel printed circuit
(Sec 15)

Fig. 12.13 Conventional dome lamp installation (Sec 16)

Fig. 12.14 Station wagon cargo lamp assembly (Sec 16)

Fig. 12.15 Later model cornering lamp installation (Sec 17)

15 Instrument printed circuit — removal and installation

1 The printed circuit that comprises the wiring of the instrument panel should be handled as little as possible to avoid damage to the circuit sheet.
2 Disconnect the negative cable at the battery.
3 Remove the instrument cluster as described in Section 18.
4 Unsnap the printed circuit from the instrument voltage regulator.
5 Remove the illumination and indicator assemblies.
6 Remove the two screws retaining the cluster resistor and remove the resistor.
7 Remove the fuel gauge attaching nuts and remove the printed circuit.
8 To install, place the printed circuit over the backplate locating pins.
9 Install the illumination and indicator assemblies and fuel gauge attaching nuts.
10 Install the instrument cluster resistor.
11 Place the instrument voltage regulator in position, install the attaching screw and snap the printed circuit to the regulator.
12 Install the instrument cluster as described in Section 18.
13 Connect the battery negative cable.

16 Bulb replacement — interior lamps

Dome lamp
1 Pull down on left side of the dome lamp assembly and remove it from its mounting.
2 Slide the bulb from its socket, using long-nose pliers.
3 Installation is the reverse of removal.

Station wagon cargo area lamp
4 Insert a small blade screwdriver between the end of the lens and the lamp body and carefully pry the lens out of the body.
5 Wrap a cloth around the bulb and slide the bulb from its socket with a pair of long-nose pliers, gripping it lightly as it could break.
6 After replacing the bulb in the socket, installation is the reverse of removal.

17 Bulb replacement — exterior lamps

Parking lamp
1 The parking lamp bulb is removed from inside the engine compartment.
2 Grasp the socket assembly, twist it counterclockwise and withdraw it from the lamp body.
3 Push in and twist to remove the bulb from the socket.
4 Install a new bulb by positioning it in the socket and turning clockwise, making sure that it locks.

Side marker lamp
5 To remove the front side marker bulbs, reach up under the fender, grasp the bulb socket, turning it counterclockwise as you withdraw it.
6 After replacing the bulb in the socket, installation is the reverse of removal.

Rear lamps
7 The various rear lamp bulbs are accessible from inside the trunk of the coupe and sedan. It may be necessary to remove some inner trim panels in the cargo area of the station wagon to reach the lamps.
8 Pull the lamp socket from the housing with a slight twisting motion.
9 Replace the bulb in the lamp socket and align the keying slot of the lamps socket with the tab of the lamp body, press down and turn clockwise to install.

12

18 Bulb replacement — instrument panel

1 The instrument cluster and trim panel must be removed to gain access to the instrument panel bulbs.
2 Disconnect the negative cable at the battery.
3 After removing the instrument cluster, remove the two screws re-

Fig. 12.16 Typical tail lamp lens and bulb installation (Sec 17)

Fig. 12.17 Conventional radio/tape player installation (Sec 19)

taining the lower access panel to gain access to the cluster bulbs.
4   To reach the instrument cluster indicator bulbs, remove the cluster trim panel.

19   Radio — removal and installation

1   Disconnect the negative cable at the battery.
2   Disconnect the electrical power leads, speaker and antenna lead-in cable.
3   Remove the control knobs, nuts and retainers and trim panel (if equipped).
4   Remove the ash tray and bracket.

5   Remove the radio rear support attaching nut.
6   Remove the instrument panel lower reinforcement and air conditioning ducts (if equipped).
7   Remove the radio receiver assembly from the bezel and the rear support, lowering it from the instrument panel.
8   Installation is the reverse of removal.

20   Radio power antenna — removal and installation

1   Lower the antenna. **Note:** *If the mast has failed in the up position and the mast or the entire antenna assembly is being replaced, the mast can be cut off at fender level to facilitate removal.*

Fig. 12.18 Fully electronic radio/tape player installation (Sec 19)

Fig. 12.19 Power antenna installation (Sec 20)

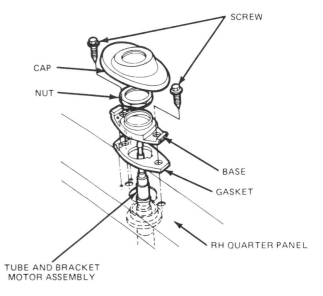

Fig. 12.20 Antenna external hardware (Sec 20)

2   Disconnect the cable from the negative battery terminal.
3   Remove the screws attaching the inner fender skirt to the fender.
4   To gain access to the antenna assembly, pull down on the rear of the fender skirt and hold it away from the fender with a block of wood.
5   Remove any clips or nuts retaining the antenna cable assembly to the fender.
6   Disconnect the electrical leads, then remove any bolts retaining the antenna assembly to the bracket and remove the assembly. Disconnect the antenna lead from the back of the radio.
7   Installation is the reverse of the removal procedure. Make sure that the mast is in the fully retracted position before installation and that the brackets are fully secured.

21 Speedometer cable — removal and installation

1   Disconnect the speedometer cable from the speedometer head.
2   Push the cable and grommet through the dash panel opening.
3   From underneath the vehicle, disengage the cable retaining clips.
4   Disconnect the cable at the transmission and remove the driven gear.
5   To install, connect the new cable to the driven gear and install to the transmission.
6   Engage the cable to the retaining clip at the marker tapes on the

Fig. 12.21 Before the antenna cable can be removed it must be disconnected from the rear of the radio (Sec 20)

12

Fig. 12.22 Speedometer cable quick-connect fitting (Sec 21)

cable housing, route it through the dash panel opening and push the grommet in place.

7   From inside the vehicle, apply a 3/16-inch diameter ball of silicone grease in the speedometer head drive hole and install the cable.

---

22   Speedometer head — removal and installation

Note: *U.S. Federal law requires that the odometer in any replacement speedometer must register the same mileage as that registered in the removed speedometer.*

1   Disconnect the negative cable at the battery.
2   Remove the instrument cluster.
3   If the cluster is equipped with a clock, remove the reset knob and retainer. Remove the screws retaining the mask and lens to the backplate and remove the mask and lens.
4   Disconnect the speedometer cable at the back of the speedometer.
5   After removing the attaching screws, remove the speedometer from the cluster.
6   To reinstall, place the speedometer in the backplate and install the retaining screws.
7   Apply a 3/16-inch ball of silicone grease to the speedometer head drive hole. Connect the speedometer cable.
8   Place mask and lens in position on the backplate and install the attaching screws. Install the clock reset knob and retainer (if equipped).
9   Install the instrument cluster.
10   Connect the battery negative cable.

---

23   Power window switch — removal and installation

1   Disconnect the negative cable at the battery.
2   Remove the switch bezel retaining screw and bezel. Remove by pivoting the bezel outward and up.
3   Pry the switch carefully from the electrical connector which retains it, using a small screwdriver.
4   To install, position the switch in alignment with the connector and press firmly in place.
5   The rest of installation is the reverse of removal.

---

24   Power window motor — removal and installation

Front door

1   Raise the window to the full up position if possible. If the glass cannot be raised to the up position, it must be supported so that it will not fall into the door well.
2   Disconnect the negative cable at the battery.
3   Remove the door trim panel and water shield as described in Chapter 11.
4   Disconnect the motor electrical leads and move them out of the way.

Fig. 12.23 Speedometer cable to transmission installation (Sec 21)

Fig. 12.24 Typical speedometer cable routing (Sec 21)

5   Use a 3/4-inch hole saw with a 1/4-inch pilot and drill a hole at the dimple.
6   Grind the sheet metal interference away from the upper motor mount screw head.
7   Prior to the motor drive assembly removal make sure that the regulator arm is in a fixed position so that the counterbalance spring can't unwind.
8   Remove the mounting screws and disengage the motor and drive assembly from the quadrant gear.
9   Install the new motor and drive assembly and tighten the motor mount screws fully.
10   Connect the electrical wiring plug and install the trim.

Rear door

11   Perform steps 1 through 3.
12   Use a 3/4-inch hole saw with a 1/4-inch pilot to drill at the existing dimples in the door inner panel.
13   Before removing the motor drive assembly, make sure that the regulator arm is in the fixed position. Remove the window motor mounting screws and disengage the motor and drive assembly from the regulator. If the window glass is in the down position, use a screwdriver to disengage the drive gear from the regulator.
14   Install the new motor and drive assembly.
15   Connect the electrical wiring plug and install the door trim as described in Chapter 11.

Fig. 12.25 Power window switch installation (Sec 23)

Fig. 12.26 It may be necessary to clamp the window regulator arm to prevent it from falling into the door when removing the power window motor (Sec 24)

VIEW A

Fig. 12.27 Power window motor installation. Note adjusting screw for regulation of window upper travel limit (Sec 24)

12

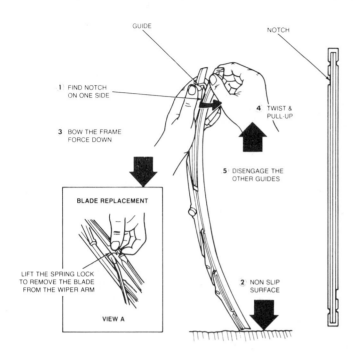

Fig. 12.28   Typical windshield wiper blade element replacement (Sec 25)

Fig. 12.29   Removing the windshield wiper arm from the pivot shaft (Sec 26)

Fig. 12.30   Windshield washer motor replacement (Sec 28)

25   Windshield wiper blade element — removal and installation

1   Locate the notch approximately one inch from the end of the blade element.
2   Stand the assembly on a firm surface with the notched end up. Be careful that the assembly is not braced against a painted surface which could be scratched.
3   Grasp the frame and push down so that the assembly is tightly bowed out and twist, which will snap the element from the retaining tab.
4   Lift the wiper assembly and slide the blade element down the frame until the notch is aligned with the locking tab. Twist the element to slip it out.
5   Installation is the reversal of removal.

26   Windshield wiper arm — removal and replacement

1   Before removing a wiper arm, turn the windshield wiper switch on and off to ensure the arms are in their normal parked position parallel with the bottom of the windshield.
2   To remove the arm, swing the arm away from the windshield, depress the spring clips in the wiper arm boss and pull the arm off the spindle.
3   When replacing the arm, position it in the parked position and push the boss onto the spindle.

27   Windshield wiper motor — removal and installation

1   Disconnect the negative cable at the battery.
2   Remove the left side wiper.
3   Remove the cowl grille screws.
4   To gain access to the linkage drive arm, raise the forward left corner of the cowl guide. Remove the retaining clip from the motor output crank and disconnect the arm.
5   Disconnect the wiper motor wire connector.
6   Remove the motor to cowl panel bolts and remove the motor.
7   Installation is the reverse of removal.

28   Windshield washer assembly — removal, installation and adjustment

1   Use a small screwdriver to unlock the tabs and disconnect the electrical connector. Remove the retaining screws and lift the washer reservoir and motor assembly from the vehicle.
2   Drain the reservoir by disconnecting the hose with a small screwdriver.
3   Pry out the retaining ring which holds the motor in the reservoir.
4   Grasp one wall around the electrical terminals with a pair of pliers and pull out the motor, seal and impeller assembly. If the impeller and seal become separated they can be reassembled.
5   Prior to installation, lubricate the outside of the seal with powdered graphite for ease of assembly.
6   Position the small projection on the motor end cap with the slot in the reservoir and assemble so that the seal seats against the bottom of the motor cavity.
7   Use a 1 inch twelve-point socket to hand press the retaining ring against the motor end plate.
8   Fill the reservoir and check for leaks.
9   The cowl mounted nozzle jets can be adjusted for the proper spray pattern by carefully bending them with needle-nose pliers, taking care not to crimp them.
10   The rear mounted (station wagon) nozzles are adjusted by inserting a paper clip into the hole and rotating the socket until the proper spray pattern is achieved.

Fig. 12.31 Rear windshield washer nozzle adjustment (Sec 28)

Fig. 12.32 Servicing the heated grid rear window defogger power supply wire (Sec 29)

Fig. 12.33 Repairing the heated rear window grid heating element with liquid splicing compound (Sec 29)

29 Defogger (rear window grid-type) — testing and repair

1   The rear window defogger consists of a rear window with a number of horizontal elements that are baked onto the glass.

2   Small breaks in the element system can be successfully repaired without removing the rear window.

3   To test the grids for proper operation, start the engine and turn on the system.

4   Use a strong light inside the vehicle to visually inspect the wire grid from the outside. A broken wire will appear as a brown spot.

5   From inside the car, use a 12-volt DC voltmeter and contact the broad reddish brown strips on the back window. The meter reading should be 10 to 13 volts. A lower voltage reading indicates a loose connection the ground side of the glass.

6   Make a good ground contact with the meter negative lead. The voltage should remain the same.

7   Ground the meter negative lead and touch each grid line at its midpoint with the positive lead. The reading should be approximately 6 volts, indicating the line is good.

8   No reading indicates that the line is broken between the midpoint of the line and the side.

9   A reading of 12 volts means that the circuit is broken between the midpoint and passenger side or the grounding pigtail on the passenger side of the glass is loose.

10   Once the area needing repair is determined, it is recommended that a grid repair kit be obtained from a dealer.

11   Clean the area to be repaired with alcohol to remove dirt, grease or other foreign material.

12   With the area clean and dry, mark the spot to be repaired on the outside of the glass.

13   Shake the bottle of grid repair compound for at least one minute and shake it frequently during use. The compound and the glass must be at room temperature.

14   Mask the area above and below the break with electrical tape so that the gap is the same as the width of the grid.

15   Apply several smooth continuous strokes of the coating, using the brush applicator cap. The repair coating should extend 1/4-inch on both sides of the break.

16   Allow the repair to dry for at least three minutes and remove the tape. The repair can be energized within three minutes. Optimum hardness occurs after 24 hours.

12

Charge, start and run system, 1975 models, 1 of 6

Charge, start and run system, 1975 models, 2 of 6

WIRING COLOR KEY
(PRIMARY COLORS)

BLACK	BK
BROWN	BR
TAN	T
RED	R
PINK	PK
ORANGE	O
YELLOW	Y
DARK GREEN	DG
LIGHT GREEN	LG
DARK BLUE	DB
LIGHT BLUE	LB
PURPLE	P
GRAY	GY
WHITE	W
HASH	(H)
DOT	(D)

The presence of a tracer on the wire is indicated by a secondary color followed by an "H" for Hash or a "D" for Dot. A stripe is understood if no letter follows.

Charge, start and run system, 1975 models, 3 of 6

Charge, start and run system, 1975 models, 4 of 6

12

Charge, start and run system, 1975 models, 5 of 6

Charge, start and run system, 1975 models, 6 of 6

Exterior lighting system, 1975 models, 1 of 4

Exterior lighting system, 1975 models, 2 of 4

12

Exterior lighting system, 1975 models, 3 of 4

Exterior lighting system, 1975 models, 4 of 4

Protection and convenience system, 1975 models, 1 of 3

Protection and convenience system, 1975 models, 2 of 3

12

Protection and convenience system, 1975 models, 3 of 3

Power seat system, 1975 models

Windshield wiper/washer system, 1975 models

Power door lock system, 1975 models

12

Power tailgate system, 1975 models

Power window system, 1975 models

Horn/speed control system, 1975 models

Immersion heater and interior lights systems, 1975 models

Air conditioner and heater systems, 1975 models

Temperature control system, 1975 models

Rear window electric defogger system, 1975 models

Radio system, 1975 models

THE FUSE PANEL IS LOCATED ON THE L.H. SIDE OF THE
STEERING COLUMN BEHIND THE LOWER STEERING COLUMN COVER.

1. (15 AMP FUSE) HAZZARD FLASHER SYSTEM, & STOP LIGHTS

2. (8.25 AMP C.B.) W/S WIPER & WASHER SYSTEM,
   INTERMITTENT WIPER, WASHER FLUID LEVEL INDICATOR

3. (BLANK)

4. (15 AMP FUSE) PARK LAMP, TAIL LAMP, LICENSE LAMP,
   INSTRUMENT PANEL AND CLUSTER ILLUMINATION,
   AUTO-LAMPS, SIDE MARKER/COACH LAMPS

5. (15 AMP FUSE) T/S FLASHER, BACK-UP LAMPS, TRAILER
   TOW RELAY COIL FEED

6. (20 AMP) HEATED BACKLITE RELAY, DECK LID RELEASE,
   SPEED CONTROL MODULE, ELECTRONIC DIGITAL CLOCK
   DISPLAY, ILLUMINATION ENTRY MODULE, CORNERING
   LAMPS, POWER WINDOW RELAY (4 DR MDLS),
   POLICE/ACCY RELAY

7. (BLANK)

8. (15 AMP FUSE) COURTESY LIGHTS, INSTRUMENT PANEL,
   R.H. & L.H. DOORS, DOME, GLOVE BOX, CARGO (STATION
   WAGON ONLY) LAMPS, LUGGAGE COMPARTMENT LAMPS, CLOCK
   FEED, ILLUMINATED ENTRY, VISOR VANITY MIRROR,
   IGNITION KEY WARNING BUZZER, ENGINE COMPARTMENT LP,
   AUTO LAMPS MODULE

9. (30 AMP FUSE) HEATER, A/C OR ATC.

10. (BLANK)

11. (20 AMP FUSE) RADIO, CB, PREMIUM SOUND SYSTEM,
    POWER ANTENNA

12. (25 AMP FUSE) TAILGATE WINDOW BATTERY FEED (KEY SWITCH)
    DOOR CIGAR LIGHTERS

12A.(30 AMP C.B.) POWER DOOR LOCKS, DOORS CIGAR LIGHTERS,
    TAILGATE WINDOW BATTERY FEED, (KEY SWITCH), POWER SEATS

13. (BLANK)

14. (25 AMP FUSE) TAILGATE WINDOW ACCY FEED (I/P SWITCH)

14A.(20 AMP FUSE) 2-DOOR POWER WINDOWS

15. (BLANK)

16. (20 AMP FUSE) HORN & I/P CIGAR LIGHTERS
    ELECTRONIC CONSOLE CLOCK

17. 15 AMP FUSE) INSTRUMENT PANEL & CLUSTER ILLUMINATION,
    RADIO, ASH TRAY, HEATER, A/C OR ATC ILLUMINATION

18. (10 AMP FUSE) WARNING LIGHTS, LOW FUEL WARNING
    MODULE, AUTO-LAMPS, THROTTLE SOLENOID POSITIONER,
    DUAL TIMER BUZZER

Power distribution system, 1981 models, 1 of 2

Power distribution system, 1981 models, 2 of 2

Charge, start and run systems, 1981 models, 1 of 7

Charge, start and run systems, 1981 models, 2 of 7

12

Charge, start and run systems, 1981 models, 3 of 7

Charge, start and run systems, 1981 models, 4 of 7

Charge, start and run systems, 1981 models, 5 of 7

Charge, start and run systems, 1981 models, 6 of 7

12

Charge, start and run systems, 1981 models, 7 of 7

Air conditioning and heater systems, 1981 models

POWER DISTRIBUTION, FUSE PANEL IF-1 — 10 LG-R H
POWER DISTRIBUTION, FUSE PANEL IF-5 — 298 P-0 H
POWER DISTRIBUTION, FUSE PANEL IF-16 — 460 Y-LB D
CHARGE START RUN, SPLICE S-309 — 640 R-Y H
POWER DISTRIBUTION, FUSE PANEL IF-6 — 296 W-P
POWER DISTRIBUTION, FUSE PANEL IF-4 — 195 T-W
POWER DISTRIBUTION, FUSE PANEL IF-8 — 38 BK-0

460 Y-LB D
10 LG-R H
298 P-0 H
296 W-P
14 BR

STOPLAMP SWITCH
C-703
C-703
511 LG
511 LG
TURN SIGNAL FLASHER
C-610
C-611
C-611
C-324
TURN AND EMERGENCY SIGNAL SWITCH
C-152
EMERGENCY WARNING FLASHER
C-611

HEADLAMP SWITCH
C-707
HEADLAMP SWITCH
C-2304   C-2306

HI BEAM INDICATOR LAMP
L.H. TURN INDICATOR LAMP
R.H. TURN INDICATOR LAMP

AUTO LAMP RELAY
AMPLIFIER AND PHOTO UNIT

INTERIOR ILLUMINATION, SPLICE S-100.
HORN & SPEED CONTROL, SPLICE S-127.
HORN & SPEED CONTROL, SPEED CONTROL AMPLIFIER.

Exterior lighting system, 1981 models, 1 of 6

460 Y-LB D — 460 Y-LB D — PROTECTION & CONVENIENCE, CIGAR LIGHTER I/P

TURNING LAMP RELAY
C-801
C-813

L.H. CORNERING LAMP

L.H. FRONT PARK & T/S LAMP
L.H. FRONT SIDE MARKER LAMP
L.H. DRIVING LAMP
L.H. LO BEAM HEAD LAMP
L.H. HI BEAM HEAD LAMP

S-803
S-801
G-801

W/WPR/WSHR W/WSHR PUMP MOTOR

Exterior lighting system, 1981 models, 2 of 6

12

Exterior lighting system, 1981 models, 3 of 6

FOR
TRAILER
LIGHTING

Exterior lighting system, 1981 models, 4 of 6

Exterior lighting system, 1981 models, 5 of 6

Exterior lighting system, 1981 models, 6 of 6

12

Power window system, 1981 models, 1 of 2

Power window system, 1981 models, 2 of 2

Windshield wiper/washer system, 1981 models

Power door lock system, 1981 models

12

Power distribution system, 1984 models, 1 of 4

Power distribution system, 1984 models, 2 of 4

Power distribution system, 1984 models, 3 of 4

Power distribution system, 1984 models, 4 of 4

12

Charge, start and run systems, 1984 models, 1 of 4

Charge, start and run systems, 1984 models, 2 of 4

Charge, start and run systems, 1984 models, 3 of 4

Charge, start and run systems, 1984 models, 4 of 4

Exterior lighting system, 1984 models, 1 of 7

Exterior lighting system, 1984 models, 2 of 7

Exterior lighting system, 1984 models, 3 of 7

Exterior lighting system, 1984 models, 4 of 7

Exterior lighting system, 1984 models, 5 of 7

Exterior lighting system, 1984 models, 6 of 7

Exterior lighting system, 1984 models, 7 of 7

Interior lamps, 1984 models, 1 of 3

Interior lamps, 1984 models, 2 of 3

Interior lamps and immersion heater, 1984 models, 3 of 3

Windshield wiper/washer system, 1984 models

Air conditioning and heater system, 1984 models

12

Speed control system, 1984 models

Power window system, 1984 models

Chapter 13 Supplement:
Revisions and information on later models

Contents

1 Introduction

This Supplement contains specifications and service procedure changes that apply to Ford mid-size models produced from 1985 on. Also included is information related to previous models that was not available at the time of original publication of this manual.

Where no differences (or very minor differences) exist between 1984 models and later models, no information is given. In those instances,

the original material included in Chapters 1 through 12 should be used.

Before beginning a service or repair procedure, check this Supplement for any new specifications or procedure changes/additions. Make note of this supplementary information and be sure to include it while following the original material in Chapters 1 through 12.

2 Specifications

Note: *The following specifications are revisions of or supplementary to those listed at the beginning of each Chapter of this manual. The original specifications apply unless alternative information is included here.*

2.3L engine

Valve springs
  Compression pressure (installed) . . . .   71 to 79 lbs @ 1.520 in
  Service limit . . . .   5% pressure loss at specified length
  Free length (approximate) . . . .   1.877 in
  Installed height . . . .   1-17/32 to 1-19/32 in
Camshaft
  Lobe lift (intake and exhaust). . . . .   0.400 in
  Theoretical valve lift @ zero lash . . . .   0.390 in
Connecting rods
  Piston pin bore diameter . . . .   0.9012 to 0.9096 in

3.8L engine

Oversize piston diameter (coded yellow) . . . .   3.8119 to 3.8125 in
Valve springs
  Compression pressure
    Loaded (without damper) . . . .   190 lbs @ 1.280 in
    Unloaded (without damper) . . . .   73 lbs @ 1.700 in
  Free length . . . .   2.020 in
Valve stem diameter (standard)
  Intake . . . .   0.3423 to 0.3716 in
  Exhaust . . . .   0.3418 to 0.3411 in

5.0L engine

Pistons
  Diameter (oversize — coded red) .... 3.9978 to 3.9984 in
  Ring-to-groove clearance
    Compression (top) .... 0.002 to 0.004 in
    Compression (bottom) .... 0.002 to 0.004 in
Valve springs
  Free length
    Intake .... 2.050 in
    Exhaust .... 1.870 in
  Compression pressure (exhaust — 2nd check) .... 195 to 215 lbs @ 1.050 in
  Installed height
    Intake .... 1-43/64 to 1-45/64 in
    Exhaust .... 1-37/64 to 1-39/64 in
Collapsed lifter gap clearance
  Allowable .... 0.098 to 0.198 in
  Desired .... 0.096 to 0.146 in

Fuel system

Torque specifications	In-lbs	Nm
Central fuel injection-to-intake manifold	120	14
Injector retainer	30 to 60	4.7
Fuel pressure regulator mounting screws	27 to 40	3 to 4.5
Throttle body mounting screws	10 to 15	1 to 2

Automatic transmission

Torque specifications	Ft-lbs	Nm
C3 transmission		
Intermediate band adjusting screw	10	14
Intermediate band adjusting screw locknut	48 to 61	35 to 45
C5 transmission		
Converter housing cover-to-converter housing	12 to 16	17 to 21
Transmission-to-engine bolts (3.8L)	28 to 38	38 to 51
AOD transmission		
Neutral start switch-to-case	8 to 11	11 to 15
Oil pan-to-case bolts	6 to 10	8 to 13.5

Brakes

Front disc brakes
  Disc diameter .... 10.080 in
  Minimum disc thickness .... 0.810 in
  Nominal disc thickness .... 0.870 in
Rear drum brakes
  Drum inside diameter .... 9.000 in
  Drum resurfacing limit (maximum diameter) .... 9.060 in

Torque specifications	Ft-lbs	Nm
Wheel cylinder-to-backing plate bolts	9 to 13	12 to 18

Suspension and steering systems

Torque specifications	Ft-lbs	Nm
Front suspension — strut type (modified MacPherson strut)		
Lower arm-to-no. 2 crossmember	110 to 150	149 to 203
Spindle-to-shock strut bolts	140 to 200	190 to 271
Rear suspension — coil spring type		
Shock absorber upper mount	17 to 27	23 to 37
Upper arm-to-frame	90 to 100	122 to 135
Lower arm-to-frame	100 to 105	135 to 142
Lower arm-to-axle	90 to 100	122 to 135
Stabilizer bar-to-lower arm	45 to 50	60 to 70

---

3 Tune-up and routine maintenance

Engine idle speed check and adjustment (Central Fuel Injection — CFI)

1   Post-1984 models with Central Fuel Injection are equipped with an electronic throttle actuator and idle tracking switch. The addition of this component eliminates the need for idle speed adjustment.
2   See Section 4 in this Chapter for additional information on the throttle actuator/idle tracking switch.

Automatic transmission intermediate band adjustment (C3 transmission)

3   Remove the downshift rod from the transmission downshift lever.
4   Clean all dirt from the band adjusting screw area, then remove and discard the locknut.
5   Install a new locknut on the adjusting screw. Using an accurate torque wrench, tighten the adjusting screw to exactly 10 ft-lbs (14 Nm), then back-off the adjusting screw exactly two (2) turns.
6   Hold the adjusting screw to keep it from turning and tighten the locknut to the specified torque.
7   Attach the downshift rod to the transmission downshift lever.

4 Fuel and exhaust systems

CFI throttle actuator/idle tracking switch — general information

Vehicles produced from 1985 on (those with a 3.8L engine) have been modified to include a DC motor-powered throttle actuator and idle tracking switch. Idle adjustment is no longer necessary or possible on these units.

The only maintenance required of this component is to check for free operation and proper lubrication. Any problems with idle speed should be referred to a dealer service department or repair shop.

5 Suspension and steering systems

Ignition switch — replacement

1   Removal and installation of the ignition switch on post-1984 models is identical to the procedure described in Chapter 10, Section 31, except for one change. Instead of turning the key to the Lock position to release the lock cylinder, turn it to the Run position. If this position is not readily apparent, it can be found by rotating the key approximately 90-degrees clockwise from the Lock position. A new factory replacement switch will be set in the Run position as received
2   It may be necessary to move the switch back and forth slightly to align the switch mounting holes with the threaded holes in the steering column lock housing.

6 Chassis electrical system

High-mount brake light — removal and installation
Sedan
1   Remove the retainer screw covers on either side of the light.
2   Remove the screws from the retainer and pull the light assembly up and forward to detach it from the retainer bracket.
3   Pull the wire assembly locator from the light body on the underside of the assembly and remove the bulb sockets on the bottom of the light by turning them counterclockwise.
4   Installation is the reverse of removal. During installation, push any excess wire into the hole in the package tray.
5   Place the light in position over the retainer bracket and snap the retainer screw covers into place.

Fig 13.1   Central Fuel Injection (CFI) throttle actuator/idle tracking switch — 3.8L engine (Sec 4)

Station wagon
6   Remove the two screws from the lens face.
7   With the light assembly detached from the bezel housing, pull the wiring grommet out of the sheet metal and disconnect the wire assembly from the harness. Detach the connector locator from the sheet metal.
8   If necessary, the bezel housing can be detached from the vehicle by removing the two retaining screws.
9   Installation is the reverse of removal. Be sure the bezel housing rubber seal is properly seated before tightening the screws or a leak may result.
10   Connect the wire assembly to the wiring harness. Make sure that the connector is secured to the sheet metal with the locator and that the grommet is securely pushed into the hole in the sheet metal.
11   Ensure that the rubber seal between the light assembly and the bezel is properly seated.

Wiring diagrams
Wiring diagrams for later models are included at the end of this Supplement.

Fig 13.2   High-mount brake light — sedan models (Sec 6)

Fig 13.3   High-mount brake light — station wagon (Sec 6)

13

Power distribution — 1986 models (1 of 4)

Power distribution — 1986 models (2 of 4)

Power distribution — 1986 models (3 of 4)

Power distribution — 1986 models (4 of 4)

364

Engine electrical system wiring diagram — 1986 models (1 of 4)

Engine electrical system wiring diagram — 1986 models (2 of 4)

Engine electrical system wiring diagram — 1986 models (3 of 4)

Engine electrical system wiring diagram — 1986 models (4 of 4)

13

Exterior lights wiring diagram — 1986 models (1 of 4)

Exterior lights wiring diagram — 1986 models (2 of 4)

Exterior lights wiring diagram — 1986 models (3 of 4)

Exterior lights wiring diagram — 1986 models (4 of 4)

Index

HAYNES AUTOMOTIVE MANUALS

NOTE: New manuals are added to this list on a periodic basis. If you do not see a listing for your vehicle, consult your local Haynes dealer for the latest product information.

ACURA
1776 Integra & Legend '86 thru '90

AMC
Jeep CJ – see JEEP (412)
694 Mid-size models, Concord, Hornet, Gremlin & Spirit '70 thru '83
934 (Renault) Alliance & Encore all models '83 thru '87

AUDI
615 4000 all models '80 thru '87
428 5000 all models '77 thru '83
1117 5000 all models '84 thru '88

AUSTIN
Healey Sprite – see MG Midget Roadster (265)

BMW
276 320i all 4 cyl models '75 thru '83
632 528i & 530i all models '75 thru '80
240 1500 thru 2002 all models except Turbo '59 thru '77
348 2500, 2800, 3.0 & Bavaria '69 thru '76

BUICK
Century (front wheel drive) – see GENERAL MOTORS A-Cars (829)
*1627 Buick, Oldsmobile & Pontiac Full-size (Front wheel drive) all models '85 thru '93
Buick Electra, LeSabre and Park Avenue; **Oldsmobile** Delta 88 Royale, Ninety Eight and Regency; **Pontiac** Bonneville
*1551 Buick Oldsmobile & Pontiac Full-size (Rear wheel drive)
Buick Electra '70 thru '84, Estate '70 thru '90, LeSabre '70 thru '79
Oldsmobile Custom Cruiser '70 thru '90, Delta 88 '70 thru '85, Ninety-eight '70 thru '84
Pontiac Bonneville '70 thru '81, Catalina '70 thru '81, Grandville '70 thru '75, Parisienne '84 thru '86
627 Mid-size all rear-drive **Regal & Century** models with V6, V8 and Turbo '74 thru '87
Regal – see GENERAL MOTORS (1671)
Skyhawk – see GENERAL MOTORS J-Cars (766)
552 Skylark all X-car models '80 thru '85

CADILLAC
*751 Cadillac Rear Wheel Drive all gasoline models '70 thru '90
Cimarron – see GENERAL MOTORS J-Cars (766)

CAPRI
296 2000 MK I Coupe all models '71 thru '75
205 2600 & 2800 V6 Coupe '71 thru '75
375 2800 Mk II V6 Coupe '75 thru '78
Mercury Capri – see FORD Mustang (654)

CHEVROLET
*1477 Astro & GMC Safari Mini-vans all models '85 thru '91
554 Camaro V8 all models '70 thru '81
*866 Camaro all models '82 thru '91
Cavalier – see GENERAL MOTORS J-Cars (766)
Celebrity – see GENERAL MOTORS A-Cars (829)
625 Chevelle, Malibu & El Camino all V6 & V8 models '69 thru '87
449 Chevette & Pontiac T1000 all models '76 thru '87
550 Citation all models '80 thru '85
*1628 Corsica/Beretta all models '87 thru '92
274 Corvette all V8 models '68 thru '82
*1336 Corvette all models '84 thru '91

704 Full-size Sedans Caprice, Impala, Biscayne, Bel Air & Wagons, all V6 & V8 models '69 thru '90
Lumina – see GENERAL MOTORS (1671)
Lumina APV – see GENERAL MOTORS (2035)
319 Luv Pick-up all 2WD & 4WD models '72 thru '82
626 Monte Carlo all V6, V8 & Turbo models '70 thru '88
241 Nova all V8 models '69 thru '79
*1642 Nova and Geo Prizm all front wheel drive models, '85 thru '90
*420 Pick-ups '67 thru '87 – Chevrolet & GMC, all full-size models '67 thru '87; Suburban, Blazer & Jimmy '67 thru '91
*1664 Pick-ups '88 thru '92 – Chevrolet & GMC all full-size (C and K) models, '88 thru '92
*1727 Sprint & Geo Metro '85 thru '91
*831 S-10 & GMC S-15 Pick-ups all models '82 thru '92
*345 Vans – Chevrolet & GMC, V8 & in-line 6 cyl models '68 thru '92

CHRYSLER
*1337 Chrysler & Plymouth Mid-size front wheel drive '82 thru '89
K-Cars – see DODGE Aries (723)
Laser – see DODGE Daytona (1140)

DATSUN
402 200SX all models '77 thru '79
647 200SX all models '80 thru '83
228 B-210 all models '73 thru '78
525 210 all models '78 thru '82
206 240Z, 260Z & 280Z Coupe & 2+2 '70 thru '78
563 280ZX Coupe & 2+2 '79 thru '83
300ZX – see NISSAN (1137)
679 310 all models '78 thru '82
123 510 & PL521 Pick-up '68 thru '73
430 510 all models '78 thru '81
372 610 all models '72 thru '76
277 620 Series Pick-up all models '73 thru '79
720 Series Pick-up – see NISSAN Pick-ups (771)
376 810/Maxima all gasoline models '77 thru '84
124 1200 all models '70 thru '73
368 F10 all models '76 thru '79
Pulsar – see NISSAN (876)
Sentra – see NISSAN (982)
Stanza – see NISSAN (981)

DODGE
*723 Aries & Plymouth Reliant all models '81 thru '89
*1231 Caravan & Plymouth Voyager Mini-Vans all models '84 thru '91
699 Challenger & Plymouth Saporro all models '78 thru '83
236 Colt all models '71 thru '77
610 Colt & Plymouth Champ (front wheel drive) all models '78 thru '87
*556 D50/Ram 50/Plymouth Arrow Pick-ups & Raider '79 thru '91
*1668 Dakota Pick-up all models '87 thru '90
234 Dart & Plymouth Valiant all 6 cyl models '67 thru '76
*1140 Daytona & Chrysler Laser all models '84 thru '89
*545 Omni & Plymouth Horizon all models '78 thru '90
*912 Pick-ups all full-size models '74 thru '91
*1726 Shadow & Plymouth Sundance '87 thru '91
*1779 Spirit & Plymouth Acclaim '89 thru '92
*349 Vans – Dodge & Plymouth V8 & 6 cyl models '71 thru '91

FIAT
094 124 Sport Coupe & Spider '68 thru '78

479 Strada all models '79 thru '82
273 X1/9 all models '74 thru '80

FORD
*1476 Aerostar Mini-vans all models '86 thru '92
788 Bronco and Pick-ups '73 thru '79
*880 Bronco and Pick-ups '80 thru '91
268 Courier Pick-up all models '72 thru '82
789 Escort & Mercury Lynx all models '81 thru '90
*2046 Escort & Mercury Tracer all models '91 thru '93
*2021 Explorer & Mazda Navajo '91 thru '92
560 Fairmont & Mercury Zephyr all in-line & V8 models '78 thru '83
334 Fiesta all models '77 thru '80
754 Ford & Mercury Full-size, Ford LTD & Mercury Marquis ('75 thru '82); Ford Custom 500, Country Squire, Crown Victoria & Mercury Colony Park ('75 thru '87); Ford LTD Crown Victoria & Mercury Gran Marquis ('83 thru '87)
359 Granada & Mercury Monarch all in-line, 6 cyl & V8 models '75 thru '80
773 Ford & Mercury Mid-size, Ford Thunderbird & Mercury Cougar ('75 thru '82); Ford LTD & Mercury Marquis ('83 thru '86); Ford Torino, Gran Torino, Elite, Ranchero pick-up, LTD II, Mercury Montego, Comet, XR-7 & Lincoln Versailles ('75 thru '86)
*654 Mustang & Mercury Capri all models including Turbo '79 thru '92
357 Mustang V8 all models '64-1/2 thru '73
231 Mustang II all 4 cyl, V6 & V8 models '74 thru '78
649 Pinto & Mercury Bobcat all models '75 thru '80
*1670 Probe all models '89 thru '92
*1026 Ranger & Bronco II all gasoline models '83 thru '92
*1421 Taurus & Mercury Sable '86 thru '92
*1418 Tempo & Mercury Topaz all gasoline models '84 thru '91
1338 Thunderbird & Mercury Cougar/XR7 '83 thru '88
*1725 Thunderbird & Mercury Cougar '89 and '90
*344 Vans all V8 Econoline models '69 thru '91

GENERAL MOTORS
*829 A-Cars – Chevrolet Celebrity, Buick Century, Pontiac 6000 & Oldsmobile Cutlass Ciera all models '82 thru '90
*766 J-Cars – Chevrolet Cavalier, Pontiac J-2000, Oldsmobile Firenza, Buick Skyhawk & Cadillac Cimarron all models '82 thru '92
*1420 N-Cars – Buick Somerset '85 thru '87; Pontiac Grand Am and Oldsmobile Calais '85 thru '91; Buick Skylark '86 thru '91
*1671 GM: Buick Regal, **Chevrolet** Lumina, **Oldsmobile** Cutlass Supreme, **Pontiac** Grand Prix, all front wheel drive models '88 thru '90
*2035 GM: Chevrolet Lumina APV, Oldsmobile Silhouette, Pontiac Trans Sport '90 thru '92

GEO
Metro – see CHEVROLET Sprint (1727)
Prizm – see CHEVROLET Nova (1642)
Tracker – see SUZUKI Samurai (1626)

GMC
Safari – see CHEVROLET ASTRO (1477)
Vans & Pick-ups – see CHEVROLET (420, 831, 345, 1664)

(continued on next page)

---

*Listings shown with an asterisk (*) indicate model coverage as of this printing. These titles will be periodically updated to include later model years – consult your Haynes dealer for more information.*

Haynes North America, Inc., 861 Lawrence Drive, Newbury Park, CA 91320 • (805) 498-6703

HAYNES AUTOMOTIVE MANUALS

(continued from previous page)

NOTE: New manuals are added to this list on a periodic basis. If you do not see a listing for your vehicle, consult your local Haynes dealer for the latest product information.

HONDA
351	**Accord CVCC** all models '76 thru '83
*1221	**Accord** all models '84 thru '89
160	**Civic 1200** all models '73 thru '79
633	**Civic 1300 & 1500 CVCC** all models '80 thru '83
297	**Civic 1500 CVCC** all models '75 thru '79
*1227	**Civic** all models '84 thru '91
*601	**Prelude CVCC** all models '79 thru '89

HYUNDAI
*1552	**Excel** all models '86 thru '91

ISUZU
*1641	**Trooper & Pick-up**, all gasoline models '81 thru '91

JAGUAR
*242	**XJ6** all 6 cyl models '68 thru '86
*478	**XJ12 & XJS** all 12 cyl models '72 thru '85

JEEP
*1553	**Cherokee, Comanche & Wagoneer Limited** all models '84 thru '91
412	**CJ** all models '49 thru '86
*1777	**Wrangler** all models '87 thru '92

LADA
*413	**1200, 1300. 1500 & 1600** all models including Riva '74 thru '86

MAZDA
648	**626** Sedan & Coupe (rear wheel drive) all models '79 thru '82
1082	**626 & MX-6 (front wheel drive)** all models '83 thru '91
370	**GLC Hatchback (rear wheel drive)** all models '77 thru '83
757	**GLC (front wheel drive)** all models '81 thru '86
*2047	**MPV** '89 thru '93
	Navajo – see FORD Explorer (2021)
*267	**Pick-ups** '72 thru '92
460	**RX-7** all models '79 thru '85
*1419	**RX-7** all models '86 thru '91

MERCEDES-BENZ
*1643	**190 Series** all four-cylinder gasoline models, '84 thru '88
346	**230, 250 & 280** Sedan, Coupe & Roadster all 6 cyl sohc models '68 thru '72
983	**280 123 Series** all gasoline models '77 thru '81
698	**350 & 450** Sedan, Coupe & Roadster all models '71 thru '80
697	**Diesel 123 Series** 200D, 220D, 240D, 240TD, 300D, 300CD, 300TD, 4- & 5-cyl incl. Turbo '76 thru '85

MERCURY
For all PLYMOUTH titles see FORD Listing

MG
111	**MGB** Roadster & GT Coupe all models '62 thru '80
265	**MG Midget & Austin Healey Sprite** Roadster '58 thru '80

MITSUBISHI
*1669	**Cordia, Tredia, Galant, Precis & Mirage** '83 thru '90
*2022	**Pick-ups & Montero** '83 thru '91

MORRIS
074	**(Austin) Marina 1.8** all models '71 thru '80
024	**Minor 1000** sedan & wagon '56 thru '71

NISSAN
1137	**300ZX** all Turbo & non-Turbo models '84 thru '89

*1341	**Maxima** all models '85 thru '91
*771	**Pick-ups/Pathfinder** gas models '80 thru '91
*876	**Pulsar** all models '83 thru '86
*982	**Sentra** all models '82 thru '90
*981	**Stanza** all models '82 thru '90

OLDSMOBILE
	Custom Cruiser – see BUICK Full-size (1551)
658	**Cutlass** all standard gasoline V6 & V8 models '74 thru '88
	Cutlass Ciera – see GENERAL MOTORS A-Cars (829)
	Cutlass Supreme – see GENERAL MOTORS (1671)
	Firenza – see GENERAL MOTORS J-Cars (766)
	Ninety-eight – see BUICK Full-size (1551)
	Omega – see PONTIAC Phoenix & Omega (551)
	Silhouette – see GENERAL MOTORS (2035)

PEUGEOT
663	**504** all diesel models '74 thru '83

PLYMOUTH
For all PLYMOUTH titles, see DODGE listing.

PONTIAC
	T1000 – see CHEVROLET Chevette (449)
	J-2000 – see GENERAL MOTORS J-Cars (766)
	6000 – see GENERAL MOTORS A-Cars (829)
1232	**Fiero** all models '84 thru '88
555	**Firebird** all V8 models except Turbo '70 thru '81
*867	**Firebird** all models '82 thru '91
	Full-size Rear Wheel Drive – see Buick, Oldsmobile, Pontiac Full-size (1551)
	Grand Prix – see GENERAL MOTORS (1671)
551	**Phoenix & Oldsmobile Omega** all X-car models '80 thru '84
	Trans Sport – see GENERAL MOTORS (2035)

PORSCHE
*264	**911** all Coupe & Targa models except Turbo & Carrera 4 '65 thru '89
239	**914** all 4 cyl models '69 thru '76
397	**924** all models including Turbo '76 thru '82
*1027	**944** all models including Turbo '83 thru '89

RENAULT
141	**5 Le Car** all models '76 thru '83
079	**8 & 10** all models with 58.4 cu in engines '62 thru '72
097	**12 Saloon & Estate** all models 1289 cc engines '70 thru '80
768	**15 & 17** all models '73 thru '79
081	**16** all models 89.7 cu in & 95.5 cu in engines '65 thru '72
	Alliance & Encore – see AMC (934)

SAAB
247	**99** all models including Turbo '69 thru '80
*980	**900** all models including Turbo '79 thru '88

SUBARU
237	**1100, 1300, 1400 & 1600** all models '71 thru '79
*681	**1600 & 1800** 2WD & 4WD all models '80 thru '89

SUZUKI
*1626	**Samurai/Sidekick and Geo Tracker** all models '86 thru '91

TOYOTA
*1023	**Camry** all models '83 thru '91
150	**Carina Sedan** all models '71 thru '74
*2038	**Celica** Front Wheel Drive '86 thru '92
935	**Celica** Rear Wheel Drive '71 thru '85
*1139	**Celica Supra** '79 thru '92
361	**Corolla** all models '75 thru '79
961	**Corolla** all models (rear wheel drive) '80 thru '87
*1025	**Corolla** all models (front wheel drive) '84 thru '91
*636	**Corolla Tercel** all models '80 thru '82
230	**Corona & MK II** all 4 cyl sohc models '69 thru '74
360	**Corona** all models '74 thru '82
*532	**Cressida** all models '78 thru '82
313	**Land Cruiser** all models '68 thru '82
200	**MK II** all 6 cyl models '72 thru '76
*1339	**MR2** all models '85 thru '87
304	**Pick-up** all models '69 thru '78
*656	**Pick-up** all models '79 thru '92

TRIUMPH
112	**GT6 & Vitesse** all models '62 thru '74
113	**Spitfire** all models '62 thru '81
322	**TR7** all models '75 thru '81

VW
159	**Beetle & Karmann Ghia** all models '54 thru '79
238	**Dasher** all gasoline models '74 thru '81
*884	**Rabbit, Jetta, Scirocco, & Pick-up** all gasoline models '74 thru '91 & **Convertible** '80 thru '91
451	**Rabbit, Jetta & Pick-up** all diesel models '77 thru '84
082	**Transporter 1600** all models '68 thru '79
226	**Transporter 1700, 1800 & 2000** all models '72 thru '79
084	**Type 3 1500 & 1600** all models '63 thru '73
1029	**Vanagon** all air-cooled models '80 thru '83

VOLVO
203	**120, 130 Series & 1800 Sports** '61 thru '73
129	**140 Series** all models '66 thru '74
*270	**240 Series** all models '74 thru '90
400	**260 Series** all models '75 thru '82
*1550	**740 & 760 Series** all models '82 thru '88

SPECIAL MANUALS
1479	**Automotive Body Repair & Painting Manual**
1654	**Automotive Electrical Manual**
1480	**Automotive Heating & Air Conditioning Manual**
1762	**Chevrolet Engine Overhaul Manual**
1736	**Diesel Engine Repair Manual**
1667	**Emission Control Manual**
1763	**Ford Engine Overhaul Manual**
482	**Fuel Injection Manual**
1666	**Small Engine Repair Manual**
299	**SU Carburetors** thru '88
393	**Weber Carburetors** thru '79
300	**Zenith/Stromberg CD Carburetors** thru '76

See your dealer for other available titles

* Listings shown with an asterisk (*) indicate model coverage as of this printing. These titles will be periodically updated to include later model years – consult your Haynes dealer for more information.

Over 100 Haynes motorcycle manuals also available

1-93

Haynes North America, Inc., 861 Lawrence Drive, Newbury Park, CA 91320 • (805) 498-6703